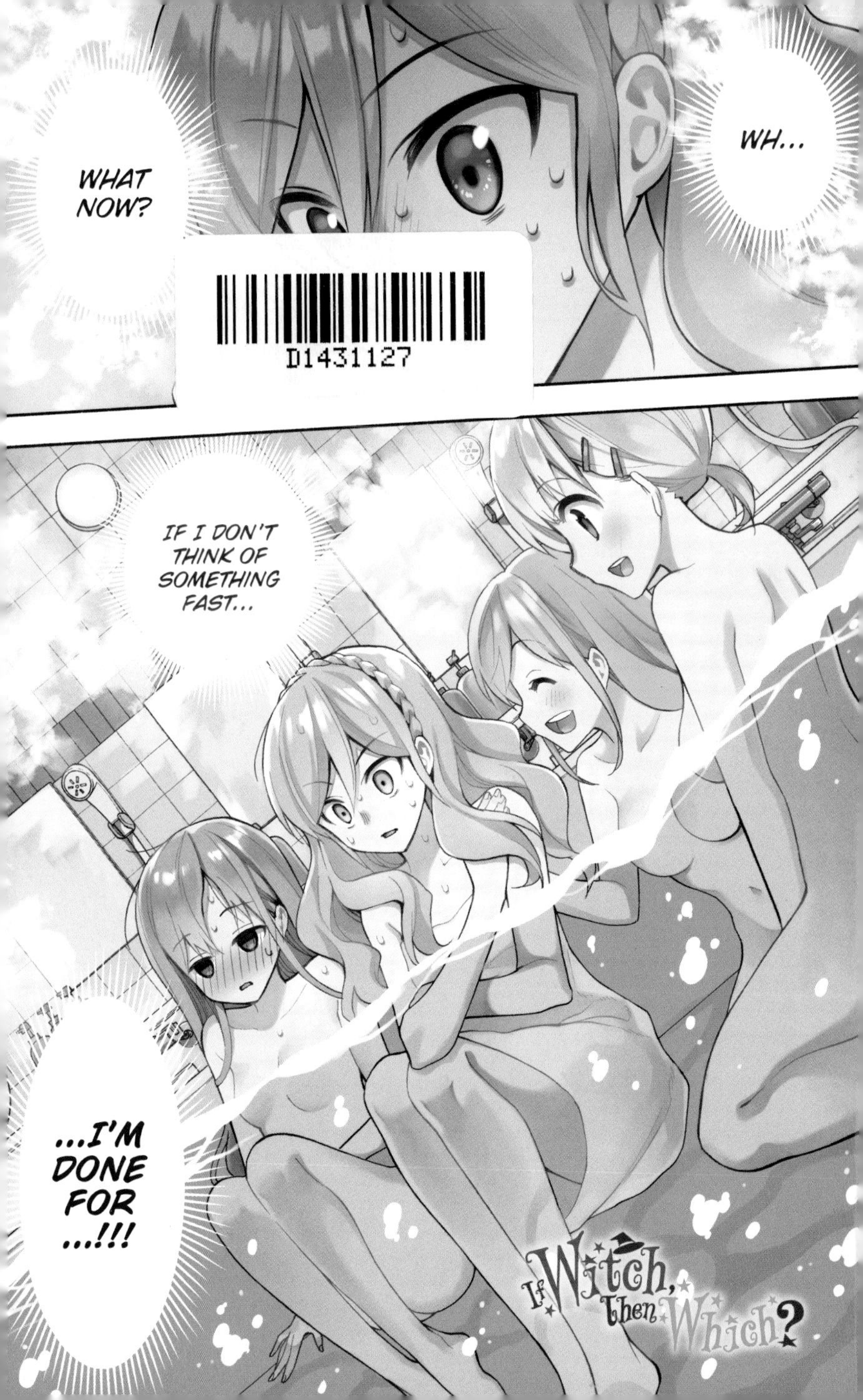
WH...
WHAT NOW?
IF I DON'T THINK OF SOMETHING FAST...
...I'M DONE FOR ...!!!
If Witch, Then Which?

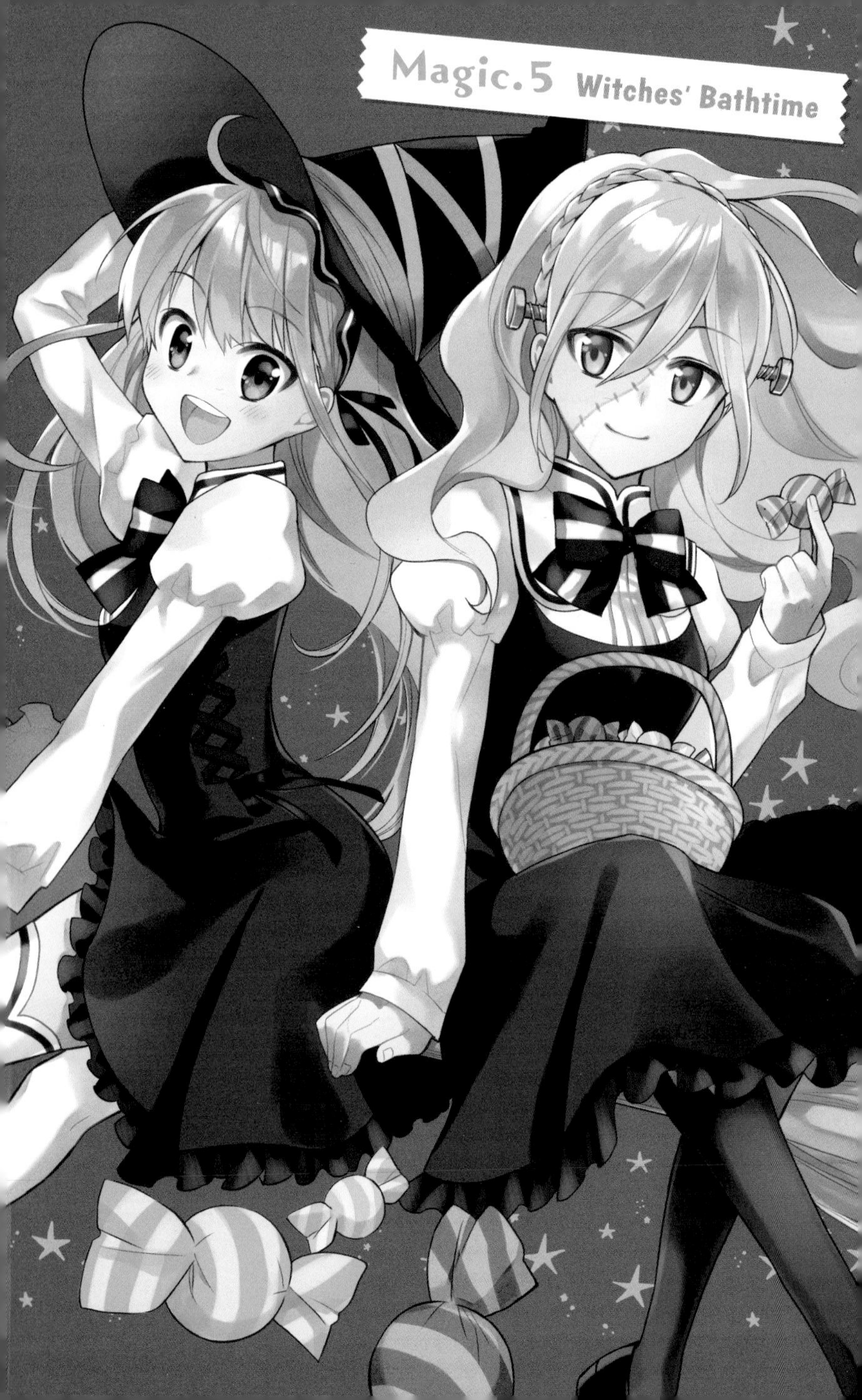
Magic.5 Witches' Bathtime

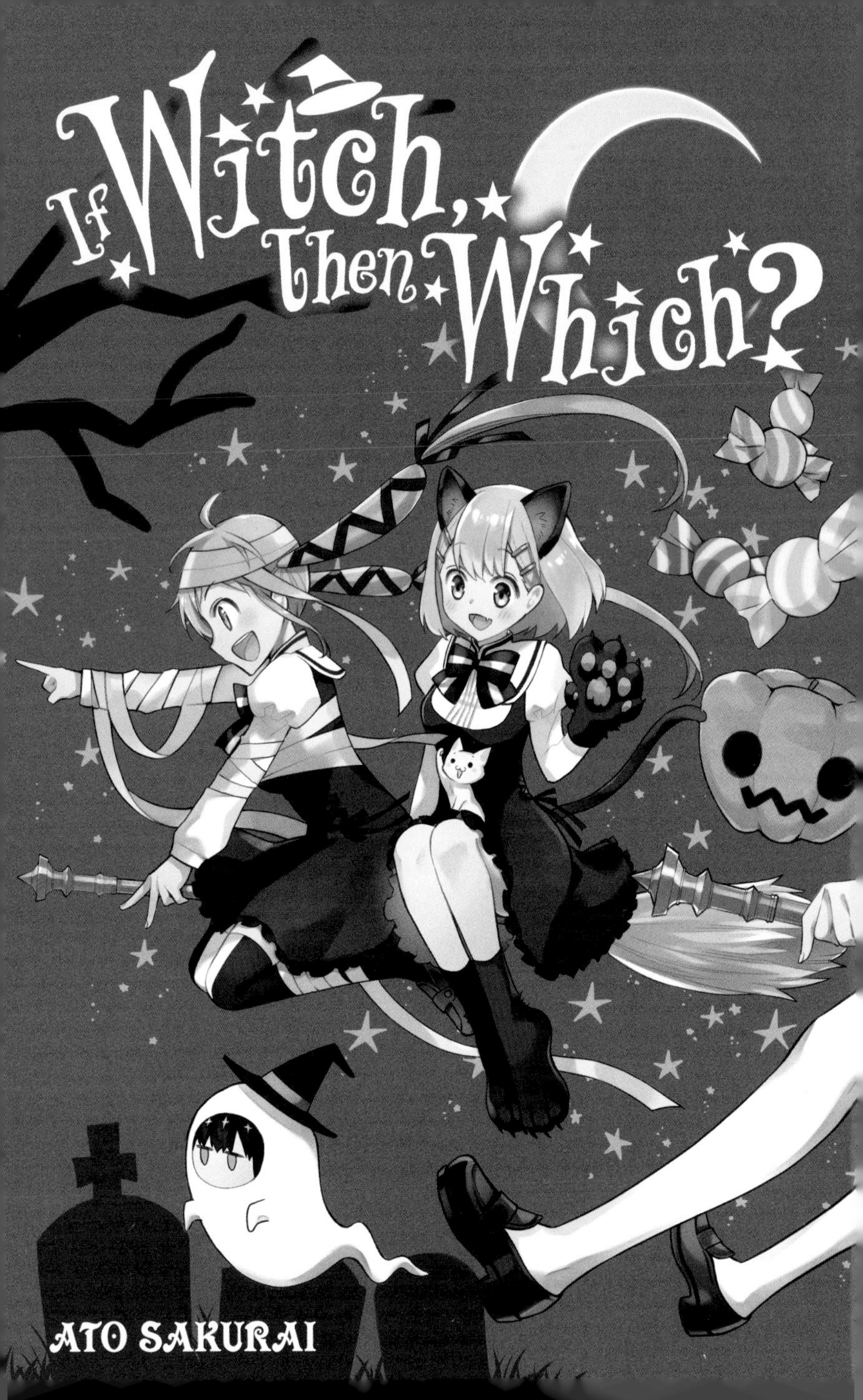
If Witch, Then Which?
ATO SAKURAI

Contents

Rin-jou!!

IF WITCH,
THEN WHICH?

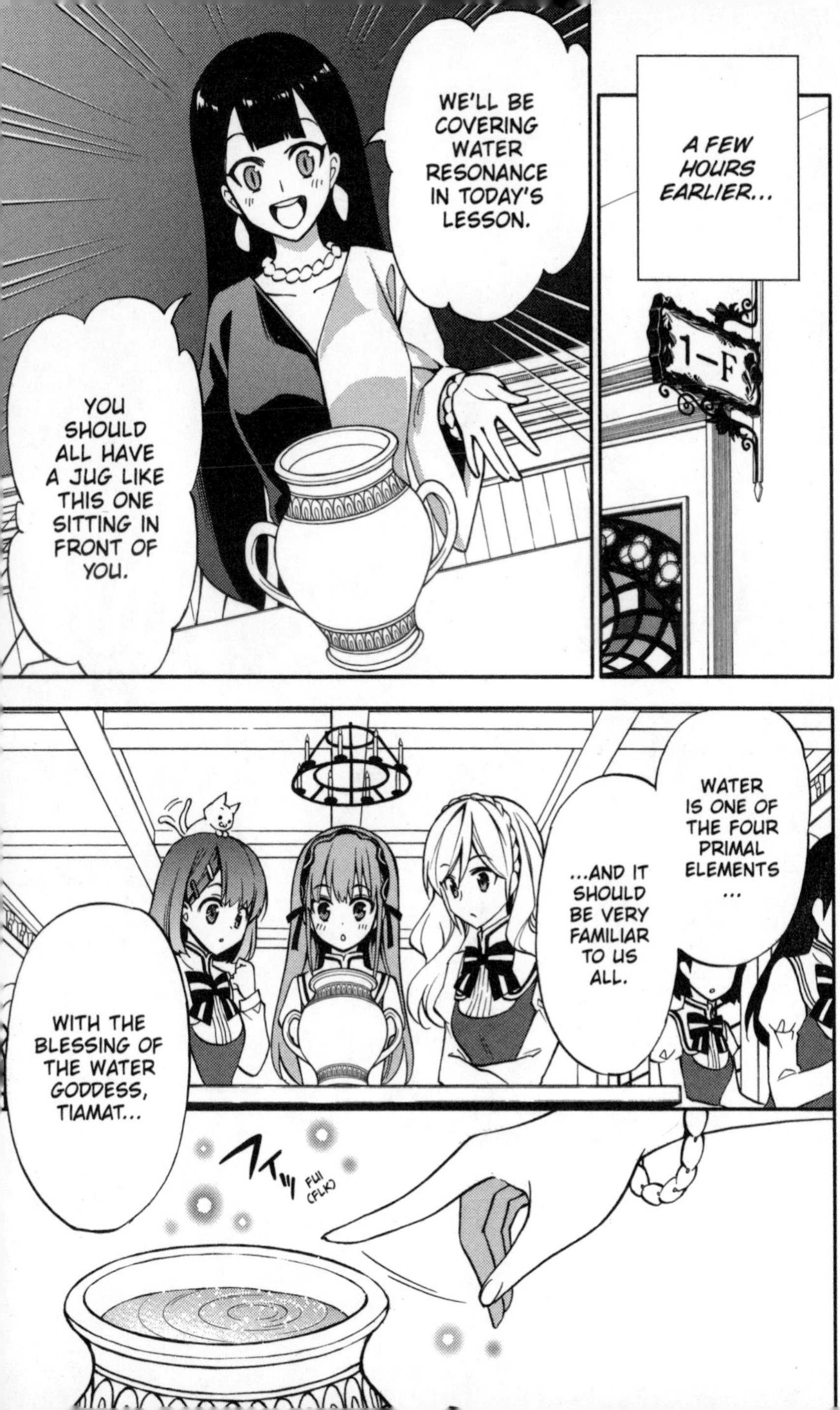
A FEW HOURS EARLIER...
1-F
WE'LL BE COVERING WATER RESONANCE IN TODAY'S LESSON.
YOU SHOULD ALL HAVE A JUG LIKE THIS ONE SITTING IN FRONT OF YOU.
WATER IS ONE OF THE FOUR PRIMAL ELEMENTS ...
...AND IT SHOULD BE VERY FAMILIAR TO US ALL.
WITH THE BLESSING OF THE WATER GODDESS, TIAMAT...
FUI (FLK)

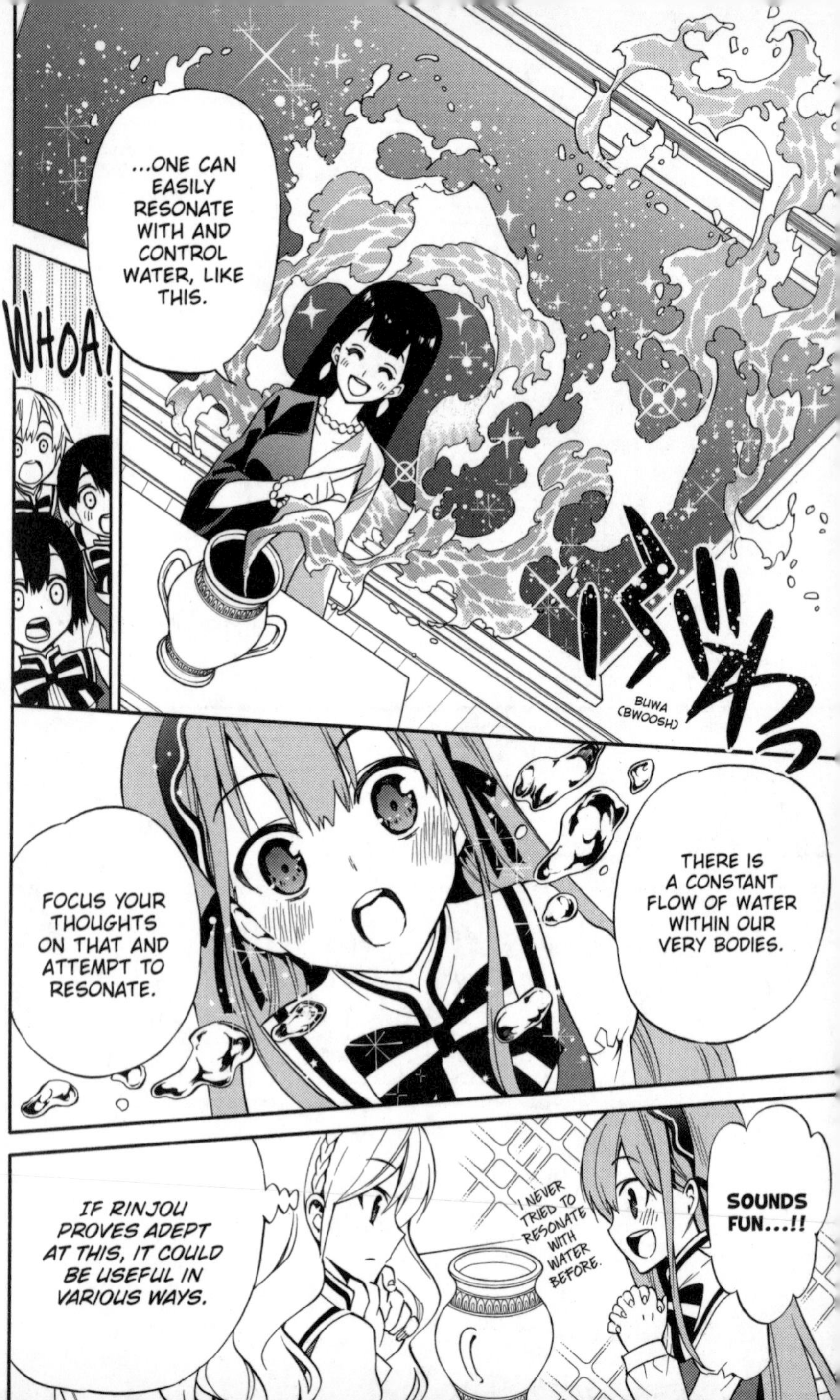
...ONE CAN EASILY RESONATE WITH AND CONTROL WATER, LIKE THIS.
BUWA (BWOOSH)
WHOA!
THERE IS A CONSTANT FLOW OF WATER WITHIN OUR VERY BODIES.
FOCUS YOUR THOUGHTS ON THAT AND ATTEMPT TO RESONATE.
SOUNDS FUN...!!
I NEVER TRIED TO RESONATE WITH WATER BEFORE.
IF RINJOU PROVES ADEPT AT THIS, IT COULD BE USEFUL IN VARIOUS WAYS.

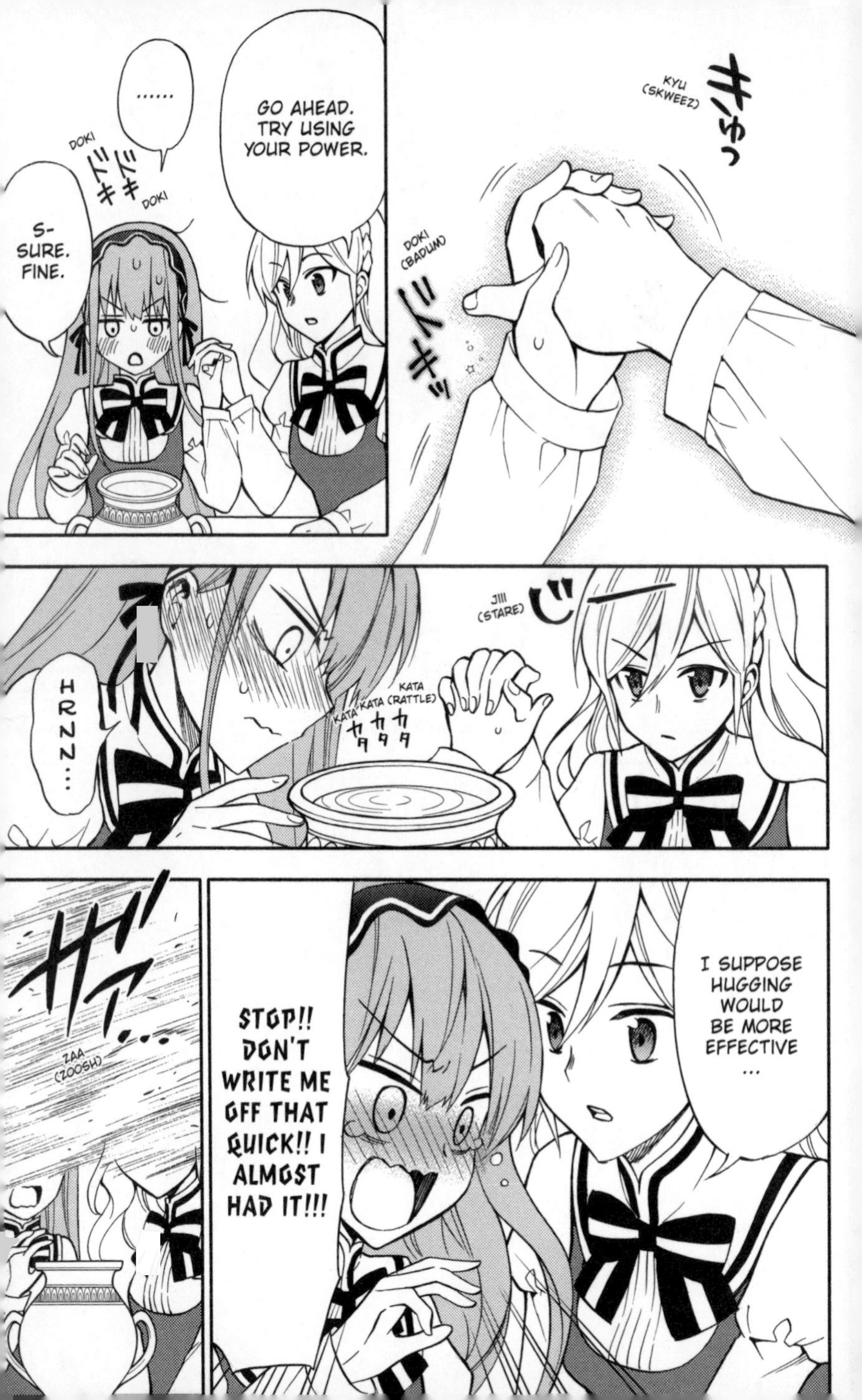
キュッ
KYU (SKWEEZ)
ドキッ
DOKI (BADUM)
GO AHEAD. TRY USING YOUR POWER.
......
ドキドキ
DOKI DOKI
S-SURE. FINE.
じー
JIII (STARE)
カタカタカタ
KATA KATA KATA (RATTLE)
HRNN...
I SUPPOSE HUGGING WOULD BE MORE EFFECTIVE ...
STOP!! DON'T WRITE ME OFF THAT QUICK!! I ALMOST HAD IT!!!
ザァ...
ZAA (ZOOSH)

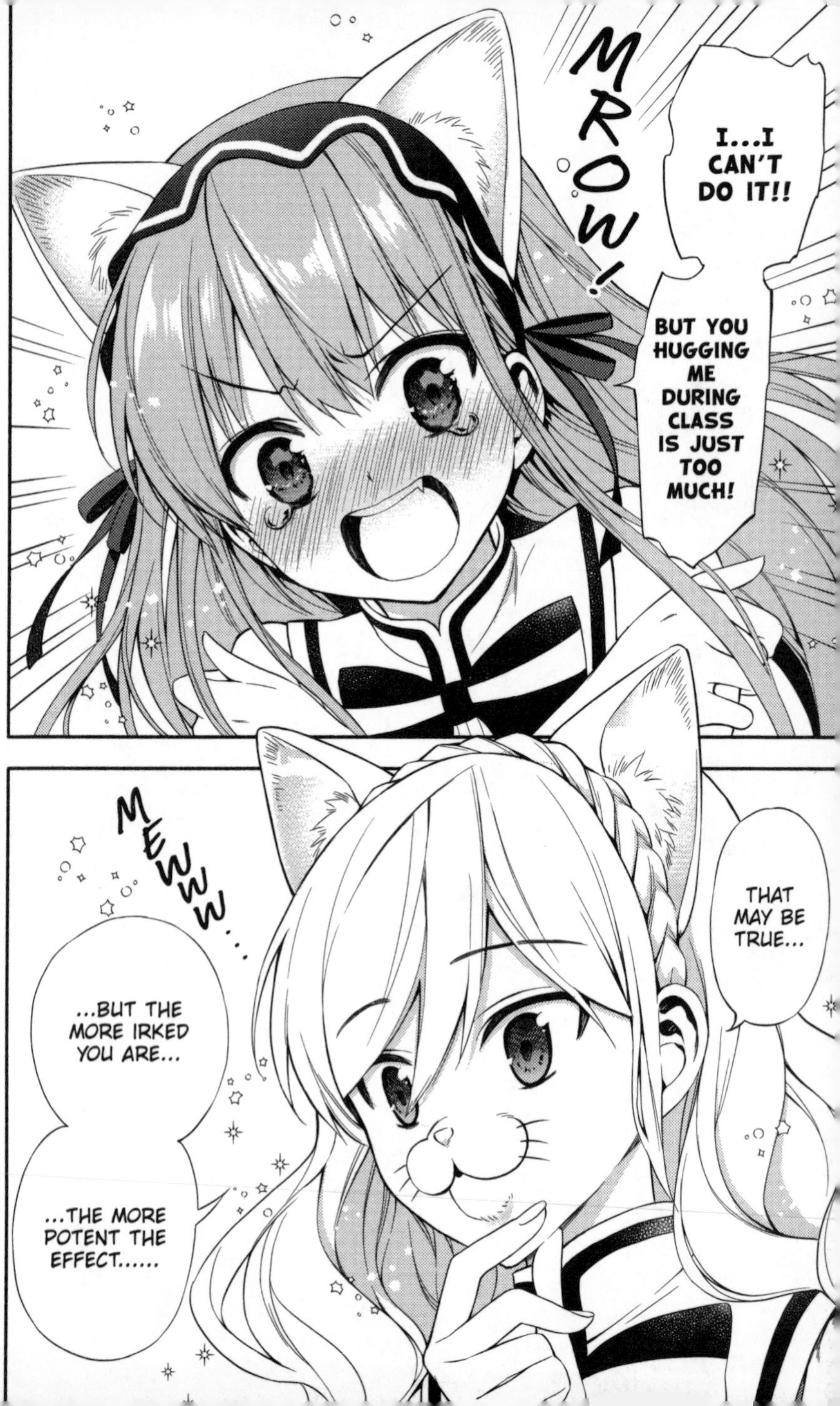
I...I CAN'T DO IT!!
BUT YOU HUGGING ME DURING CLASS IS JUST TOO MUCH!
MROW!
THAT MAY BE TRUE...
MEWWW...
...BUT THE MORE IRKED YOU ARE...
...THE MORE POTENT THE EFFECT......

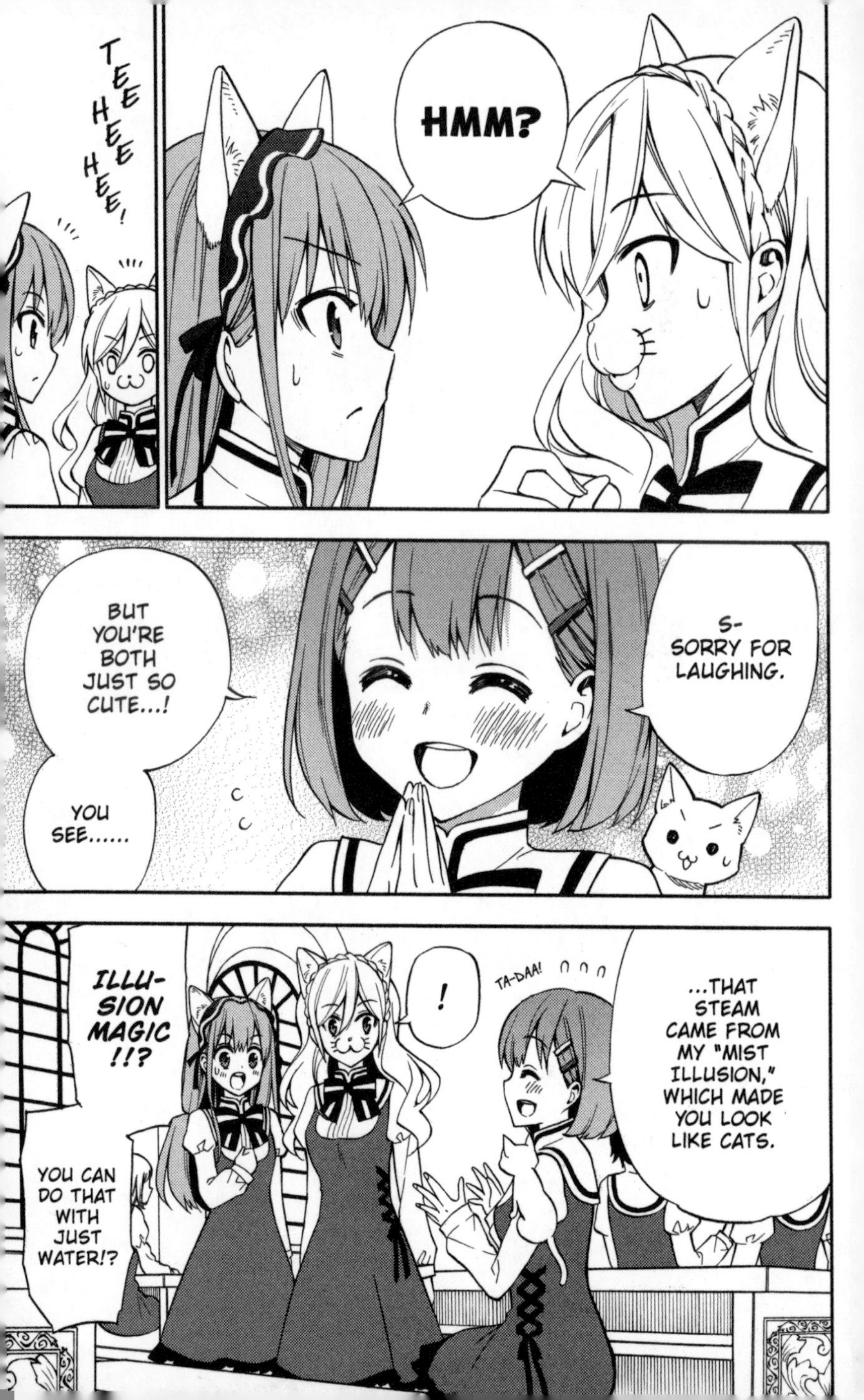
HMM?
TEE HEE HEE!
S-SORRY FOR LAUGHING.
BUT YOU'RE BOTH JUST SO CUTE...!
YOU SEE......
...THAT STEAM CAME FROM MY "MIST ILLUSION," WHICH MADE YOU LOOK LIKE CATS.
TA-DAA!
!
ILLUSION MAGIC!!?
YOU CAN DO THAT WITH JUST WATER!?

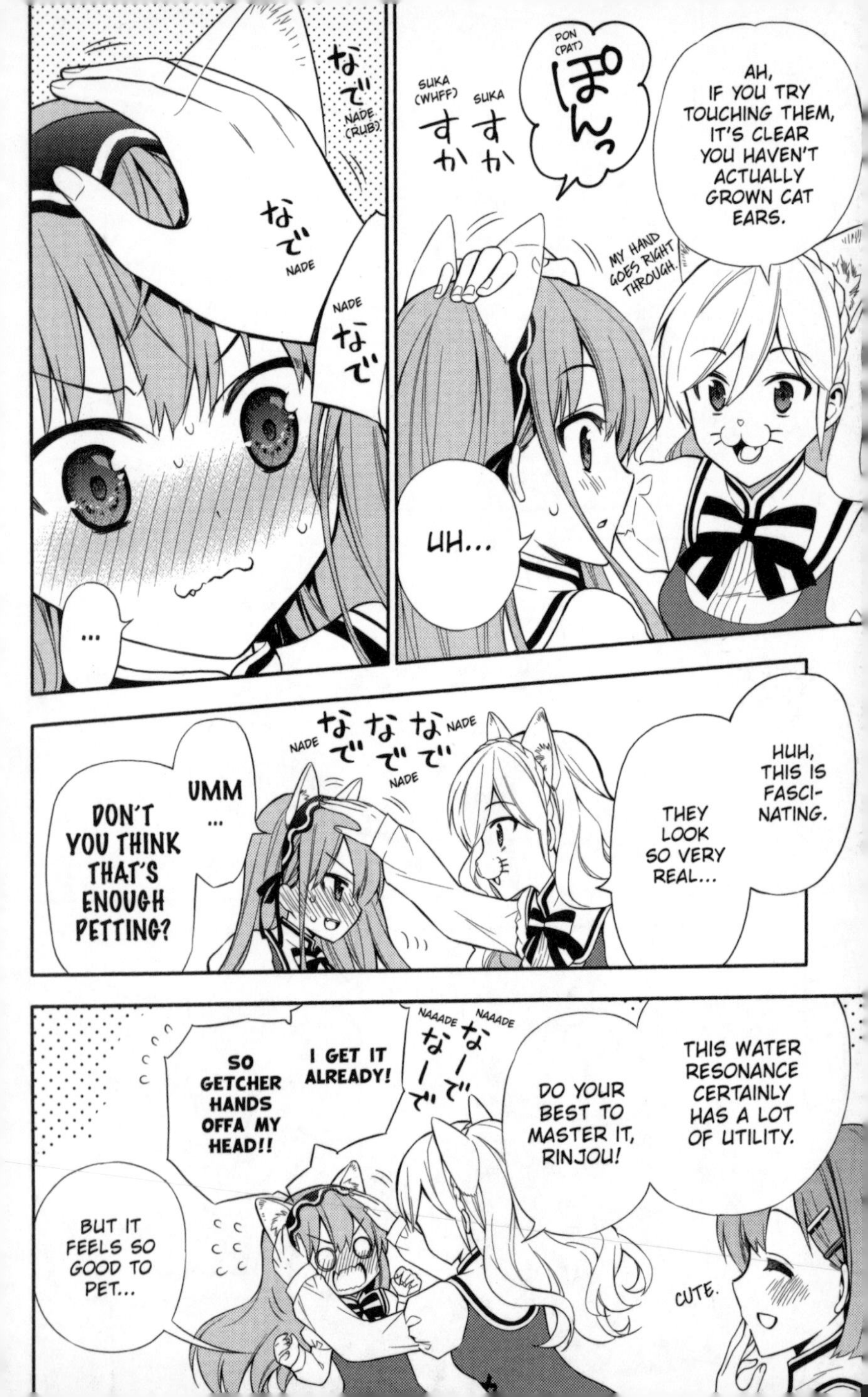
AH, IF YOU TRY TOUCHING THEM, IT'S CLEAR YOU HAVEN'T ACTUALLY GROWN CAT EARS.
PON (PAT)
ぽんっ
SUKA
すか
SUKA (WHFF)
すか
MY HAND GOES RIGHT THROUGH.
UH...
なで
NADE (RUB)
なで
NADE
NADE
なで
...
HUH, THIS IS FASCINATING.
THEY LOOK SO VERY REAL...
なで
NADE
なで
NADE
なで
NADE
UMM...
DON'T YOU THINK THAT'S ENOUGH PETTING?
THIS WATER RESONANCE CERTAINLY HAS A LOT OF UTILITY.
DO YOUR BEST TO MASTER IT, RINJOU!
なーで
NAAADE
なーで
NAAADE
I GET IT ALREADY!
SO GETCHER HANDS OFFA MY HEAD!!
BUT IT FEELS SO GOOD TO PET...
CUTE.

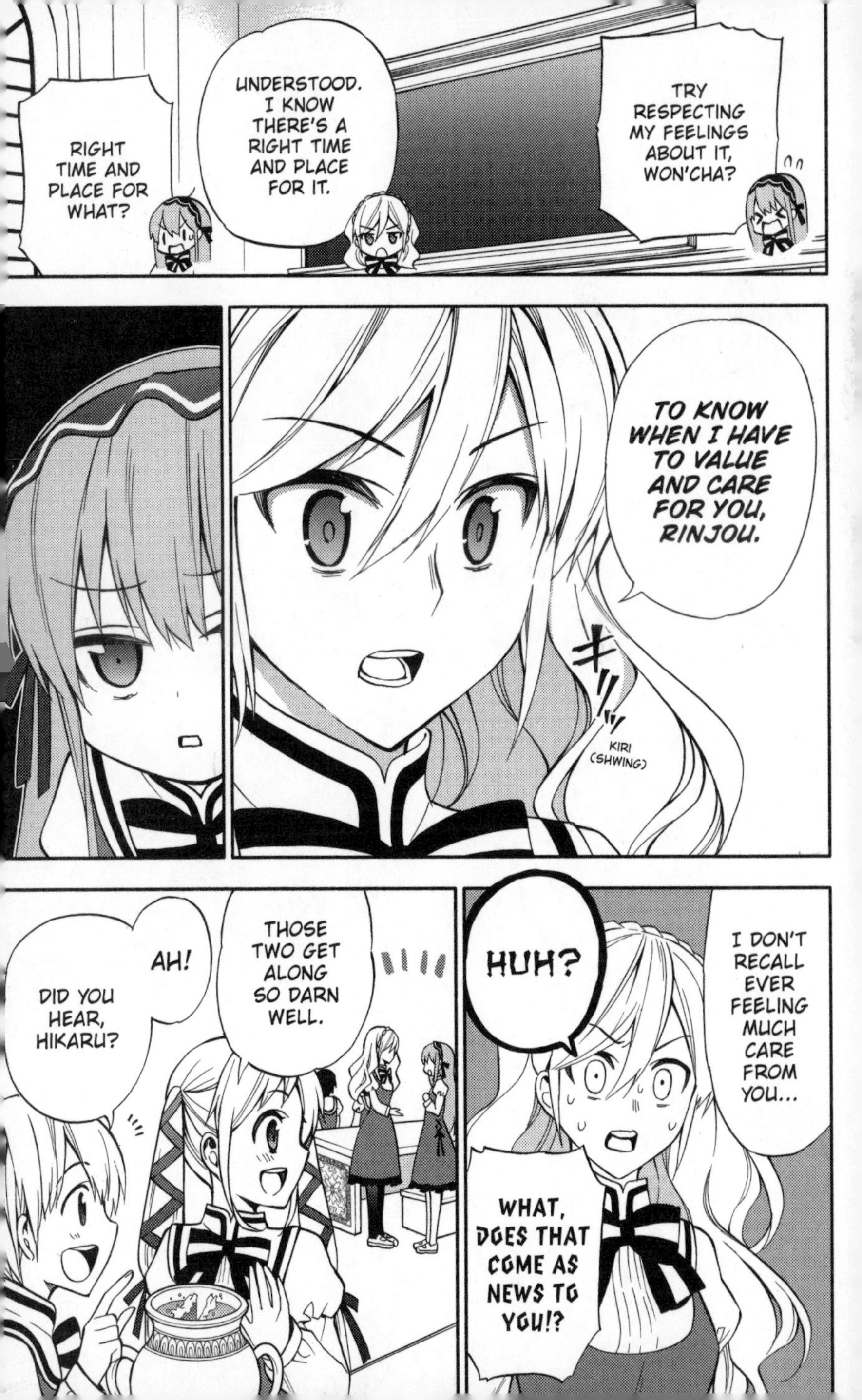
TRY RESPECTING MY FEELINGS ABOUT IT, WON'CHA?
UNDERSTOOD. I KNOW THERE'S A RIGHT TIME AND PLACE FOR IT.
RIGHT TIME AND PLACE FOR WHAT?
TO KNOW WHEN I HAVE TO VALUE AND CARE FOR YOU, RINJOU.
KIRI (SHWING)
I DON'T RECALL EVER FEELING MUCH CARE FROM YOU...
HUH?
WHAT, DOES THAT COME AS NEWS TO YOU!?
THOSE TWO GET ALONG SO DARN WELL.
AH!
DID YOU HEAR, HIKARU?

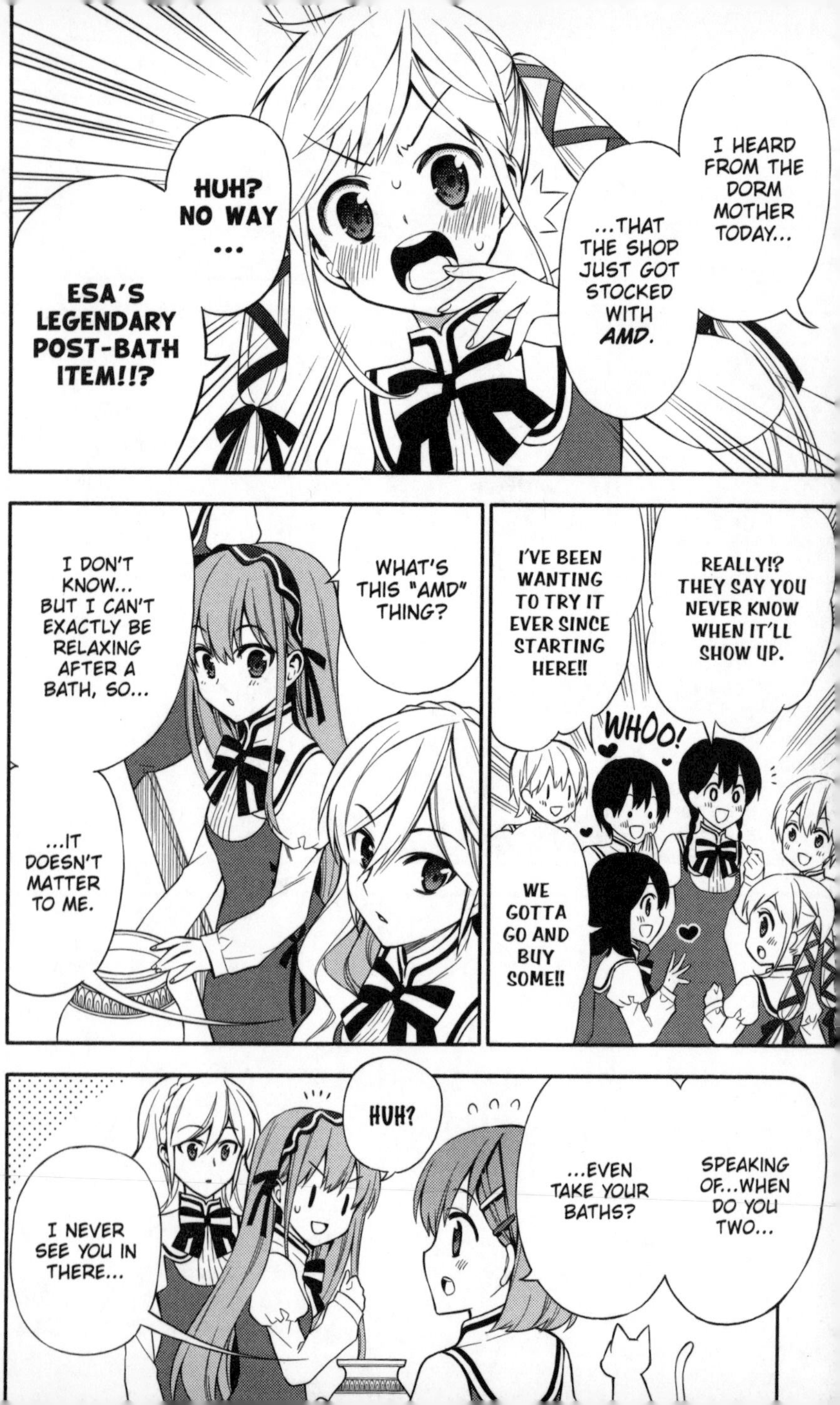
I HEARD FROM THE DORM MOTHER TODAY...
...THAT THE SHOP JUST GOT STOCKED WITH AMD.
HUH? NO WAY ...
ESA'S LEGENDARY POST-BATH ITEM!!?
REALLY!? THEY SAY YOU NEVER KNOW WHEN IT'LL SHOW UP.
I'VE BEEN WANTING TO TRY IT EVER SINCE STARTING HERE!!
WHOO!
WE GOTTA GO AND BUY SOME!!
WHAT'S THIS "AMD" THING?
I DON'T KNOW... BUT I CAN'T EXACTLY BE RELAXING AFTER A BATH, SO...
...IT DOESN'T MATTER TO ME.
SPEAKING OF...WHEN DO YOU TWO...
...EVEN TAKE YOUR BATHS?
HUH?
I NEVER SEE YOU IN THERE...

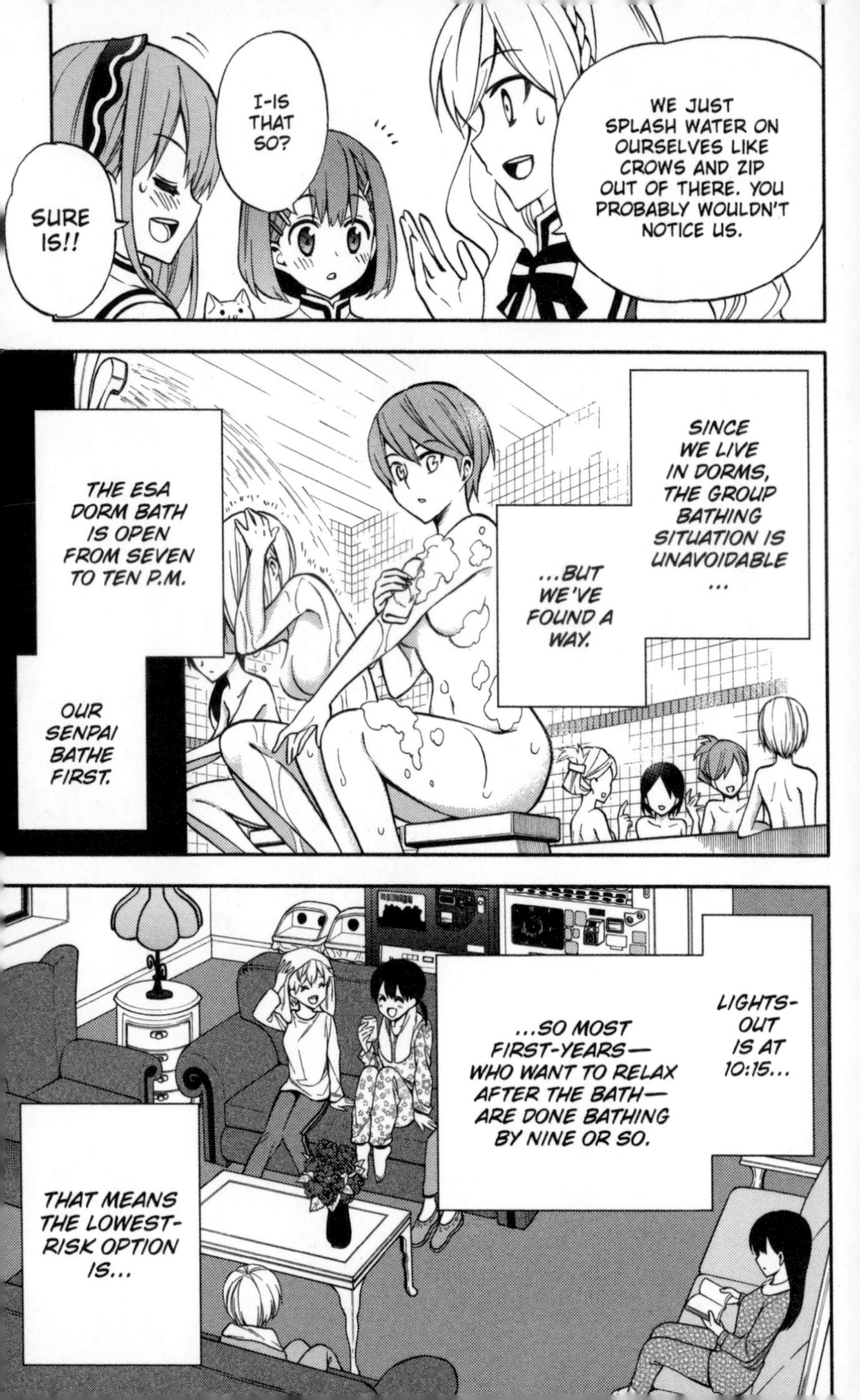
WE JUST SPLASH WATER ON OURSELVES LIKE CROWS AND ZIP OUT OF THERE. YOU PROBABLY WOULDN'T NOTICE US.
I-IS THAT SO?
SURE IS!!
SINCE WE LIVE IN DORMS, THE GROUP BATHING SITUATION IS UNAVOIDABLE...
...BUT WE'VE FOUND A WAY.
THE ESA DORM BATH IS OPEN FROM SEVEN TO TEN P.M.
OUR SENPAI BATHE FIRST.
LIGHTS-OUT IS AT 10:15...
...SO MOST FIRST-YEARS—WHO WANT TO RELAX AFTER THE BATH—ARE DONE BATHING BY NINE OR SO.
THAT MEANS THE LOWEST-RISK OPTION IS...

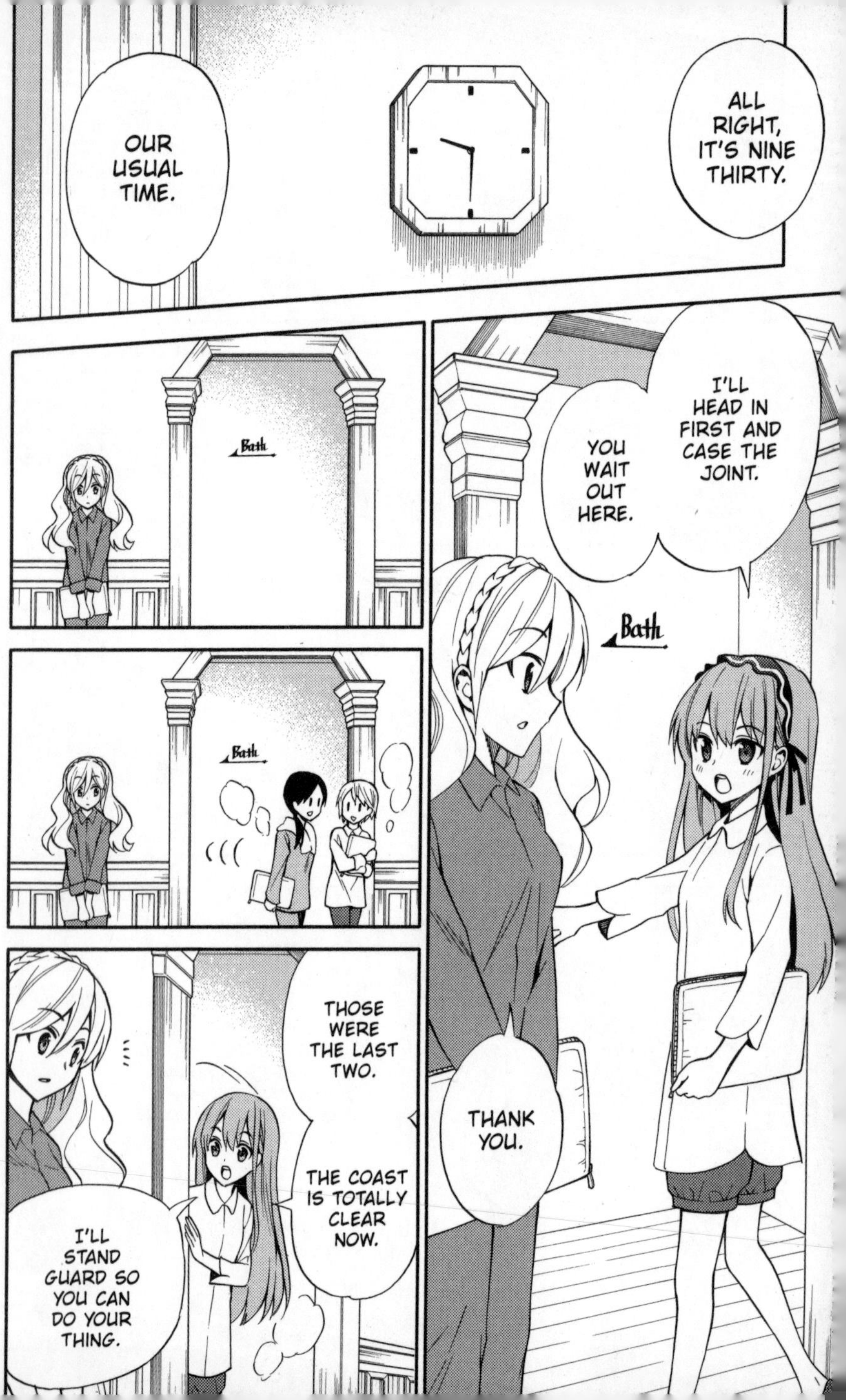
ALL RIGHT, IT'S NINE THIRTY.
OUR USUAL TIME.
I'LL HEAD IN FIRST AND CASE THE JOINT.
YOU WAIT OUT HERE.
Bath
THANK YOU.
Bath
Bath
THOSE WERE THE LAST TWO.
THE COAST IS TOTALLY CLEAR NOW.
I'LL STAND GUARD SO YOU CAN DO YOUR THING.

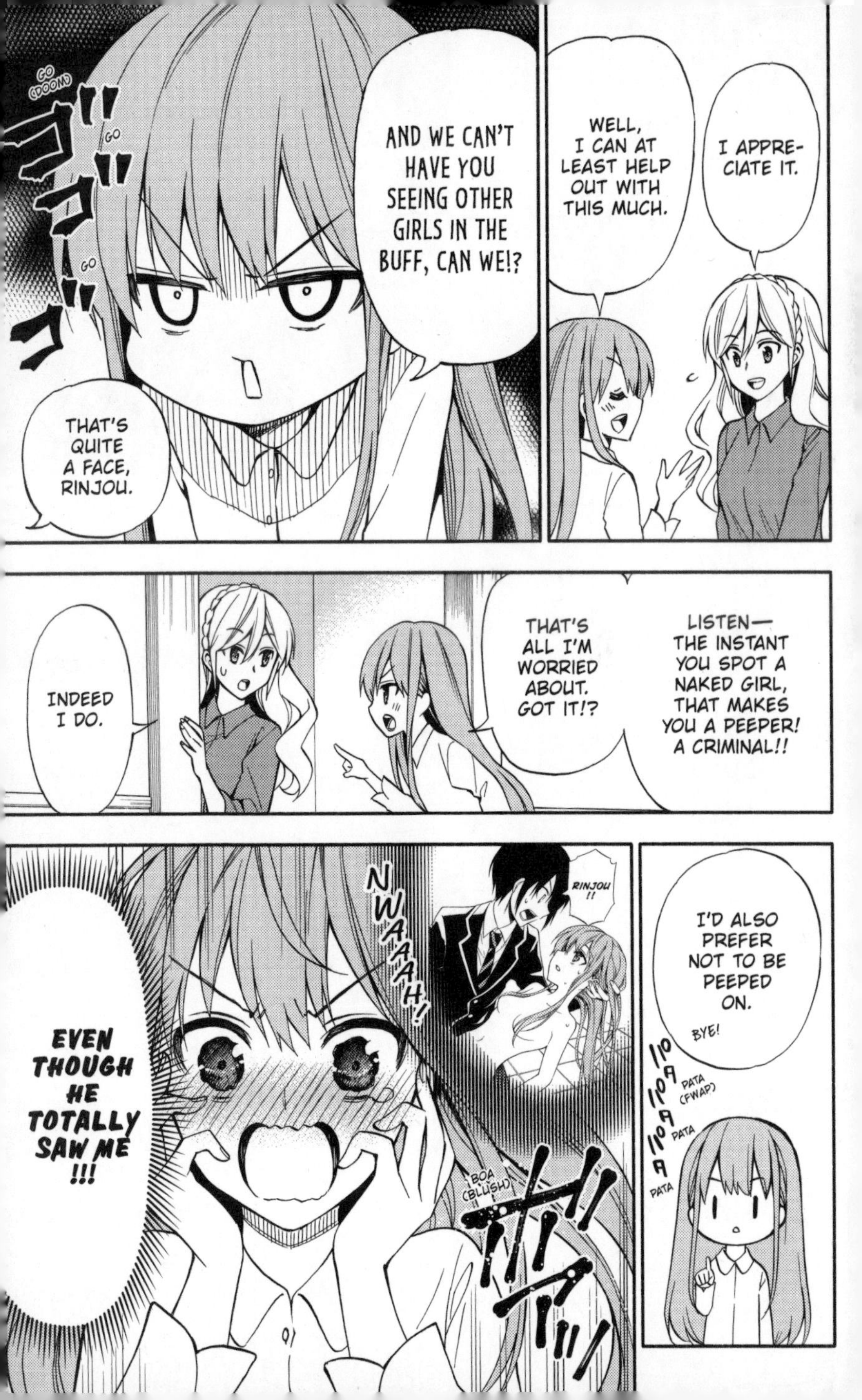
I APPRE-CIATE IT.
WELL, I CAN AT LEAST HELP OUT WITH THIS MUCH.
AND WE CAN'T HAVE YOU SEEING OTHER GIRLS IN THE BUFF, CAN WE!?
GO (DOOM)
GO
GO
THAT'S QUITE A FACE, RINJOU.
LISTEN— THE INSTANT YOU SPOT A NAKED GIRL, THAT MAKES YOU A PEEPER! A CRIMINAL!!
THAT'S ALL I'M WORRIED ABOUT. GOT IT!?
INDEED I DO.
I'D ALSO PREFER NOT TO BE PEEPED ON.
BYE!
PATA (FWAP)
PATA
PATA
RINJOU!!
NWAAAAH!
BOA (BLUSH)
EVEN THOUGH HE TOTALLY SAW ME!!!

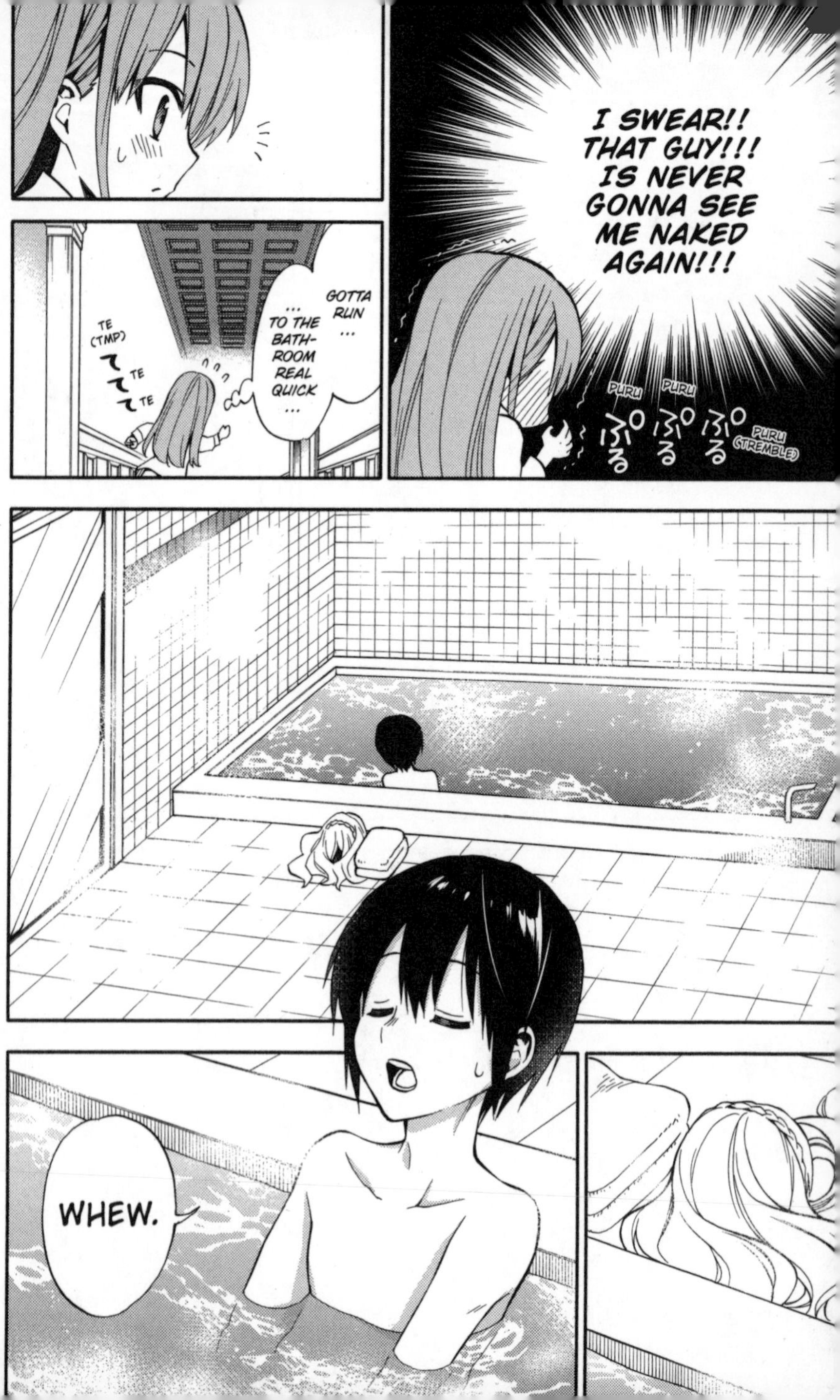
I SWEAR!! THAT GUY!!! IS NEVER GONNA SEE ME NAKED AGAIN!!!
PURU ぷる
PURU ぷる
PURU ぷる (TREMBLE)
GOTTA RUN ...
... TO THE BATH-ROOM REAL QUICK ...
TE (TMP) て
TE て
TE て
WHEW.

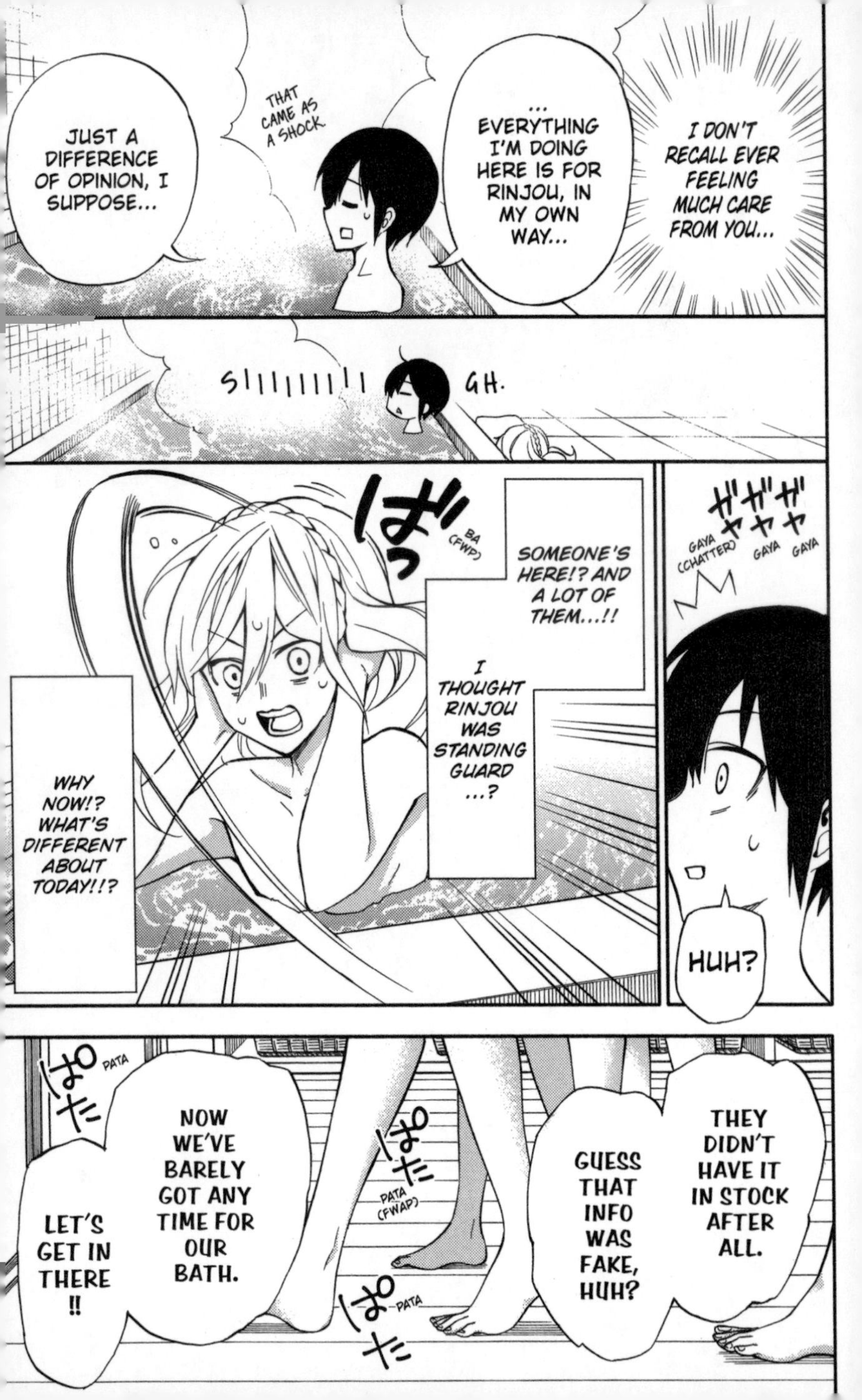
I DON'T RECALL EVER FEELING MUCH CARE FROM YOU...
... EVERYTHING I'M DOING HERE IS FOR RINJOU, IN MY OWN WAY...
THAT CAME AS A SHOCK
JUST A DIFFERENCE OF OPINION, I SUPPOSE...
SIIIIIIIII
GH.
ガヤガヤガヤ
GAYA (CHATTER) GAYA GAYA
HUH?
ばっ
BA (FWP)
SOMEONE'S HERE!? AND A LOT OF THEM...!!
I THOUGHT RINJOU WAS STANDING GUARD...?
WHY NOW!? WHAT'S DIFFERENT ABOUT TODAY!!?
THEY DIDN'T HAVE IT IN STOCK AFTER ALL.
GUESS THAT INFO WAS FAKE, HUH?
ぱた
PATA (FWAP)
NOW WE'VE BARELY GOT ANY TIME FOR OUR BATH.
ぱた
PATA
LET'S GET IN THERE !!
ぱた
PATA

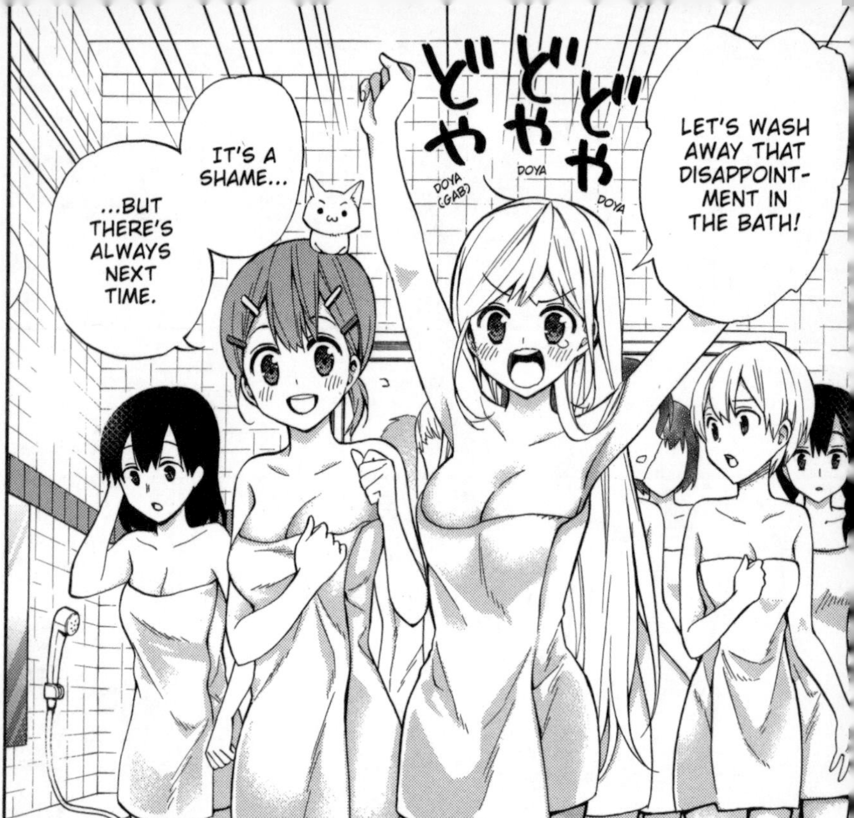
LET'S WASH AWAY THAT DISAPPOINTMENT IN THE BATH!
DOYA DOYA DOYA (GAB)
IT'S A SHAME...
...BUT THERE'S ALWAYS NEXT TIME.

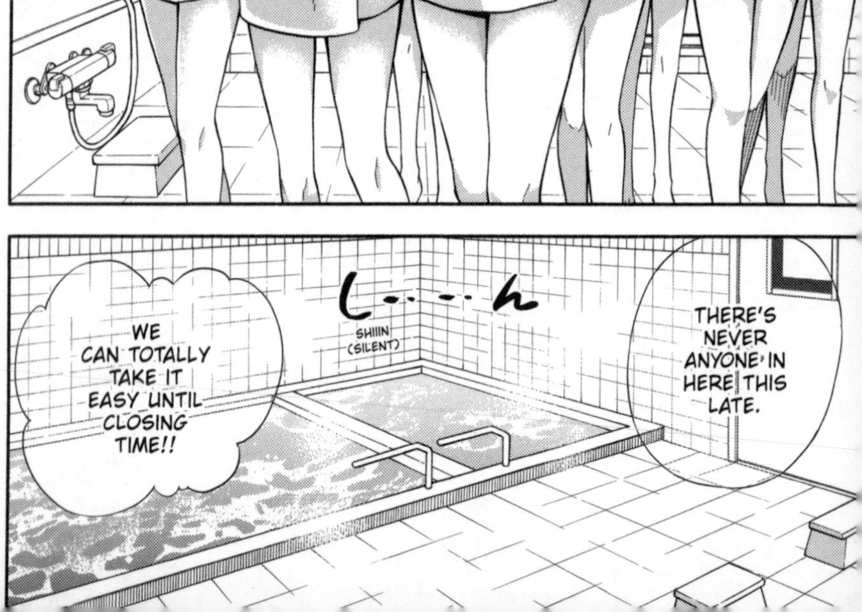
THERE'S NEVER ANYONE IN HERE THIS LATE.
SHIIIN (SILENT)
WE CAN TOTALLY TAKE IT EASY UNTIL CLOSING TIME!!

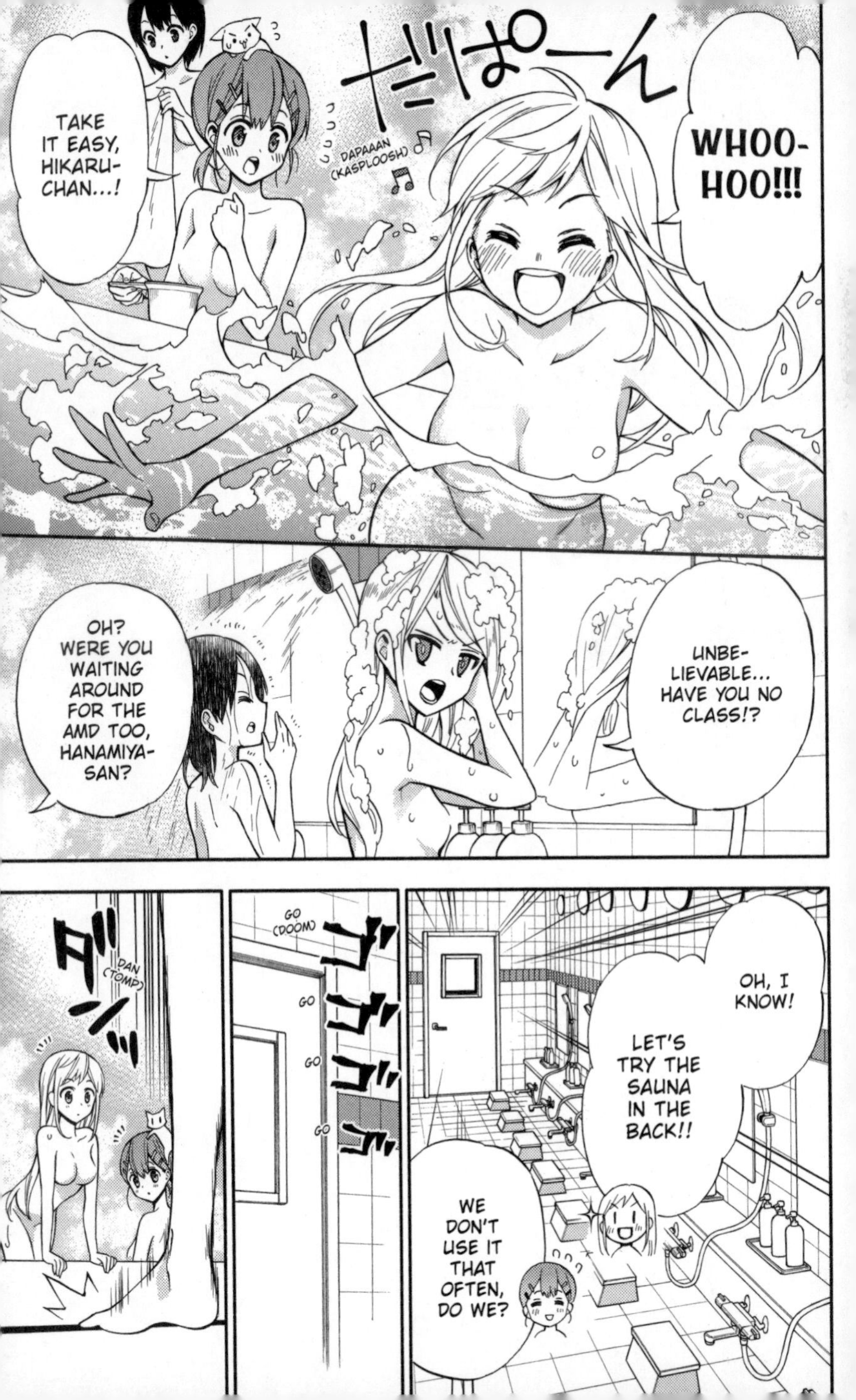
WHOO-HOO!!!
だぱーん
DAPAAAN (KASPLOOSH)
TAKE IT EASY, HIKARU-CHAN...!
UNBE-LIEVABLE... HAVE YOU NO CLASS!?
OH? WERE YOU WAITING AROUND FOR THE AMD TOO, HANAMIYA-SAN?
OH, I KNOW!
LET'S TRY THE SAUNA IN THE BACK!!
WE DON'T USE IT THAT OFTEN, DO WE?
GO (DOOM)
GO
GO
GO
DAN (TOMP)

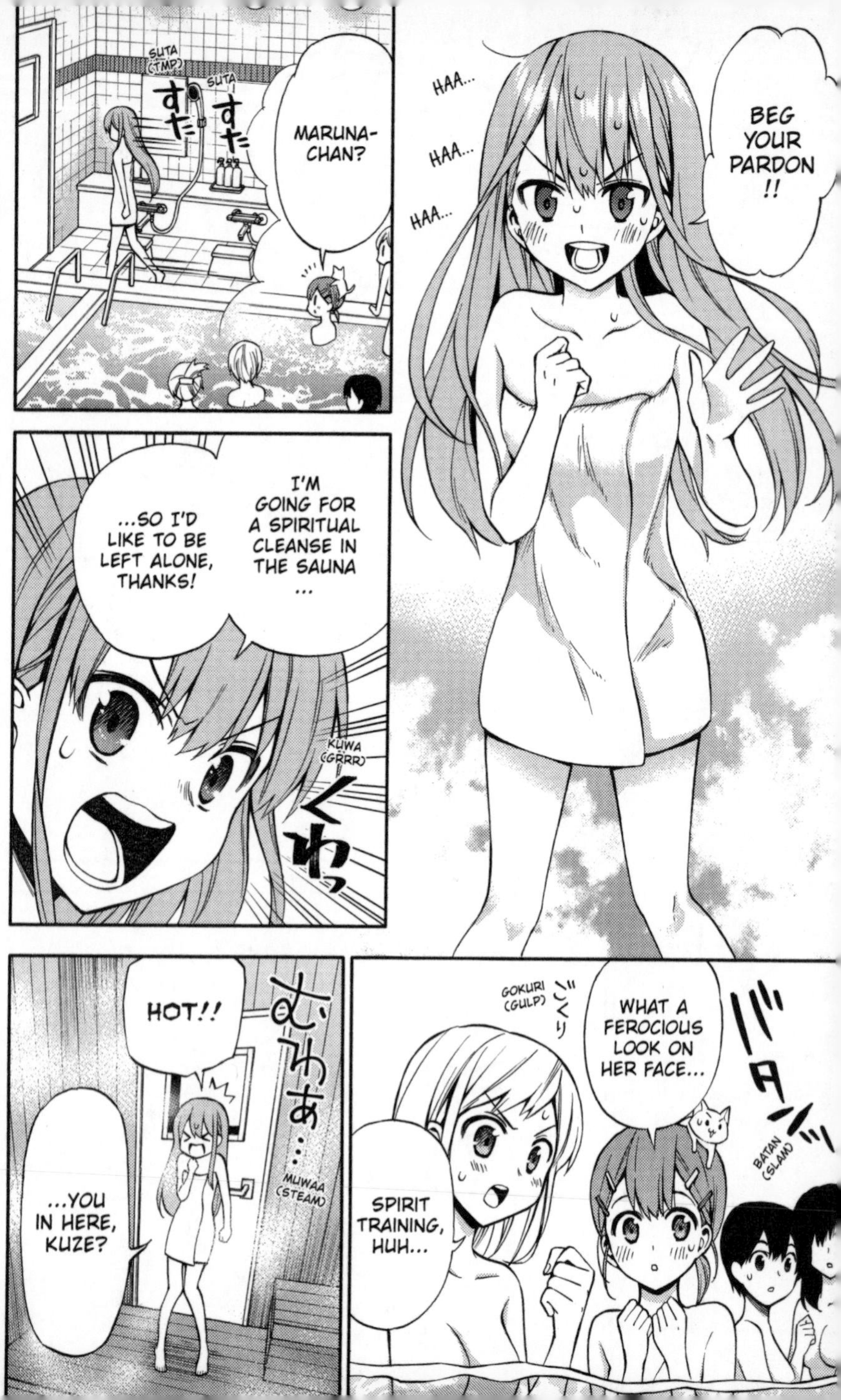
BEG YOUR PARDON!!
HAA...
HAA...
HAA...
SUTA (TMP)
すた
SUTA
すた
MARUNA-CHAN?
I'M GOING FOR A SPIRITUAL CLEANSE IN THE SAUNA...
...SO I'D LIKE TO BE LEFT ALONE, THANKS!
KUWA (GRRR)
くわっ
バタンッ
BATAN (SLAM)
WHAT A FEROCIOUS LOOK ON HER FACE...
GOKURI (GULP)
ごくり
SPIRIT TRAINING, HUH...
むわぁ…
MUWAA (STEAM)
HOT!!
...YOU IN HERE, KUZE?

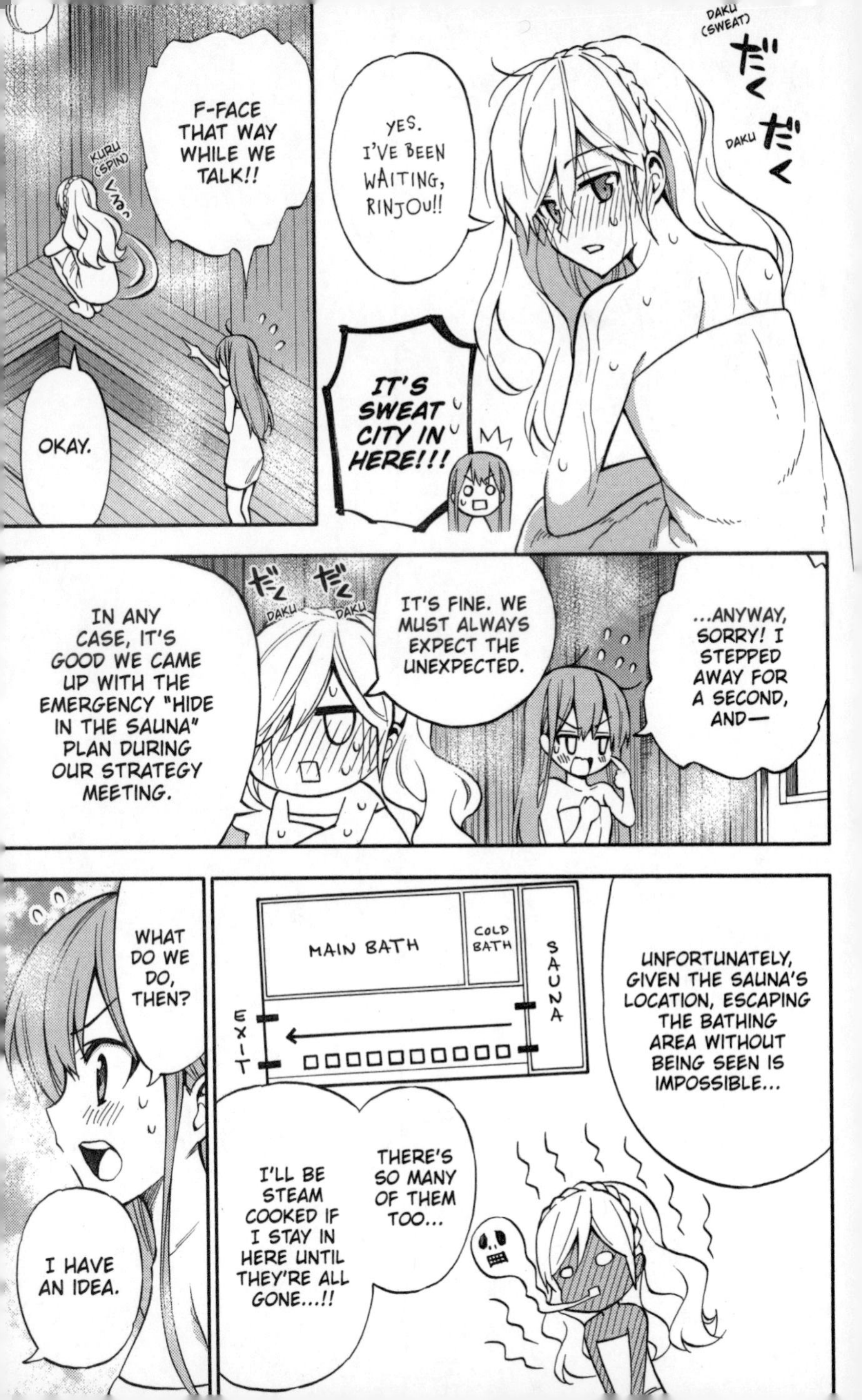

DAKU (SWEAT)
だく
DAKU
だく
YES. I'VE BEEN WAITING, RINJOU!!
IT'S SWEAT CITY IN HERE!!!
F-FACE THAT WAY WHILE WE TALK!!
KURU (SPIN)
くるっ
OKAY.
...ANYWAY, SORRY! I STEPPED AWAY FOR A SECOND, AND—
IT'S FINE. WE MUST ALWAYS EXPECT THE UNEXPECTED.
だく
DAKU
だく
DAKU
IN ANY CASE, IT'S GOOD WE CAME UP WITH THE EMERGENCY "HIDE IN THE SAUNA" PLAN DURING OUR STRATEGY MEETING.
UNFORTUNATELY, GIVEN THE SAUNA'S LOCATION, ESCAPING THE BATHING AREA WITHOUT BEING SEEN IS IMPOSSIBLE...
SAUNA
COLD BATH
MAIN BATH
EXIT
THERE'S SO MANY OF THEM TOO...
I'LL BE STEAM COOKED IF I STAY IN HERE UNTIL THEY'RE ALL GONE...!!
WHAT DO WE DO, THEN?
I HAVE AN IDEA.

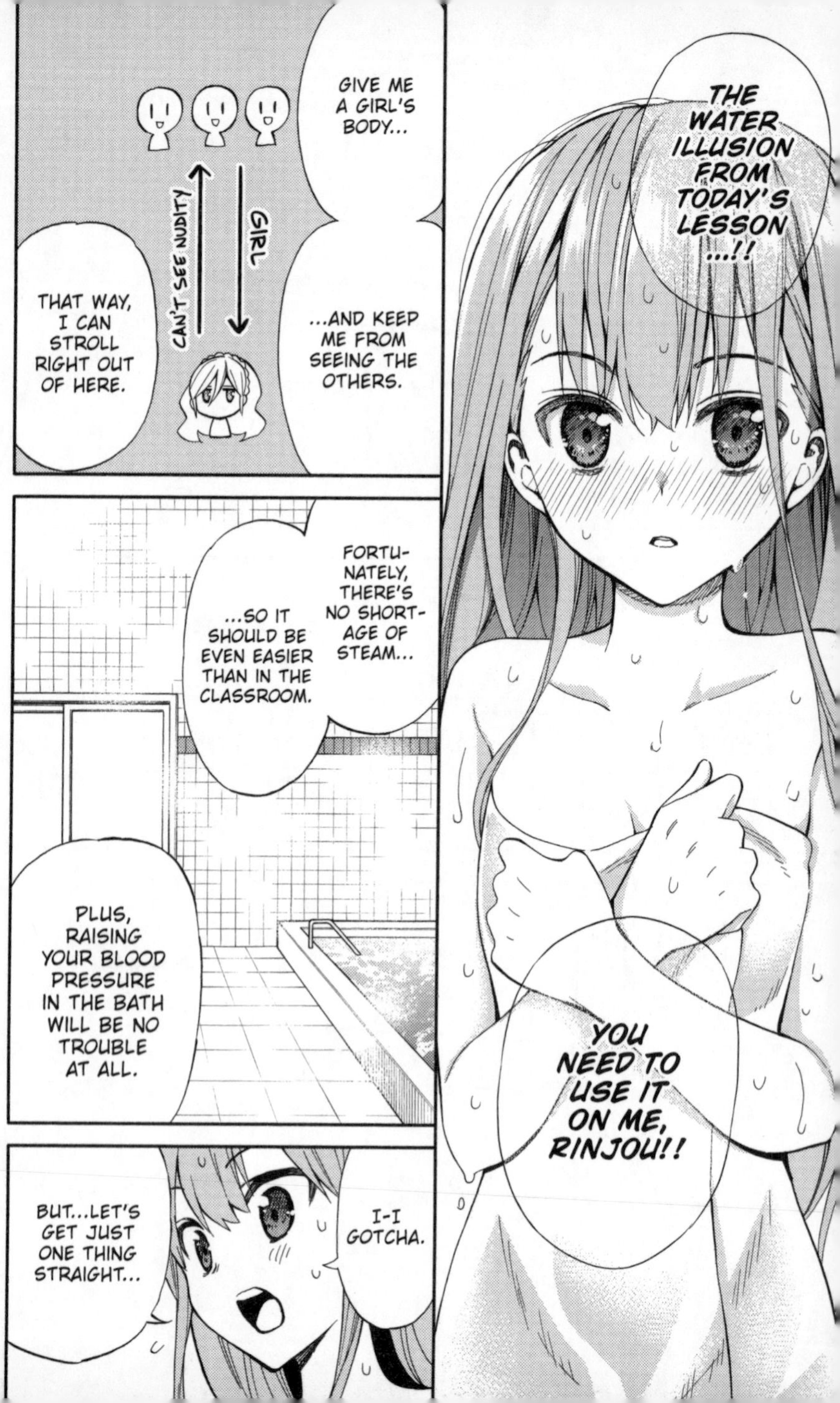
THE WATER ILLUSION FROM TODAY'S LESSON...!!
YOU NEED TO USE IT ON ME, RINJOU!!
GIVE ME A GIRL'S BODY...
...AND KEEP ME FROM SEEING THE OTHERS.
GIRL
CAN'T SEE NUDITY
THAT WAY, I CAN STROLL RIGHT OUT OF HERE.
FORTU-NATELY, THERE'S NO SHORT-AGE OF STEAM...
...SO IT SHOULD BE EVEN EASIER THAN IN THE CLASSROOM.
PLUS, RAISING YOUR BLOOD PRESSURE IN THE BATH WILL BE NO TROUBLE AT ALL.
I-I GOTCHA.
BUT...LET'S GET JUST ONE THING STRAIGHT...

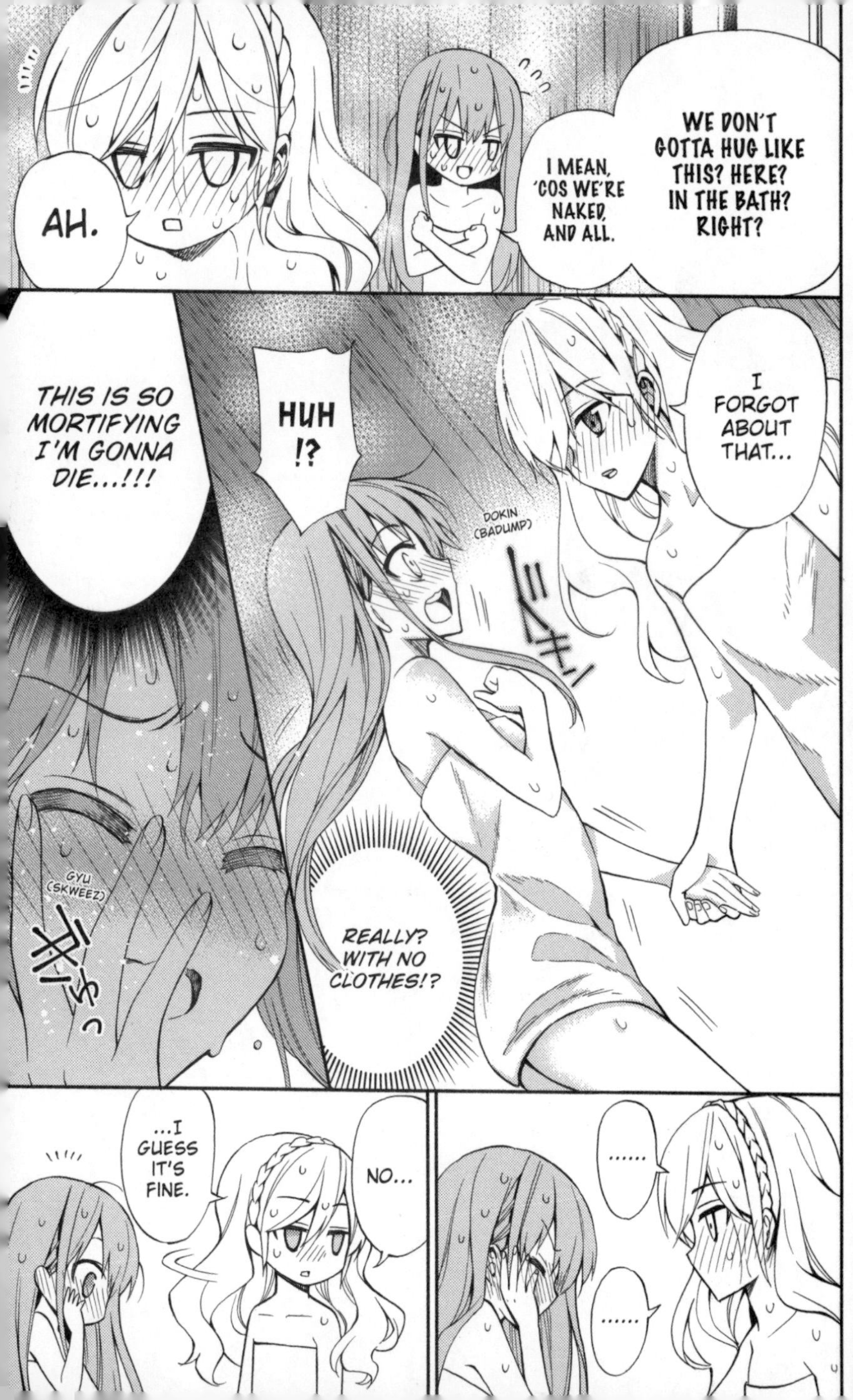
WE DON'T GOTTA HUG LIKE THIS? HERE? IN THE BATH? RIGHT?
I MEAN, 'COS WE'RE NAKED, AND ALL.
AH.
I FORGOT ABOUT THAT...
DOKIN (BADUMP)
HUH !?
REALLY? WITH NO CLOTHES!?
THIS IS SO MORTIFYING I'M GONNA DIE...!!!
GYU (SKWEEZ)
......
......
NO...
...I GUESS IT'S FINE.

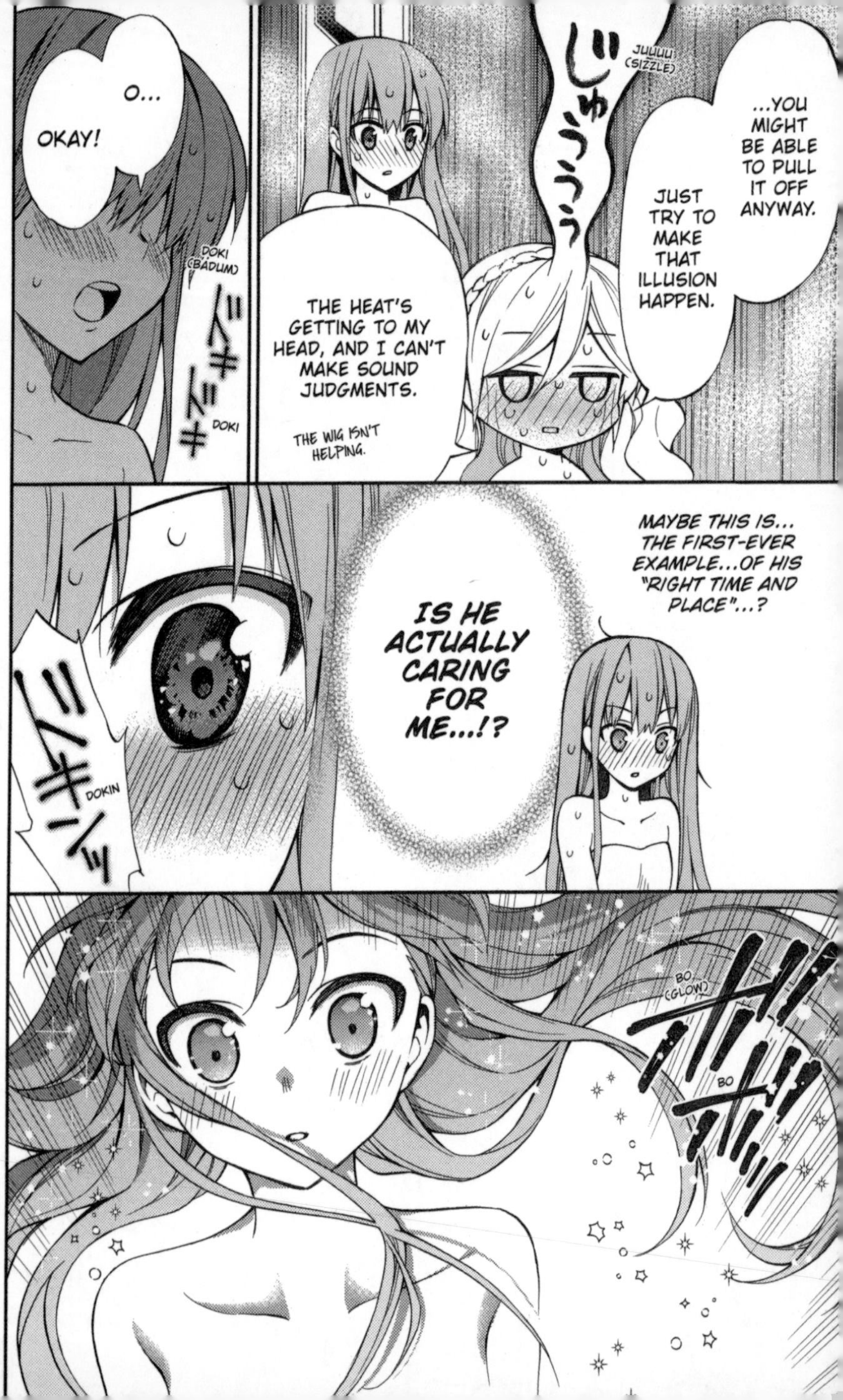
...YOU MIGHT BE ABLE TO PULL IT OFF ANYWAY.
JUST TRY TO MAKE THAT ILLUSION HAPPEN.
JUUUUU (SIZZLE)
THE HEAT'S GETTING TO MY HEAD, AND I CAN'T MAKE SOUND JUDGMENTS.
THE WIG ISN'T HELPING.
O... OKAY!
DOKI (BADUM)
DOKI
MAYBE THIS IS... THE FIRST-EVER EXAMPLE...OF HIS "RIGHT TIME AND PLACE"...?
IS HE ACTUALLY CARING FOR ME...!?
DOKIN
BO (GLOW)
BO

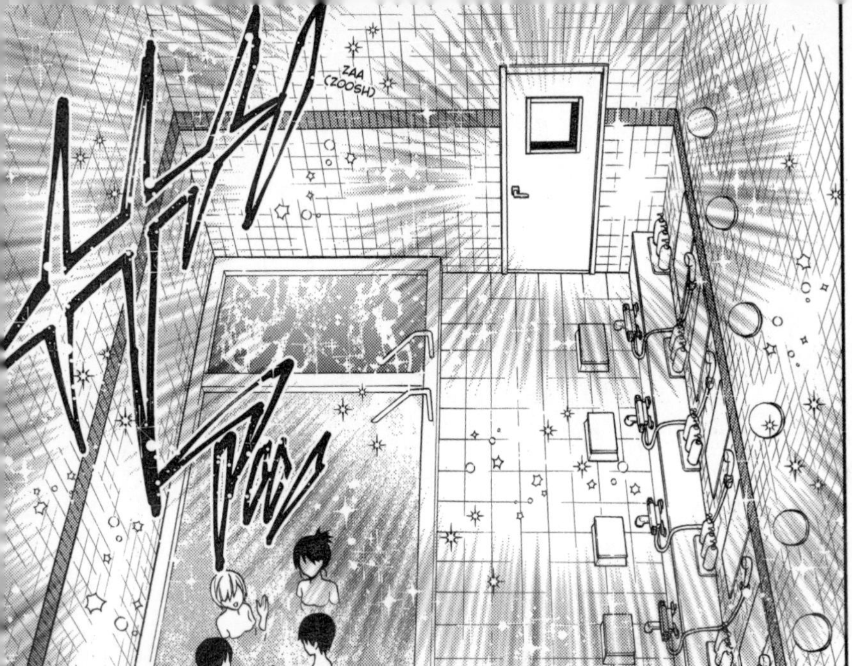
ZAA (ZOOSH)

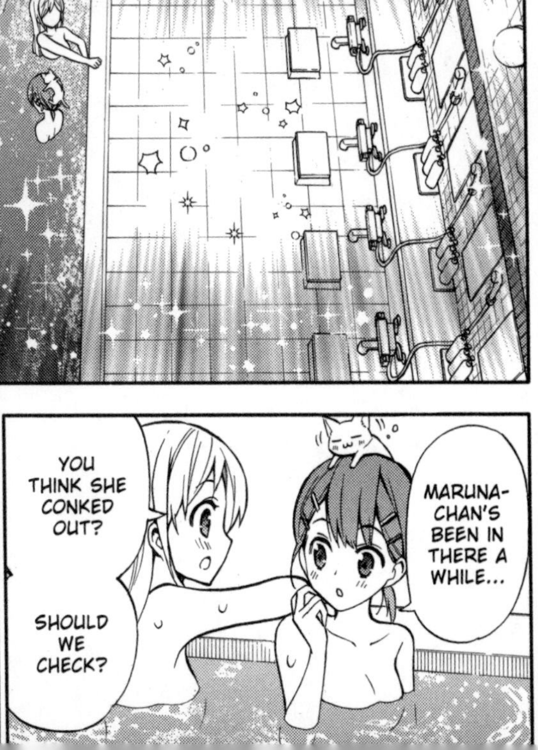
MARUNA-CHAN'S BEEN IN THERE A WHILE...
YOU THINK SHE CONKED OUT?
SHOULD WE CHECK?

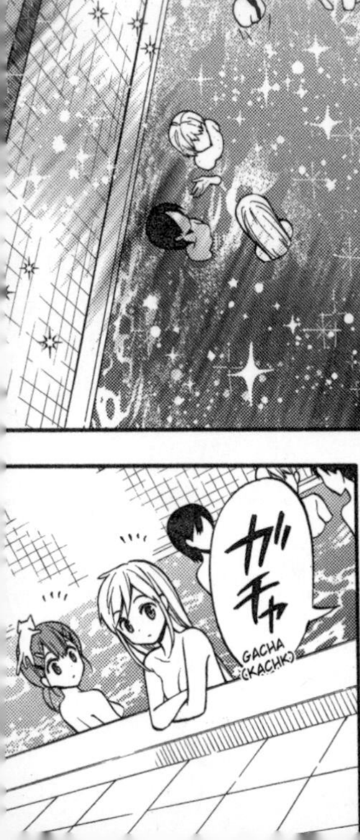
ガチャ
GACHA (KACHK)

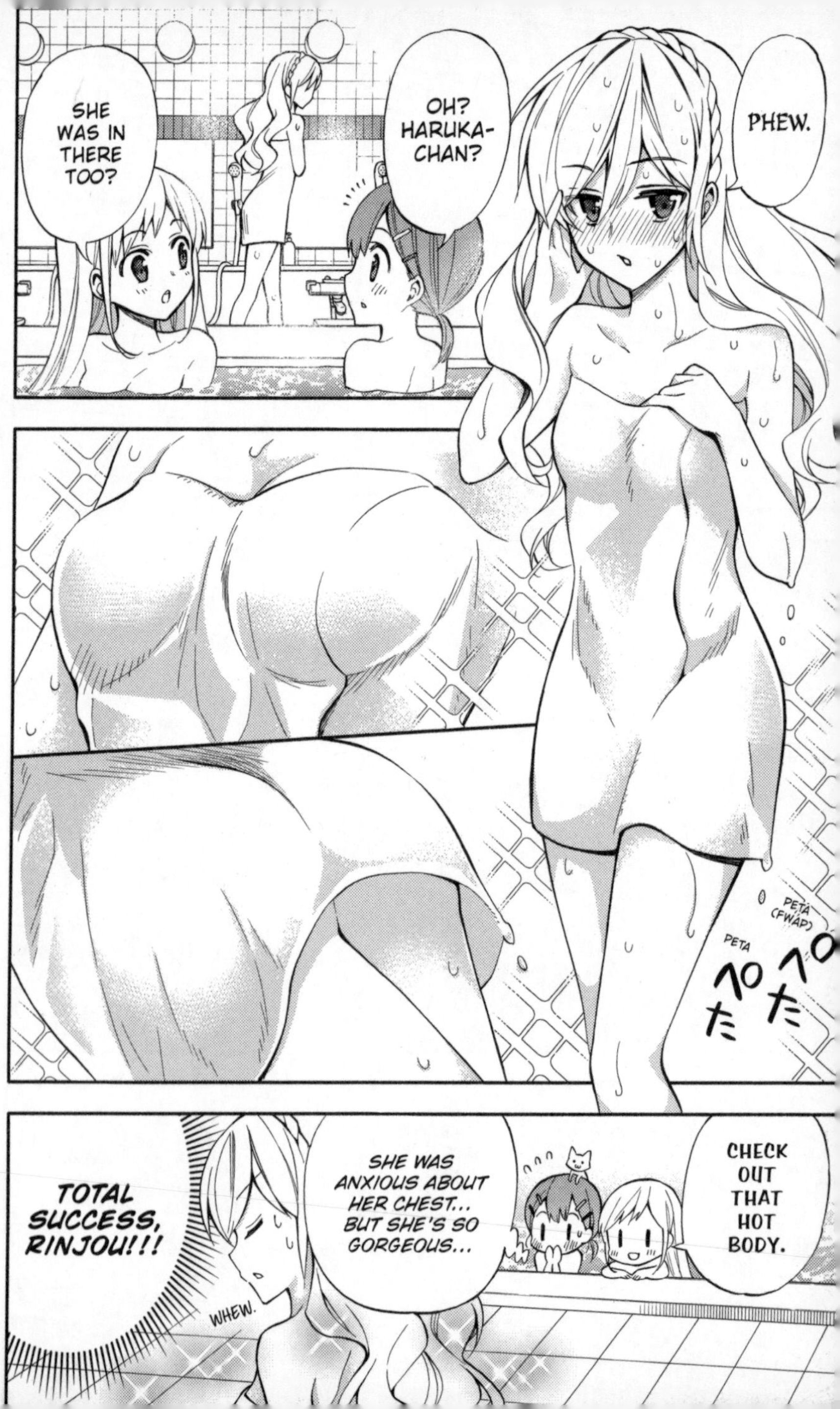
PHEW.
PETA (FWAP)
PETA
ぺた ぺた
OH? HARUKA-CHAN?
SHE WAS IN THERE TOO?
CHECK OUT THAT HOT BODY.
SHE WAS ANXIOUS ABOUT HER CHEST... BUT SHE'S SO GORGEOUS...
TOTAL SUCCESS, RINJOU!!!
WHEW.

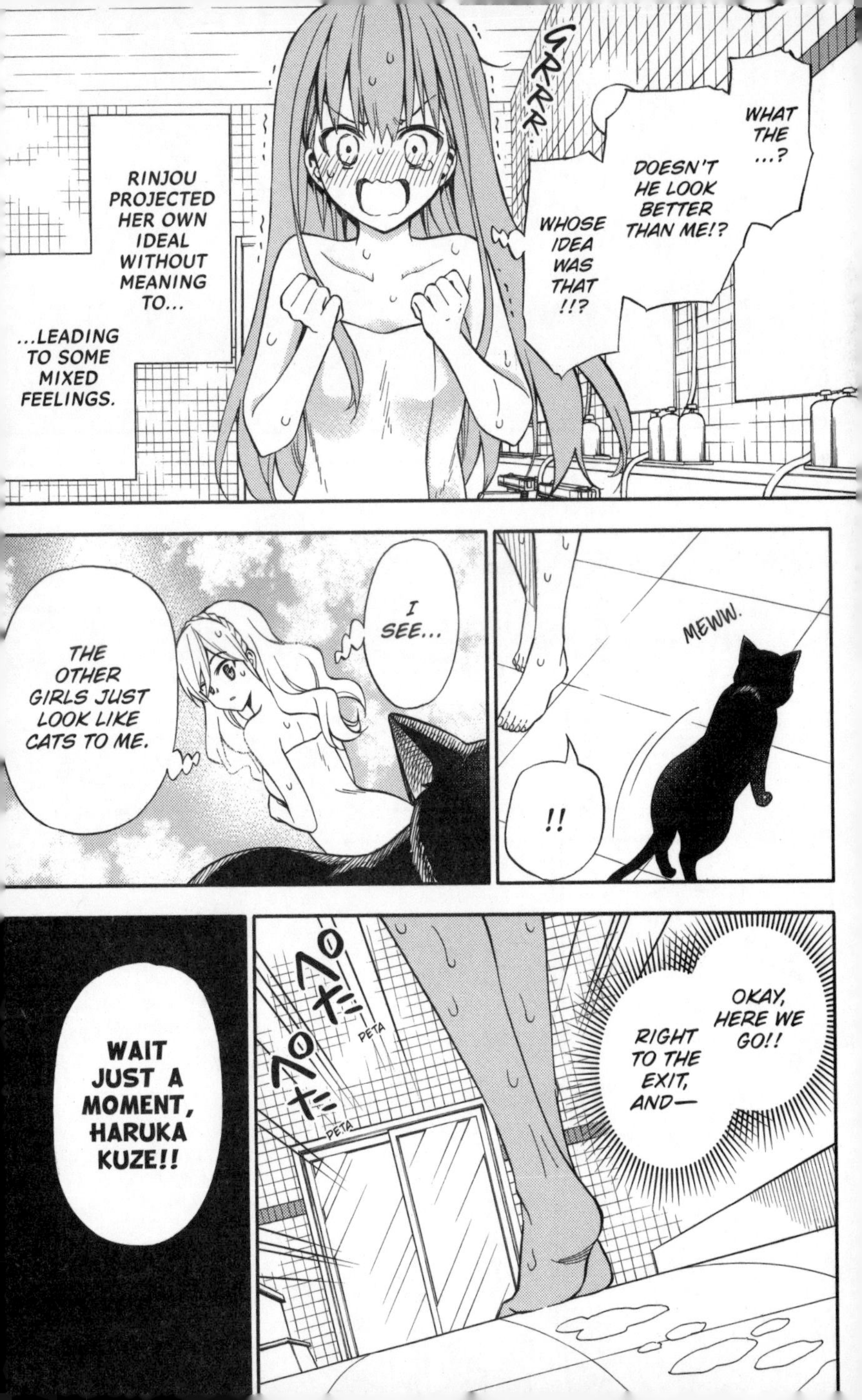
GRRR
WHAT THE ...?
DOESN'T HE LOOK BETTER THAN ME!?
WHOSE IDEA WAS THAT!!?
RINJOU PROJECTED HER OWN IDEAL WITHOUT MEANING TO...
...LEADING TO SOME MIXED FEELINGS.
MEWW.
!!
I SEE...
THE OTHER GIRLS JUST LOOK LIKE CATS TO ME.
OKAY, HERE WE GO!!
RIGHT TO THE EXIT, AND—
ぺた PETA
ぺた PETA
WAIT JUST A MOMENT, HARUKA KUZE!!

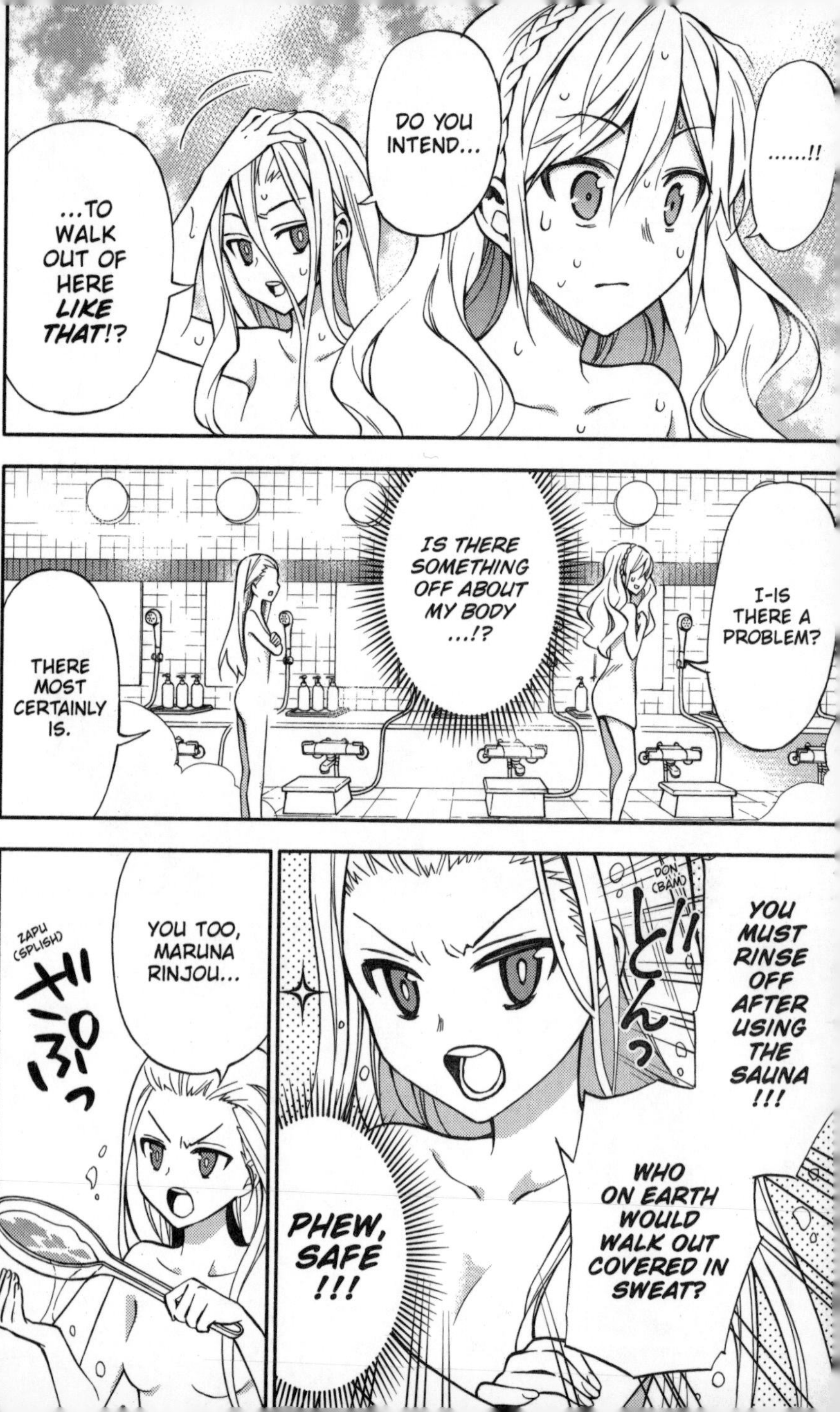
......!!
DO YOU INTEND...
...TO WALK OUT OF HERE LIKE THAT!?
I-IS THERE A PROBLEM?
IS THERE SOMETHING OFF ABOUT MY BODY ...!?
THERE MOST CERTAINLY IS.
YOU MUST RINSE OFF AFTER USING THE SAUNA !!!
DON (BAM)
どんっ
WHO ON EARTH WOULD WALK OUT COVERED IN SWEAT?
PHEW, SAFE !!!
YOU TOO, MARUNA RINJOU...
ZAPU (SPLISH)
ざぷっ

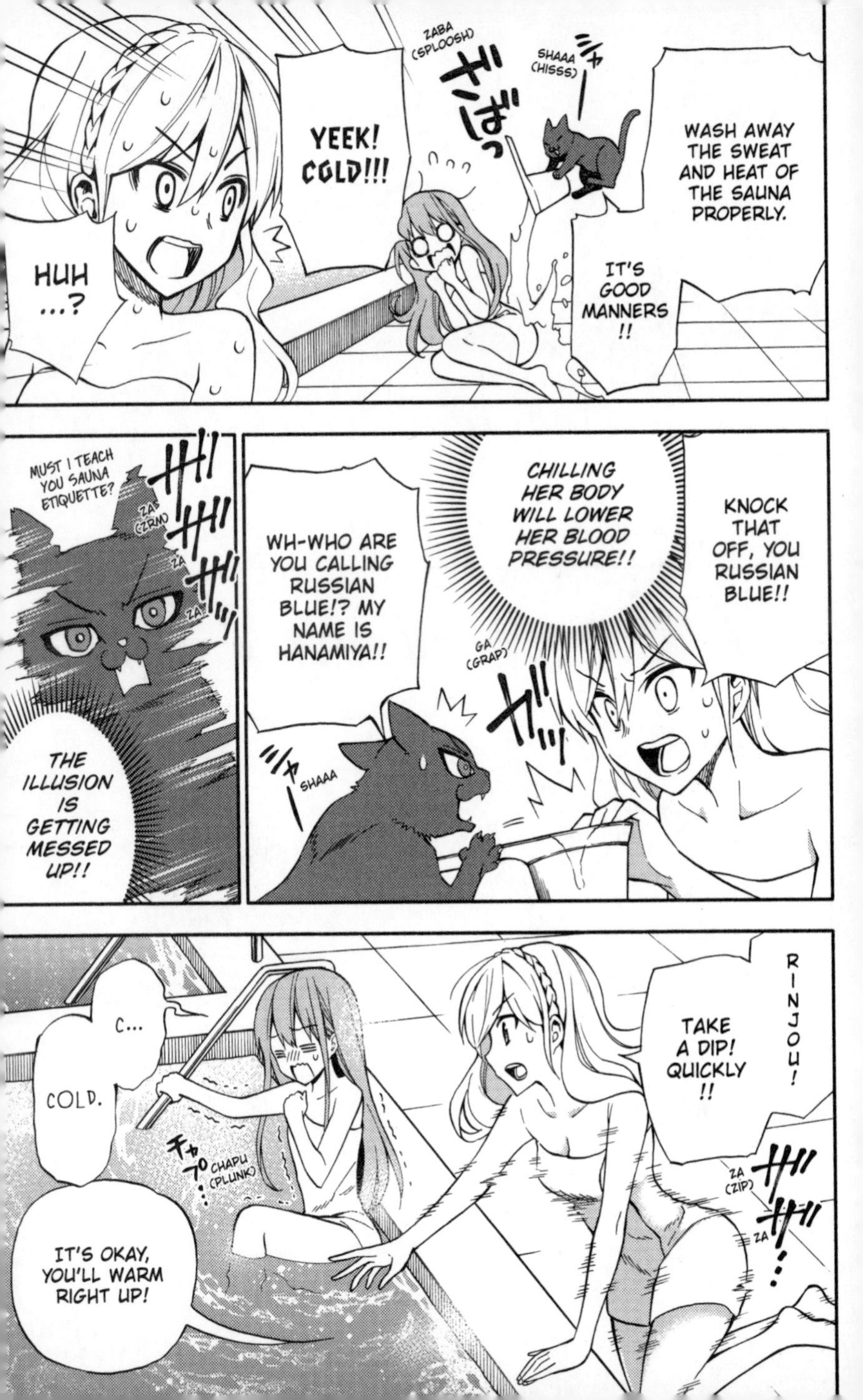
WASH AWAY THE SWEAT AND HEAT OF THE SAUNA PROPERLY.
IT'S GOOD MANNERS!!
SHAAA (HISSS)
ZABA (SPLOOSH)
YEEK! COLD!!!
HUH ...?
KNOCK THAT OFF, YOU RUSSIAN BLUE!!
CHILLING HER BODY WILL LOWER HER BLOOD PRESSURE!!
WH-WHO ARE YOU CALLING RUSSIAN BLUE!? MY NAME IS HANAMIYA!!
GA (GRAP)
SHAAA
MUST I TEACH YOU SAUNA ETIQUETTE?
ZA (ZRM)
ZA
ZA
THE ILLUSION IS GETTING MESSED UP!!
RINJOU!
TAKE A DIP! QUICKLY!!
ZA (ZIP)
ZA
CHAPU (PLUNK)
C... COLD.
IT'S OKAY, YOU'LL WARM RIGHT UP!

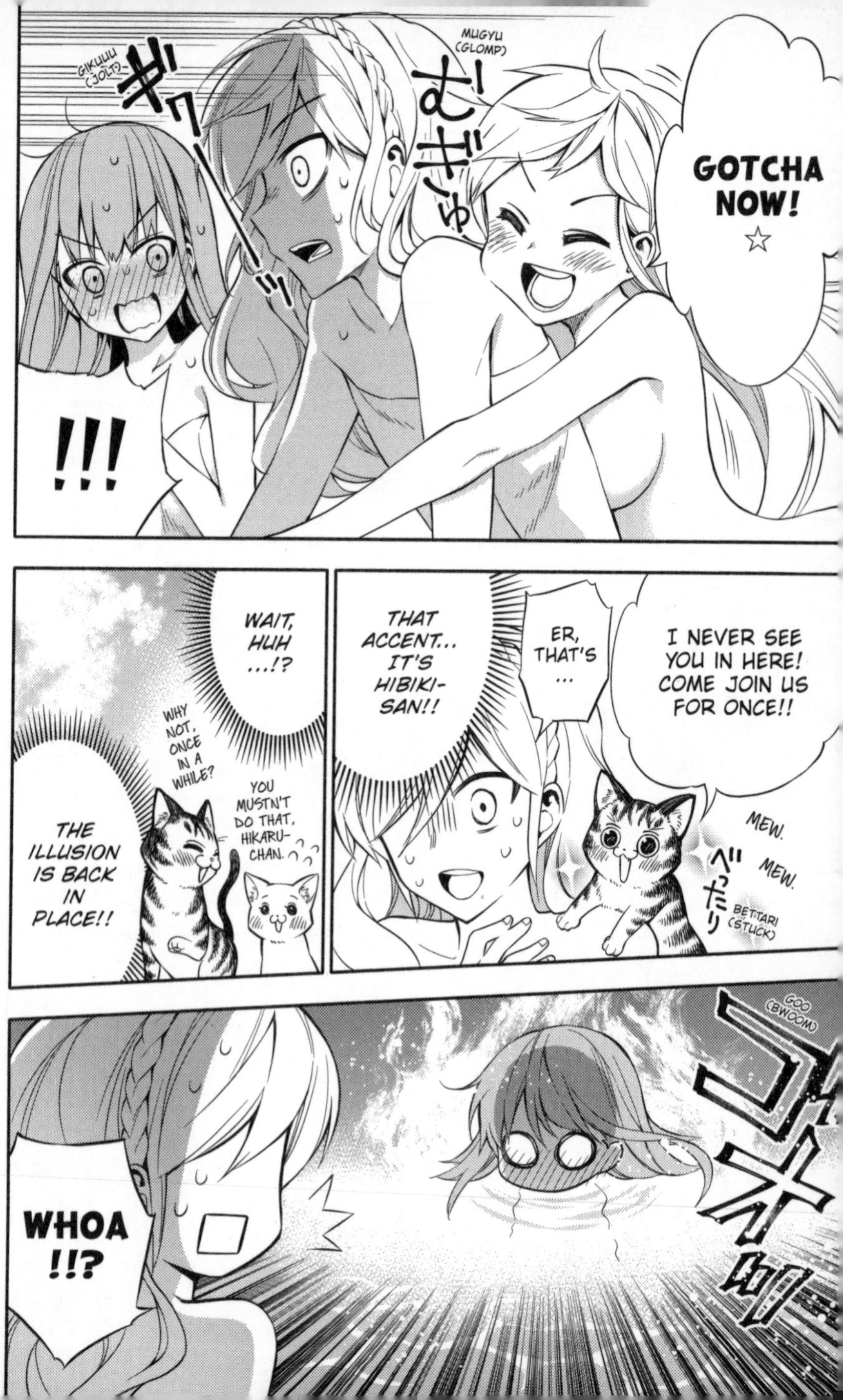
GOTCHA NOW! ☆
むぎゅ
MUGYU (GLOMP)
ギクッ
GIKUUU (JOLT)
!!!
I NEVER SEE YOU IN HERE! COME JOIN US FOR ONCE!!
ER, THAT'S ...
THAT ACCENT... IT'S HIBIKI-SAN!!
MEW.
MEW.
べったり
BETTARI (STUCK)
WAIT, HUH ...!?
WHY NOT, ONCE IN A WHILE?
YOU MUSTN'T DO THAT, HIKARU-CHAN.
THE ILLUSION IS BACK IN PLACE!!
GOO (BWOOM)
WHOA !!?

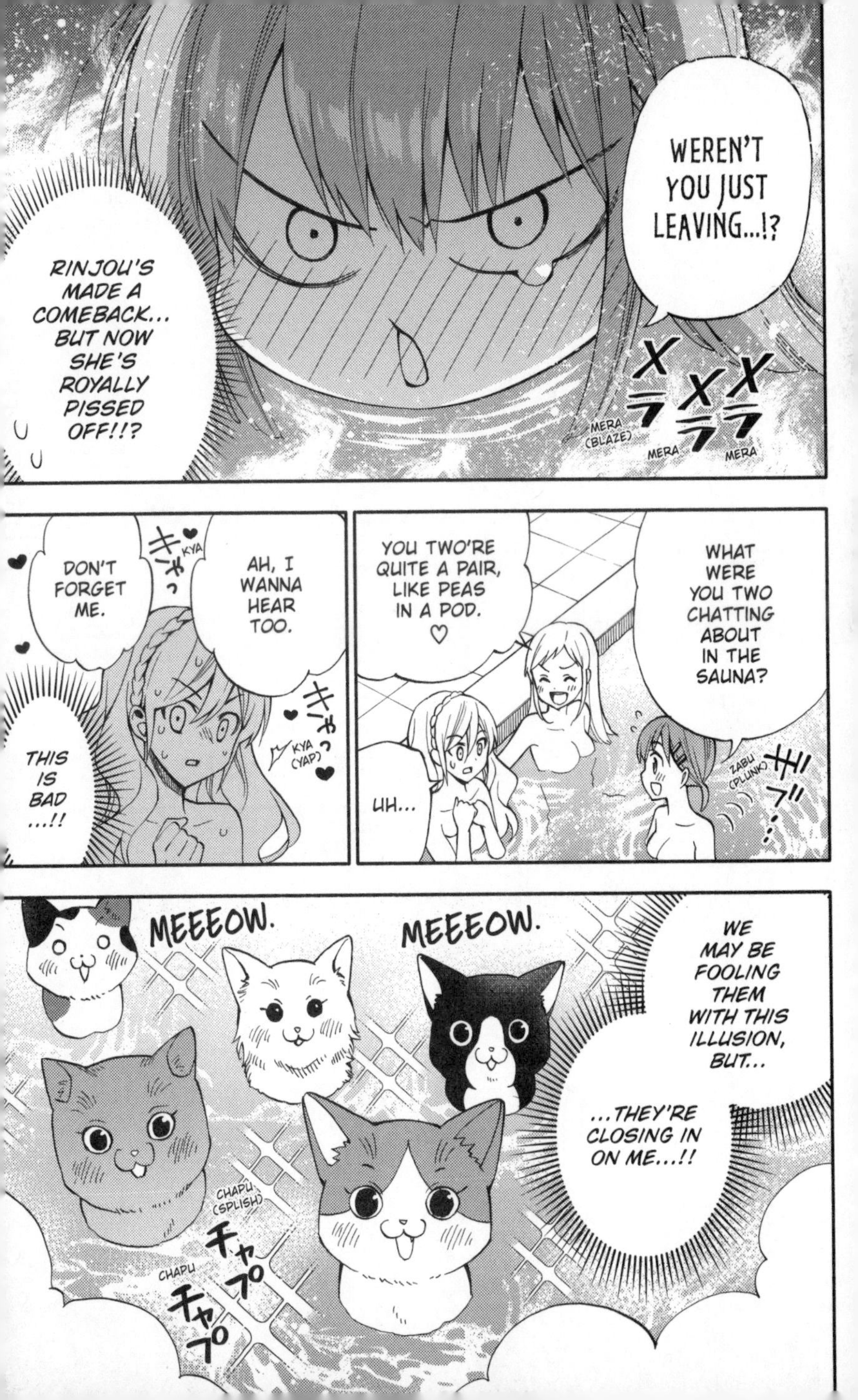
WEREN'T YOU JUST LEAVING...!?
MERA (BLAZE)
MERA
MERA
RINJOU'S MADE A COMEBACK... BUT NOW SHE'S ROYALLY PISSED OFF!!?
WHAT WERE YOU TWO CHATTING ABOUT IN THE SAUNA?
ZABU (PLUNK)
YOU TWO'RE QUITE A PAIR, LIKE PEAS IN A POD. ♡
UH...
AH, I WANNA HEAR TOO.
KYA
DON'T FORGET ME.
KYA (YAP)
THIS IS BAD ...!!
WE MAY BE FOOLING THEM WITH THIS ILLUSION, BUT...
...THEY'RE CLOSING IN ON ME...!!
MEEEOW.
MEEEOW.
CHAPU (SPLISH)
CHAPU

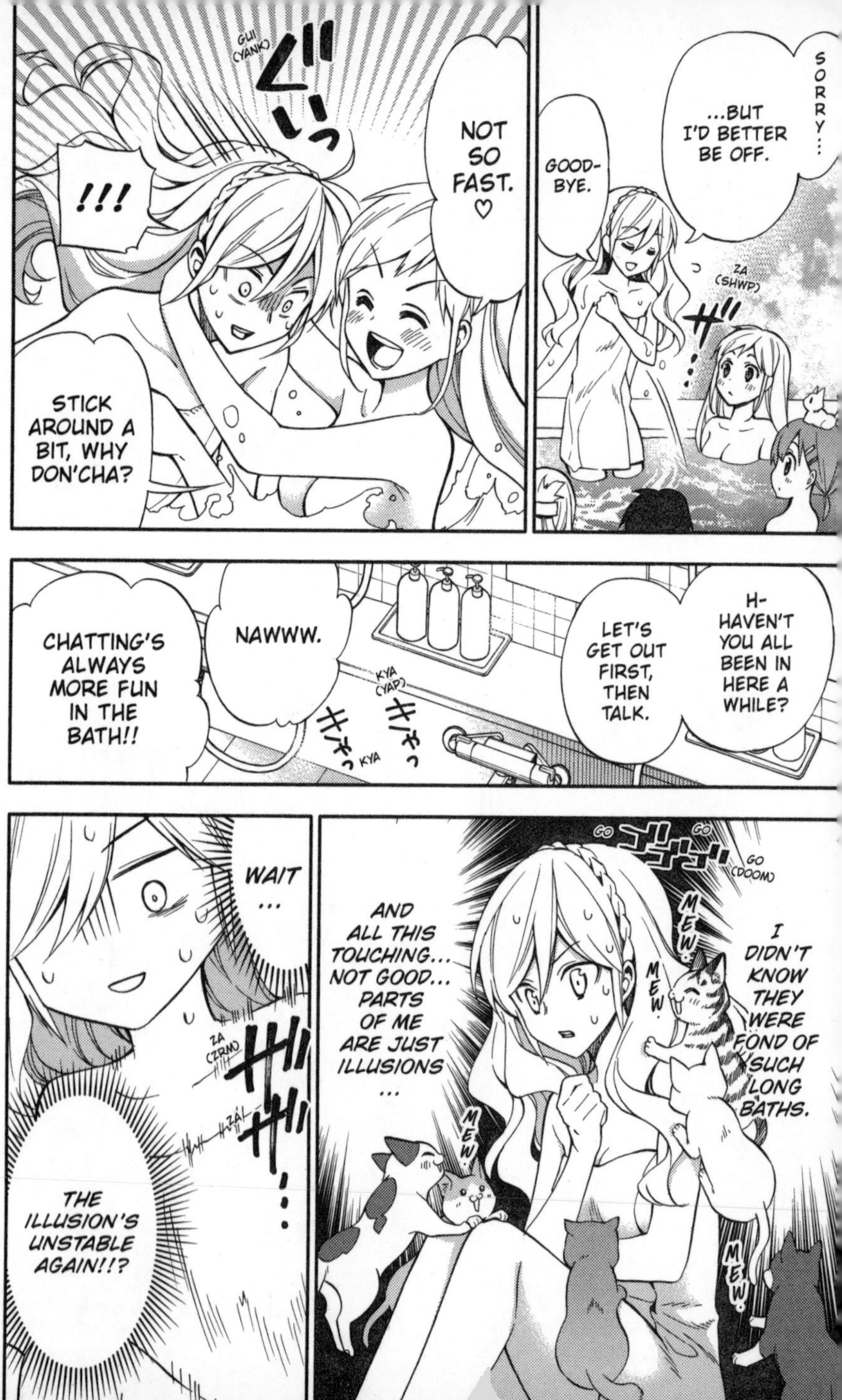
SORRY...
...BUT I'D BETTER BE OFF.
GOOD-BYE.
ZA (SHWP)
NOT SO FAST. ♡
GUI (YANK)
!!!
STICK AROUND A BIT, WHY DON'CHA?
H-HAVEN'T YOU ALL BEEN IN HERE A WHILE?
LET'S GET OUT FIRST, THEN TALK.
KYA (YAP)
KYA
NAWWW.
CHATTING'S ALWAYS MORE FUN IN THE BATH!!
GO GO GO (DOOM)
I DIDN'T KNOW THEY WERE FOND OF SUCH LONG BATHS.
MEW.
MEW.
AND ALL THIS TOUCHING... NOT GOOD... PARTS OF ME ARE JUST ILLUSIONS...
MEW.
MEW.
WAIT...
ZA
ZA
THE ILLUSION'S UNSTABLE AGAIN!!?

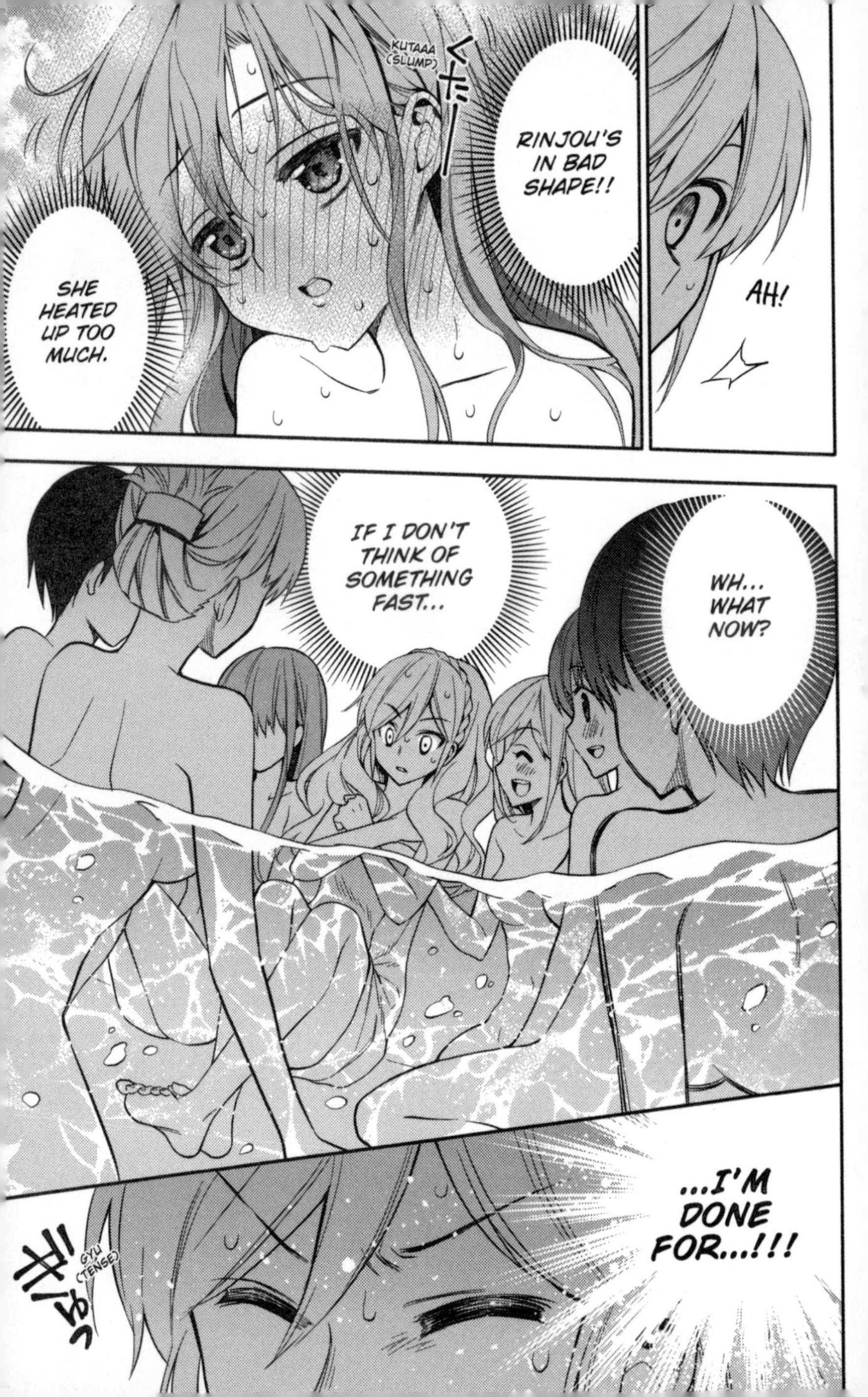
AH!
KUTAAA (SLUMP)
RINJOU'S IN BAD SHAPE!!
SHE HEATED UP TOO MUCH.
WH... WHAT NOW?
IF I DON'T THINK OF SOMETHING FAST...
...I'M DONE FOR...!!!
GYU (TENSE)

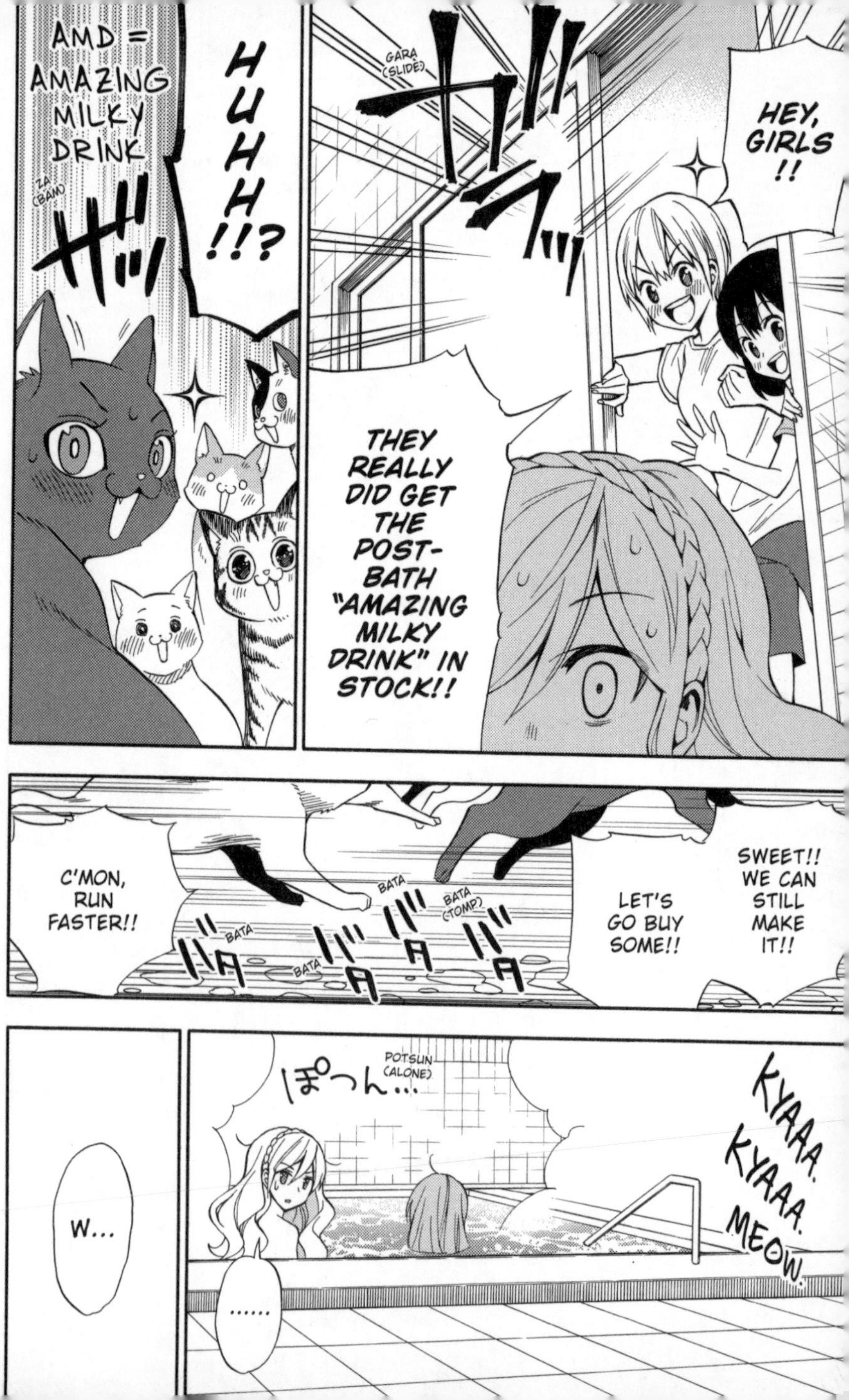
GARA (SLIDE)
HEY, GIRLS!!
THEY REALLY DID GET THE POST-BATH "AMAZING MILKY DRINK" IN STOCK!!
HUHHH!!?
ZA (BAM)
AMD = AMAZING MILKY DRINK
SWEET!! WE CAN STILL MAKE IT!!
LET'S GO BUY SOME!!
BATA (TOMP)
BATA
BATA
BATA
C'MON, RUN FASTER!!
KYAAA. KYAAA. MEOW.
POTSUN (ALONE)
ぽつん…
......
W...

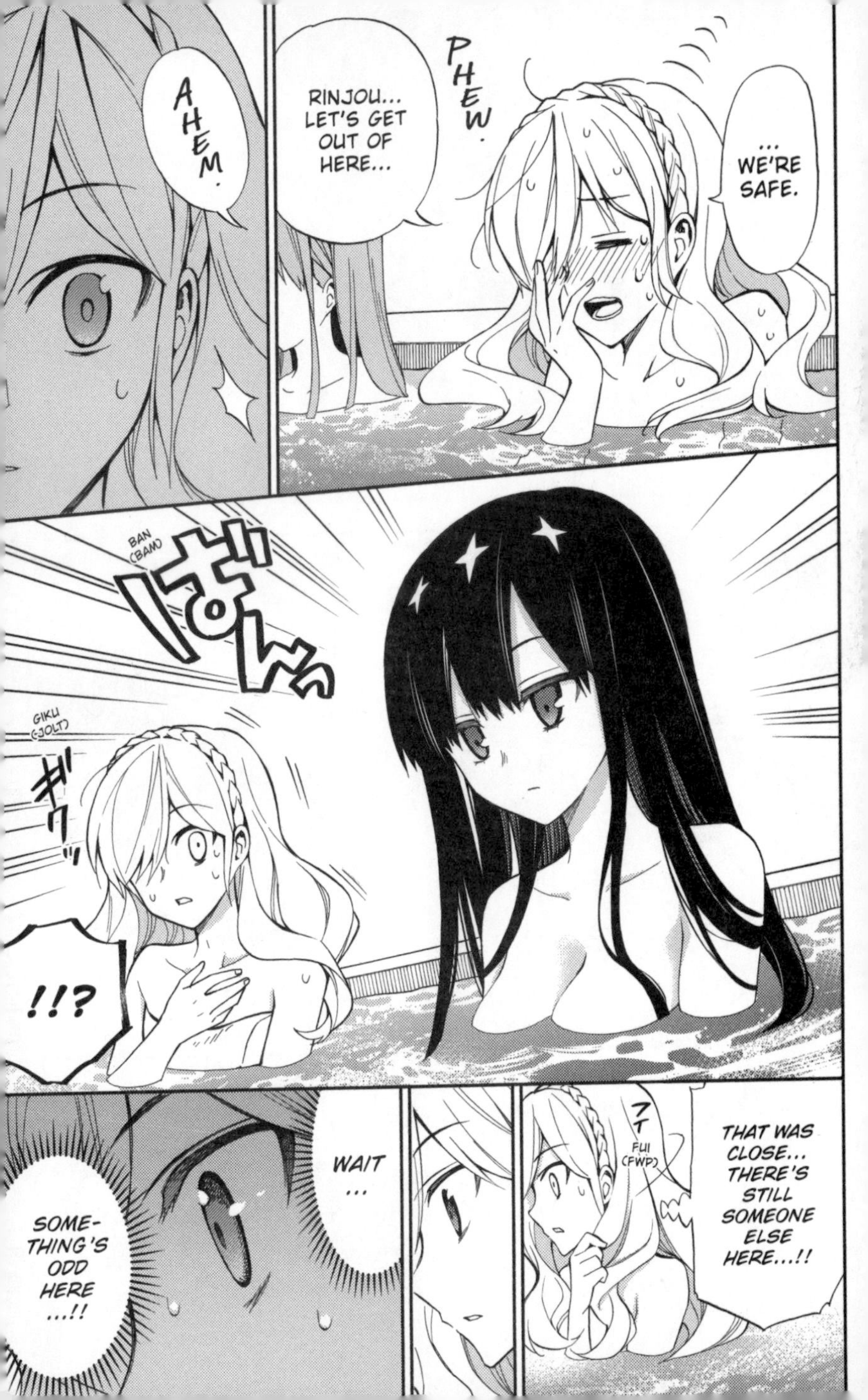
...WE'RE SAFE.
PHEW.
RINJOU... LET'S GET OUT OF HERE...
AHEM.
BAN (BAM)
GIKU (-JOLT)
!!?
THAT WAS CLOSE... THERE'S STILL SOMEONE ELSE HERE...!!
FUI (FWP)
WAIT...
SOME-THING'S ODD HERE...!!

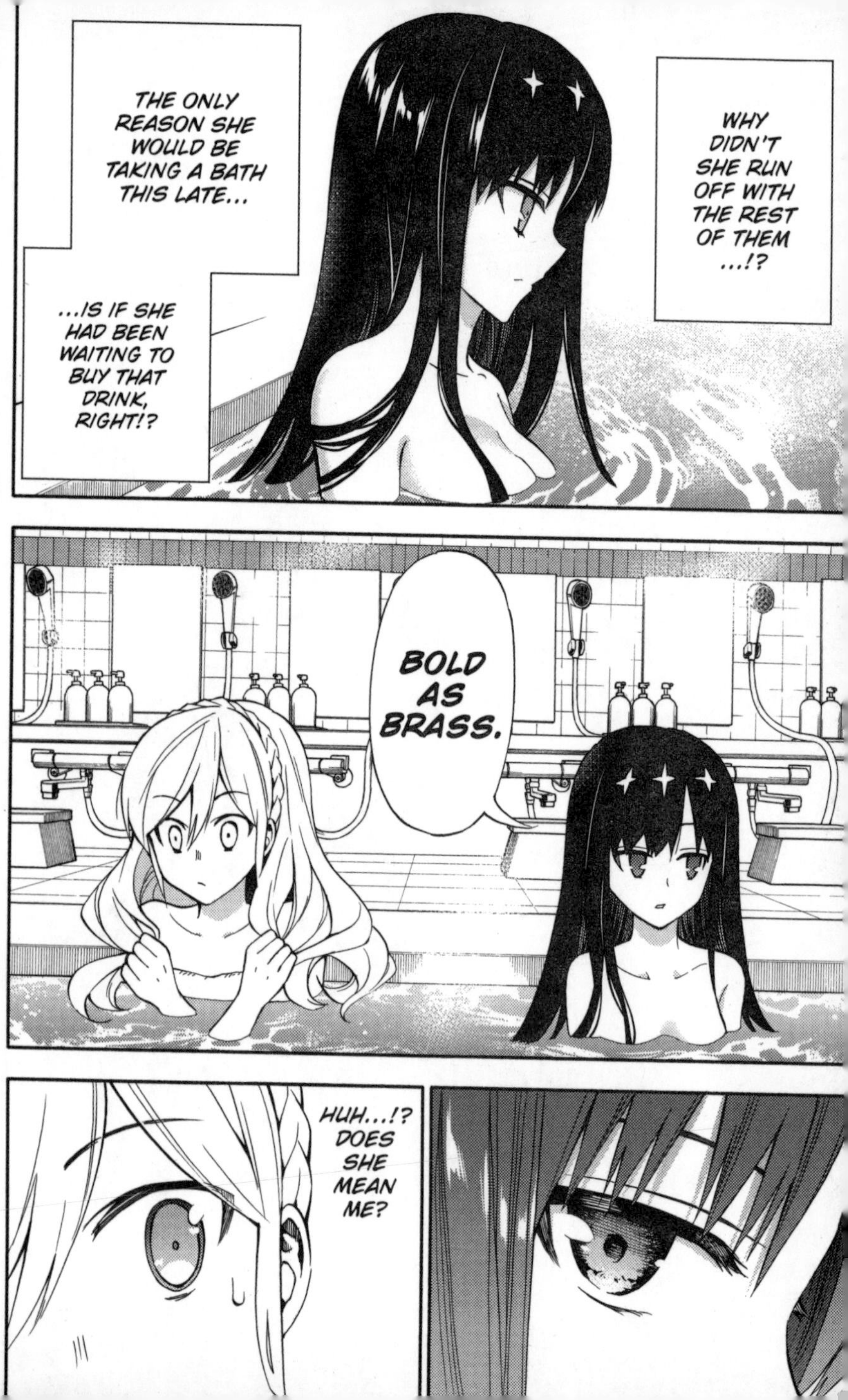
WHY DIDN'T SHE RUN OFF WITH THE REST OF THEM ...!?
THE ONLY REASON SHE WOULD BE TAKING A BATH THIS LATE...
...IS IF SHE HAD BEEN WAITING TO BUY THAT DRINK, RIGHT!?
BOLD AS BRASS.
HUH...!? DOES SHE MEAN ME?

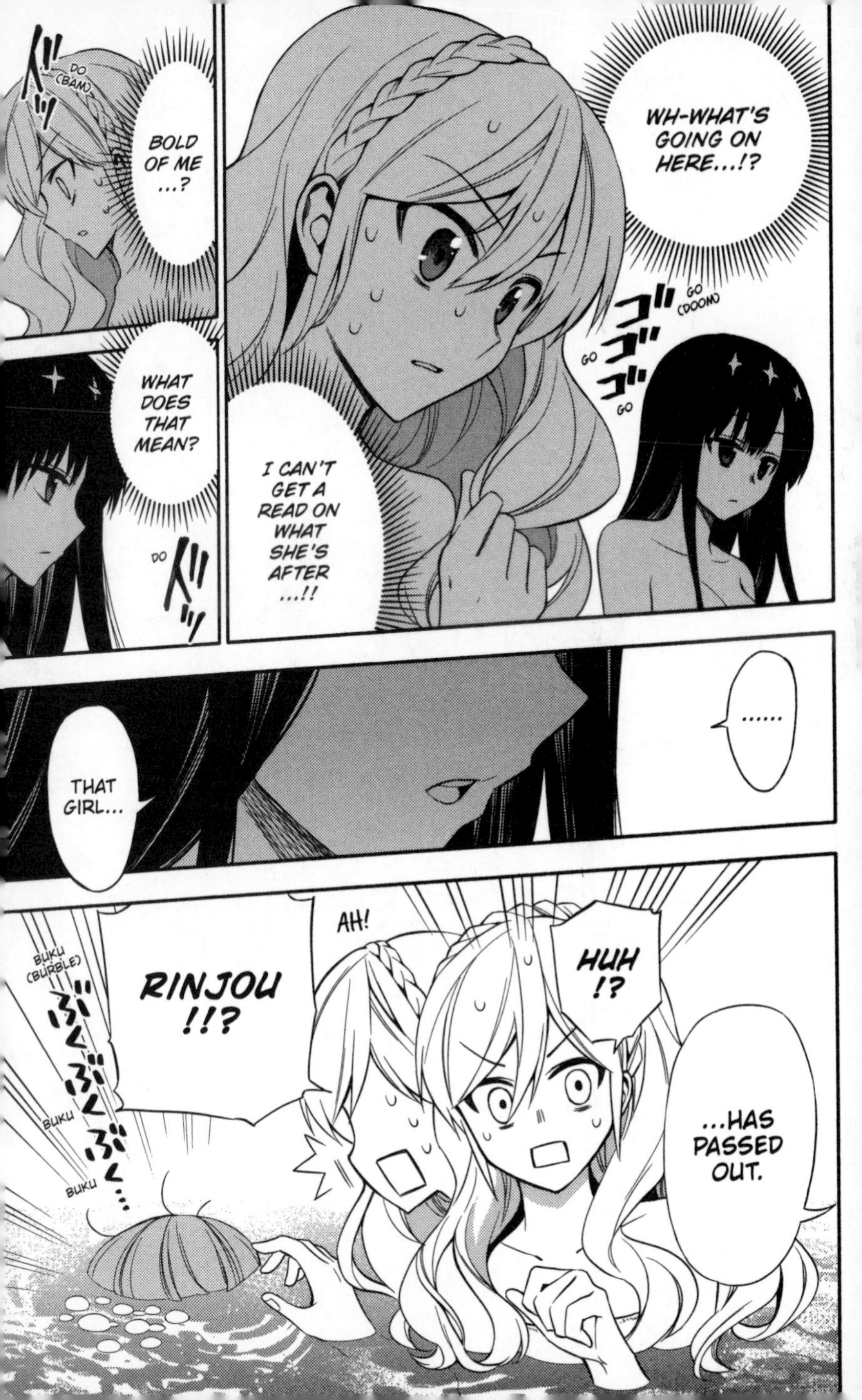
WH-WHAT'S GOING ON HERE...!?
GO (DOOM)
GO
GO
I CAN'T GET A READ ON WHAT SHE'S AFTER...!!
DO (BAM)
BOLD OF ME...?
WHAT DOES THAT MEAN?
DO
......
THAT GIRL...
...HAS PASSED OUT.
HUH!?
AH!
RINJOU!!?
BUKU (BURBLE)
BUKU
BUKU

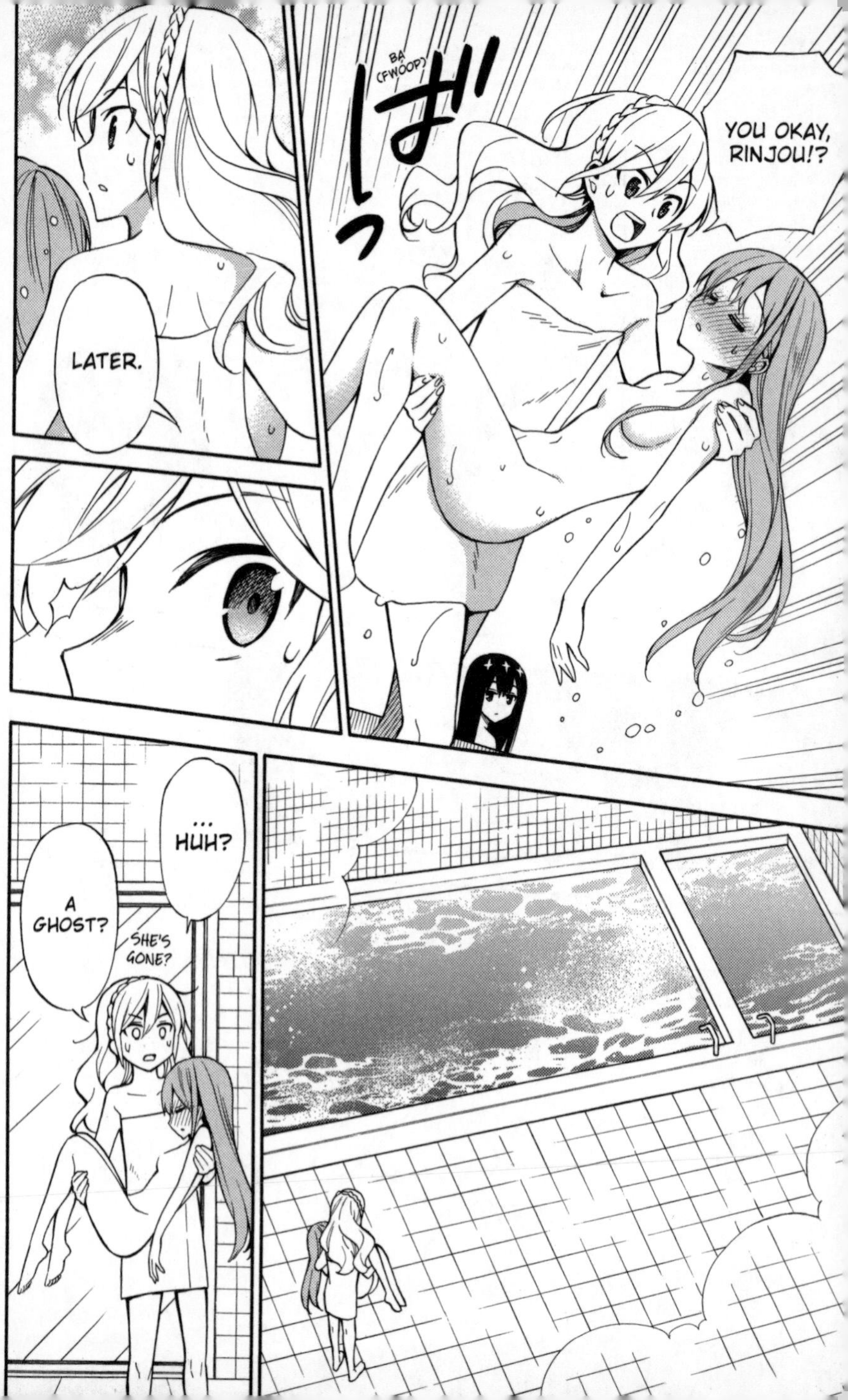
YOU OKAY, RINJOU!?
BA (FWOOP)
LATER.
... HUH?
A GHOST?
SHE'S GONE?

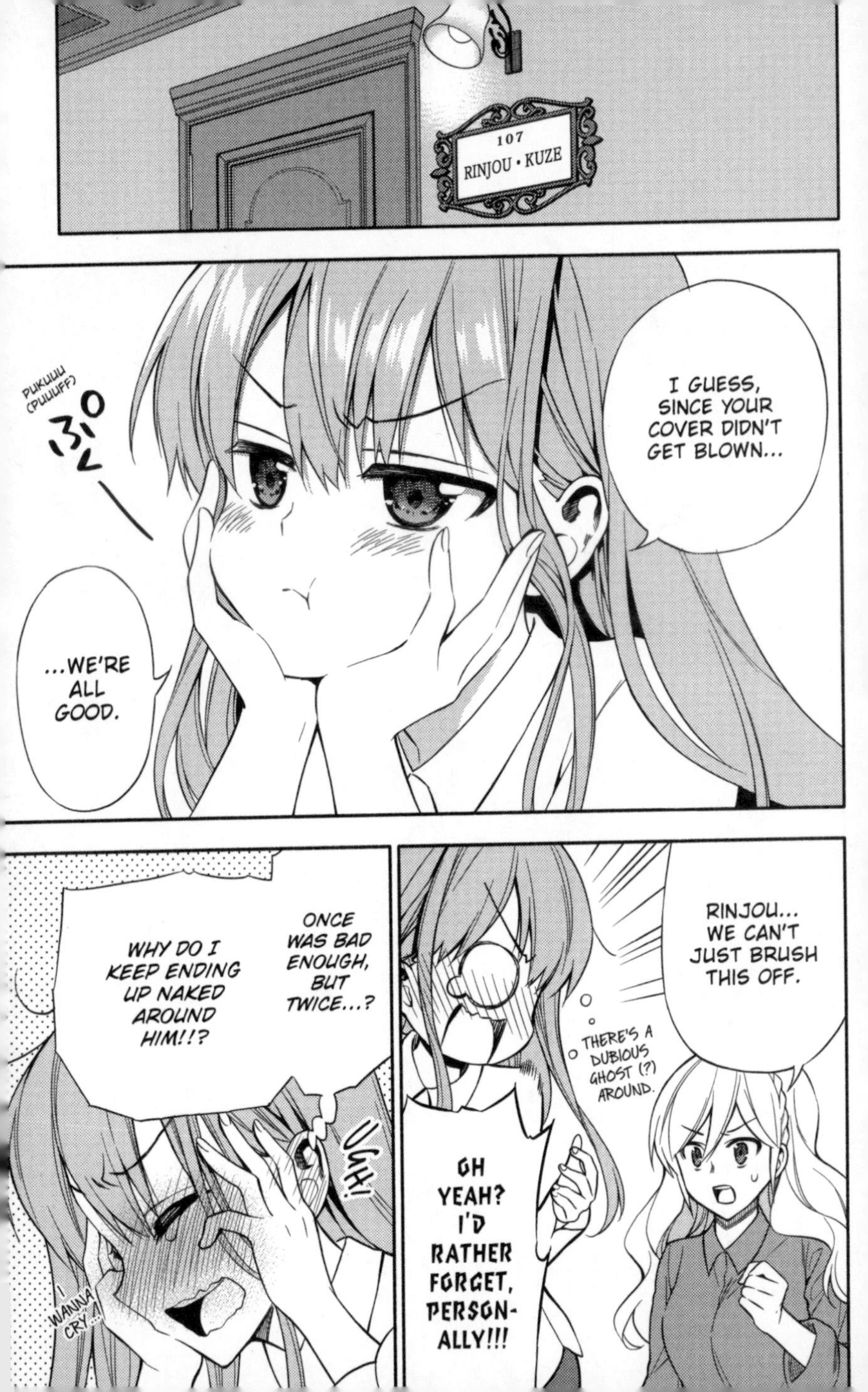
107
RINJOU • KUZE
I GUESS, SINCE YOUR COVER DIDN'T GET BLOWN...
PUKUUU (PUUUFF)
...WE'RE ALL GOOD.
RINJOU... WE CAN'T JUST BRUSH THIS OFF.
THERE'S A DUBIOUS GHOST (?) AROUND.
OH YEAH? I'D RATHER FORGET, PERSON-ALLY!!!
ONCE WAS BAD ENOUGH, BUT TWICE...?
WHY DO I KEEP ENDING UP NAKED AROUND HIM!!?
UGH!
I WANNA CRY...!

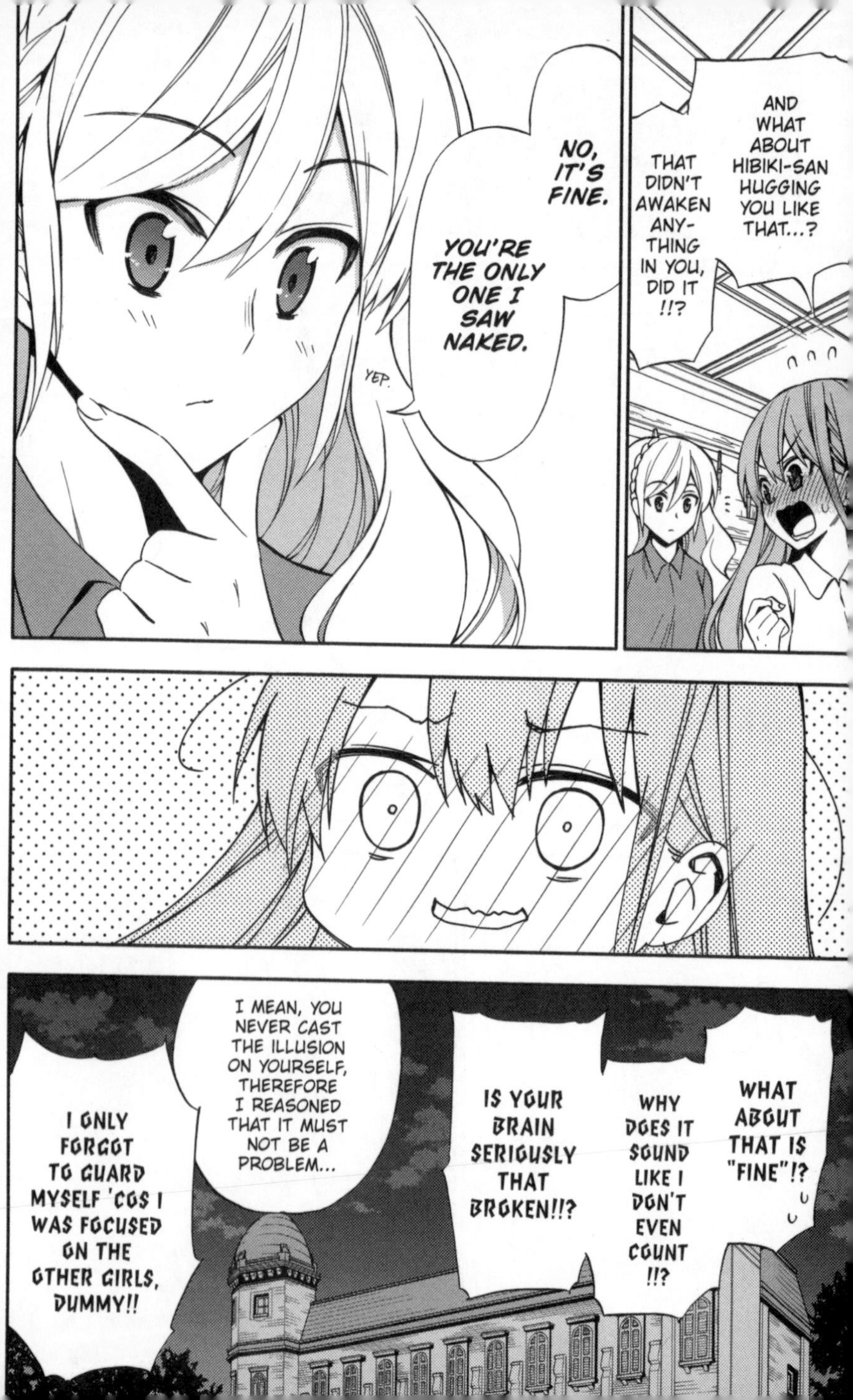
AND WHAT ABOUT HIBIKI-SAN HUGGING YOU LIKE THAT...?
THAT DIDN'T AWAKEN ANY-THING IN YOU, DID IT !!?
NO, IT'S FINE.
YOU'RE THE ONLY ONE I SAW NAKED.
YEP.
WHAT ABOUT THAT IS "FINE"!?
WHY DOES IT SOUND LIKE I DON'T EVEN COUNT !!?
IS YOUR BRAIN SERIOUSLY THAT BROKEN!!?
I MEAN, YOU NEVER CAST THE ILLUSION ON YOURSELF, THEREFORE I REASONED THAT IT MUST NOT BE A PROBLEM...
I ONLY FORGOT TO GUARD MYSELF 'COS I WAS FOCUSED ON THE OTHER GIRLS, DUMMY!!

If Witch, then Which?

YUMMY! ♡ ♡

PWAAH!

If Witch, Then Which?

PULLING IT OFF THAT EASILY...YOU MUST HAVE A REAL SENSE FOR WATER, SUZUNARI-SAN.
WELL, THE HUMAN BODY IS 60% WATER, SO...
HUH? YOU MEAN THAT MATTERS!?

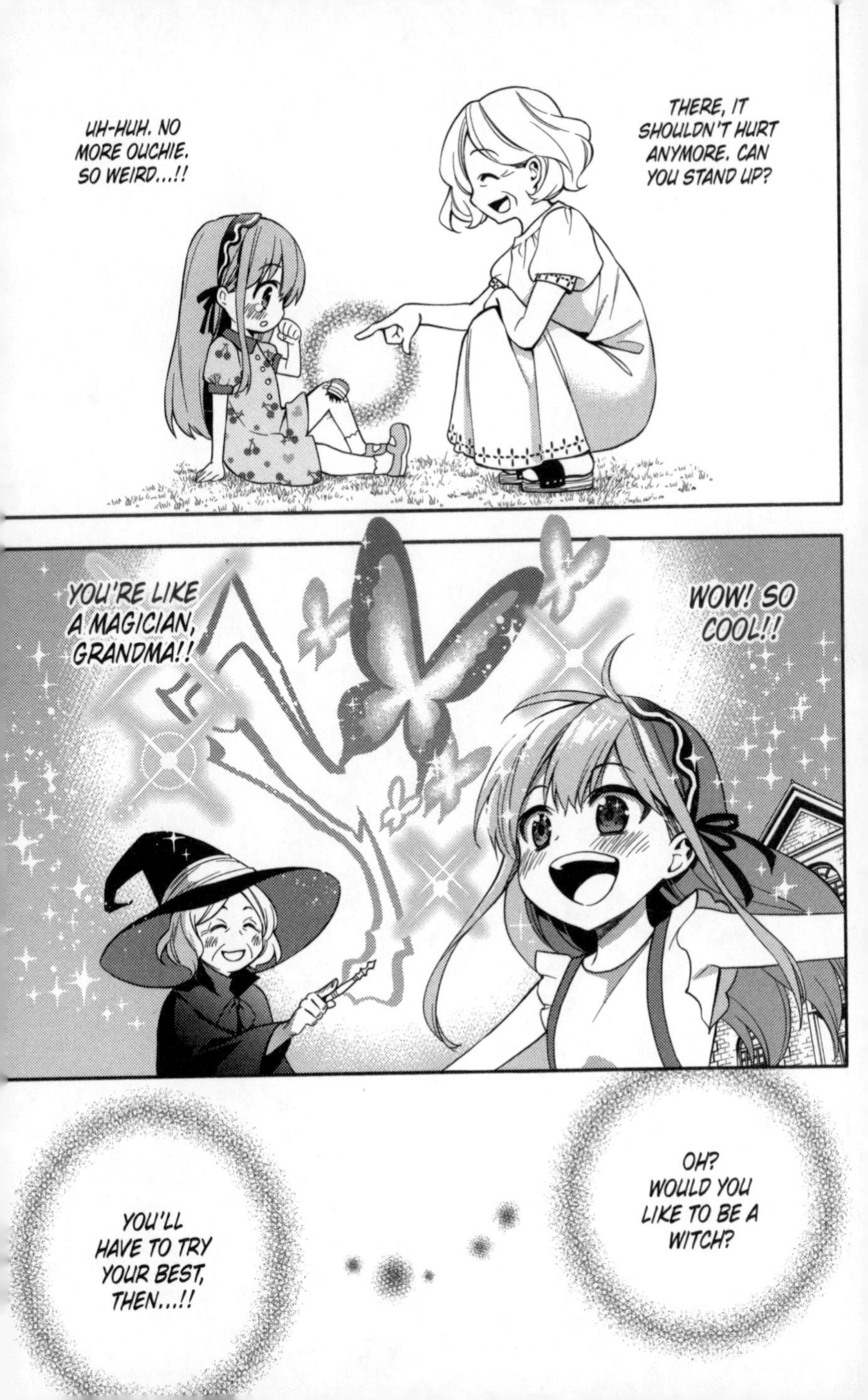
THERE, IT SHOULDN'T HURT ANYMORE. CAN YOU STAND UP?
UH-HUH. NO MORE OUCHIE. SO WEIRD...!!
WOW! SO COOL!!
YOU'RE LIKE A MAGICIAN, GRANDMA!!
OH? WOULD YOU LIKE TO BE A WITCH?
YOU'LL HAVE TO TRY YOUR BEST, THEN...!!

MAGIC.6 **Makings of a Witch and Herbal Tea**

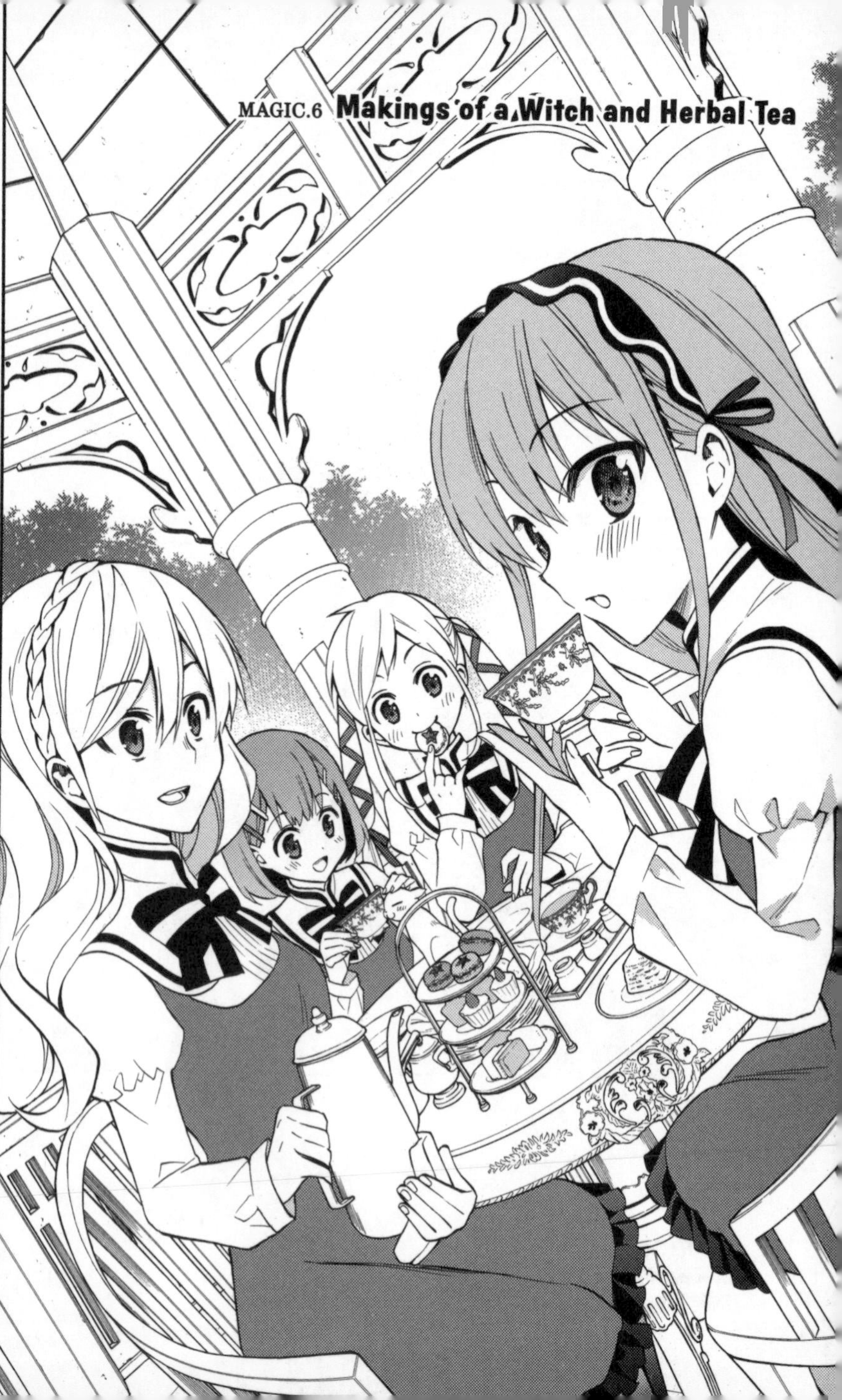

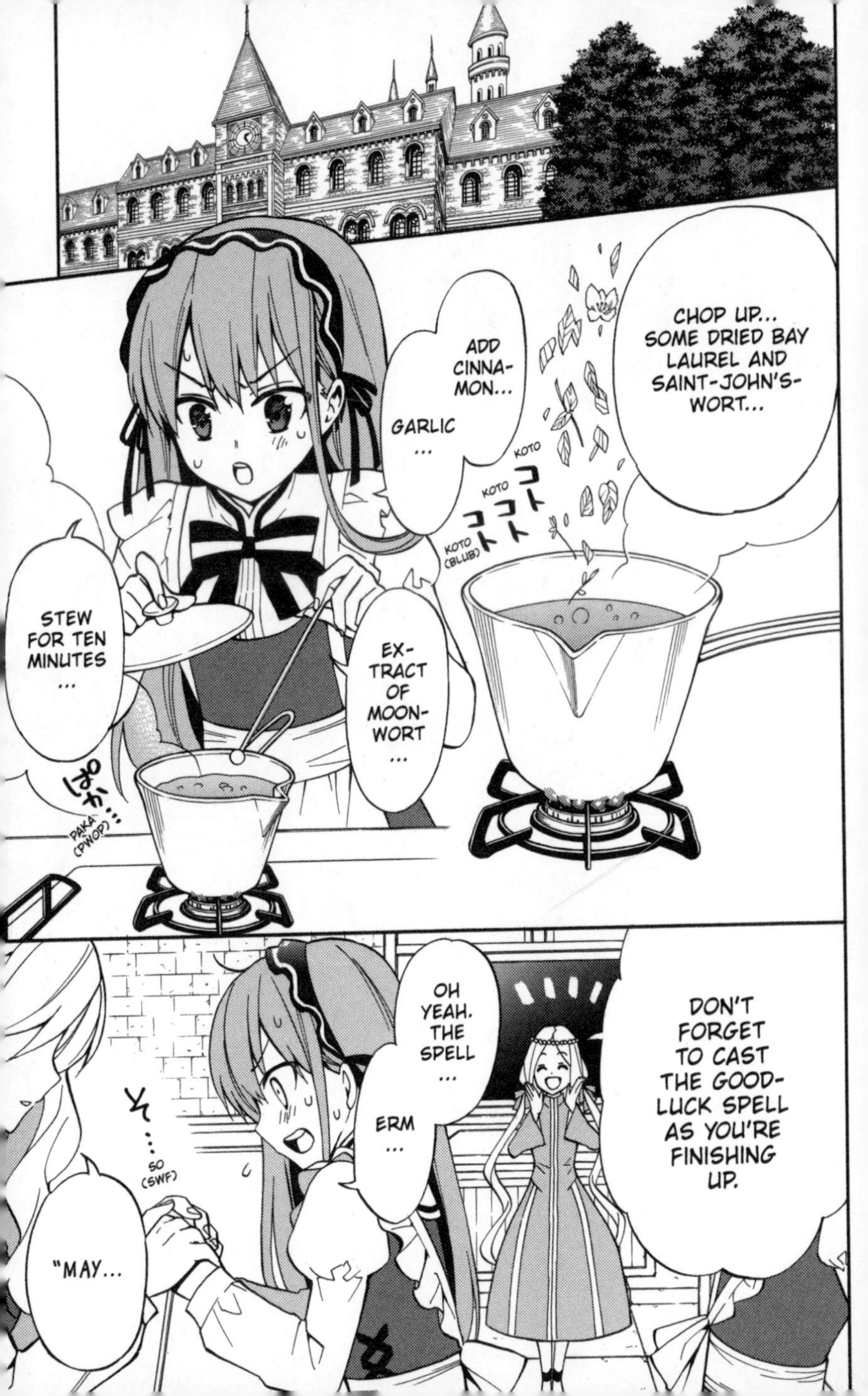
CHOP UP... SOME DRIED BAY LAUREL AND SAINT-JOHN'S-WORT...
コトコトコト
KOTO KOTO KOTO (BLUB)
ADD CINNAMON... GARLIC...
EXTRACT OF MOONWORT...
STEW FOR TEN MINUTES...
ぱか
PAKA (PWOP)
DON'T FORGET TO CAST THE GOOD-LUCK SPELL AS YOU'RE FINISHING UP.
OH YEAH. THE SPELL... ERM...
そ…
SO (SWF)
"MAY...

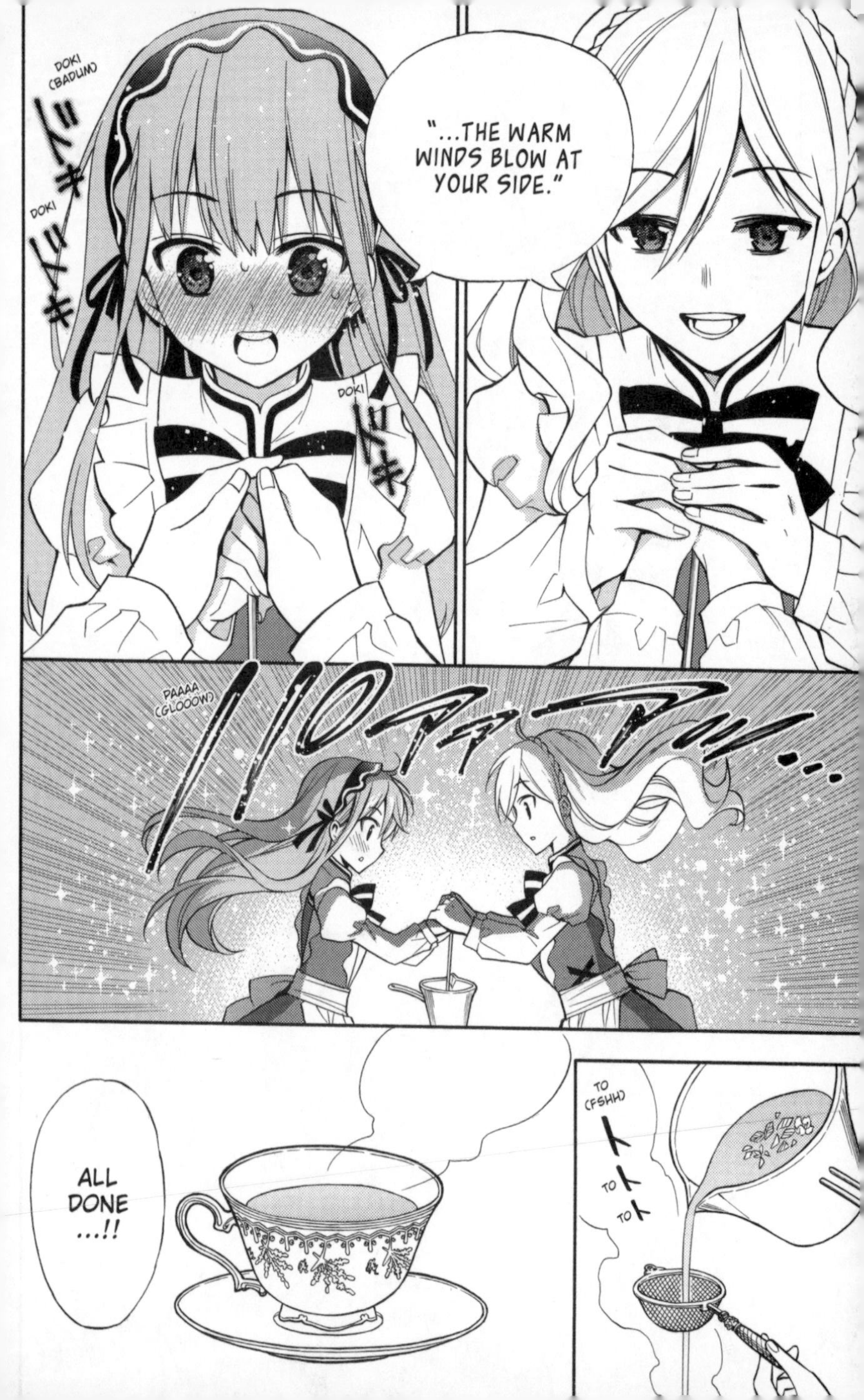
"...THE WARM WINDS BLOW AT YOUR SIDE."
DOKI (BADUM)
DOKI
DOKI
PAAAA (GLOOOW)
TO (FSHH)
TO
TO
ALL DONE ...!!

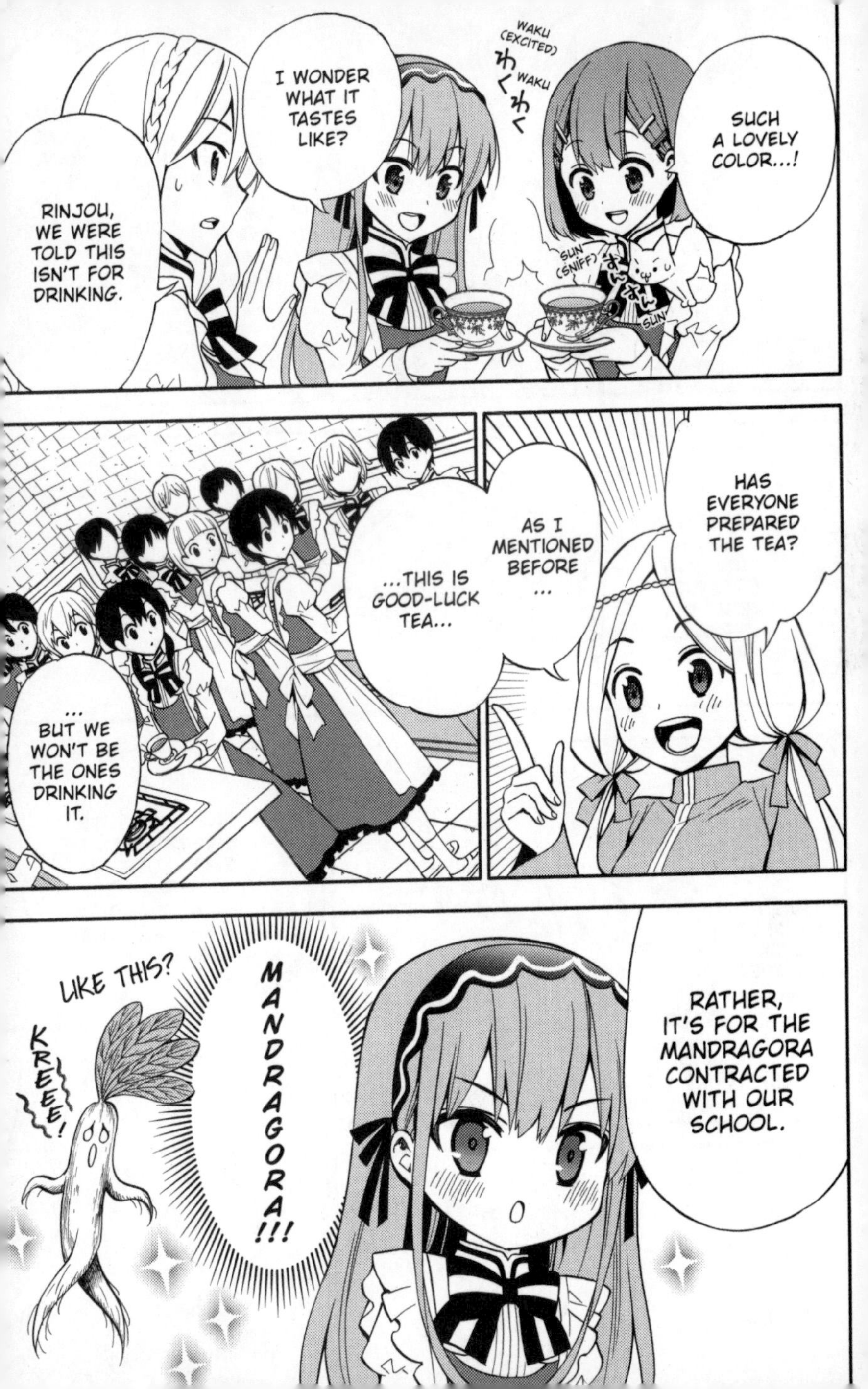
SUCH A LOVELY COLOR...!
WAKU (EXCITED) WAKU
わくわく
I WONDER WHAT IT TASTES LIKE?
SUN (SNIFF) SUN
すんすん
RINJOU, WE WERE TOLD THIS ISN'T FOR DRINKING.
HAS EVERYONE PREPARED THE TEA?
AS I MENTIONED BEFORE ...
...THIS IS GOOD-LUCK TEA...
... BUT WE WON'T BE THE ONES DRINKING IT.
RATHER, IT'S FOR THE MANDRAGORA CONTRACTED WITH OUR SCHOOL.
MANDRAGORA!!!
LIKE THIS?
KREEE!

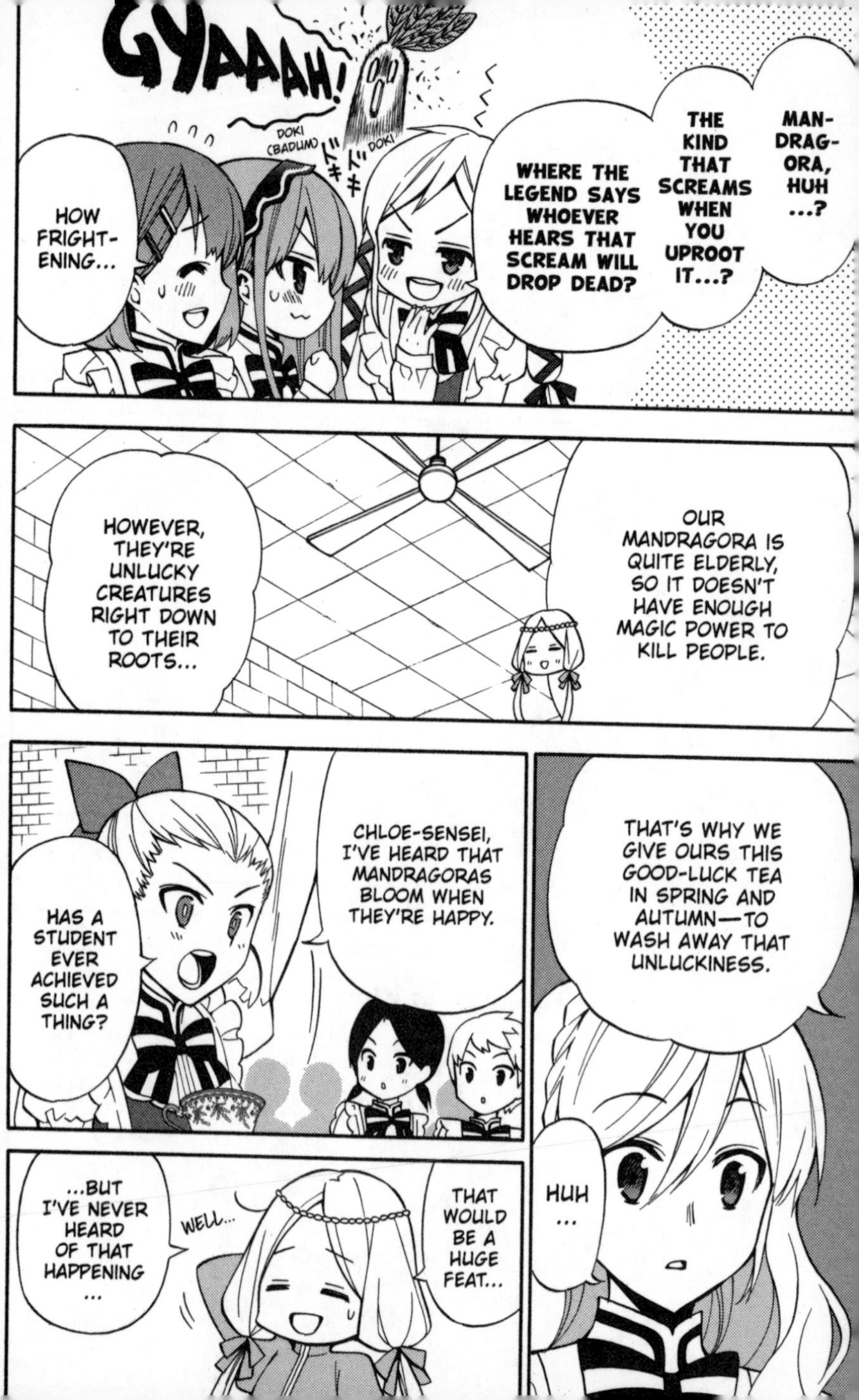

MAN-DRAG-ORA, HUH...?
THE KIND THAT SCREAMS WHEN YOU UPROOT IT...?
WHERE THE LEGEND SAYS WHOEVER HEARS THAT SCREAM WILL DROP DEAD?
GYAAAH!
DOKI (BADUM) DOKI
HOW FRIGHT-ENING...
OUR MANDRAGORA IS QUITE ELDERLY, SO IT DOESN'T HAVE ENOUGH MAGIC POWER TO KILL PEOPLE.
HOWEVER, THEY'RE UNLUCKY CREATURES RIGHT DOWN TO THEIR ROOTS...
THAT'S WHY WE GIVE OURS THIS GOOD-LUCK TEA IN SPRING AND AUTUMN—TO WASH AWAY THAT UNLUCKINESS.
HUH...
CHLOE-SENSEI, I'VE HEARD THAT MANDRAGORAS BLOOM WHEN THEY'RE HAPPY.
HAS A STUDENT EVER ACHIEVED SUCH A THING?
THAT WOULD BE A HUGE FEAT...
WELL...
...BUT I'VE NEVER HEARD OF THAT HAPPENING...

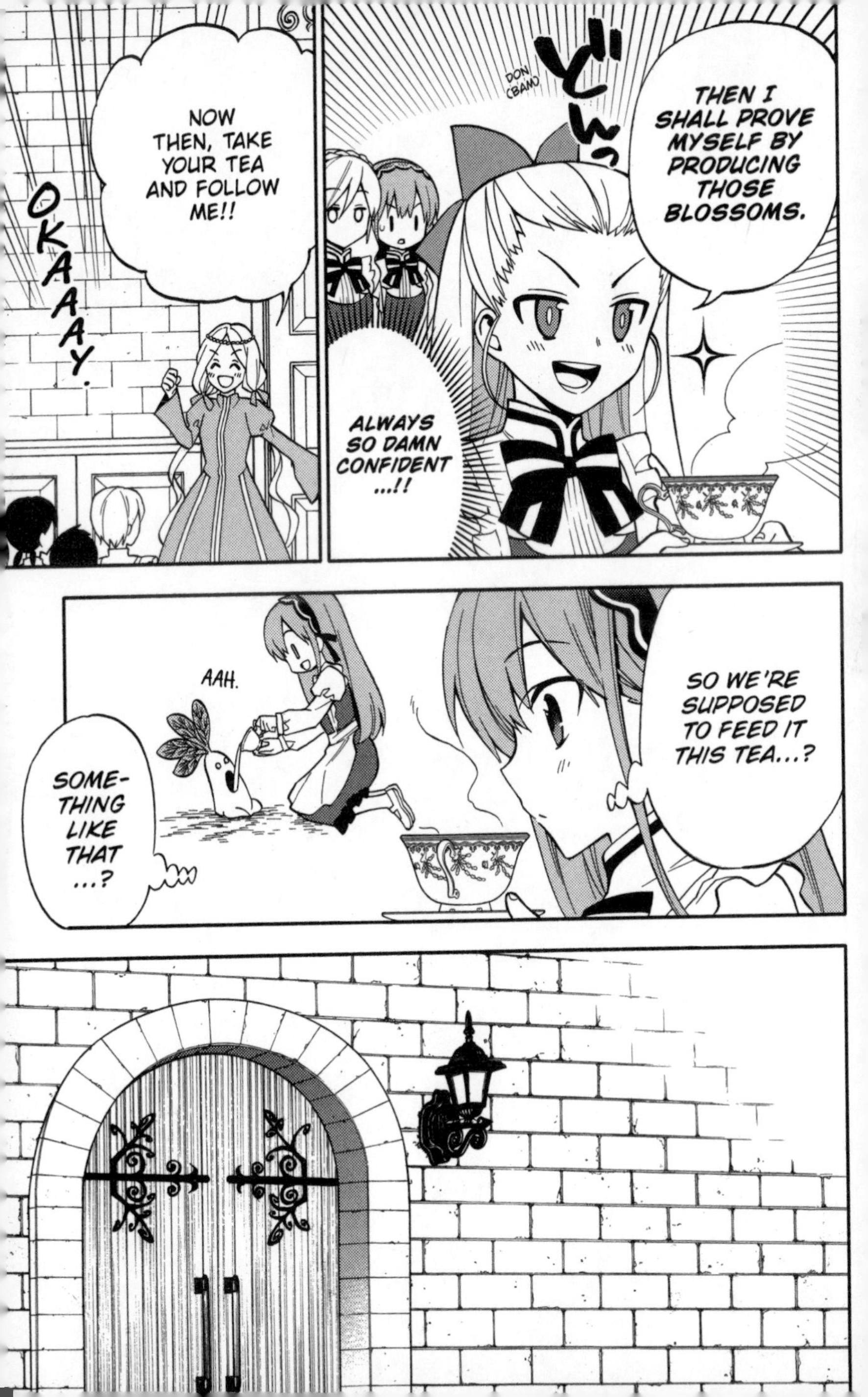
DON (BAM)
THEN I SHALL PROVE MYSELF BY PRODUCING THOSE BLOSSOMS.
ALWAYS SO DAMN CONFIDENT ...!!
NOW THEN, TAKE YOUR TEA AND FOLLOW ME!!
OKAAAY.
SO WE'RE SUPPOSED TO FEED IT THIS TEA...?
AAH.
SOME-THING LIKE THAT ...?

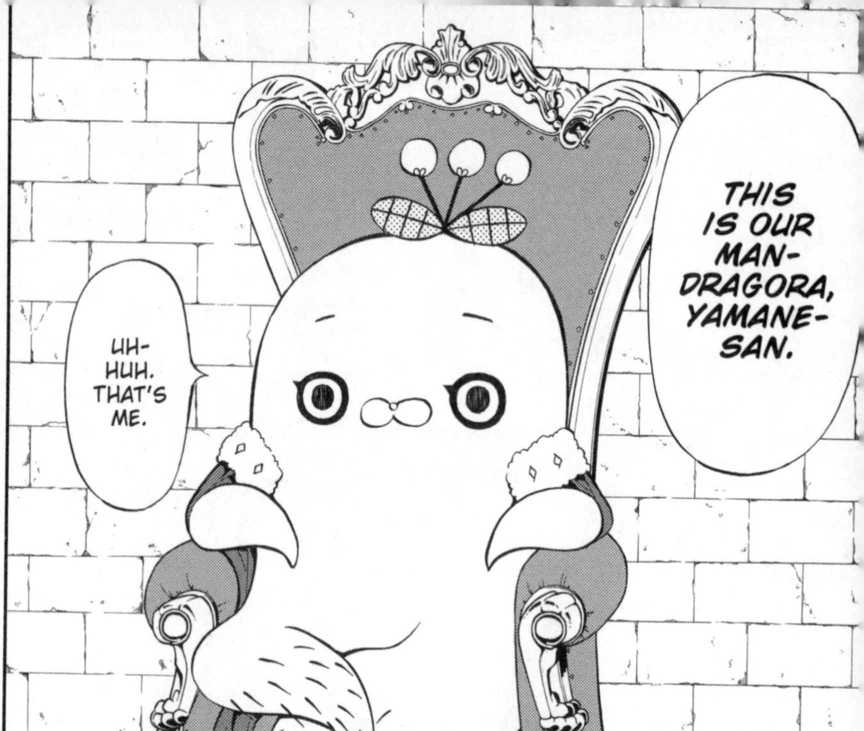
THIS IS OUR MAN-DRAGORA, YAMANE-SAN.
UH-HUH. THAT'S ME.

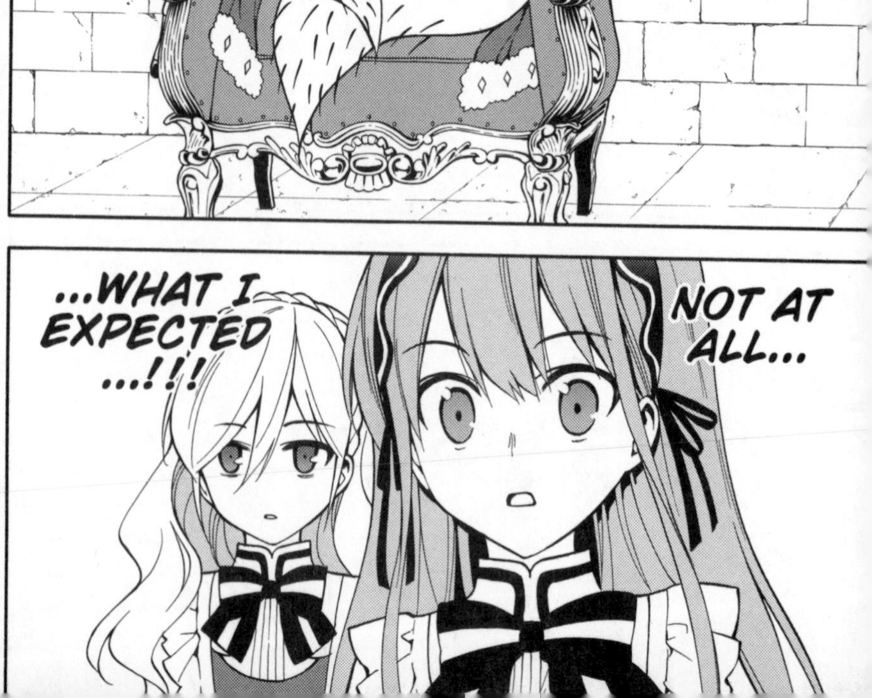
NOT AT ALL...
...WHAT I EXPECTED ...!!!

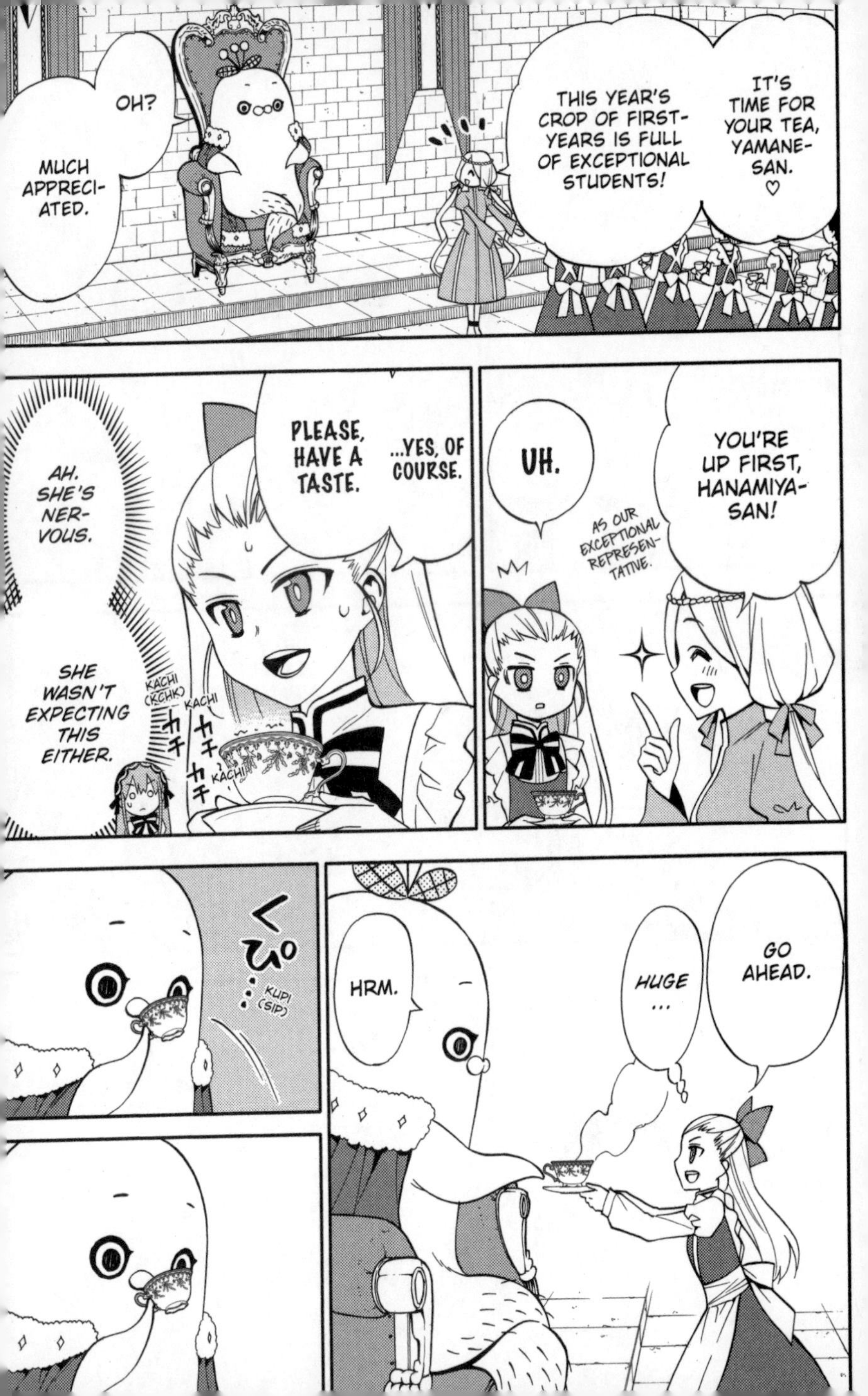
IT'S TIME FOR YOUR TEA, YAMANE-SAN. ♡
THIS YEAR'S CROP OF FIRST-YEARS IS FULL OF EXCEPTIONAL STUDENTS!
OH?
MUCH APPRECIATED.
YOU'RE UP FIRST, HANAMIYA-SAN!
AS OUR EXCEPTIONAL REPRESENTATIVE.
UH.
...YES, OF COURSE.
PLEASE, HAVE A TASTE.
AH. SHE'S NERVOUS.
KACHI (KCHK)
KACHI
KACHI
SHE WASN'T EXPECTING THIS EITHER.
GO AHEAD.
HUGE...
HRM.
KUPI (SIP)

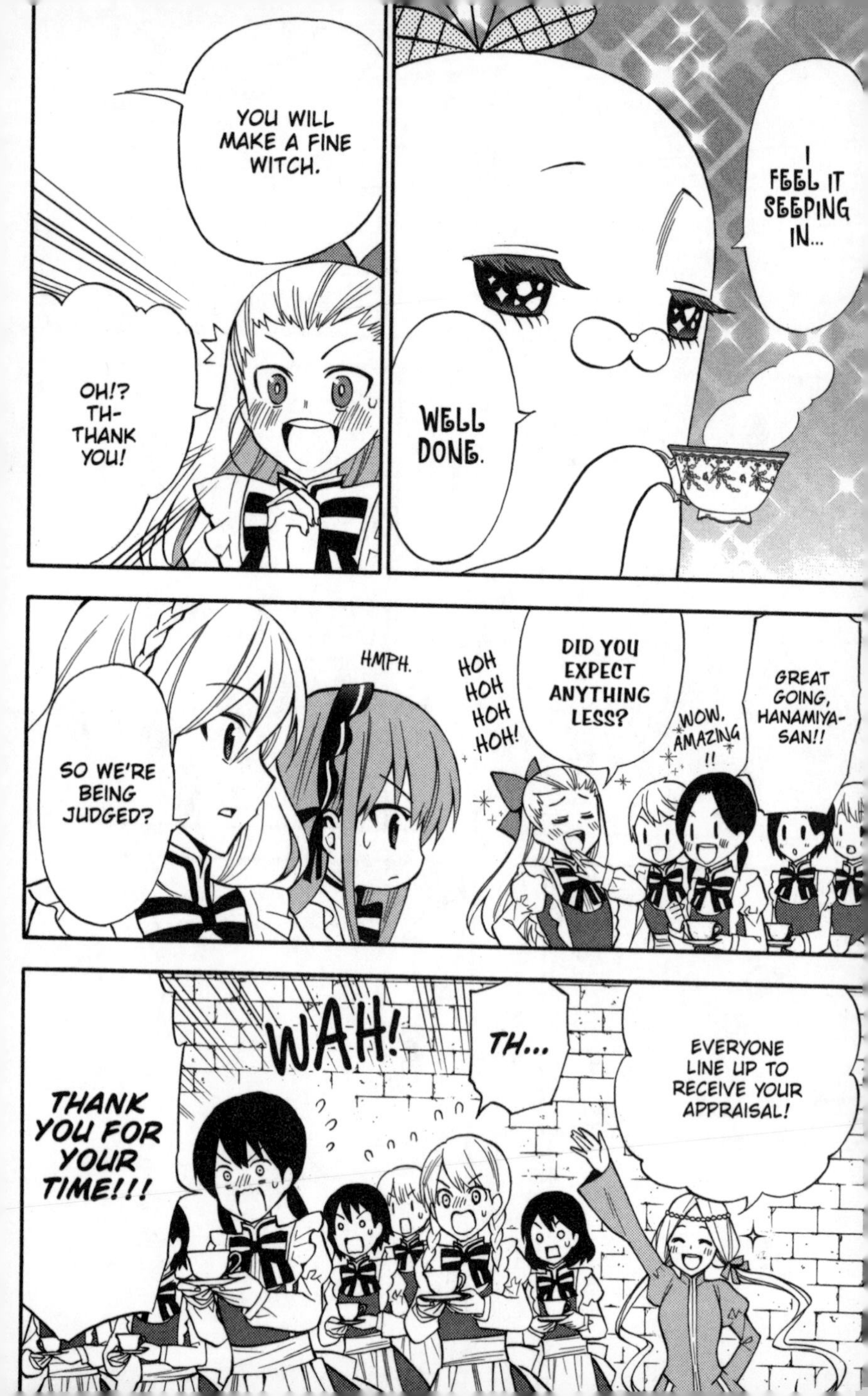
I FEEL IT SEEPING IN...
WELL DONE.
YOU WILL MAKE A FINE WITCH.
OH!? TH-THANK YOU!
GREAT GOING, HANAMIYA-SAN!!
WOW, AMAZING!!
DID YOU EXPECT ANYTHING LESS?
HOH HOH HOH HOH!
HMPH.
SO WE'RE BEING JUDGED?
EVERYONE LINE UP TO RECEIVE YOUR APPRAISAL!
TH...
WAH!
THANK YOU FOR YOUR TIME!!!

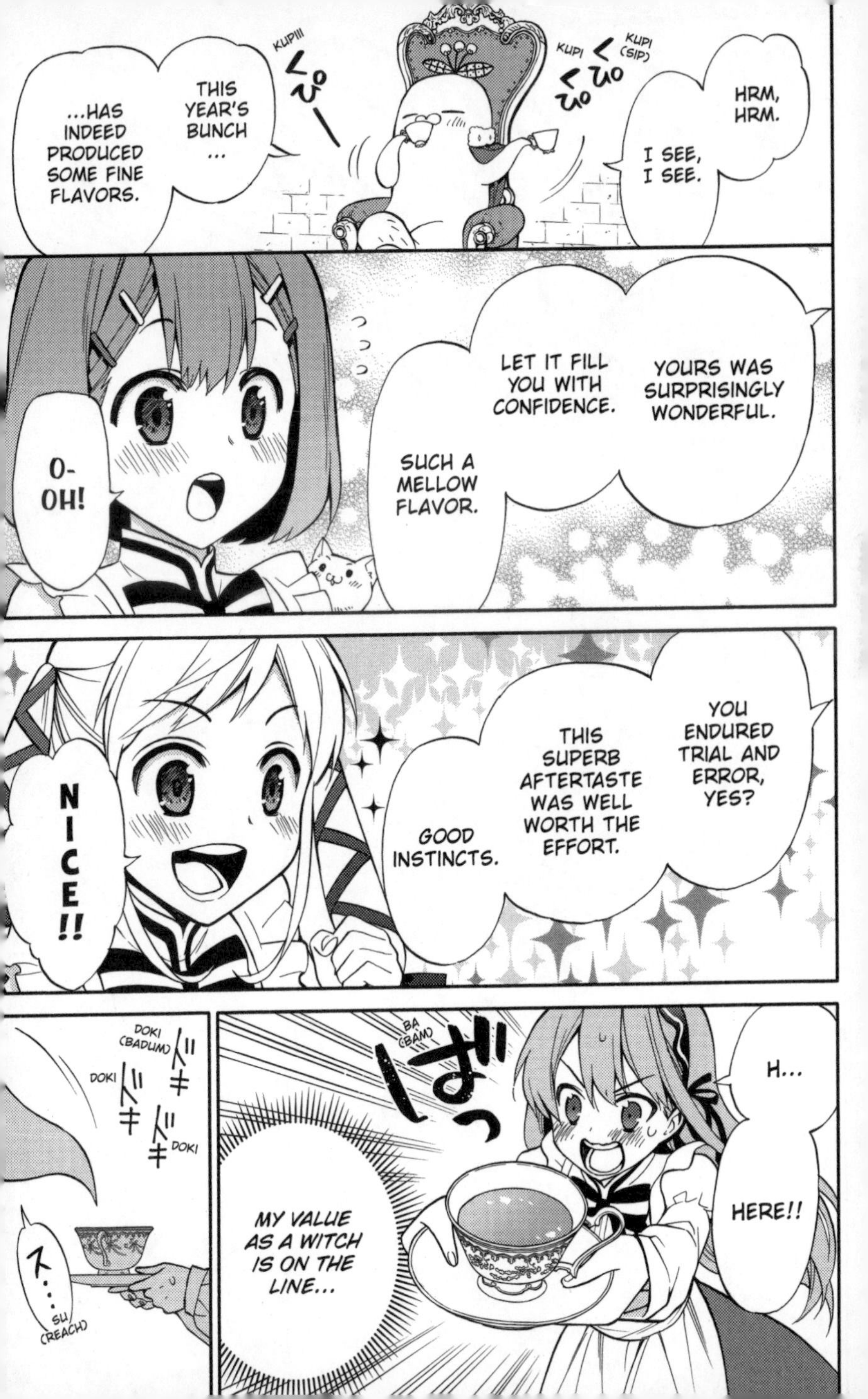

HRM, HRM.
I SEE, I SEE.
KUPI KUPI (SIP)
KUPIIII
THIS YEAR'S BUNCH...
...HAS INDEED PRODUCED SOME FINE FLAVORS.
YOURS WAS SURPRISINGLY WONDERFUL.
LET IT FILL YOU WITH CONFIDENCE.
SUCH A MELLOW FLAVOR.
O-OH!
YOU ENDURED TRIAL AND ERROR, YES?
THIS SUPERB AFTERTASTE WAS WELL WORTH THE EFFORT.
GOOD INSTINCTS.
NICE!!
H...
HERE!!
BA (BAM)
MY VALUE AS A WITCH IS ON THE LINE...
DOKI (BADUM) DOKI DOKI
SU (REACH)

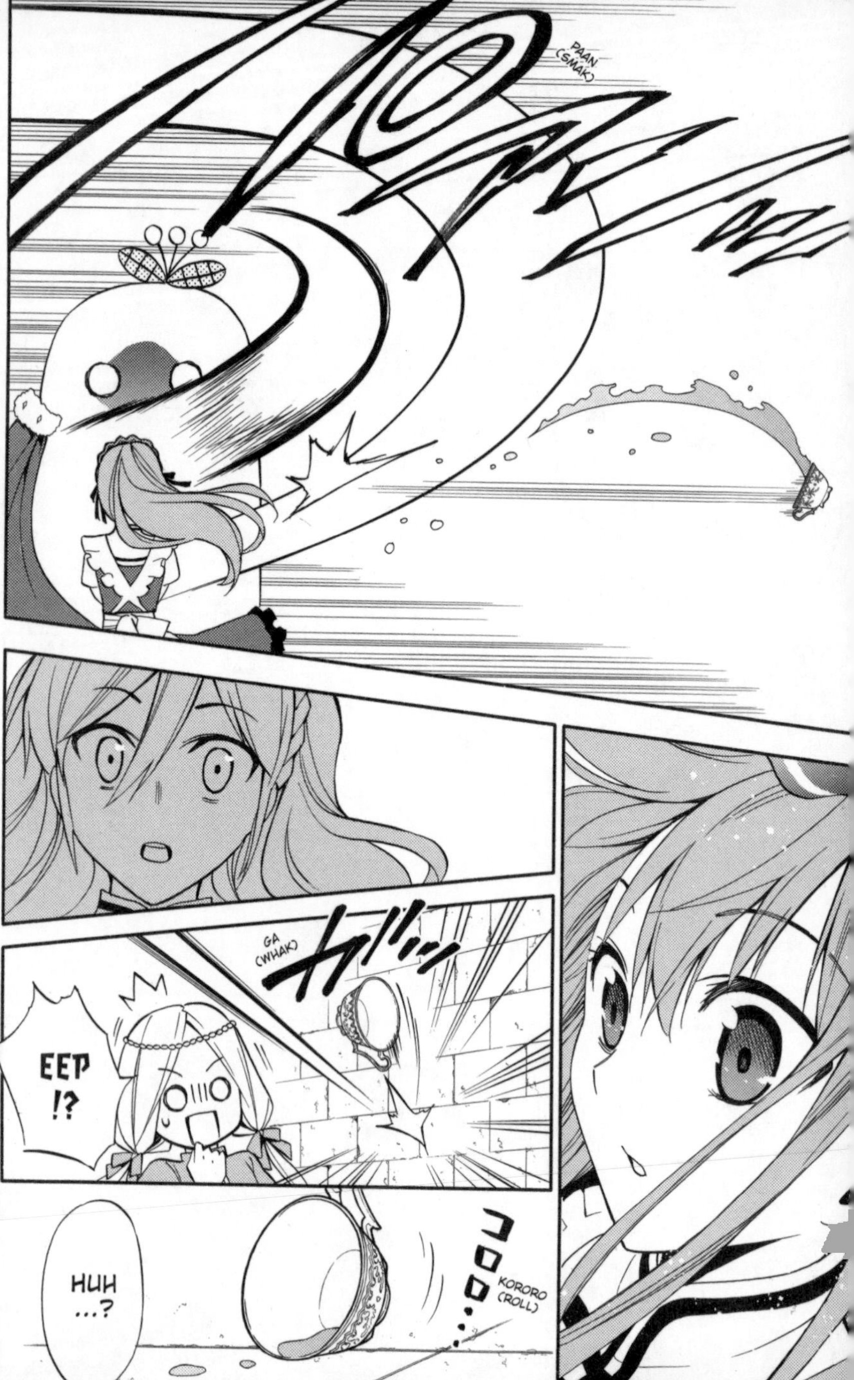
PAAN (SMAK)
GA (WHAK)
EEP!?
KORORO (ROLL)
HUH...?

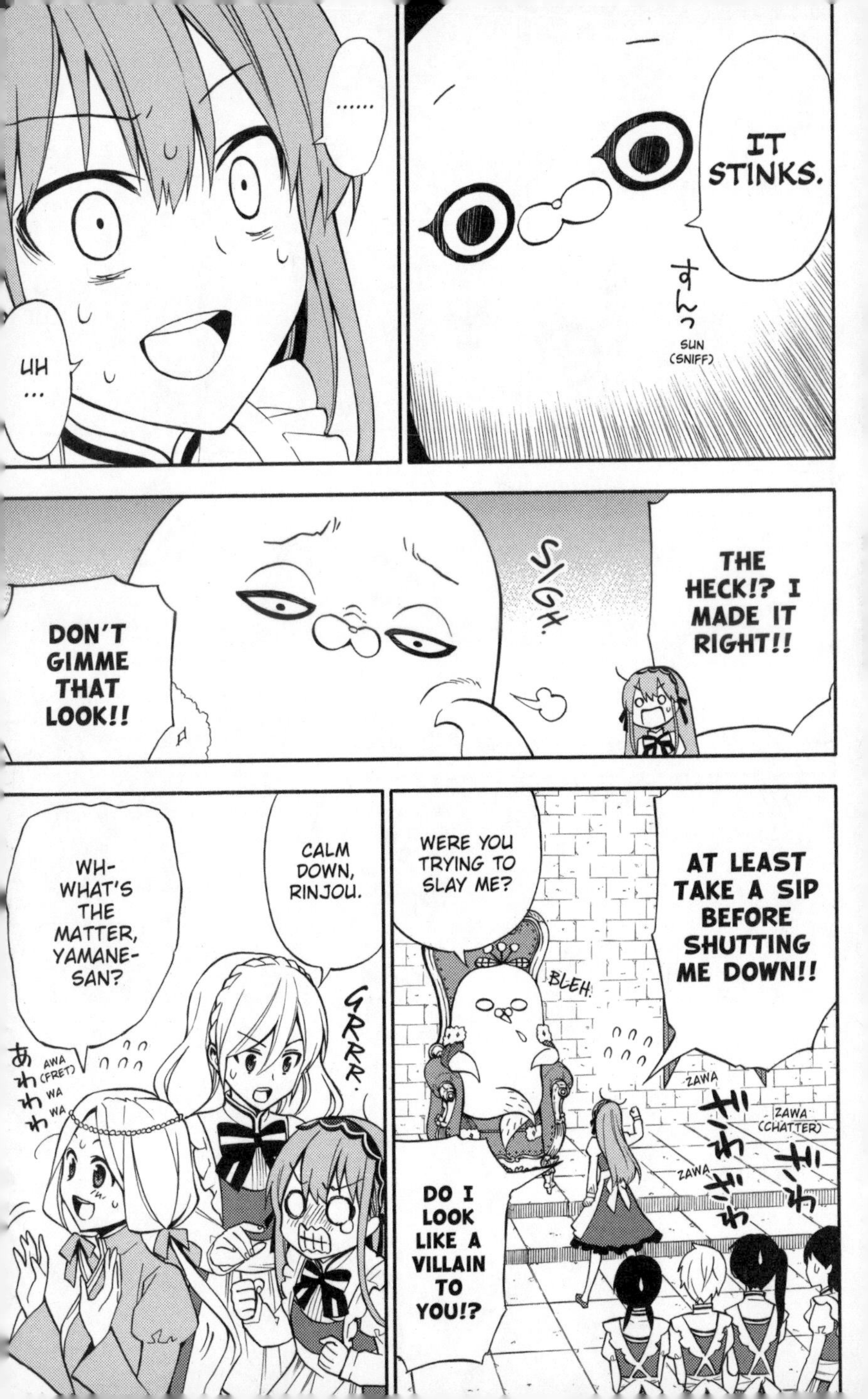
IT STINKS.
すんっ
SUN (SNIFF)
......
UH ...
THE HECK!? I MADE IT RIGHT!!
SIGH.
DON'T GIMME THAT LOOK!!
AT LEAST TAKE A SIP BEFORE SHUTTING ME DOWN!!
WERE YOU TRYING TO SLAY ME?
BLEH.
ざわ
ZAWA
ざわ
ZAWA (CHATTER)
ざわ
ZAWA
DO I LOOK LIKE A VILLAIN TO YOU!?
CALM DOWN, RINJOU.
GRRR.
WH- WHAT'S THE MATTER, YAMANE-SAN?
あわわわ
AWA (FRET) WA WA

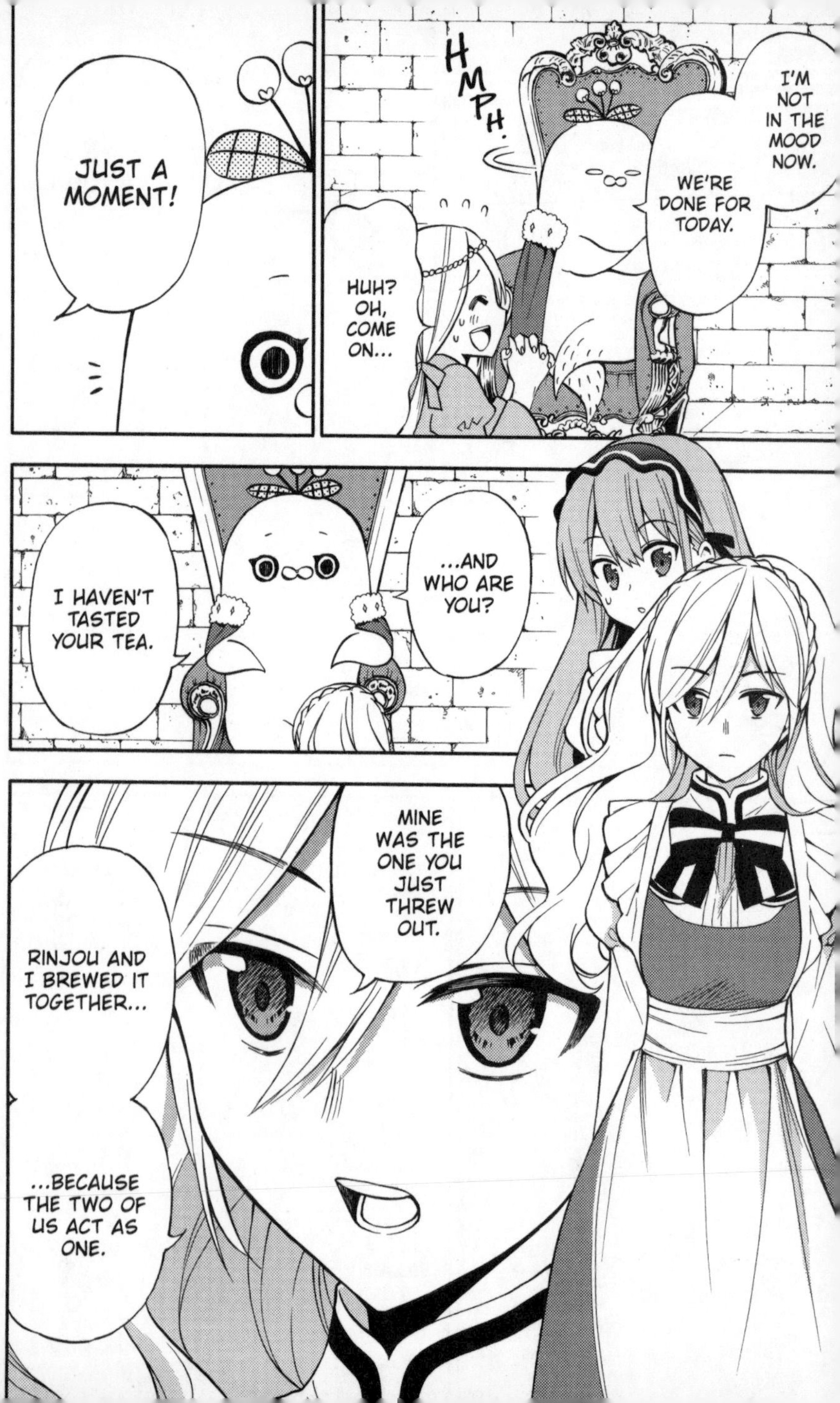
HMPH.
I'M NOT IN THE MOOD NOW.
WE'RE DONE FOR TODAY.
HUH? OH, COME ON...
JUST A MOMENT!
...AND WHO ARE YOU?
I HAVEN'T TASTED YOUR TEA.
MINE WAS THE ONE YOU JUST THREW OUT.
RINJOU AND I BREWED IT TOGETHER...
...BECAUSE THE TWO OF US ACT AS ONE.

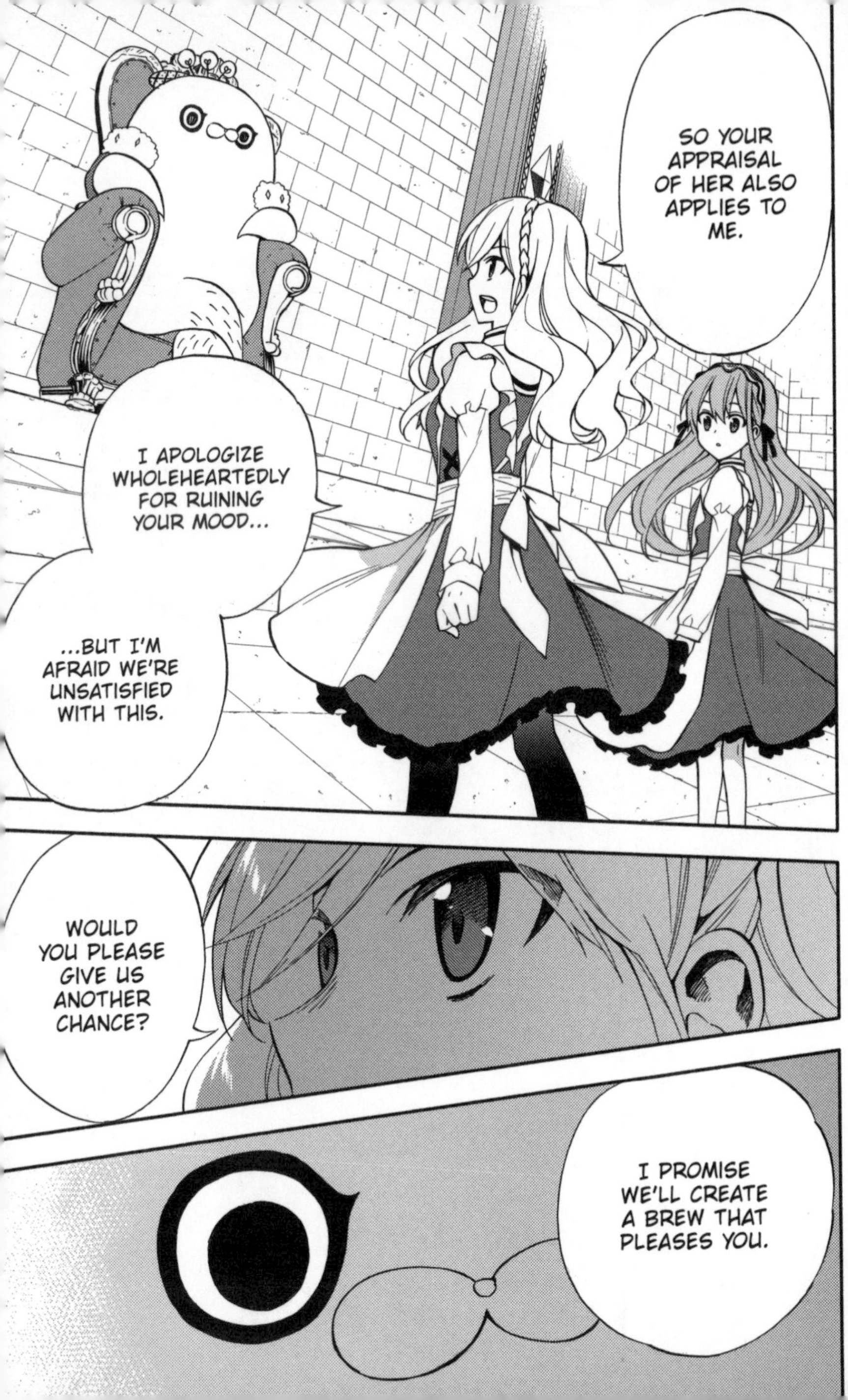
SO YOUR APPRAISAL OF HER ALSO APPLIES TO ME.
I APOLOGIZE WHOLEHEARTEDLY FOR RUINING YOUR MOOD...
...BUT I'M AFRAID WE'RE UNSATISFIED WITH THIS.
WOULD YOU PLEASE GIVE US ANOTHER CHANCE?
I PROMISE WE'LL CREATE A BREW THAT PLEASES YOU.

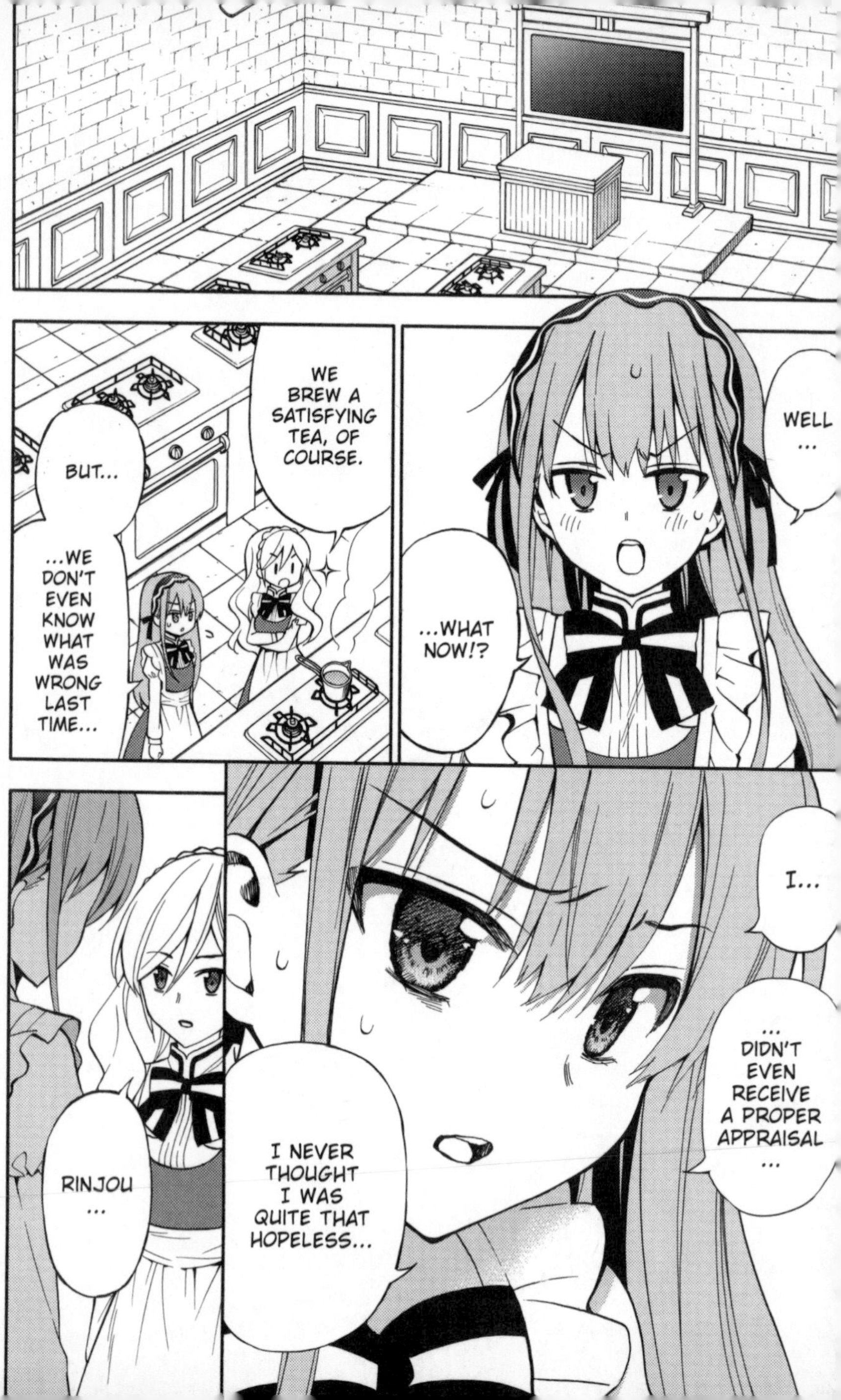
WELL ...
...WHAT NOW!?
WE BREW A SATISFYING TEA, OF COURSE.
BUT...
...WE DON'T EVEN KNOW WHAT WAS WRONG LAST TIME...
I...
...DIDN'T EVEN RECEIVE A PROPER APPRAISAL ...
I NEVER THOUGHT I WAS QUITE THAT HOPELESS...
RINJOU ...

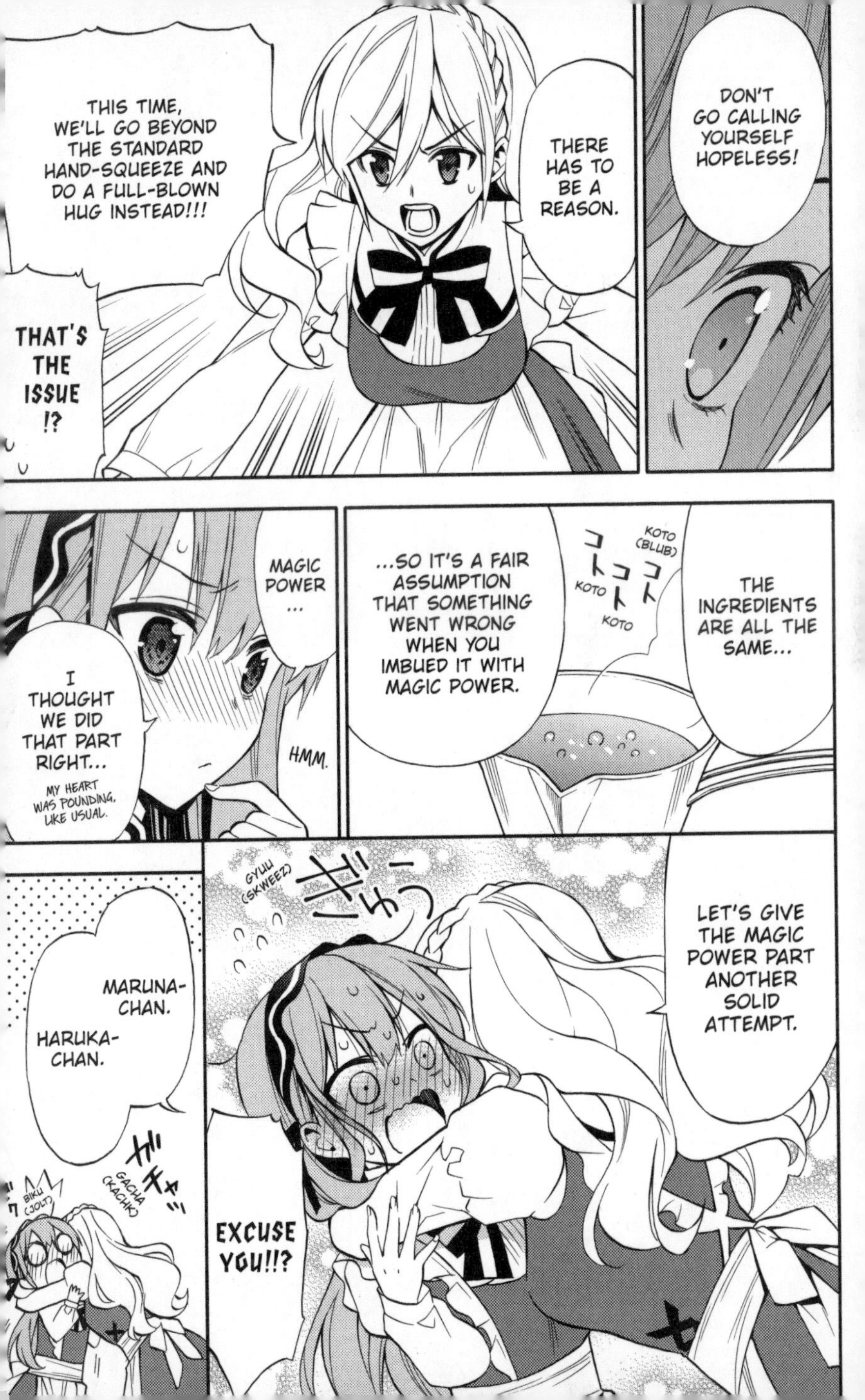
DON'T GO CALLING YOURSELF HOPELESS!
THERE HAS TO BE A REASON.
THIS TIME, WE'LL GO BEYOND THE STANDARD HAND-SQUEEZE AND DO A FULL-BLOWN HUG INSTEAD!!!
THAT'S THE ISSUE!?
KOTO (BLUB)
KOTO
KOTO
THE INGREDIENTS ARE ALL THE SAME...
...SO IT'S A FAIR ASSUMPTION THAT SOMETHING WENT WRONG WHEN YOU IMBUED IT WITH MAGIC POWER.
MAGIC POWER...
HMM.
I THOUGHT WE DID THAT PART RIGHT...
MY HEART WAS POUNDING, LIKE USUAL.
LET'S GIVE THE MAGIC POWER PART ANOTHER SOLID ATTEMPT.
GYUU (SKWEEZ)
EXCUSE YOU!!?
MARUNA-CHAN.
HARUKA-CHAN.
GACHA (KACHK)
BIKU (JOLT)

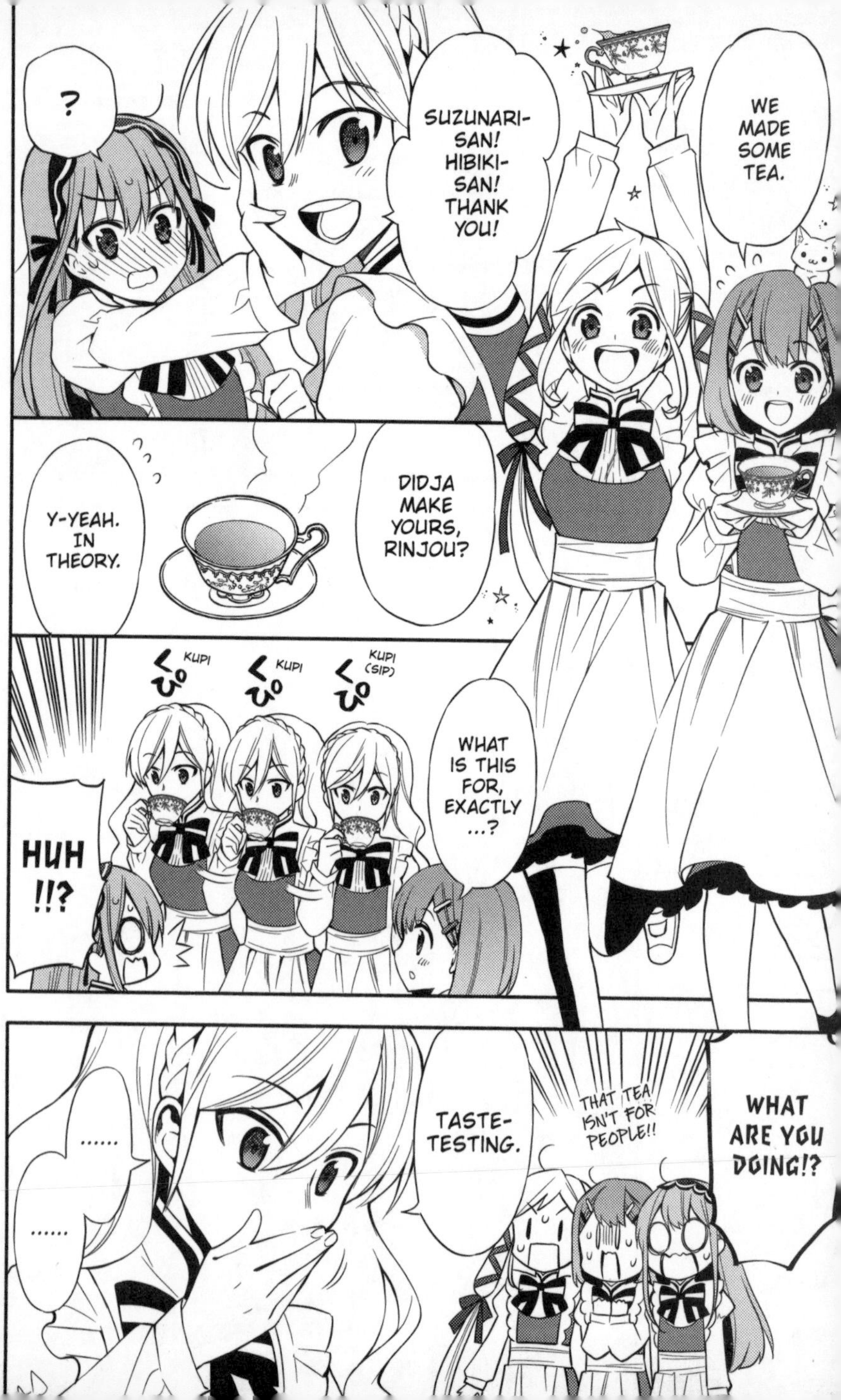

WE MADE SOME TEA.
SUZUNARI-SAN! HIBIKI-SAN! THANK YOU!
?
DIDJA MAKE YOURS, RINJOU?
Y-YEAH. IN THEORY.
WHAT IS THIS FOR, EXACTLY ...?
くぴ
KUPI (SIP)
くぴ
KUPI
くぴ
KUPI
HUH !!?
WHAT ARE YOU DOING!?
THAT TEA ISN'T FOR PEOPLE!!
TASTE-TESTING.
......
......

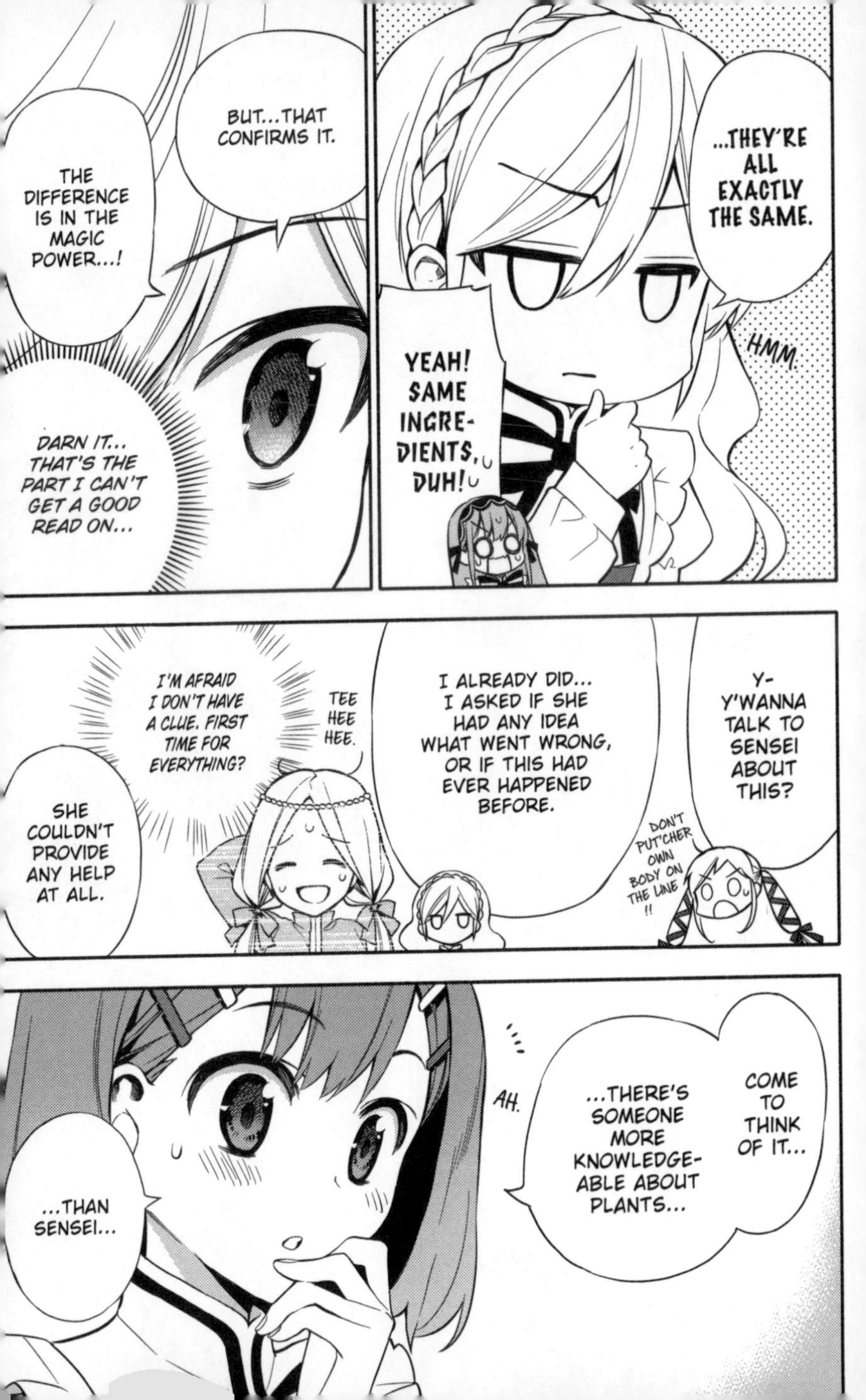
...THEY'RE ALL EXACTLY THE SAME.
HMM
YEAH! SAME INGREDIENTS, DUH!
BUT...THAT CONFIRMS IT.
THE DIFFERENCE IS IN THE MAGIC POWER...!
DARN IT... THAT'S THE PART I CAN'T GET A GOOD READ ON...
Y-Y'WANNA TALK TO SENSEI ABOUT THIS?
DON'T PUT'CHER OWN BODY ON THE LINE !!
I ALREADY DID... I ASKED IF SHE HAD ANY IDEA WHAT WENT WRONG, OR IF THIS HAD EVER HAPPENED BEFORE.
TEE HEE HEE.
I'M AFRAID I DON'T HAVE A CLUE. FIRST TIME FOR EVERYTHING?
SHE COULDN'T PROVIDE ANY HELP AT ALL.
...
AH.
COME TO THINK OF IT...
...THERE'S SOMEONE MORE KNOWLEDGE-ABLE ABOUT PLANTS...
...THAN SENSEI...

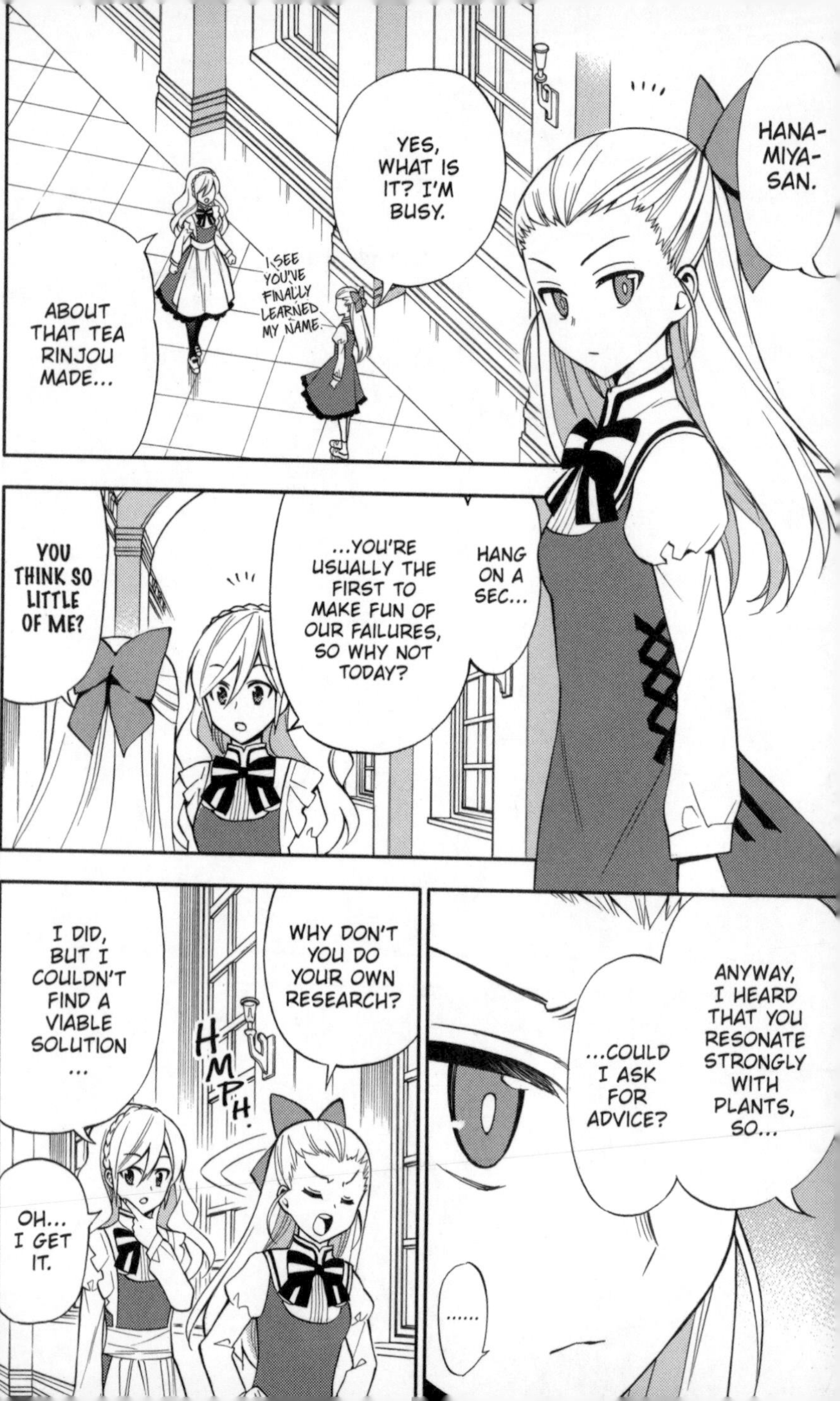
HANA-MIYA-SAN.
YES, WHAT IS IT? I'M BUSY.
I SEE YOU'VE FINALLY LEARNED MY NAME.
ABOUT THAT TEA RINJOU MADE...
HANG ON A SEC...
...YOU'RE USUALLY THE FIRST TO MAKE FUN OF OUR FAILURES, SO WHY NOT TODAY?
YOU THINK SO LITTLE OF ME?
ANYWAY, I HEARD THAT YOU RESONATE STRONGLY WITH PLANTS, SO...
...COULD I ASK FOR ADVICE?
......
WHY DON'T YOU DO YOUR OWN RESEARCH?
HMPH!
I DID, BUT I COULDN'T FIND A VIABLE SOLUTION...
OH... I GET IT.

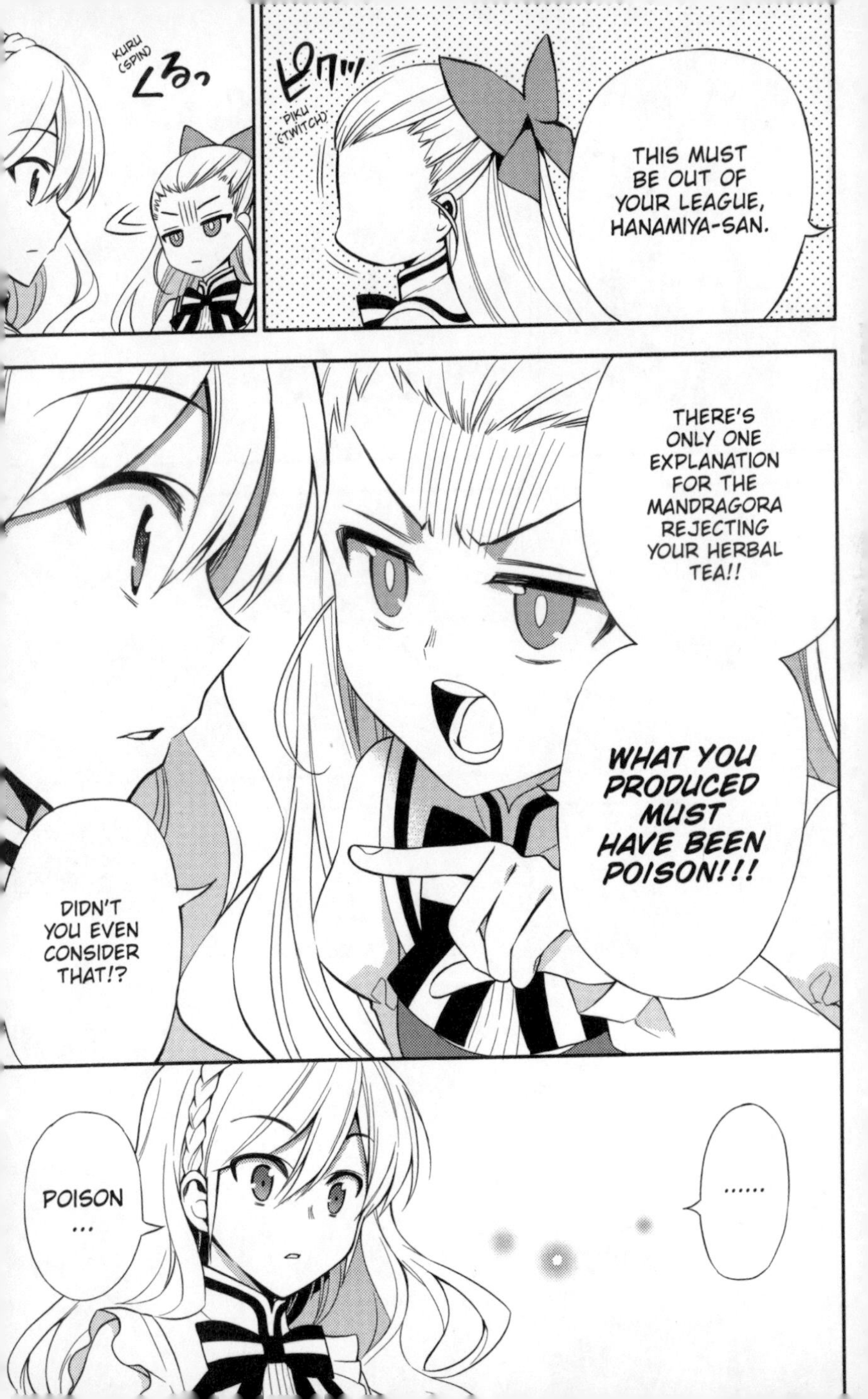
ピクッ
PIKU (TWITCH)
THIS MUST BE OUT OF YOUR LEAGUE, HANAMIYA-SAN.
くるっ
KURU (SPIN)
THERE'S ONLY ONE EXPLANATION FOR THE MANDRAGORA REJECTING YOUR HERBAL TEA!!
WHAT YOU PRODUCED MUST HAVE BEEN POISON!!!
DIDN'T YOU EVEN CONSIDER THAT!?
......
POISON ...

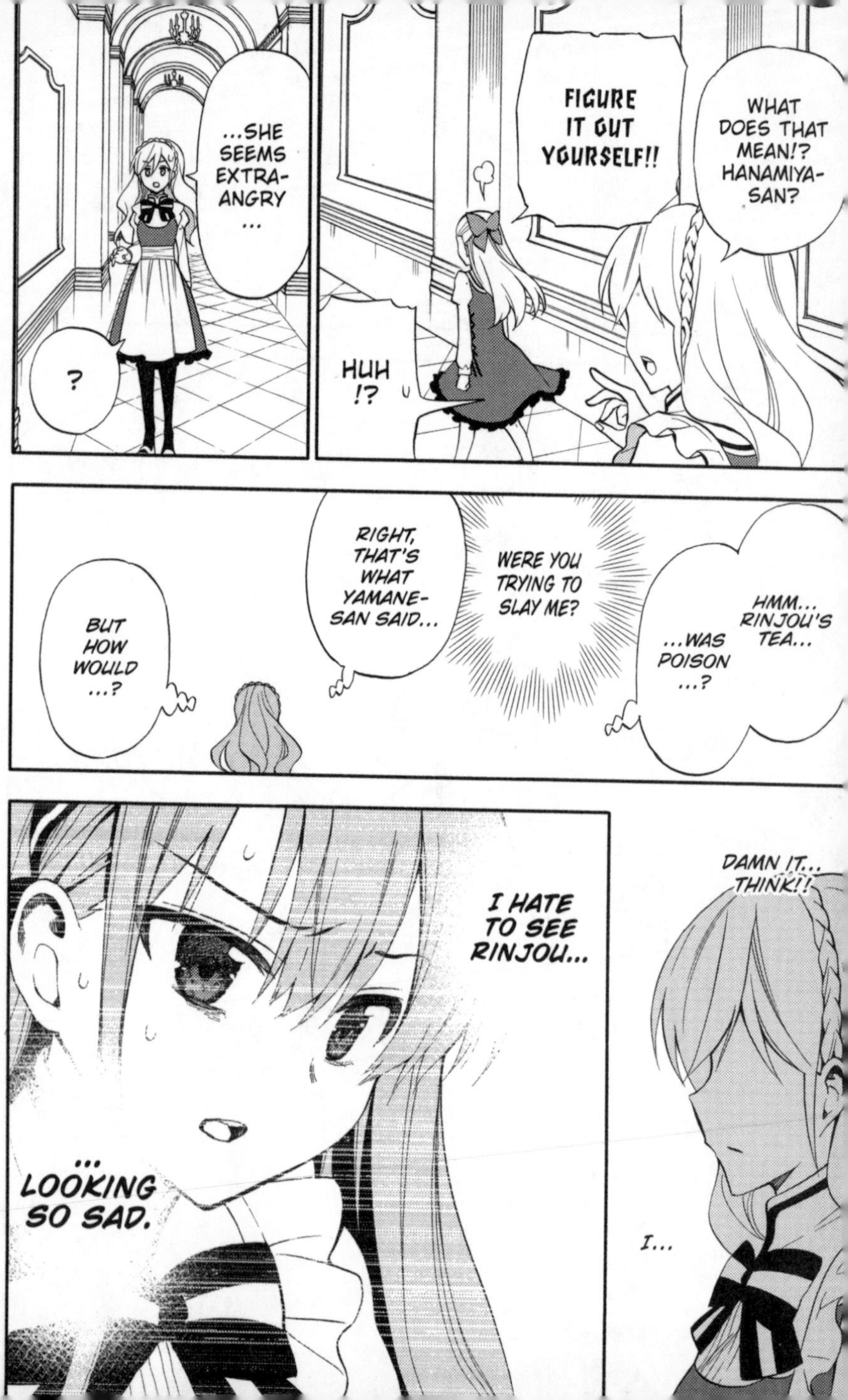
WHAT DOES THAT MEAN!? HANAMIYA-SAN?
FIGURE IT OUT YOURSELF!!
HUH !?
...SHE SEEMS EXTRA-ANGRY ...
?
HMM... RINJOU'S TEA...
...WAS POISON ...?
WERE YOU TRYING TO SLAY ME?
RIGHT, THAT'S WHAT YAMANE-SAN SAID...
BUT HOW WOULD ...?
DAMN IT... THINK!!
I...
I HATE TO SEE RINJOU...
...LOOKING SO SAD.

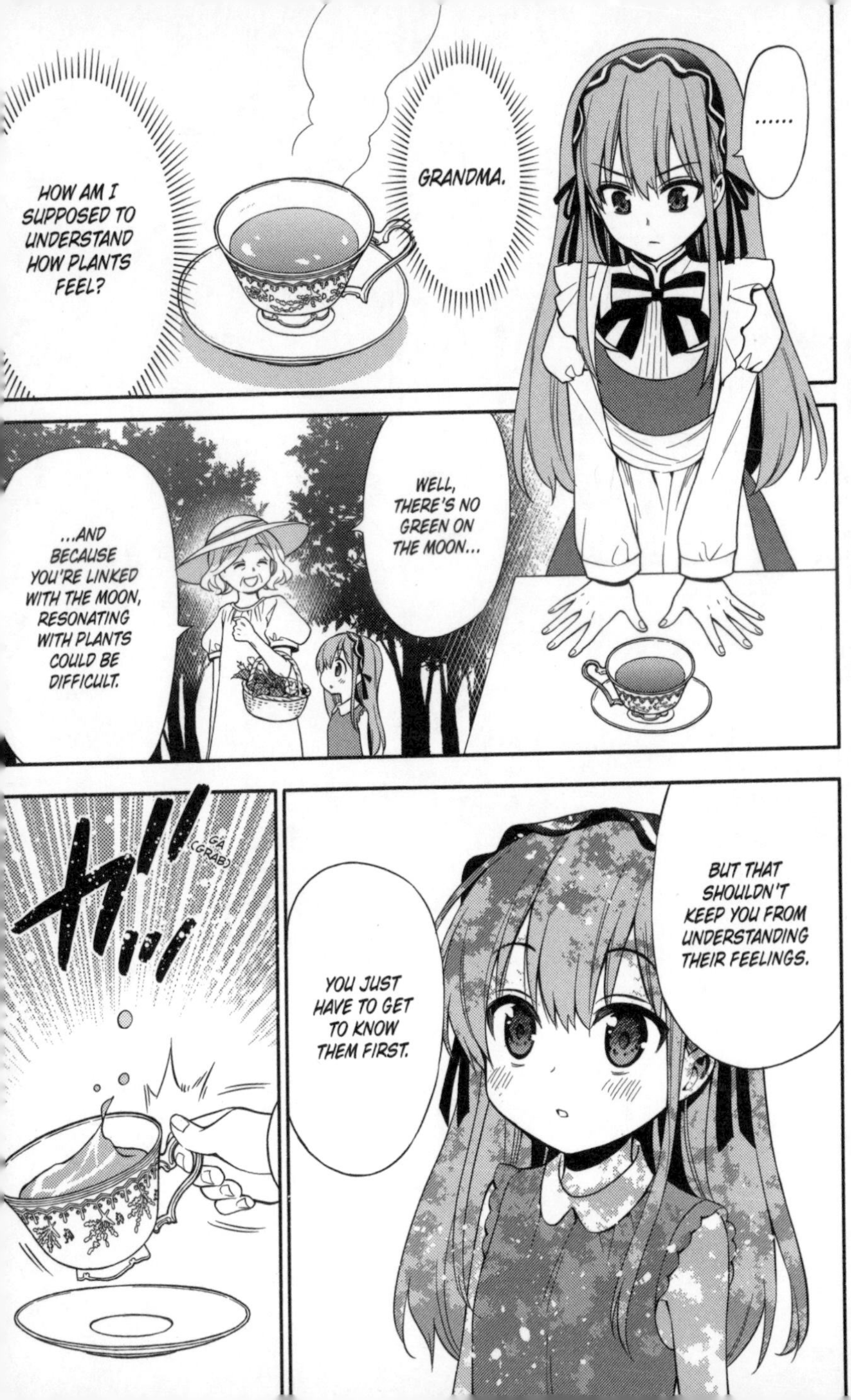
......
GRANDMA.
HOW AM I SUPPOSED TO UNDERSTAND HOW PLANTS FEEL?
WELL, THERE'S NO GREEN ON THE MOON...
...AND BECAUSE YOU'RE LINKED WITH THE MOON, RESONATING WITH PLANTS COULD BE DIFFICULT.
BUT THAT SHOULDN'T KEEP YOU FROM UNDERSTANDING THEIR FEELINGS.
YOU JUST HAVE TO GET TO KNOW THEM FIRST.
GA (GRAB)

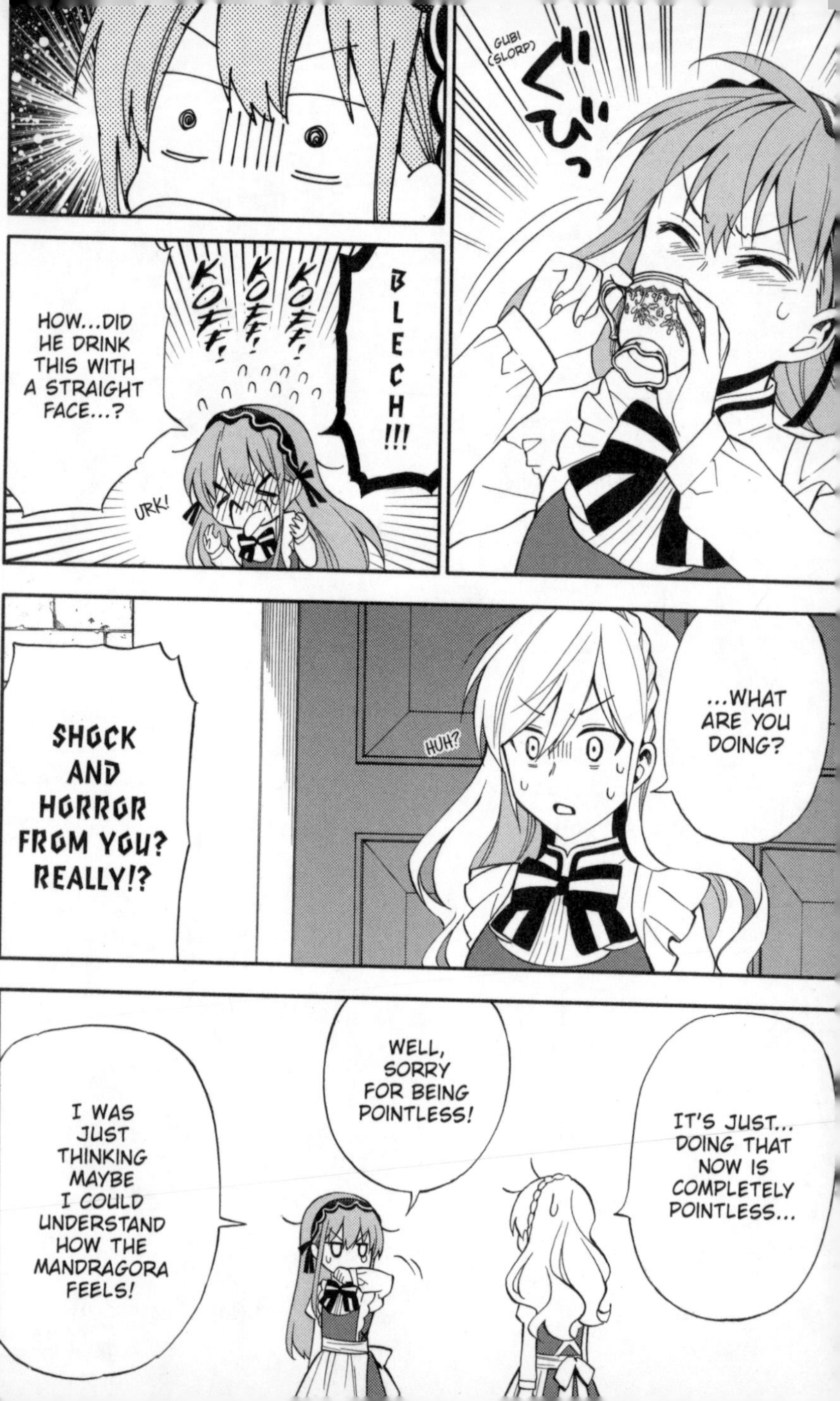
GUBI (SLORP)
BLECH!!!
KOFF!
KOFF!
KOFF!
HOW...DID HE DRINK THIS WITH A STRAIGHT FACE...?
URK!
...WHAT ARE YOU DOING?
HUH?
SHOCK AND HORROR FROM YOU? REALLY!?
IT'S JUST... DOING THAT NOW IS COMPLETELY POINTLESS...
WELL, SORRY FOR BEING POINTLESS!
I WAS JUST THINKING MAYBE I COULD UNDERSTAND HOW THE MANDRAGORA FEELS!

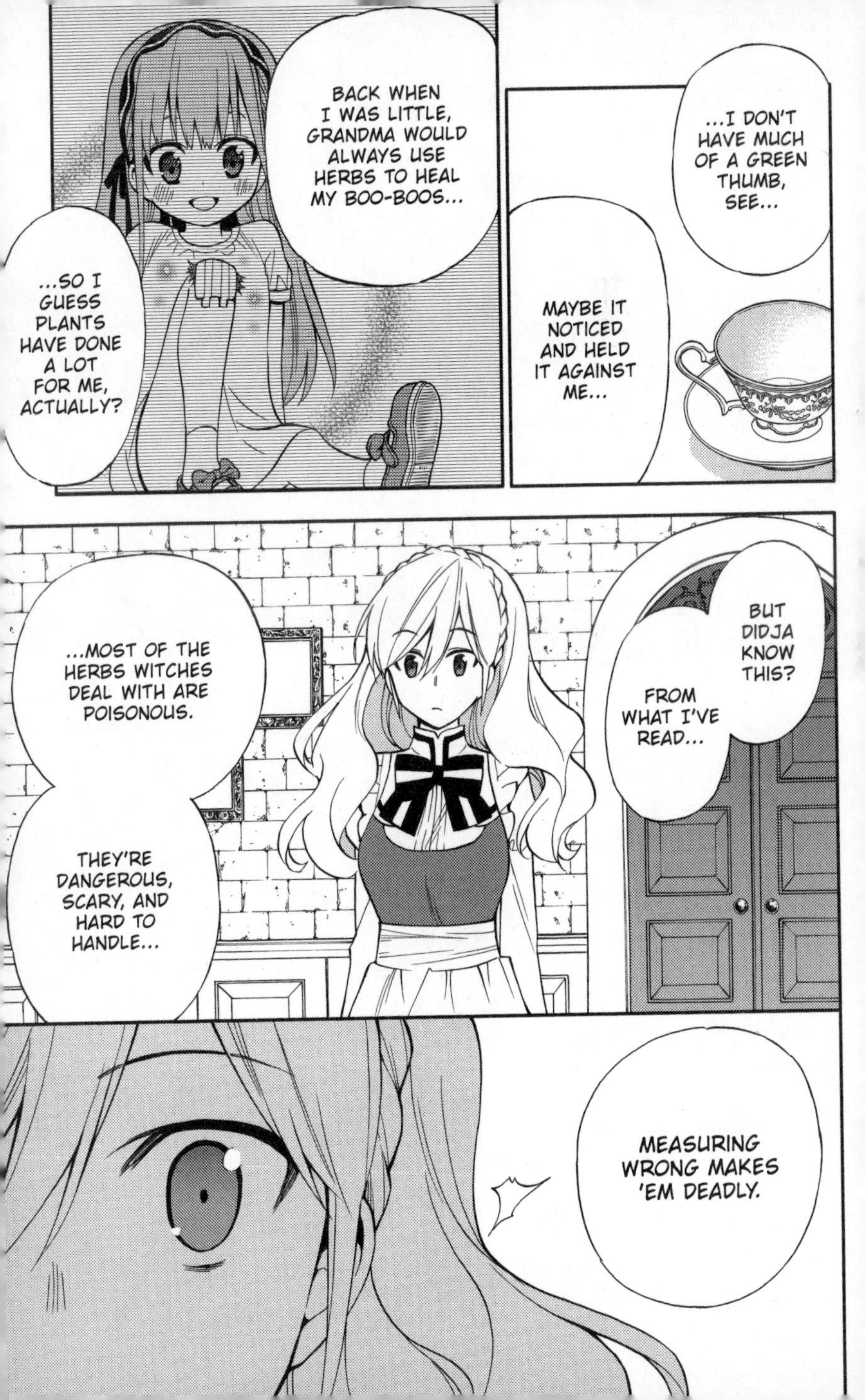
...I DON'T HAVE MUCH OF A GREEN THUMB, SEE...
MAYBE IT NOTICED AND HELD IT AGAINST ME...
BACK WHEN I WAS LITTLE, GRANDMA WOULD ALWAYS USE HERBS TO HEAL MY BOO-BOOS...
...SO I GUESS PLANTS HAVE DONE A LOT FOR ME, ACTUALLY?
BUT DIDJA KNOW THIS?
FROM WHAT I'VE READ...
...MOST OF THE HERBS WITCHES DEAL WITH ARE POISONOUS.
THEY'RE DANGEROUS, SCARY, AND HARD TO HANDLE...
MEASURING WRONG MAKES 'EM DEADLY.

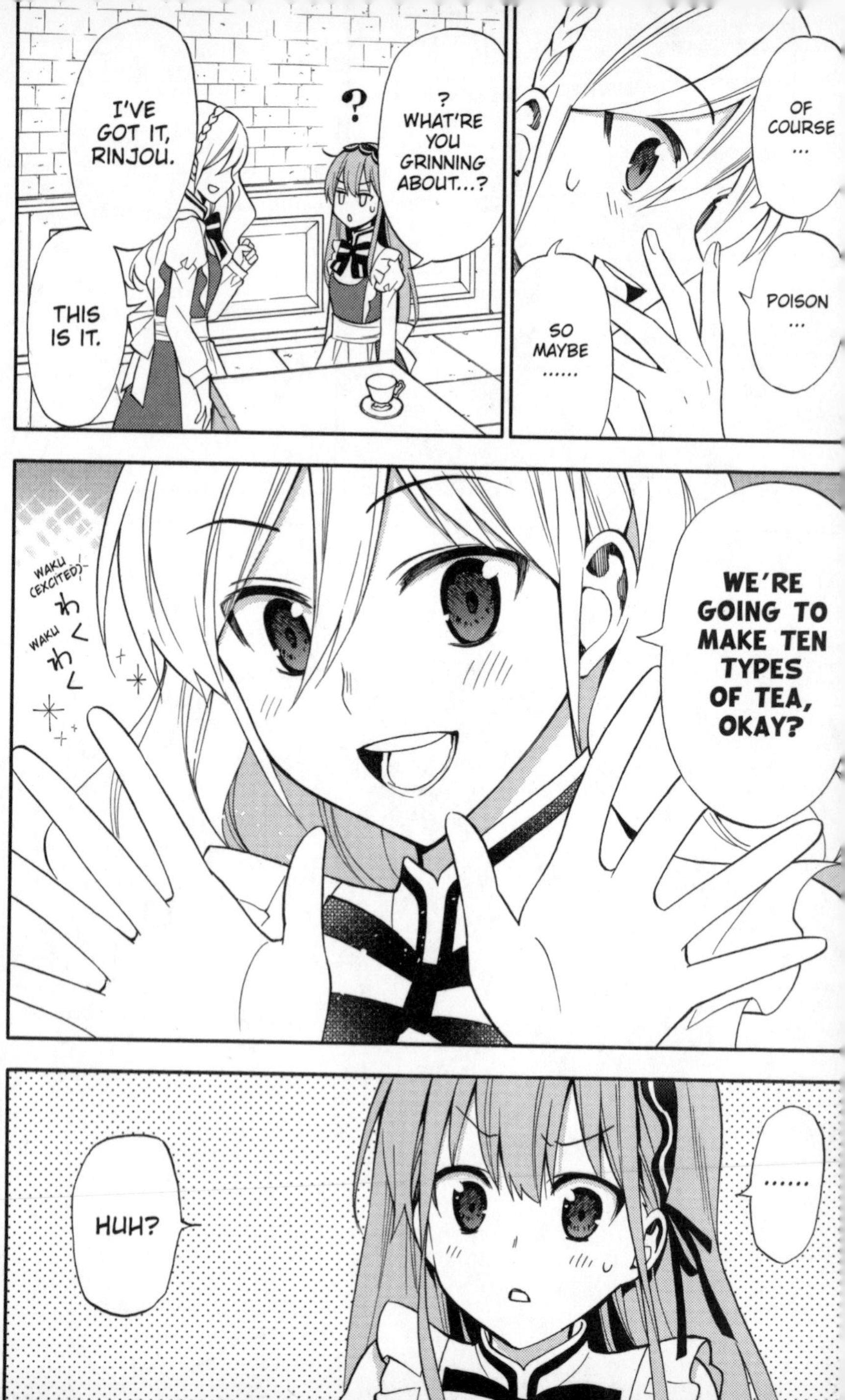
OF COURSE ...
POISON ...
SO MAYBE ......
? WHAT'RE YOU GRINNING ABOUT...?
?
I'VE GOT IT, RINJOU.
THIS IS IT.
WE'RE GOING TO MAKE TEN TYPES OF TEA, OKAY?
WAKU (EXCITED)
わく
WAKU
わく
......
HUH?

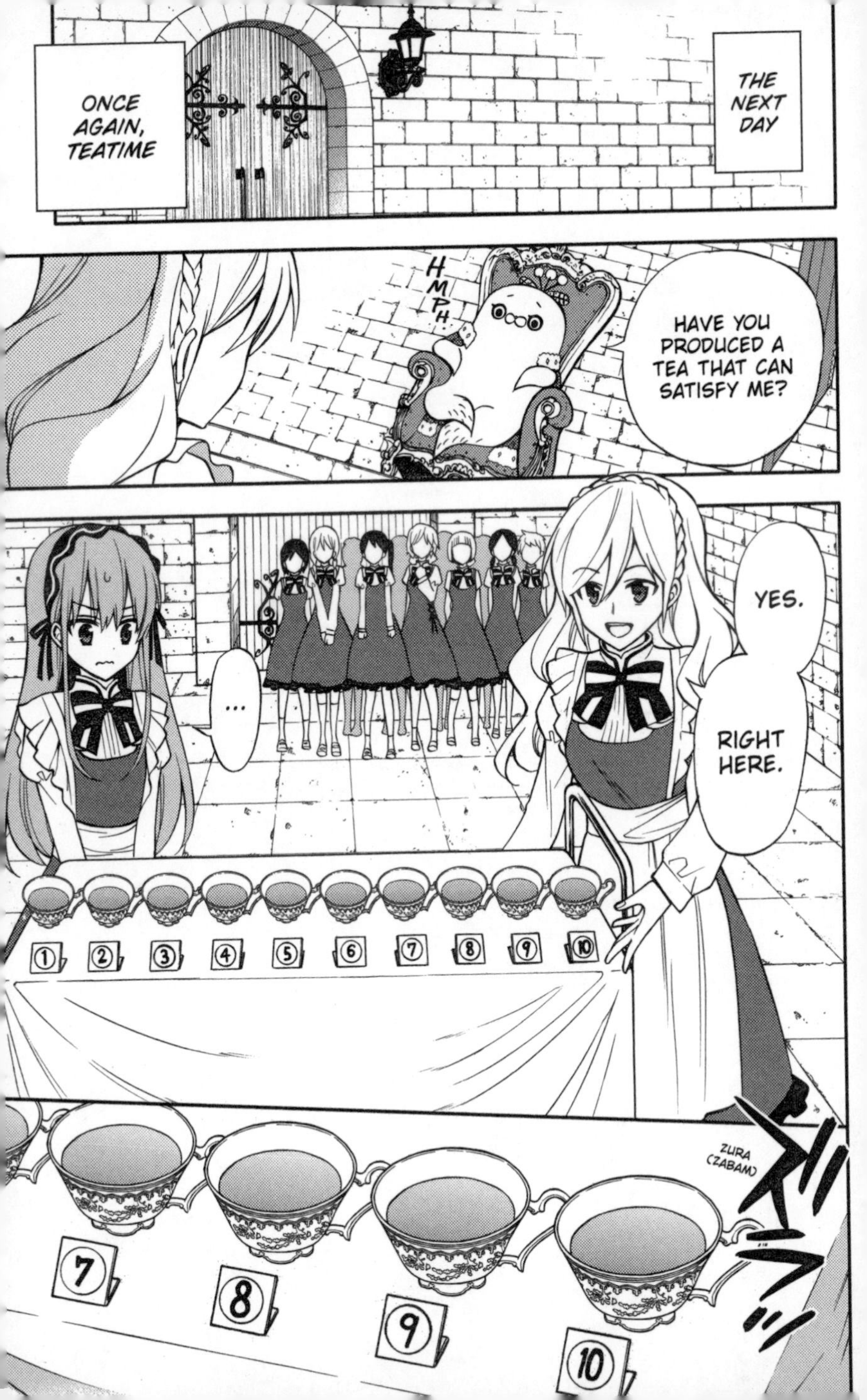
THE NEXT DAY
ONCE AGAIN, TEATIME
HAVE YOU PRODUCED A TEA THAT CAN SATISFY ME?
HMPH
YES.
RIGHT HERE.
...
1
2
3
4
5
6
7
8
9
10
ZURA (ZABAM)
10
9
8
7

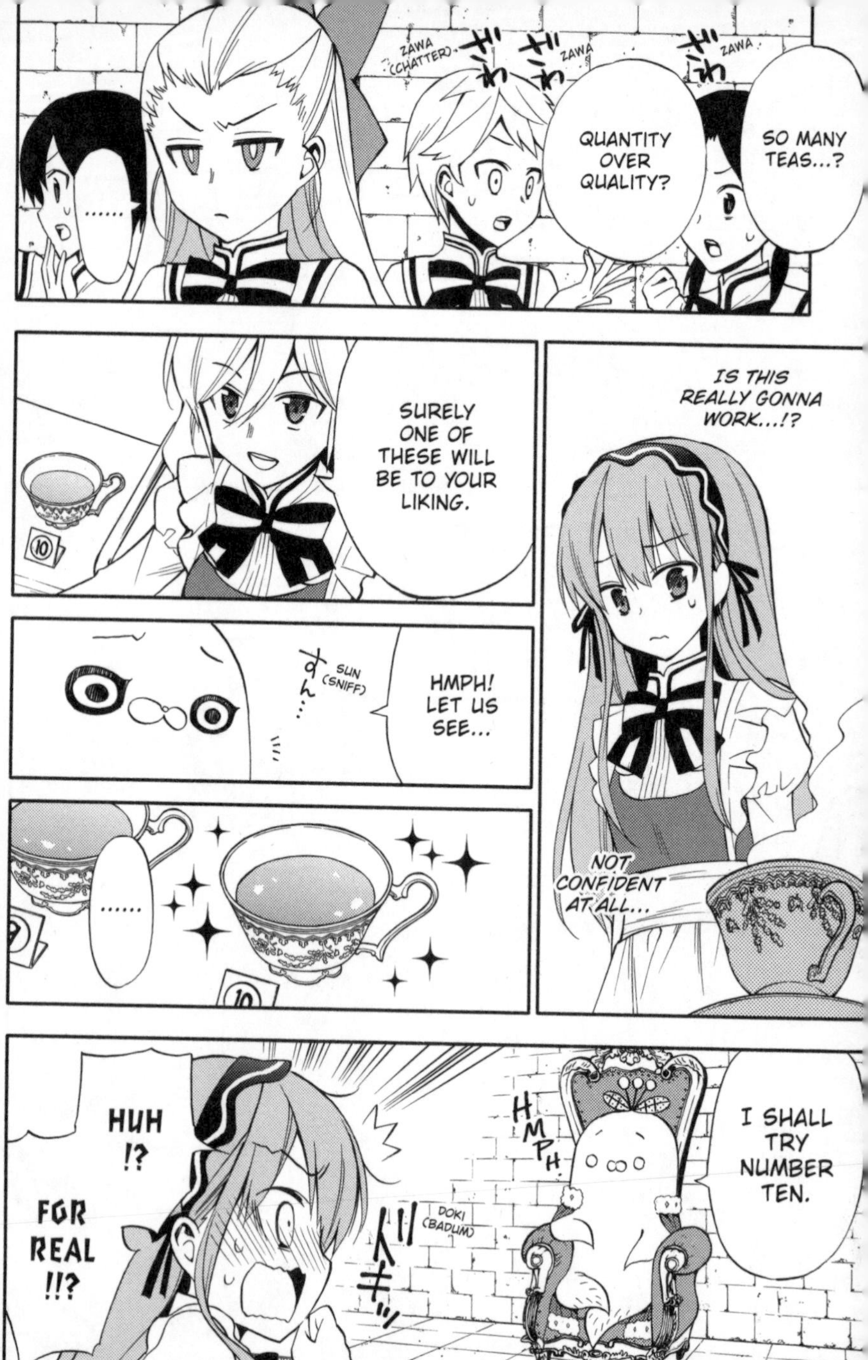
ZAWA
ZAWA
ZAWA (CHATTER)
SO MANY TEAS...?
QUANTITY OVER QUALITY?
......
IS THIS REALLY GONNA WORK...!?
NOT CONFIDENT AT ALL...
SURELY ONE OF THESE WILL BE TO YOUR LIKING.
HMPH! LET US SEE...
SUN (SNIFF)
......
I SHALL TRY NUMBER TEN.
HMPH
DOKI (BADUM)
HUH !?
FOR REAL !!?

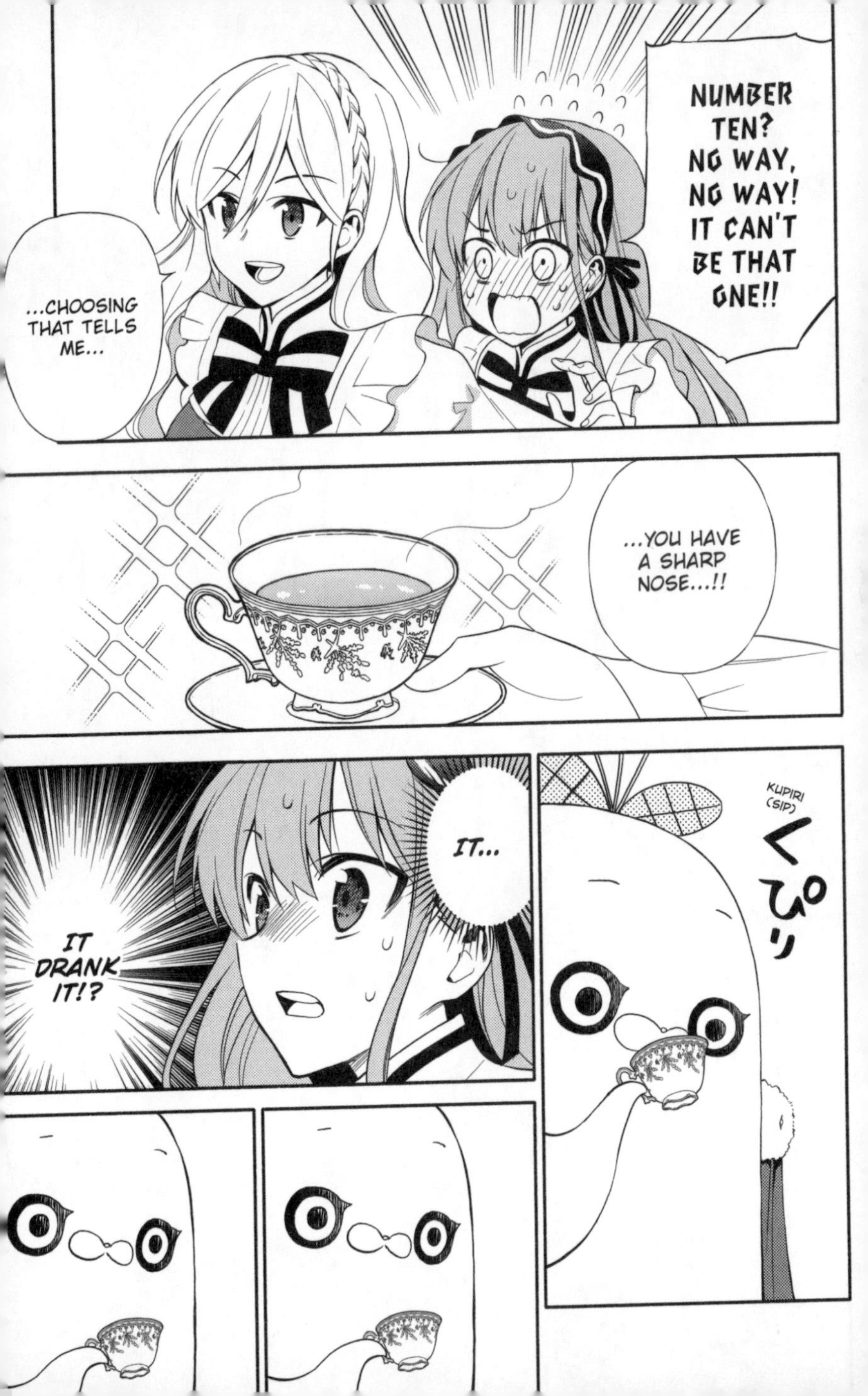
NUMBER TEN? NO WAY, NO WAY! IT CAN'T BE THAT ONE!!
...CHOOSING THAT TELLS ME...
...YOU HAVE A SHARP NOSE...!!
KUPIRI (SIP)
くぴり
IT...
IT DRANK IT!?

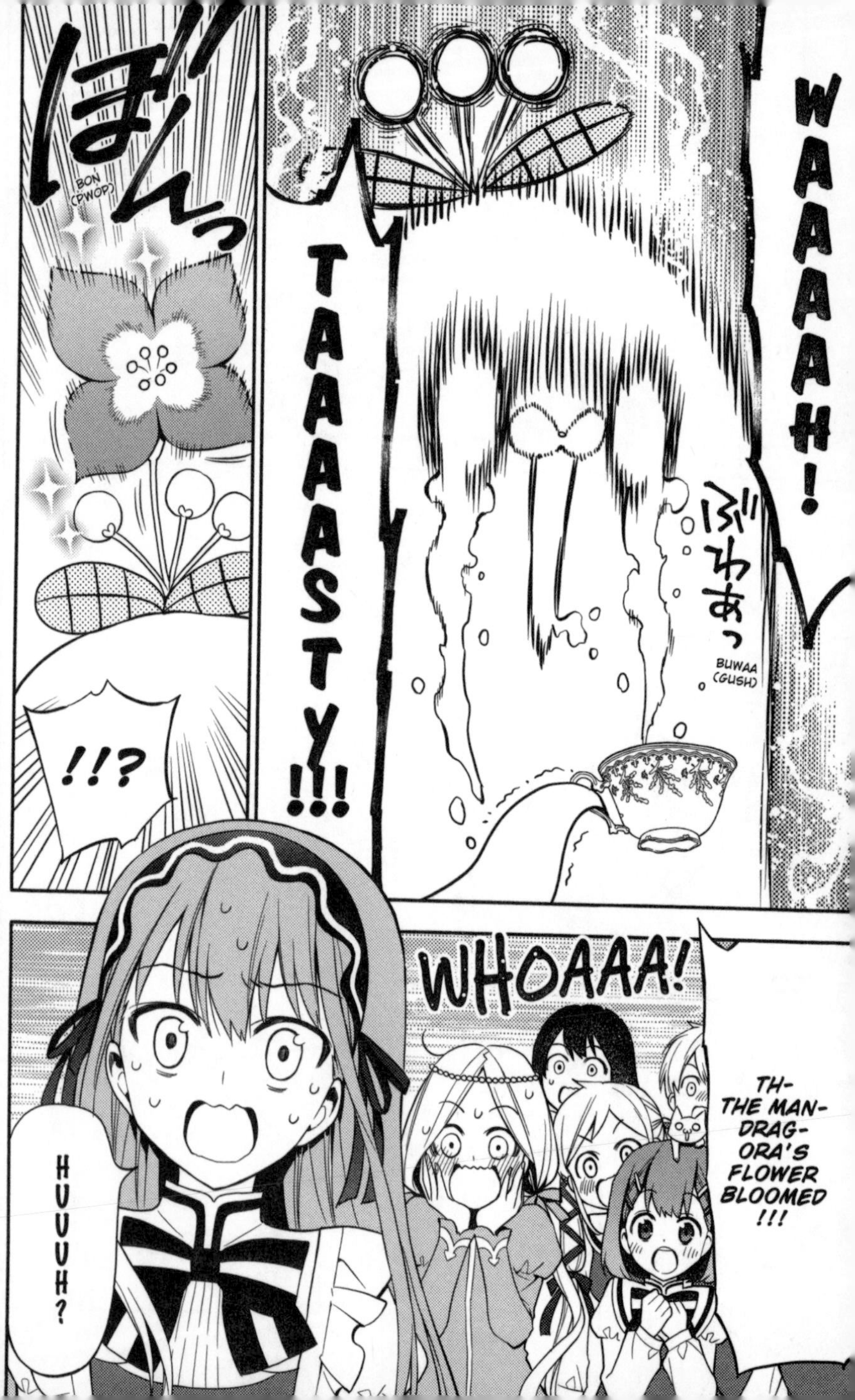

WAAAAH!
ぶわあっ
BUWAA (GUSH)
TAAAASTY!!!
ぼんっ
BON (PWOP)
!!?
TH-THE MAN-DRAG-ORA'S FLOWER BLOOMED!!!
WHOAAA!
HUUUUH?

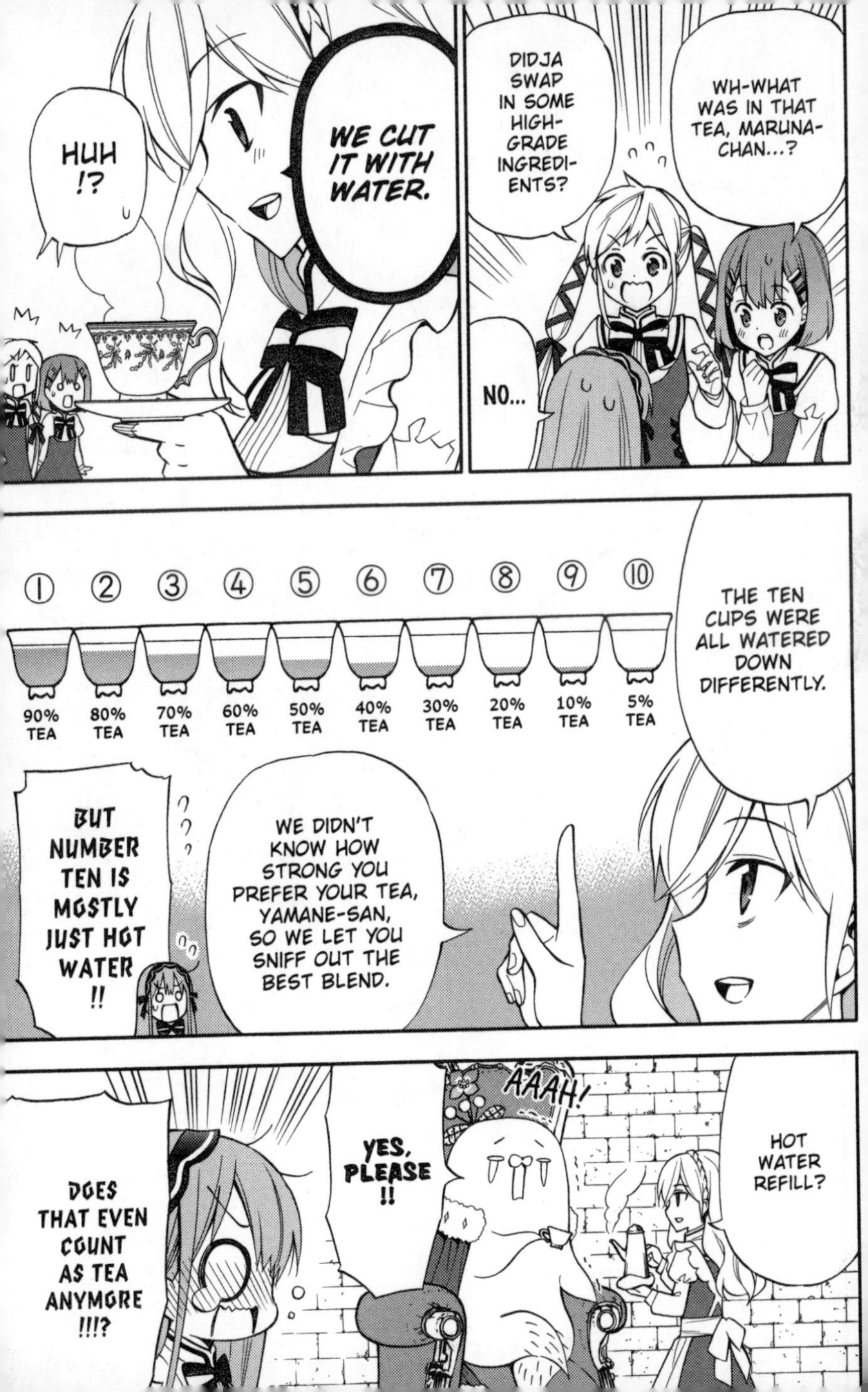
WH-WHAT WAS IN THAT TEA, MARUNA-CHAN...?
DIDJA SWAP IN SOME HIGH-GRADE INGREDI-ENTS?
NO...
WE CUT IT WITH WATER.
HUH!?
THE TEN CUPS WERE ALL WATERED DOWN DIFFERENTLY.
① ② ③ ④ ⑤ ⑥ ⑦ ⑧ ⑨ ⑩
90% TEA
80% TEA
70% TEA
60% TEA
50% TEA
40% TEA
30% TEA
20% TEA
10% TEA
5% TEA
WE DIDN'T KNOW HOW STRONG YOU PREFER YOUR TEA, YAMANE-SAN, SO WE LET YOU SNIFF OUT THE BEST BLEND.
BUT NUMBER TEN IS MOSTLY JUST HOT WATER!!
HOT WATER REFILL?
AAAH!
YES, PLEASE!!
DOES THAT EVEN COUNT AS TEA ANYMORE!!!?

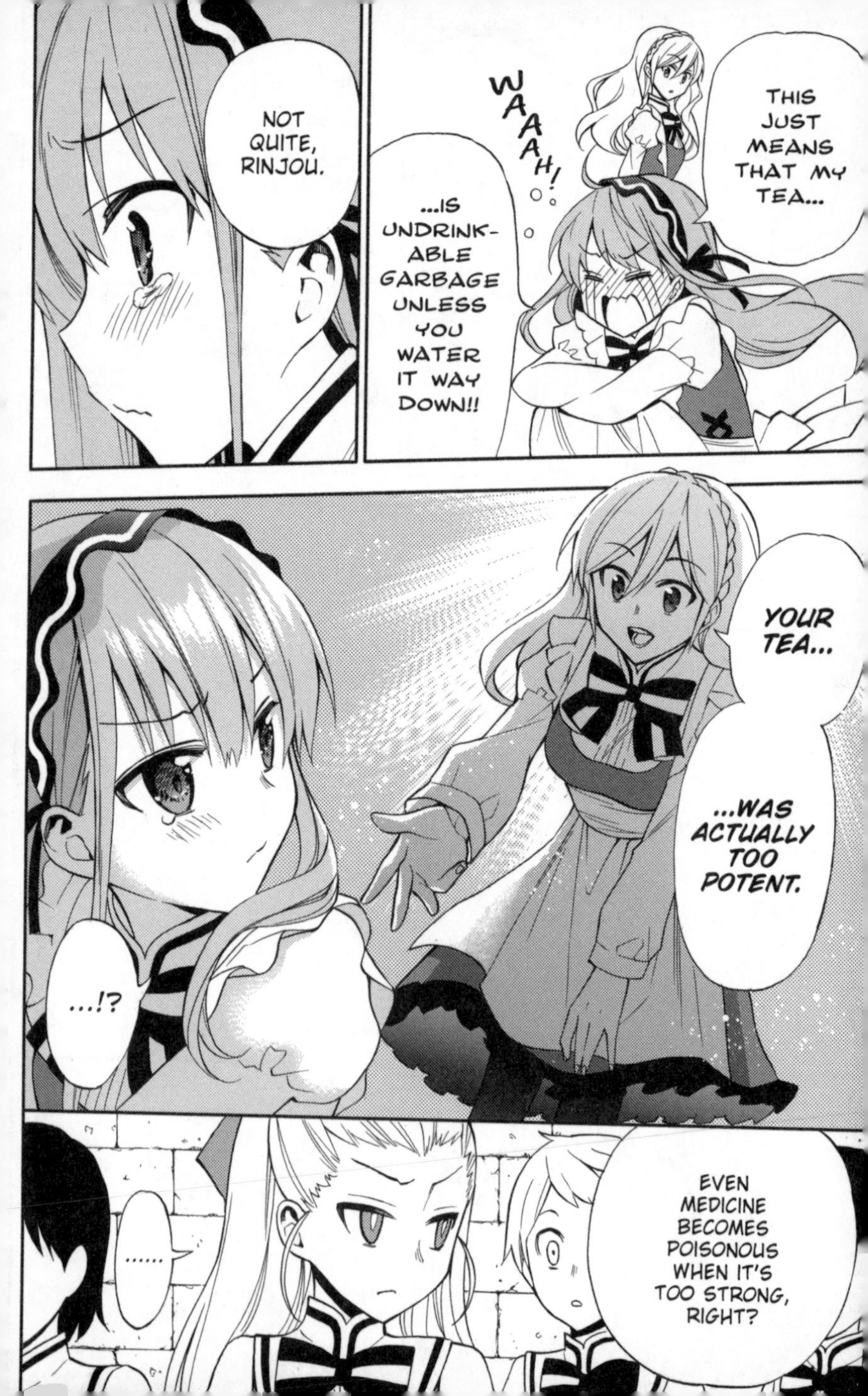
THIS JUST MEANS THAT MY TEA...
WAAAAH!
...IS UNDRINKABLE GARBAGE UNLESS YOU WATER IT WAY DOWN!!
NOT QUITE, RINJOU.
YOUR TEA...
...WAS ACTUALLY TOO POTENT.
...!?
EVEN MEDICINE BECOMES POISONOUS WHEN IT'S TOO STRONG, RIGHT?
......

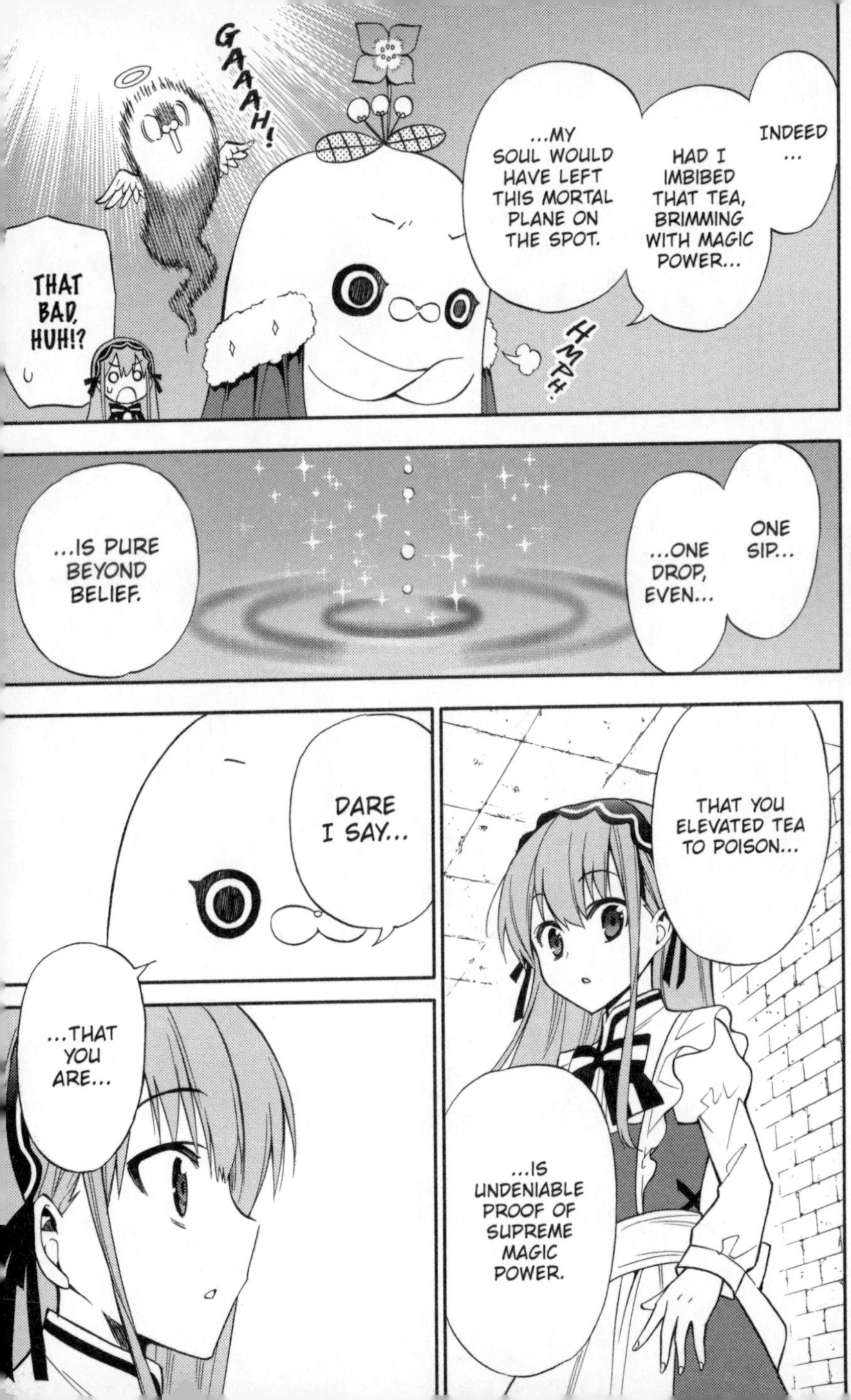
INDEED ...
HAD I IMBIBED THAT TEA, BRIMMING WITH MAGIC POWER...
...MY SOUL WOULD HAVE LEFT THIS MORTAL PLANE ON THE SPOT.
HMPH.
GAAAAH!
THAT BAD, HUH!?
ONE SIP...
...ONE DROP, EVEN...
...IS PURE BEYOND BELIEF.
THAT YOU ELEVATED TEA TO POISON...
...IS UNDENIABLE PROOF OF SUPREME MAGIC POWER.
DARE I SAY...
...THAT YOU ARE...

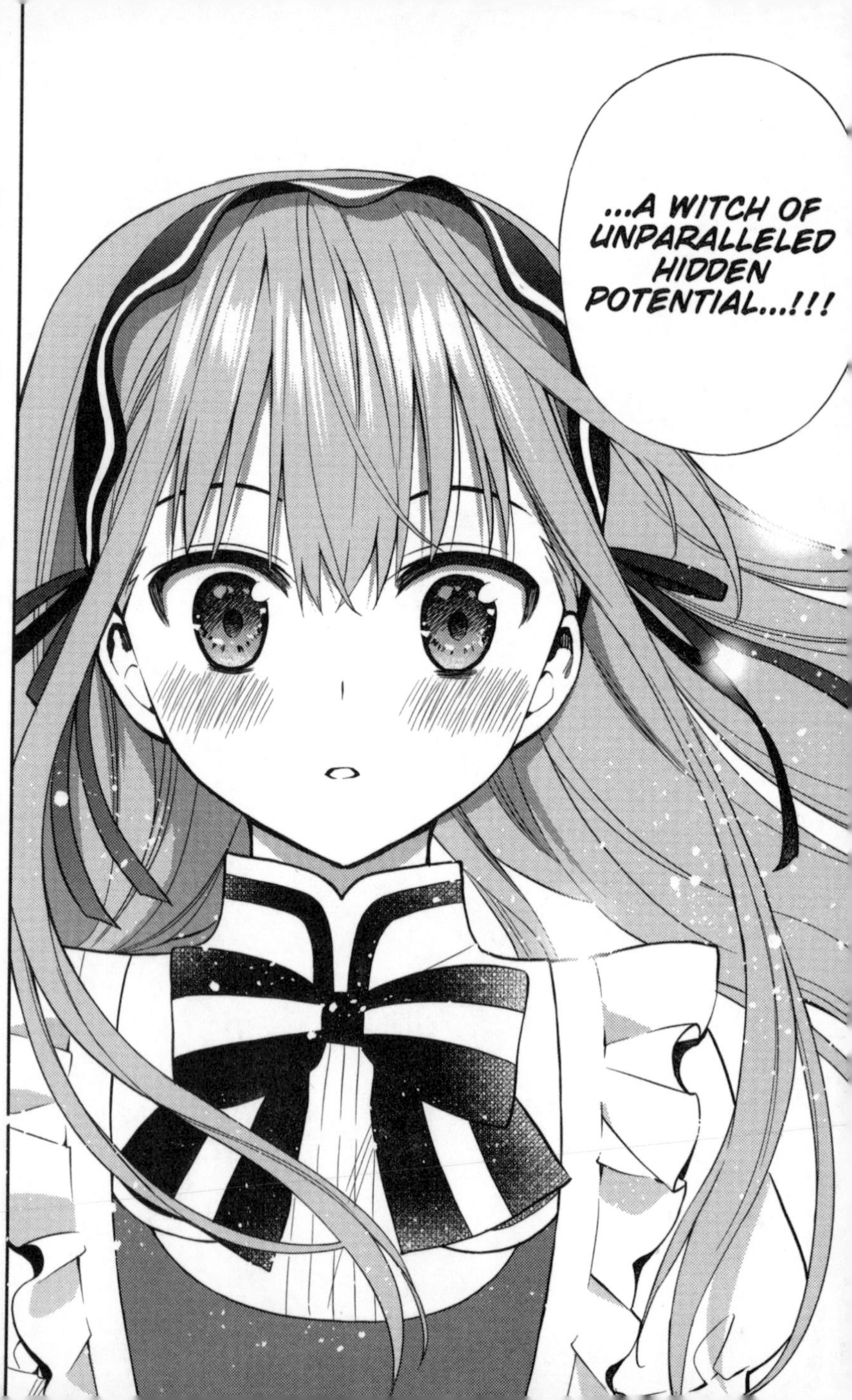
...A WITCH OF UNPARALLELED HIDDEN POTENTIAL...!!!

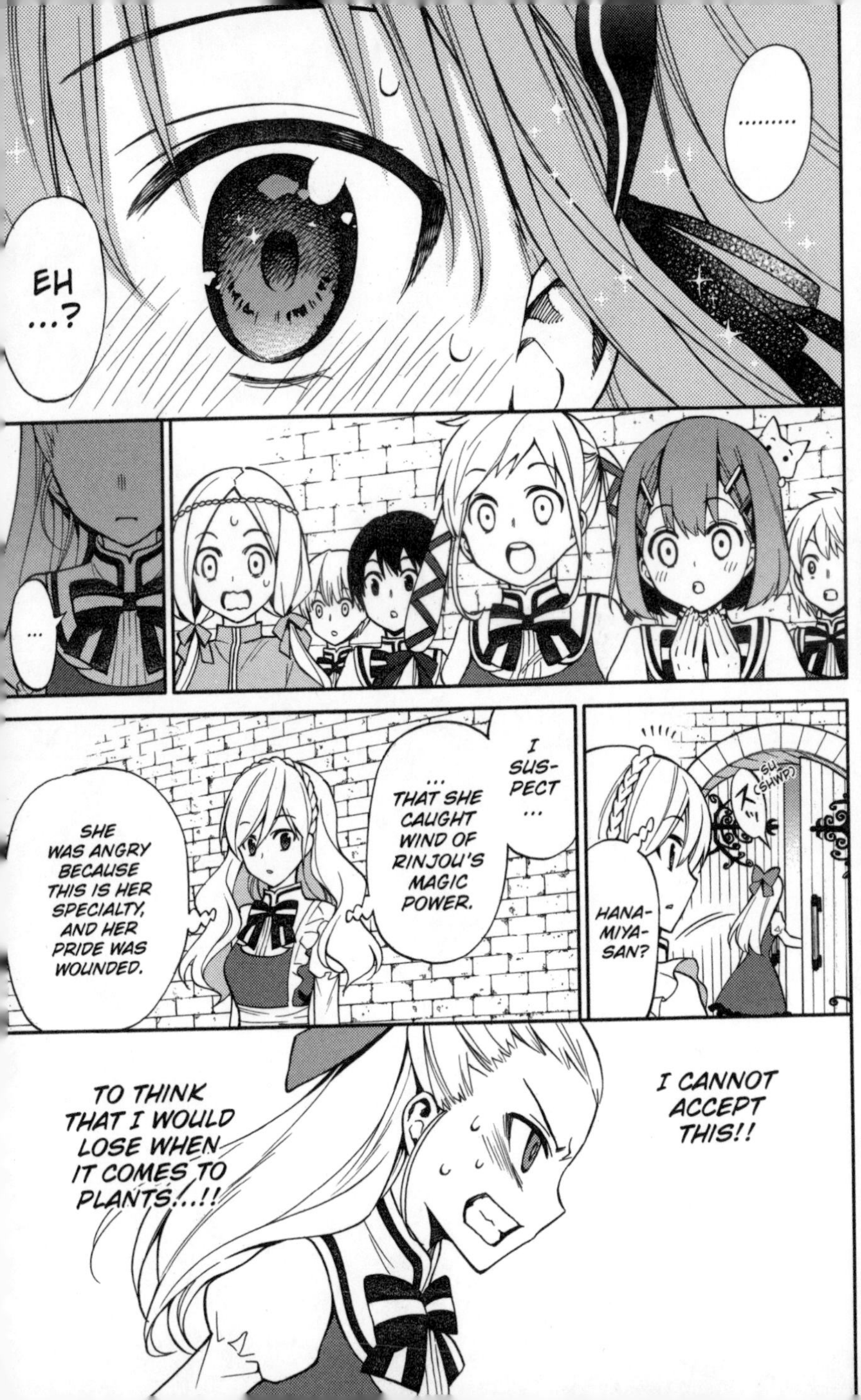
....
EH ...?
...
SU (SHWP)
HANA-MIYA-SAN?
I SUS-PECT ...
... THAT SHE CAUGHT WIND OF RINJOU'S MAGIC POWER.
SHE WAS ANGRY BECAUSE THIS IS HER SPECIALTY, AND HER PRIDE WAS WOUNDED.
I CANNOT ACCEPT THIS!!
TO THINK THAT I WOULD LOSE WHEN IT COMES TO PLANTS...!!

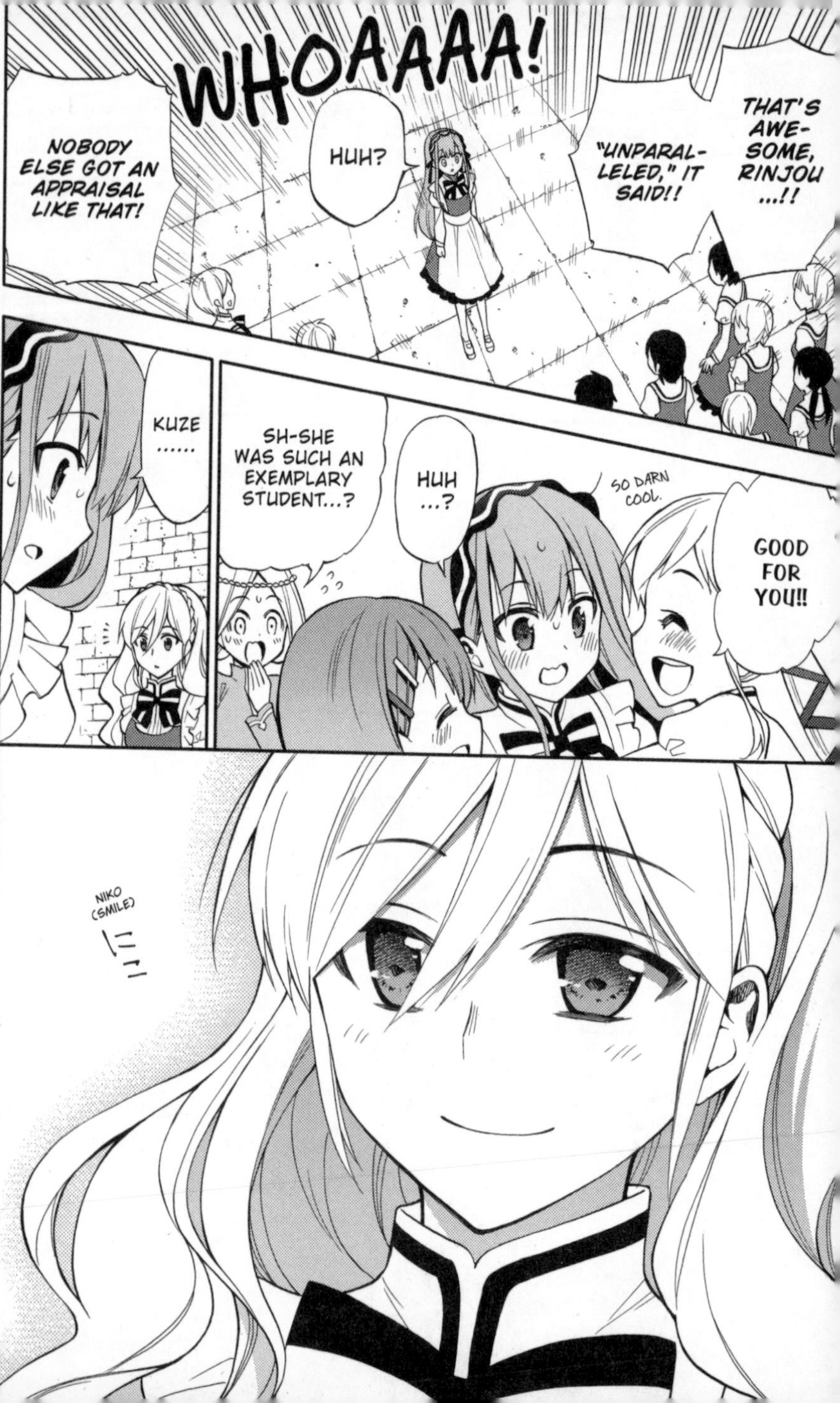
WHOAAAA!
THAT'S AWE-SOME, RINJOU ...!!
"UNPARAL-LELED," IT SAID!!
HUH?
NOBODY ELSE GOT AN APPRAISAL LIKE THAT!
GOOD FOR YOU!!
SO DARN COOL.
HUH ...?
SH-SHE WAS SUCH AN EXEMPLARY STUDENT...?
KUZE ......
NIKO (SMILE)

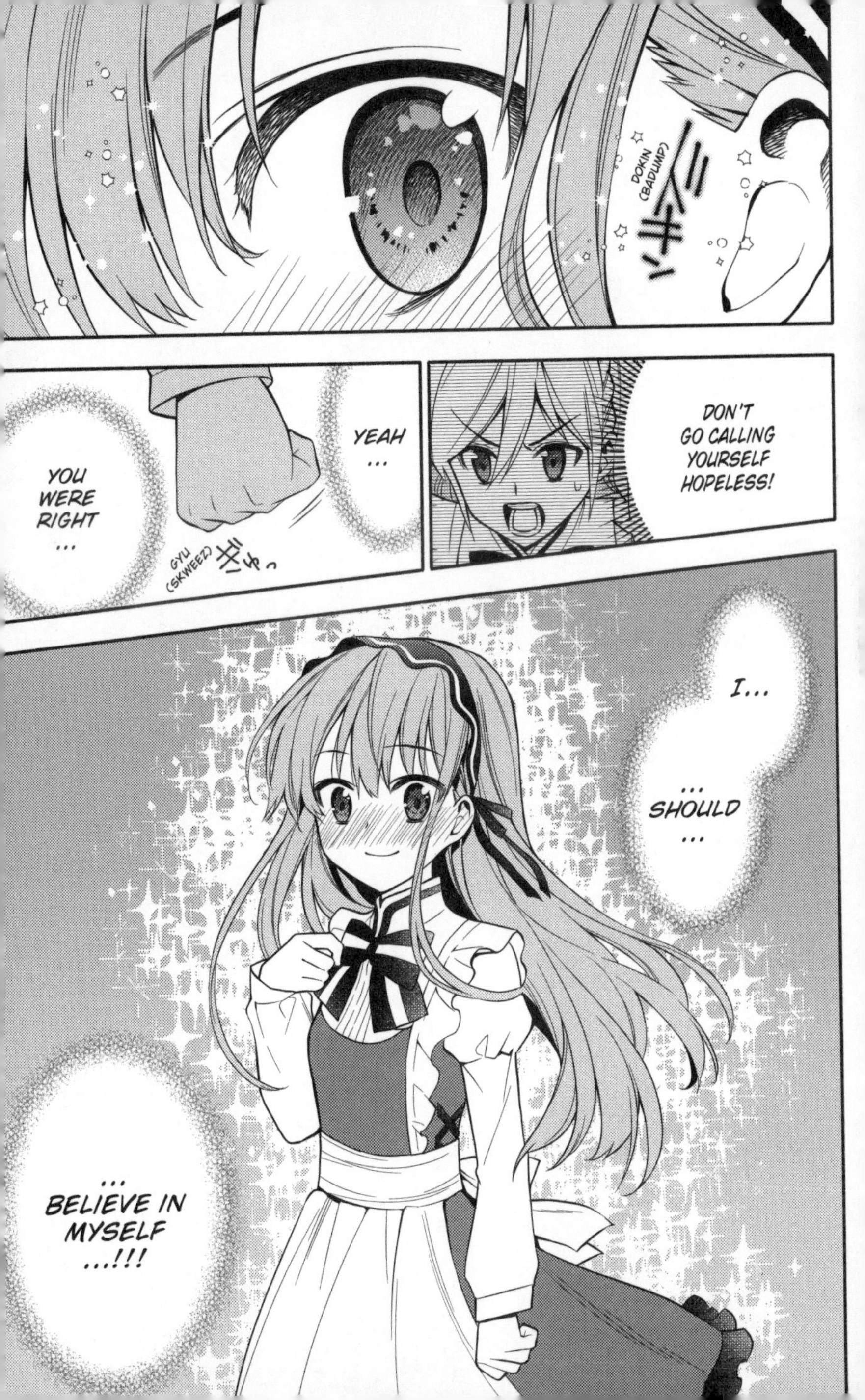
ドキン
DOKIN (BADUMP)
DON'T GO CALLING YOURSELF HOPELESS!
YEAH ...
YOU WERE RIGHT ...
ぎゅっ
GYU (SKWEEZ)
I...
... SHOULD ...
... BELIEVE IN MYSELF ...!!!

If Witch, Then Which?

INITIAL DESIGN FOR YAMANE-SAN THE MANDRAGORA
GOOD THING I ABANDONED THIS DESIGN.

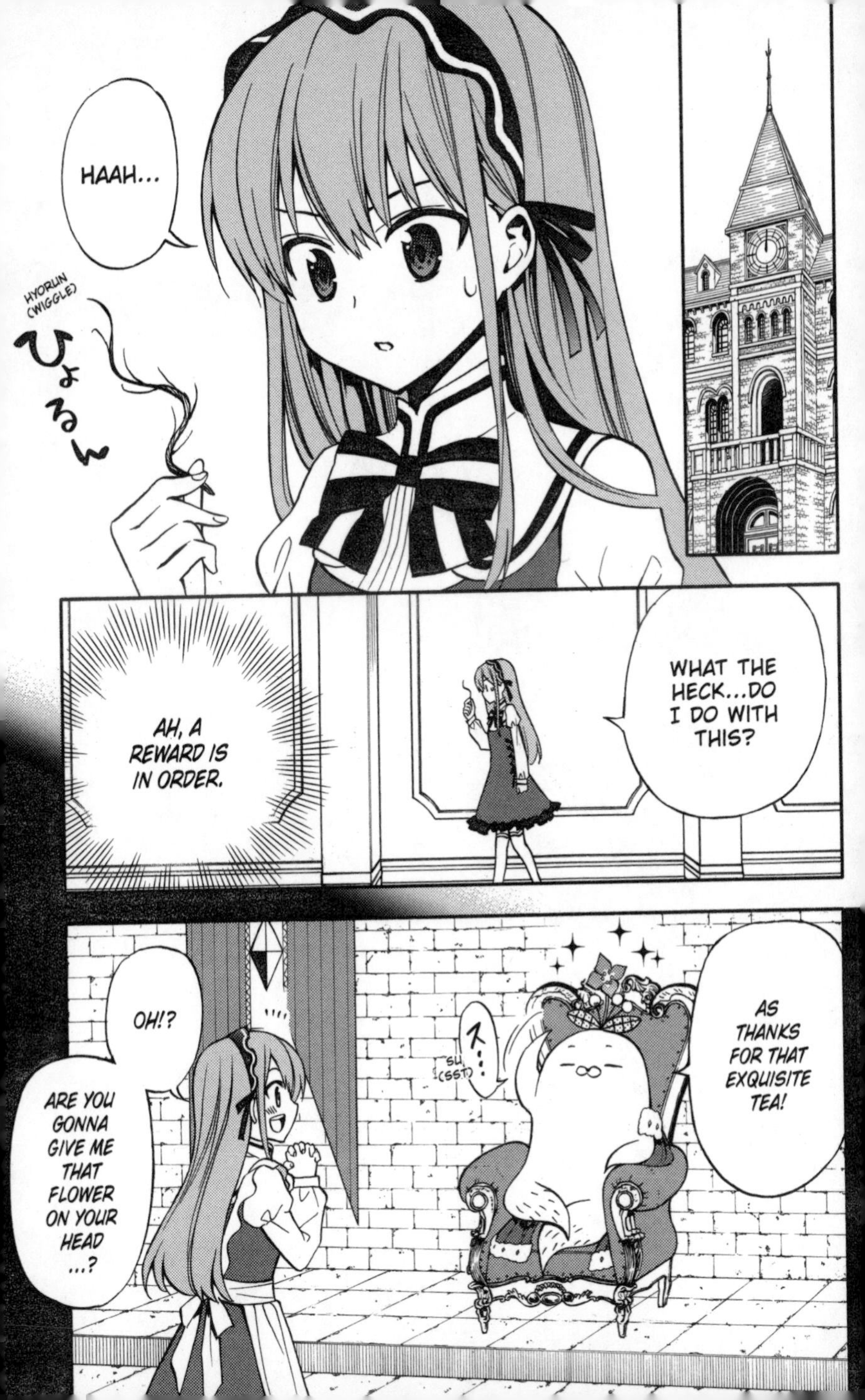
HAAH...
HYORUN (WIGGLE)
ひょるん
WHAT THE HECK...DO I DO WITH THIS?
AH, A REWARD IS IN ORDER.
AS THANKS FOR THAT EXQUISITE TEA!
ス…
SU (SSST)
...
OH!?
ARE YOU GONNA GIVE ME THAT FLOWER ON YOUR HEAD ...?

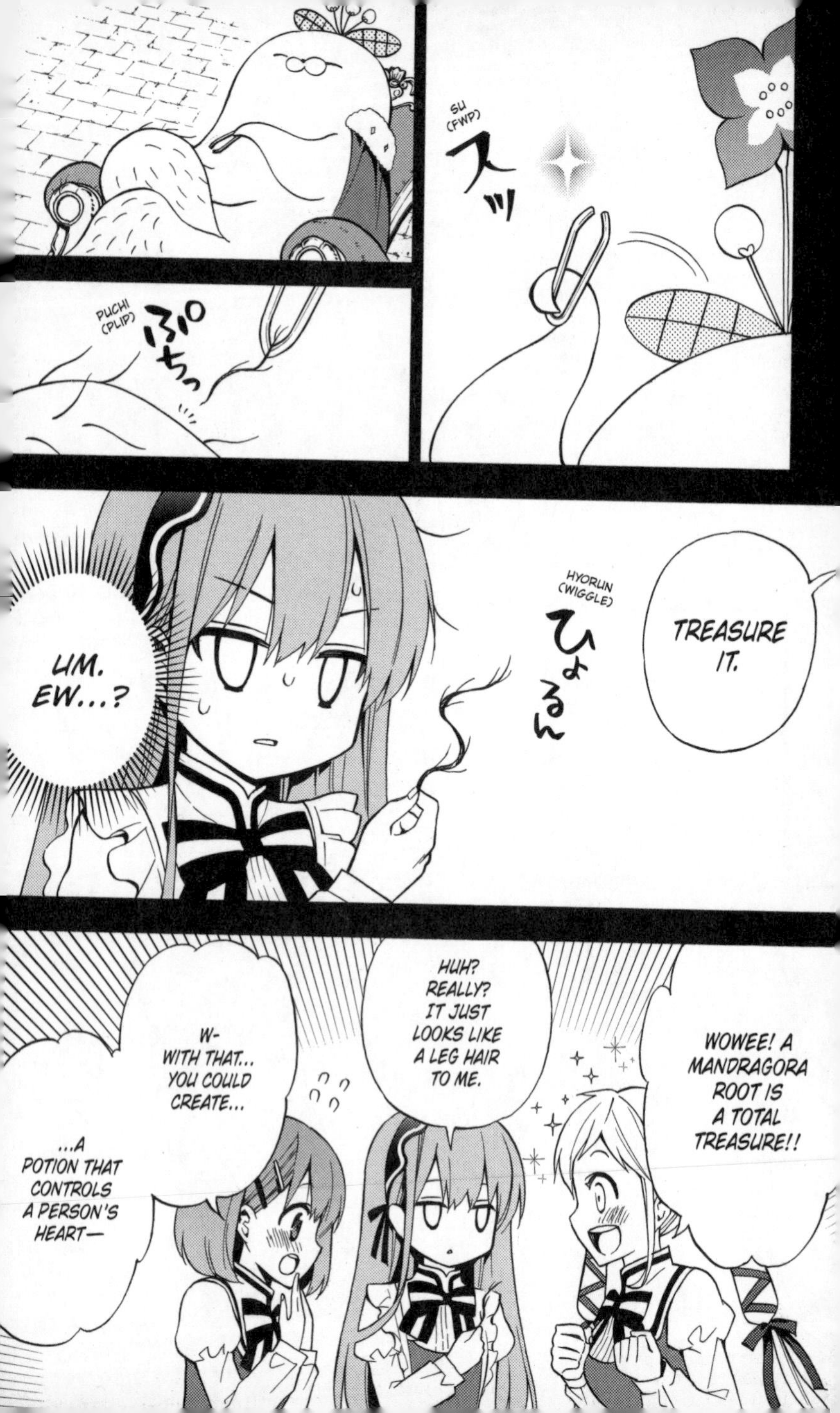
SU (FWP)
スッ
PUCHI (PLIP)
ぷちっ
TREASURE IT.
HYORUN (WIGGLE)
ひょるん
UM. EW...?
WOWEE! A MANDRAGORA ROOT IS A TOTAL TREASURE!!
HUH? REALLY? IT JUST LOOKS LIKE A LEG HAIR TO ME.
W- WITH THAT... YOU COULD CREATE...
...A POTION THAT CONTROLS A PERSON'S HEART—

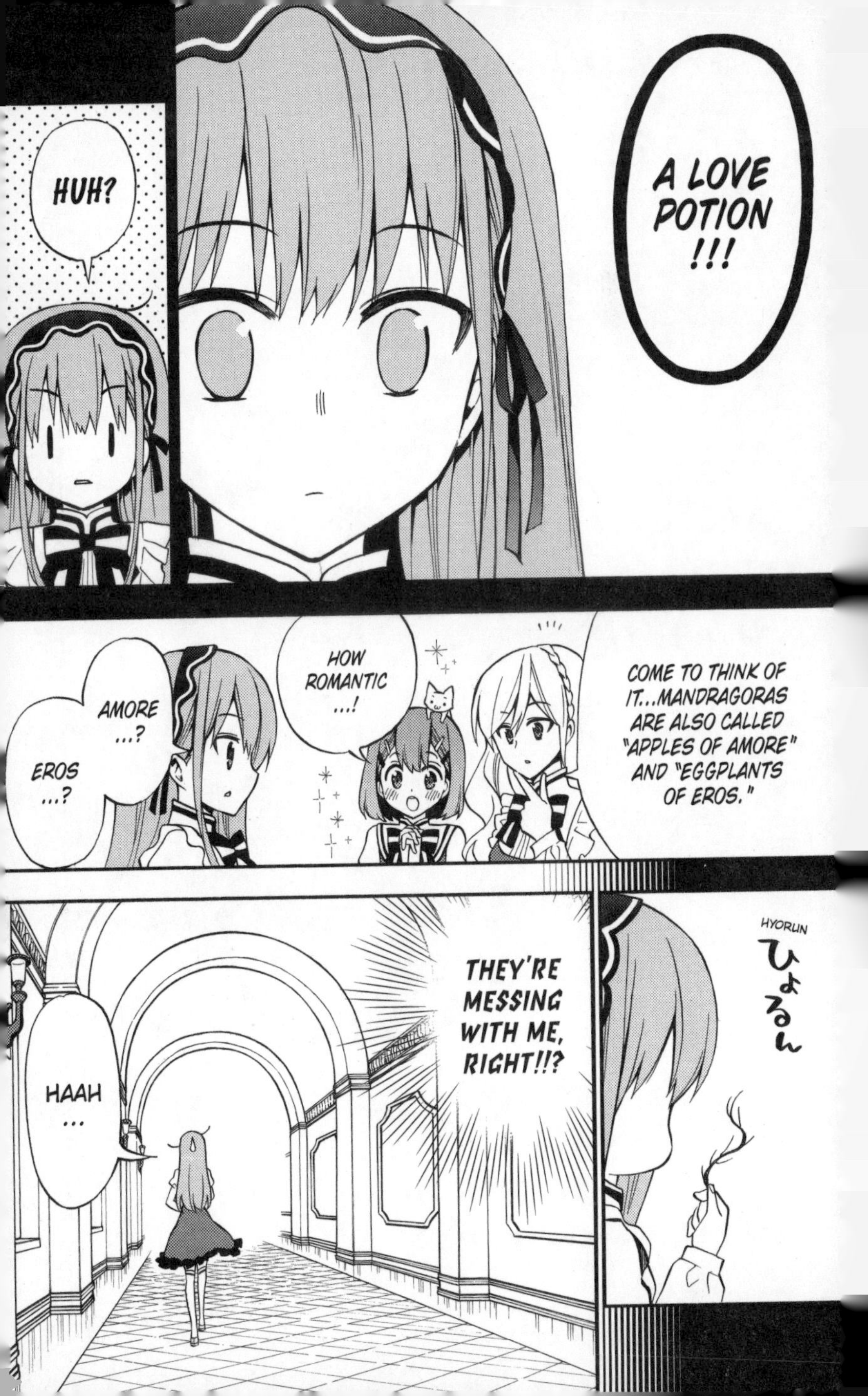
A LOVE POTION !!!
HUH?
COME TO THINK OF IT...MANDRAGORAS ARE ALSO CALLED "APPLES OF AMORE" AND "EGGPLANTS OF EROS."
HOW ROMANTIC ...!
AMORE ...?
EROS ...?
HYORUN
ひょるん
THEY'RE MESSING WITH ME, RIGHT!!?
HAAH ...

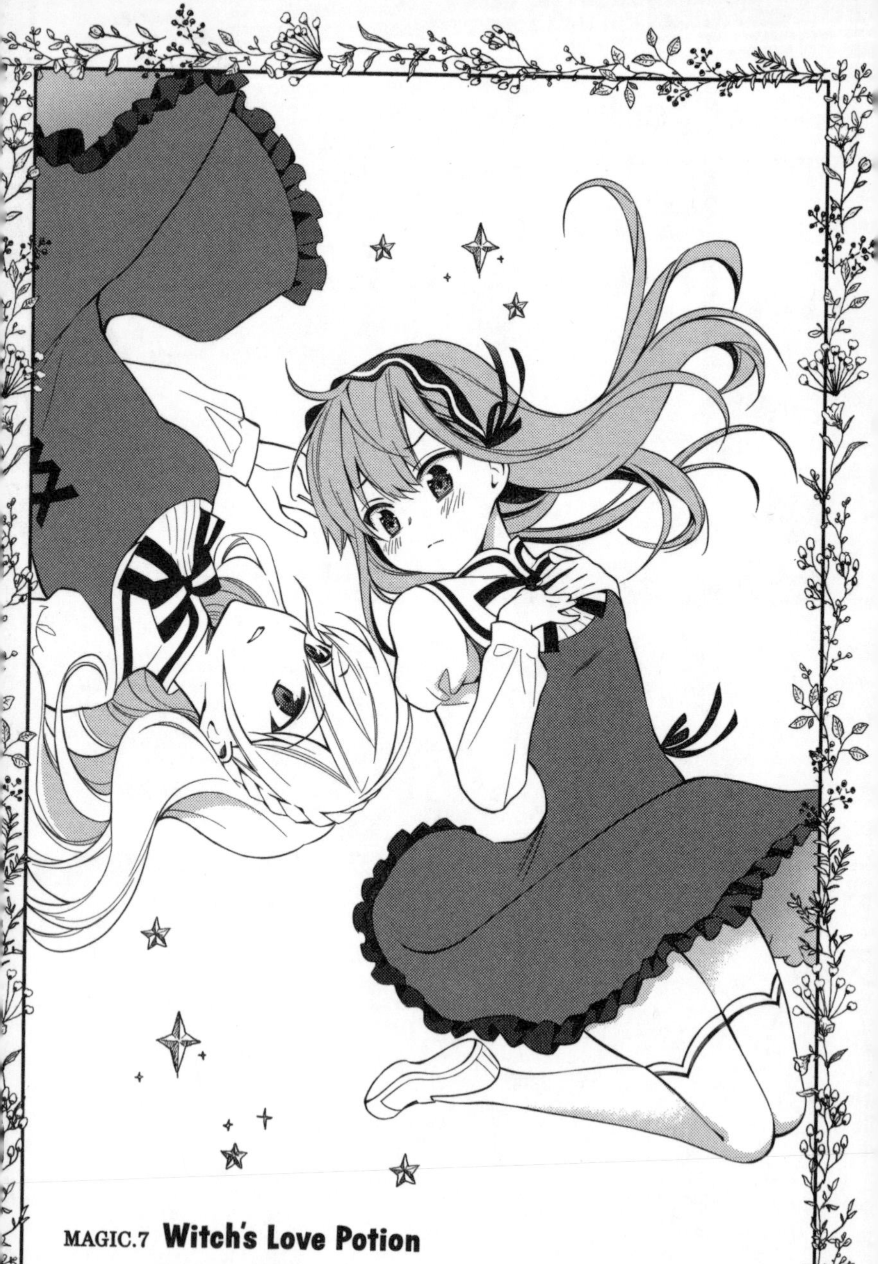

MAGIC.7 **Witch's Love Potion**

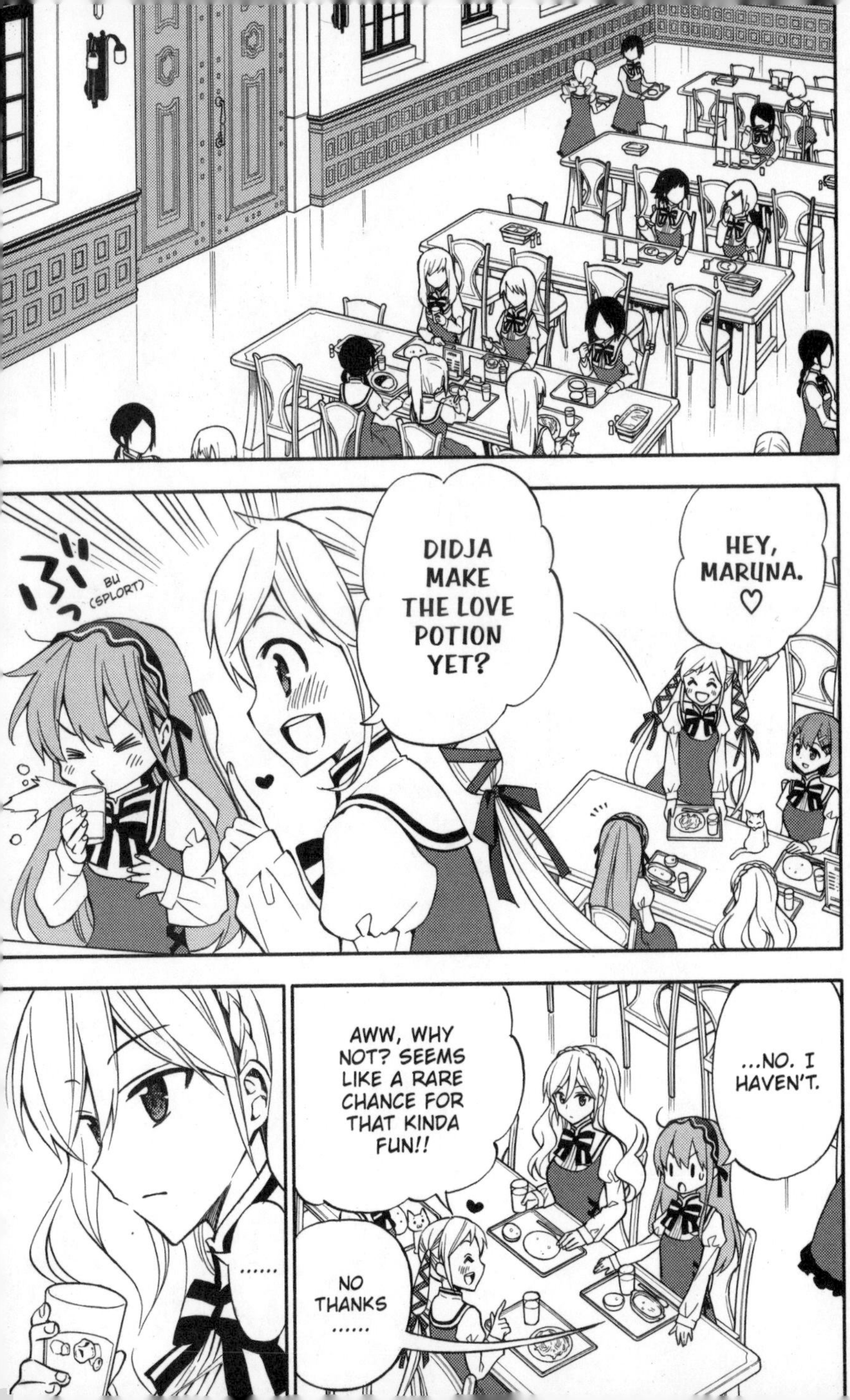
HEY, MARUNA. ♡
DIDJA MAKE THE LOVE POTION YET?
ぶっ
BU (SPLORT)
...NO. I HAVEN'T.
AWW, WHY NOT? SEEMS LIKE A RARE CHANCE FOR THAT KINDA FUN!!
NO THANKS ......
......

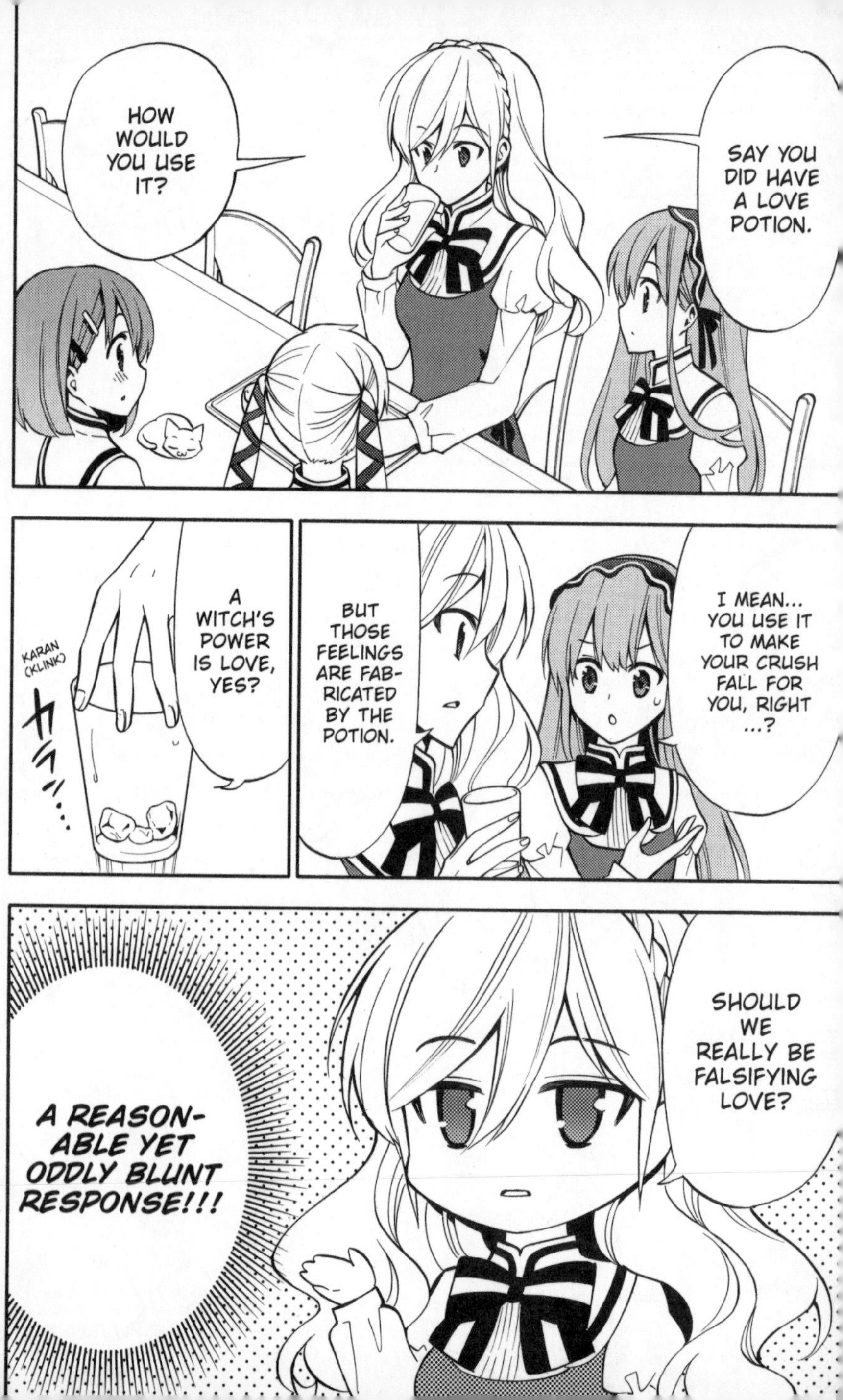
SAY YOU DID HAVE A LOVE POTION.
HOW WOULD YOU USE IT?
I MEAN... YOU USE IT TO MAKE YOUR CRUSH FALL FOR YOU, RIGHT ...?
BUT THOSE FEELINGS ARE FAB-RICATED BY THE POTION.
A WITCH'S POWER IS LOVE, YES?
KARAN (KLINK)
SHOULD WE REALLY BE FALSIFYING LOVE?
A REASON-ABLE YET ODDLY BLUNT RESPONSE!!!

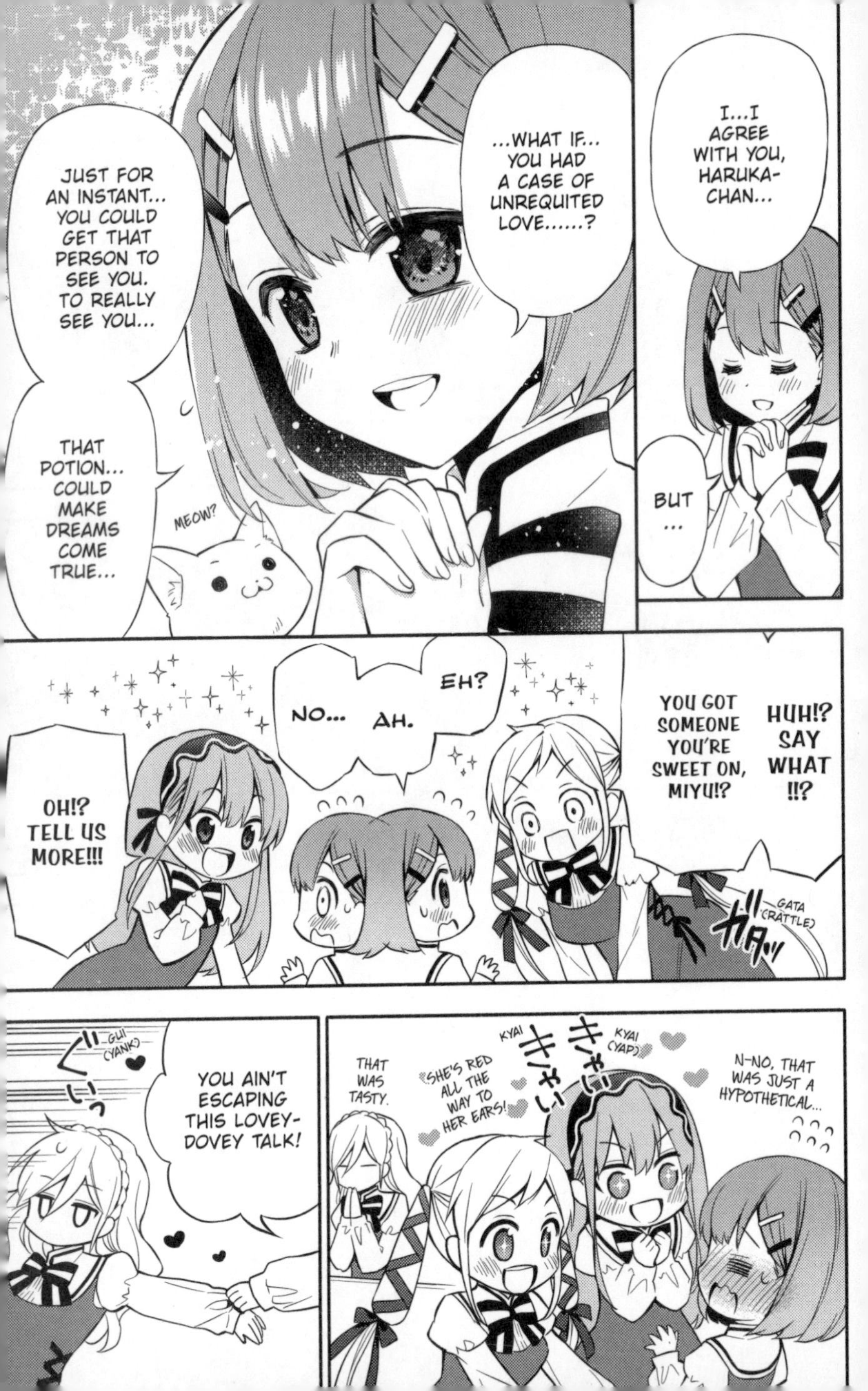
I...I AGREE WITH YOU, HARUKA-CHAN...
BUT ...
...WHAT IF... YOU HAD A CASE OF UNREQUITED LOVE......?
JUST FOR AN INSTANT... YOU COULD GET THAT PERSON TO SEE YOU. TO REALLY SEE YOU...
THAT POTION... COULD MAKE DREAMS COME TRUE...
MEOW?
HUH!? SAY WHAT!!?
YOU GOT SOMEONE YOU'RE SWEET ON, MIYU!?
ガタッ
GATA (RATTLE)
EH?
NO... AH.
OH!? TELL US MORE!!!
N-NO, THAT WAS JUST A HYPOTHETICAL...
きゃいきゃい
KYAI (YAP)
KYAI
SHE'S RED ALL THE WAY TO HER EARS!
THAT WAS TASTY.
ぐいっ
GUI (YANK)
YOU AIN'T ESCAPING THIS LOVEY-DOVEY TALK!

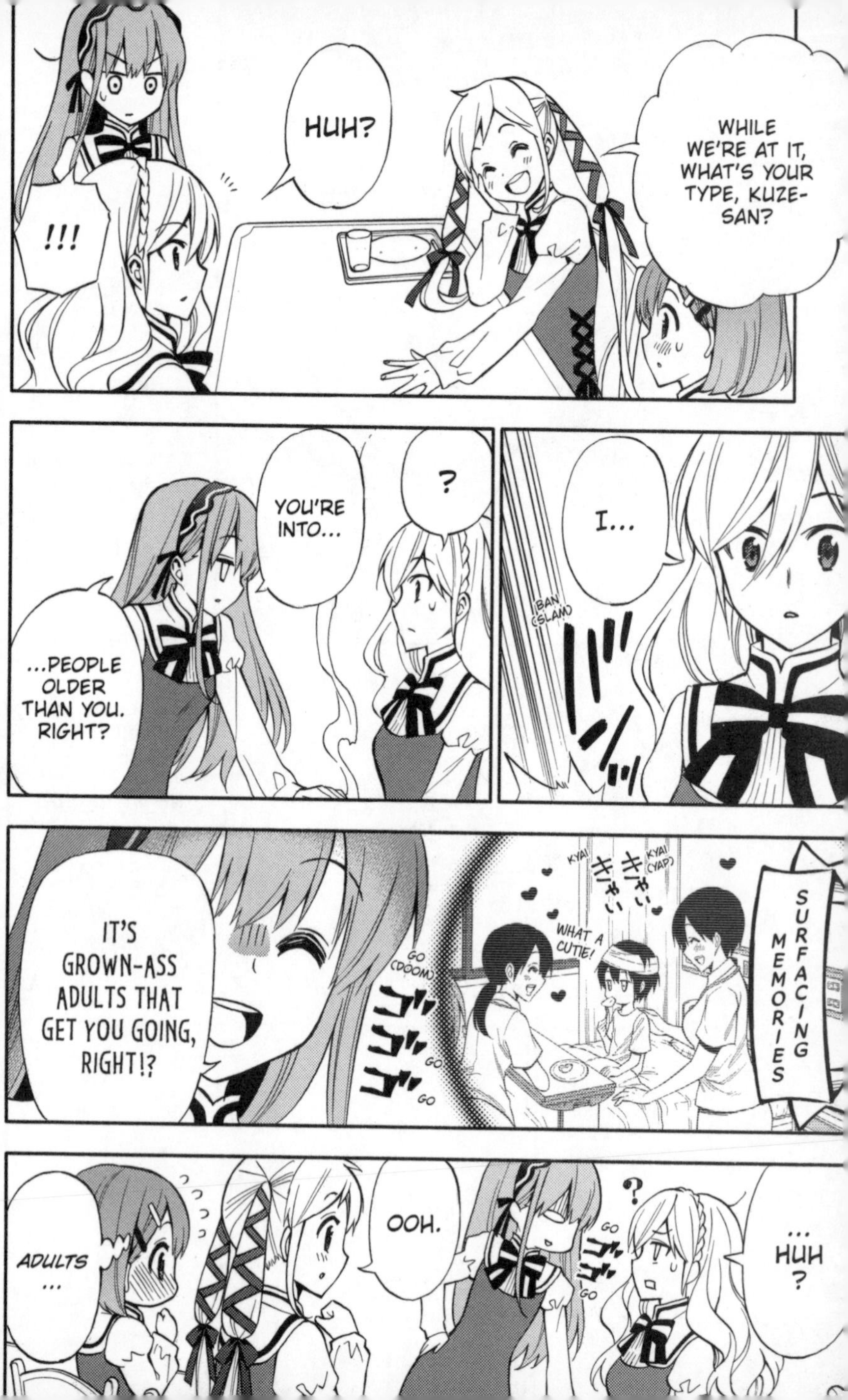
WHILE WE'RE AT IT, WHAT'S YOUR TYPE, KUZE-SAN?
HUH?
!!!
I...
BAN (SLAM)
?
YOU'RE INTO...
...PEOPLE OLDER THAN YOU. RIGHT?
SURFACING MEMORIES
KYA! (YAP)
KYA!
WHAT A CUTIE!
GO (DOOM) GO GO
IT'S GROWN-ASS ADULTS THAT GET YOU GOING, RIGHT!?
... HUH ?
?
GO GO
OOH.
ADULTS ...

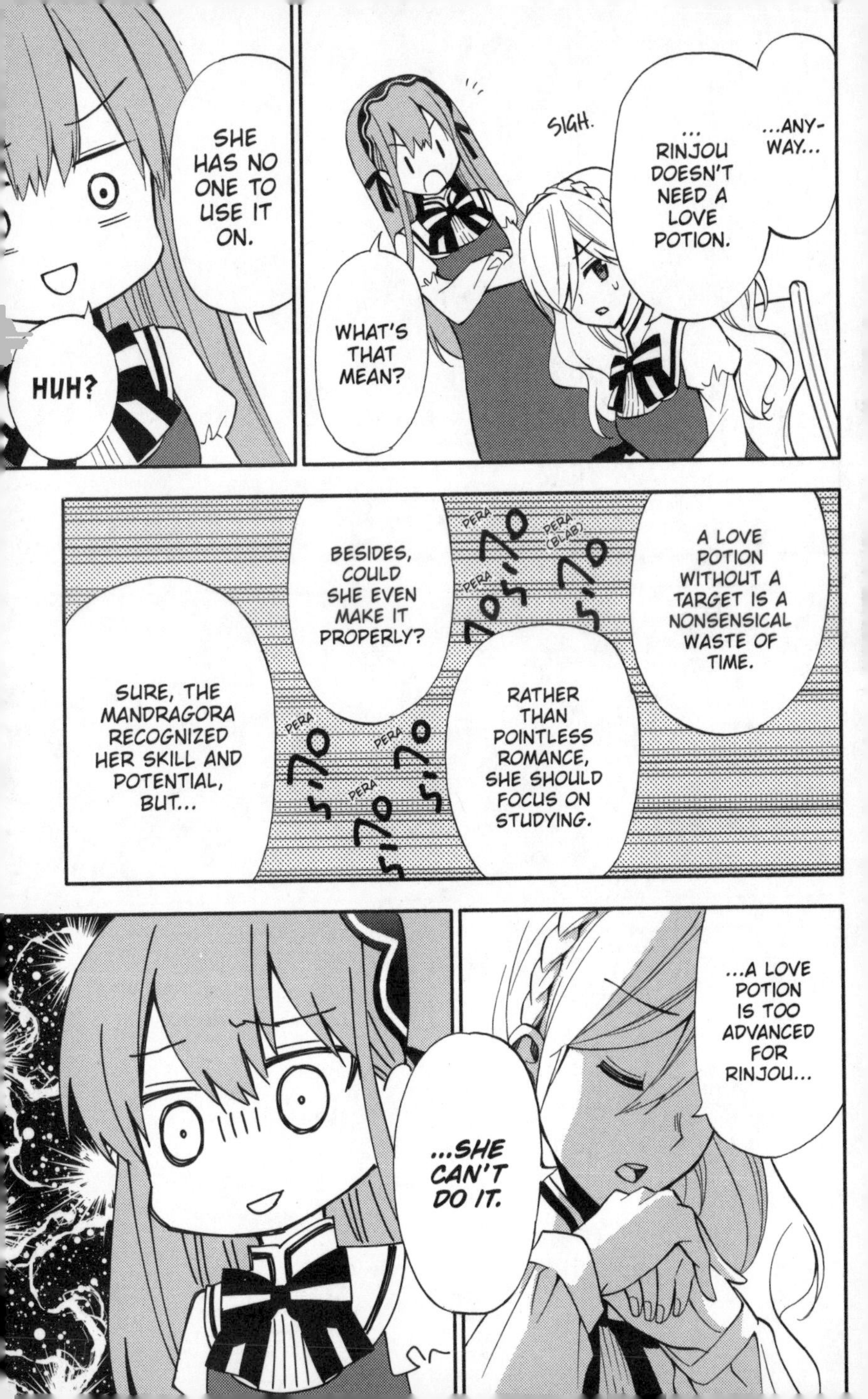
...ANY-WAY...
... RINJOU DOESN'T NEED A LOVE POTION.
SIGH.
WHAT'S THAT MEAN?
SHE HAS NO ONE TO USE IT ON.
HUH?
A LOVE POTION WITHOUT A TARGET IS A NONSENSICAL WASTE OF TIME.
PERA (BLAB)
PERA
PERA
BESIDES, COULD SHE EVEN MAKE IT PROPERLY?
RATHER THAN POINTLESS ROMANCE, SHE SHOULD FOCUS ON STUDYING.
PERA
PERA
PERA
SURE, THE MANDRAGORA RECOGNIZED HER SKILL AND POTENTIAL, BUT...
...A LOVE POTION IS TOO ADVANCED FOR RINJOU...
...SHE CAN'T DO IT.

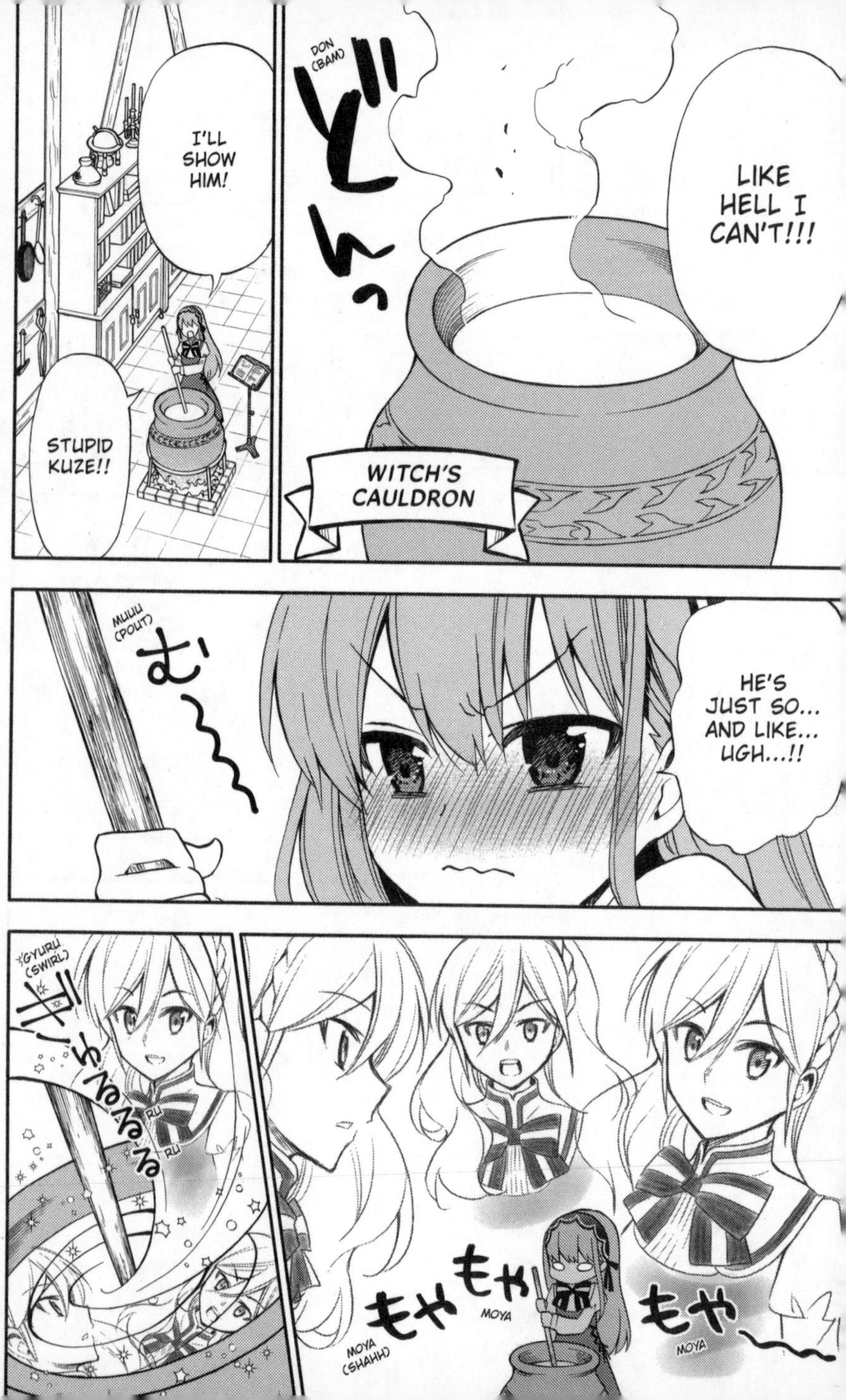
LIKE HELL I CAN'T!!!
DON (BAM)
WITCH'S CAULDRON
I'LL SHOW HIM!
STUPID KUZE!!
HE'S JUST SO... AND LIKE... UGH...!!
MUUU (POUT)
MOYA
MOYA
MOYA (SHAHH)
GYURU (SWIRL)
RU
RU

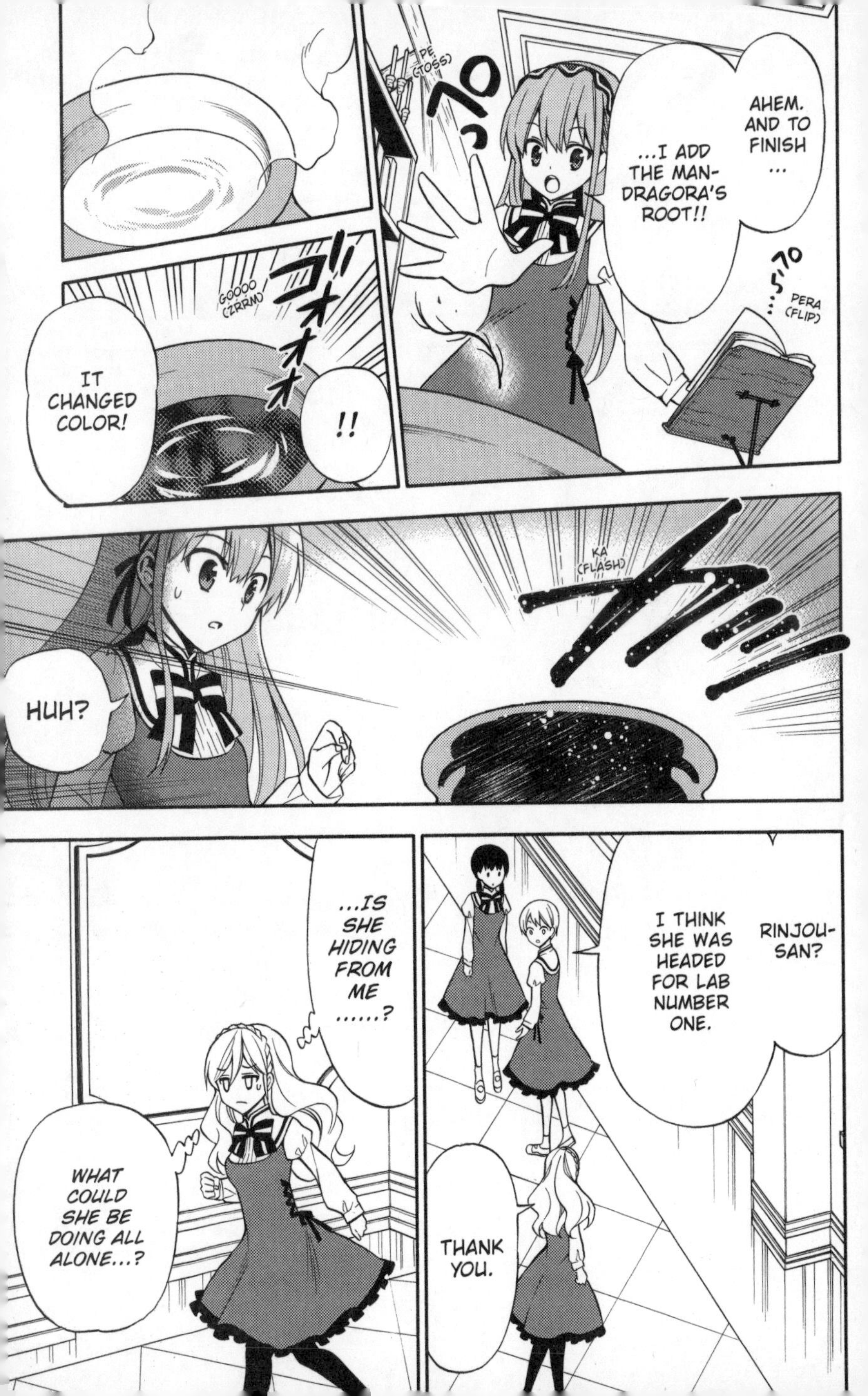
AHEM. AND TO FINISH ...
...I ADD THE MAN-DRAGORA'S ROOT!!
PE (TOSS)
PERA (FLIP)
GOOOO (ZRRM)
!!
IT CHANGED COLOR!
KA (FLASH)
HUH?
RINJOU-SAN?
I THINK SHE WAS HEADED FOR LAB NUMBER ONE.
THANK YOU.
...IS SHE HIDING FROM ME ......?
WHAT COULD SHE BE DOING ALL ALONE...?

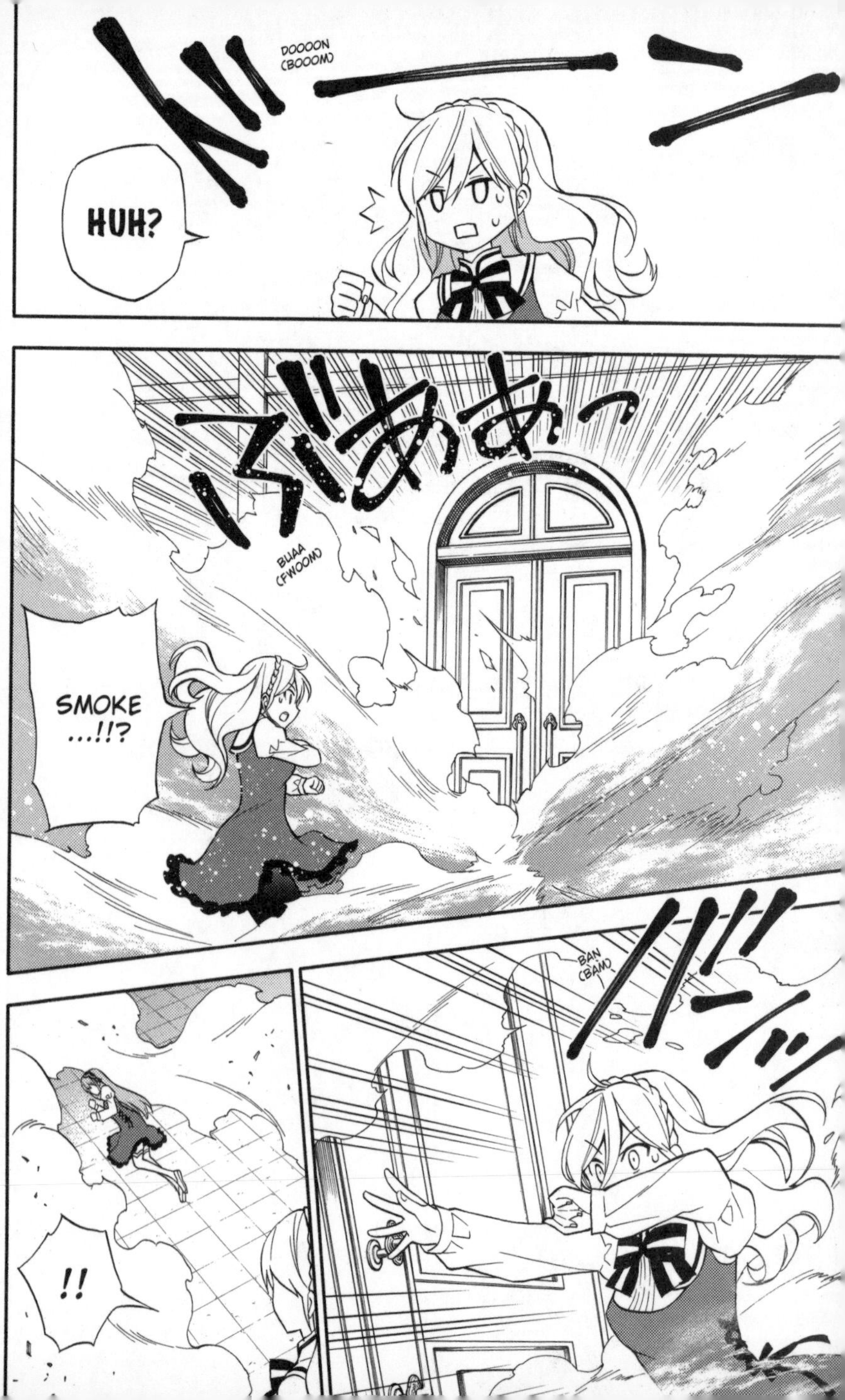
DOOOON (BOOOM)
HUH?
BUAA (FWOOM)
SMOKE ...!!?
BAN (BAM)
!!

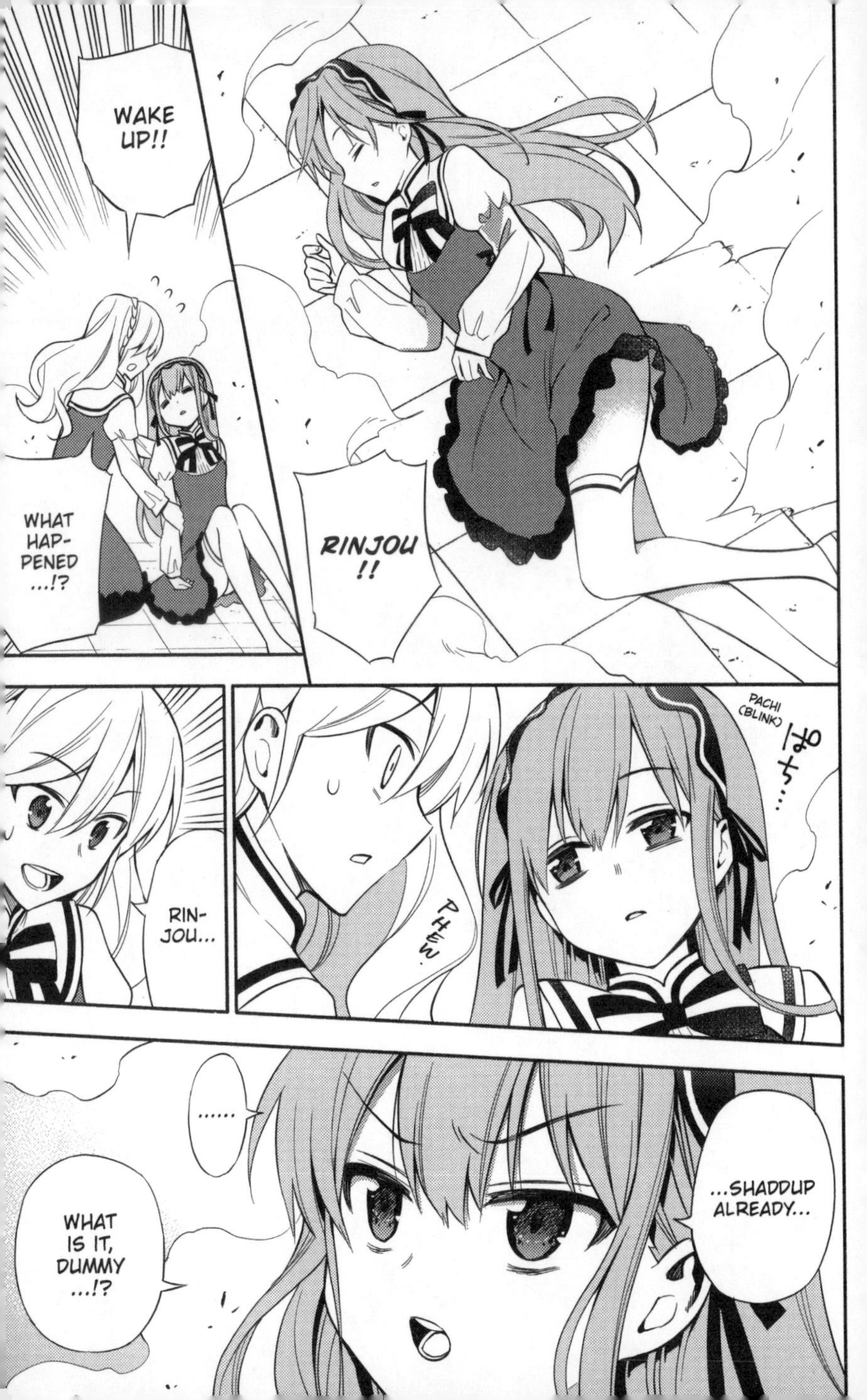
RINJOU !!
WAKE UP!!
WHAT HAP-PENED ...!?
PACHI (BLINK)
ぱち…
PHEW.
RIN-JOU...
...SHADDUP ALREADY...
......
WHAT IS IT, DUMMY ...!?

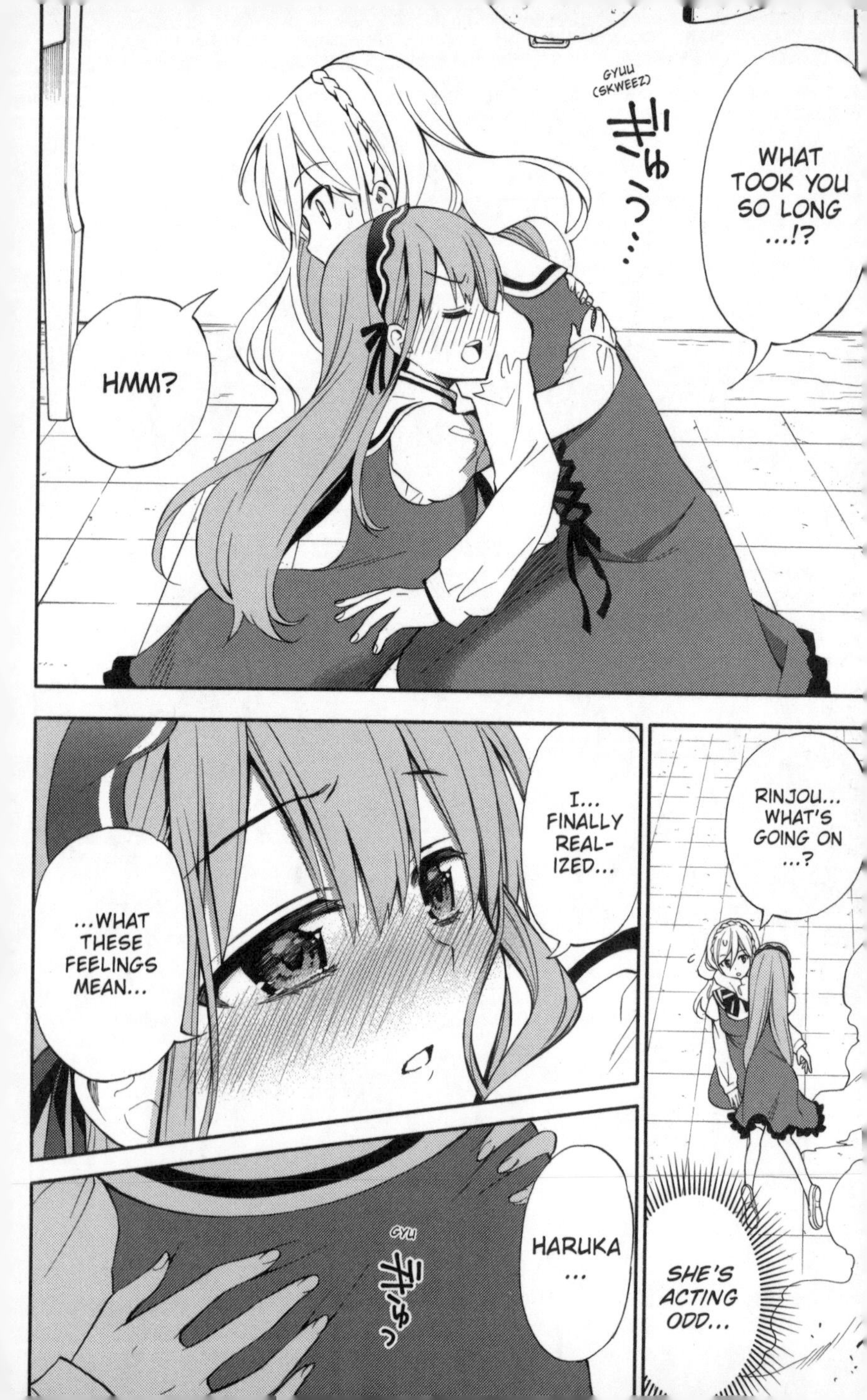
WHAT TOOK YOU SO LONG ...!?
GYUU (SKWEEZ)
ぎゅう…
HMM?
RINJOU... WHAT'S GOING ON ...?
SHE'S ACTING ODD...
I... FINALLY REAL-IZED...
...WHAT THESE FEELINGS MEAN...
HARUKA ...
GYU
ぎゅっ

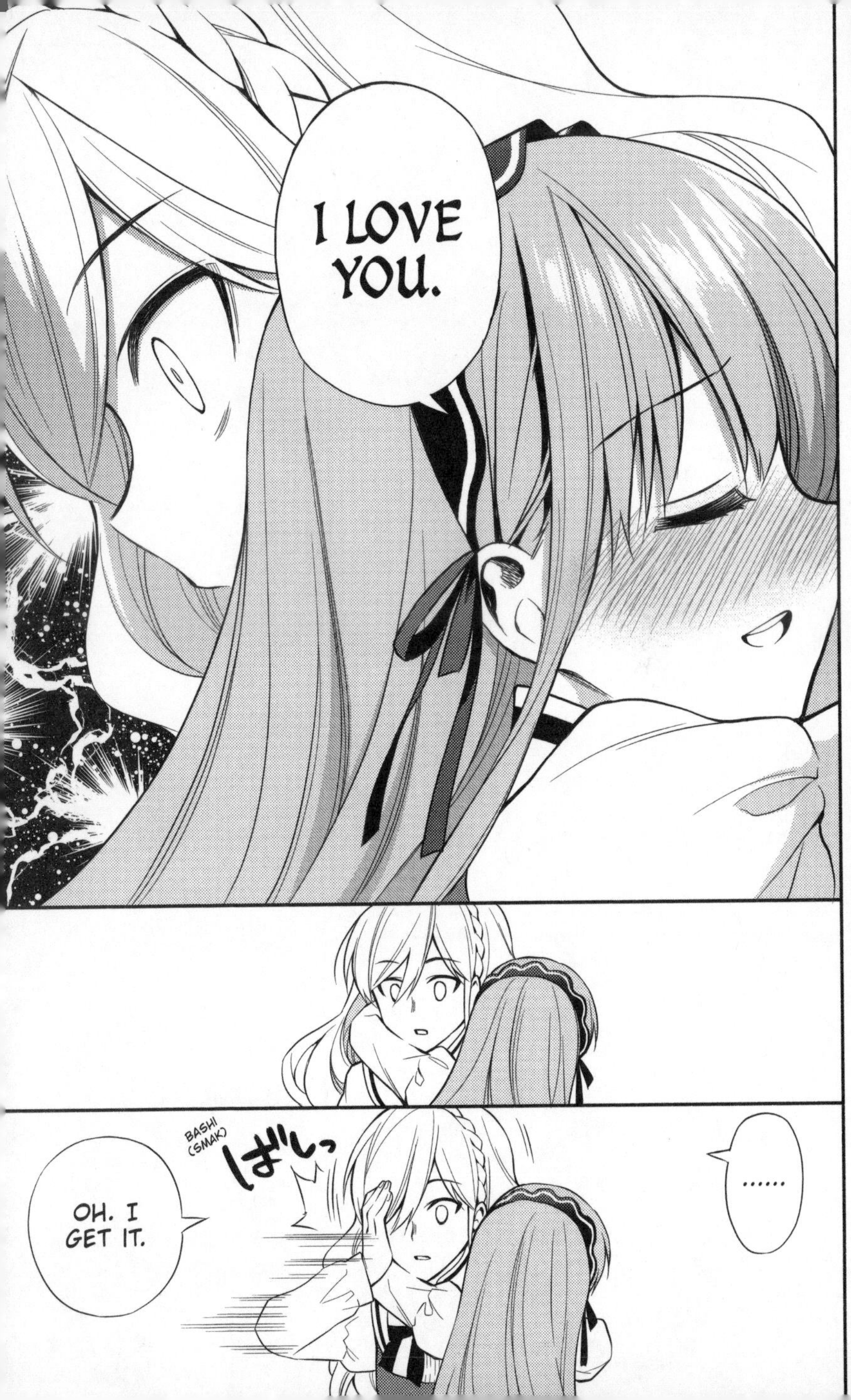
I LOVE YOU.
......
ばしっ
BASHI (SMAK)
OH. I GET IT.

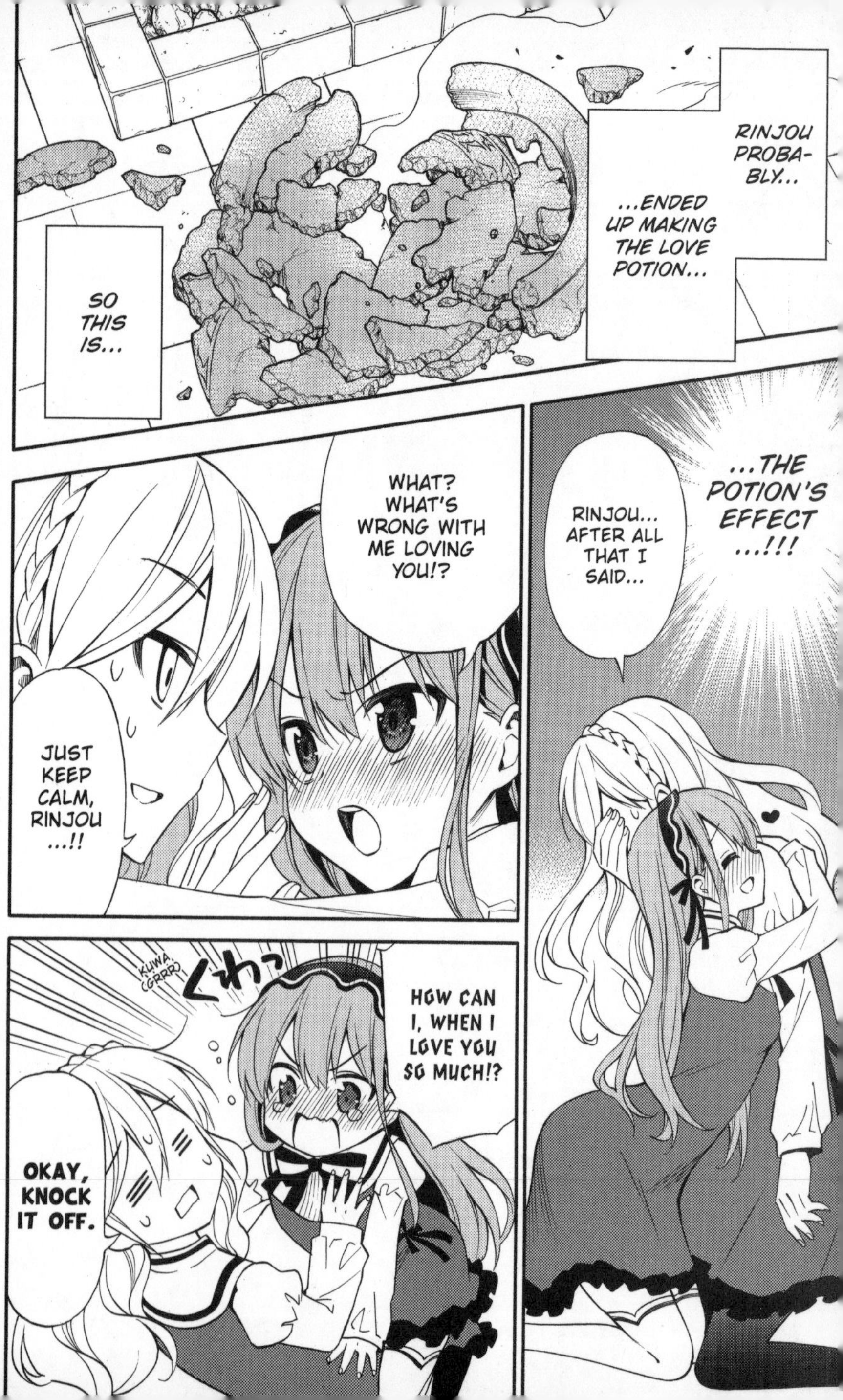
RINJOU PROBA-BLY...
...ENDED UP MAKING THE LOVE POTION...
SO THIS IS...
...THE POTION'S EFFECT ...!!!
RINJOU... AFTER ALL THAT I SAID...
WHAT? WHAT'S WRONG WITH ME LOVING YOU!?
JUST KEEP CALM, RINJOU ...!!
KUWA (GRRR)
くわっ
HOW CAN I, WHEN I LOVE YOU SO MUCH!?
OKAY, KNOCK IT OFF.

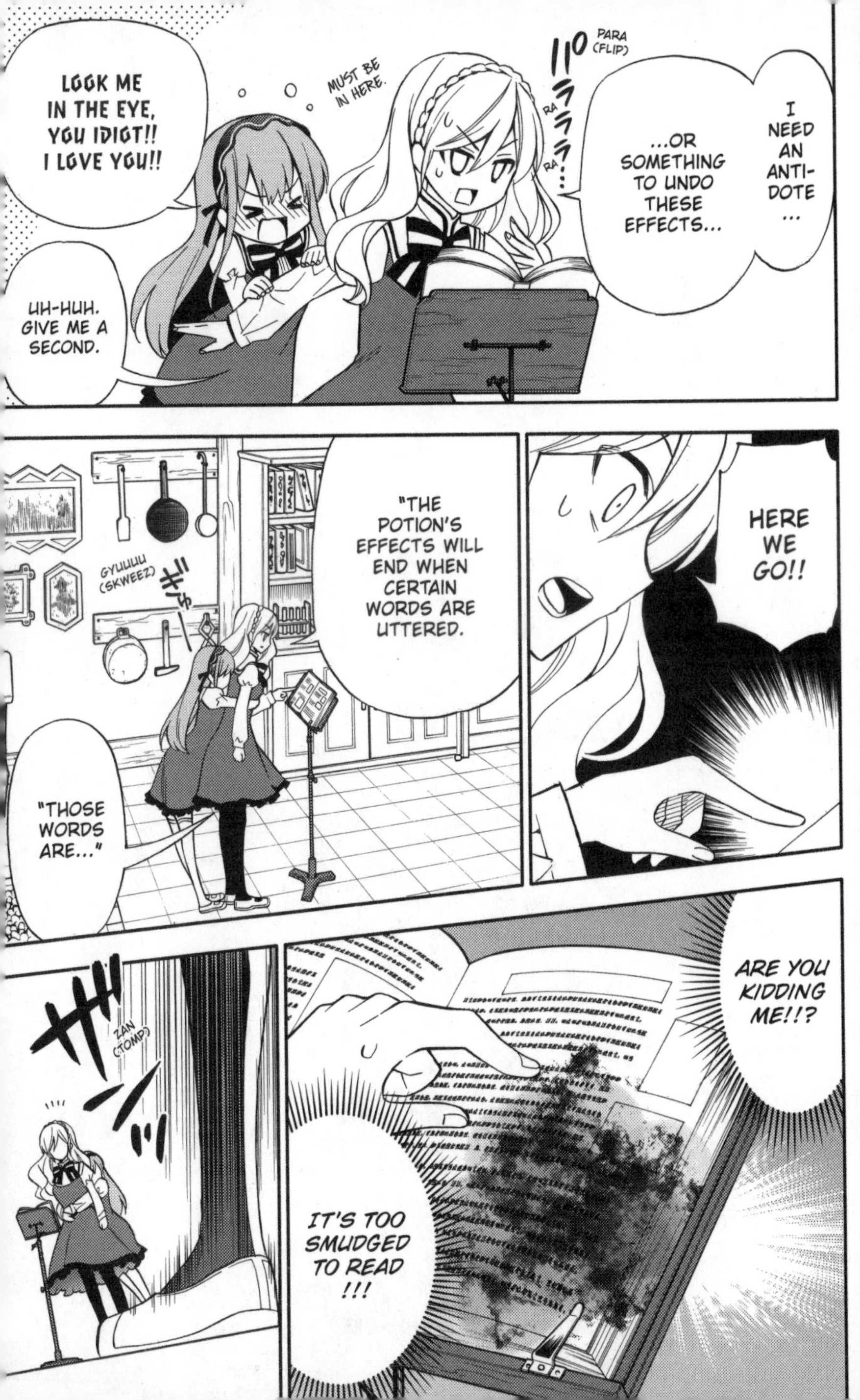
PARA (FLIP)
I NEED AN ANTI-DOTE ...
...OR SOMETHING TO UNDO THESE EFFECTS...
MUST BE IN HERE.
LOOK ME IN THE EYE, YOU IDIOT!! I LOVE YOU!!
UH-HUH. GIVE ME A SECOND.
HERE WE GO!!
"THE POTION'S EFFECTS WILL END WHEN CERTAIN WORDS ARE UTTERED.
GYUUUU (SKWEEZ)
"THOSE WORDS ARE..."
ARE YOU KIDDING ME!!?
IT'S TOO SMUDGED TO READ !!!
ZAN (TOMP)

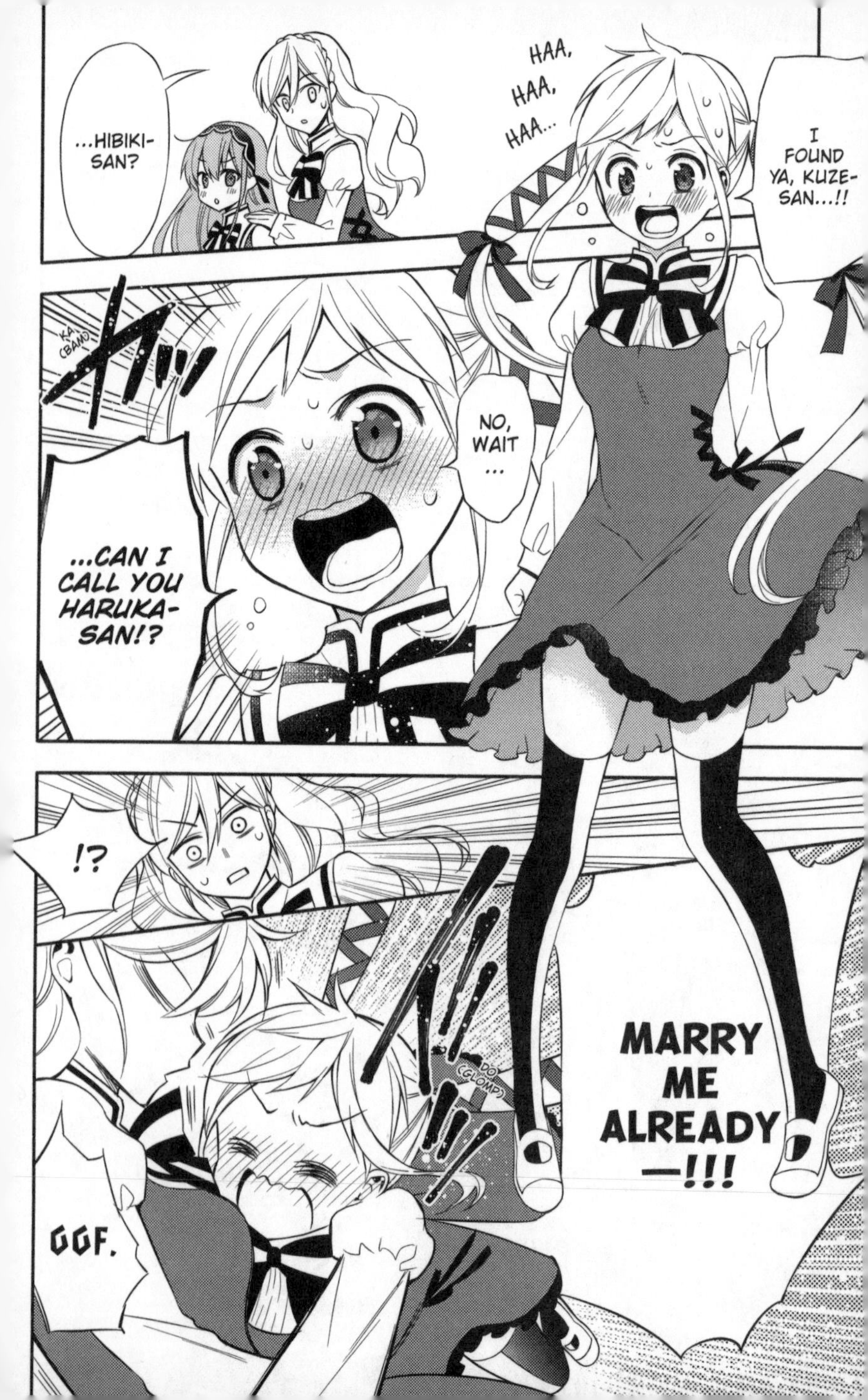

I FOUND YA, KUZE-SAN...!!
HAA, HAA, HAA...
...HIBIKI-SAN?
KA (BAM)
NO, WAIT ...
...CAN I CALL YOU HARUKA-SAN!?
!?
MARRY ME ALREADY —!!!
DO (GLOMP)
GGF.

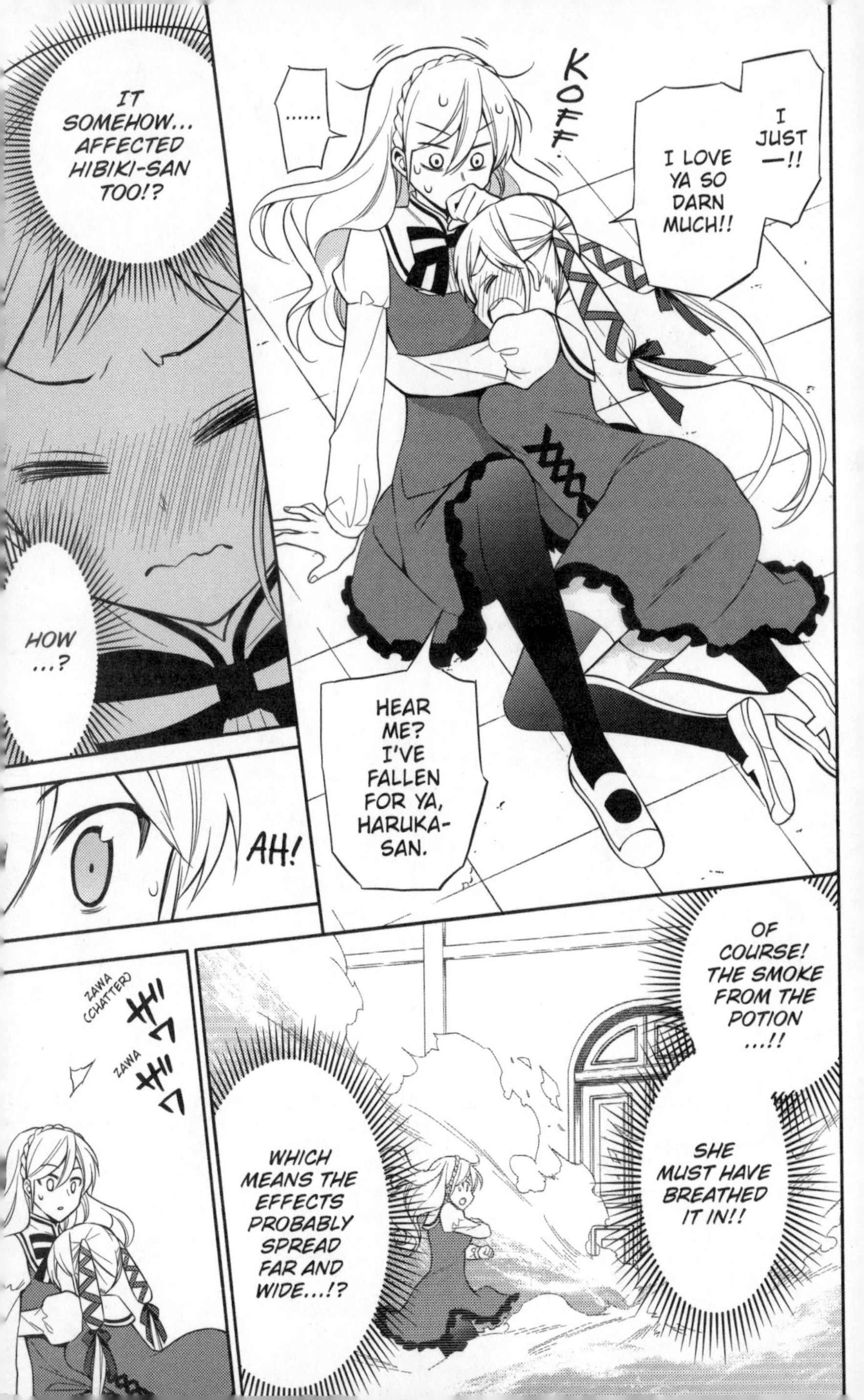

I JUST—!!
I LOVE YA SO DARN MUCH!!
KOFF
......
HEAR ME? I'VE FALLEN FOR YA, HARUKA-SAN.
IT SOMEHOW... AFFECTED HIBIKI-SAN TOO!?
HOW...?
AH!
OF COURSE! THE SMOKE FROM THE POTION...!!
SHE MUST HAVE BREATHED IT IN!!
WHICH MEANS THE EFFECTS PROBABLY SPREAD FAR AND WIDE...!?
ZAWA (CHATTER)
ZAWA

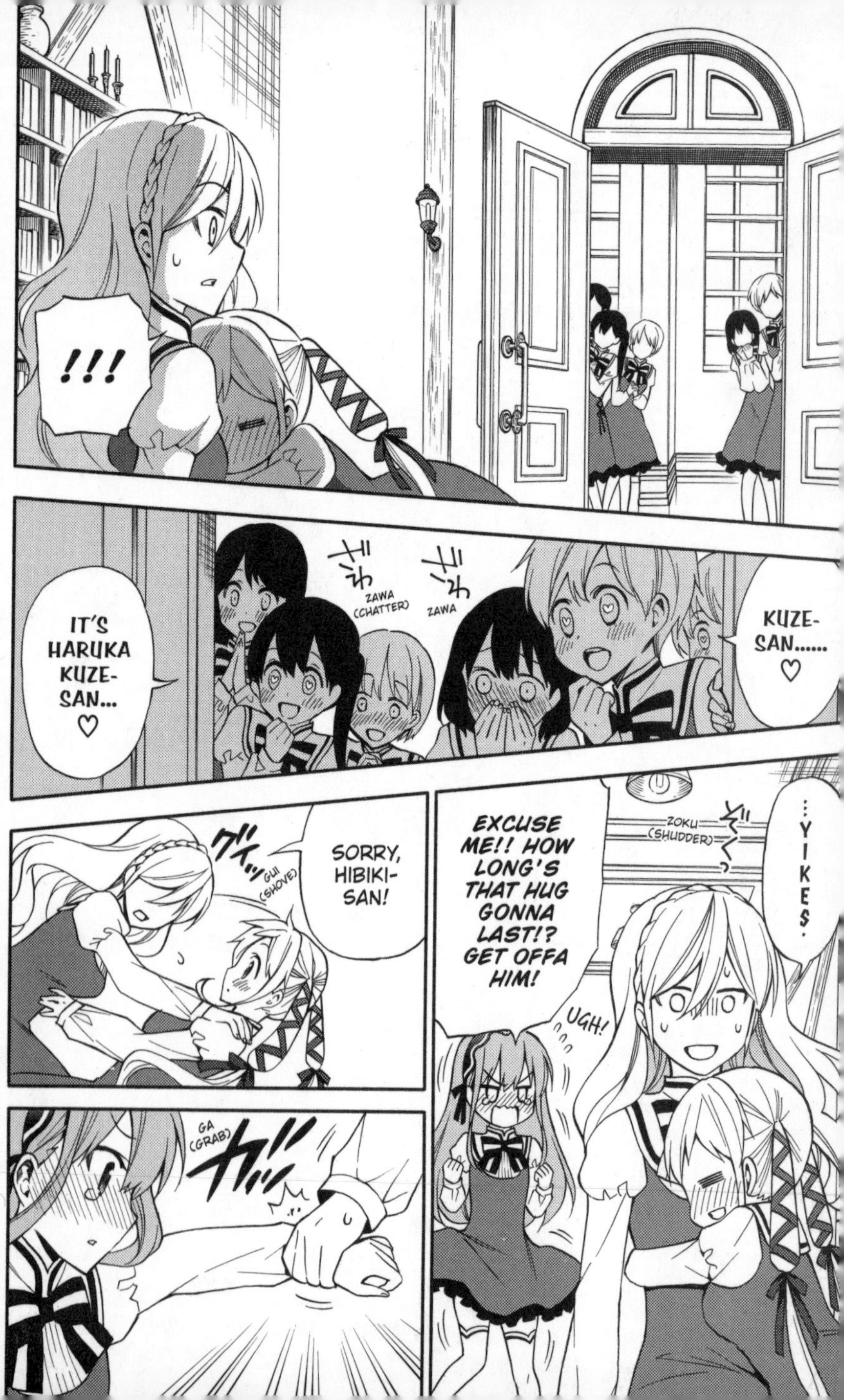
!!!
KUZE-SAN...... ♡
ざわ
ZAWA
ざわ
ZAWA (CHATTER)
IT'S HARUKA KUZE-SAN... ♡
...YIKES.
ぞくっ
ZOKU (SHUDDER)
EXCUSE ME!! HOW LONG'S THAT HUG GONNA LAST!? GET OFFA HIM!
UGH!
SORRY, HIBIKI-SAN!
グイッ
GUI (SHOVE)
ガッ
GA (GRAB)

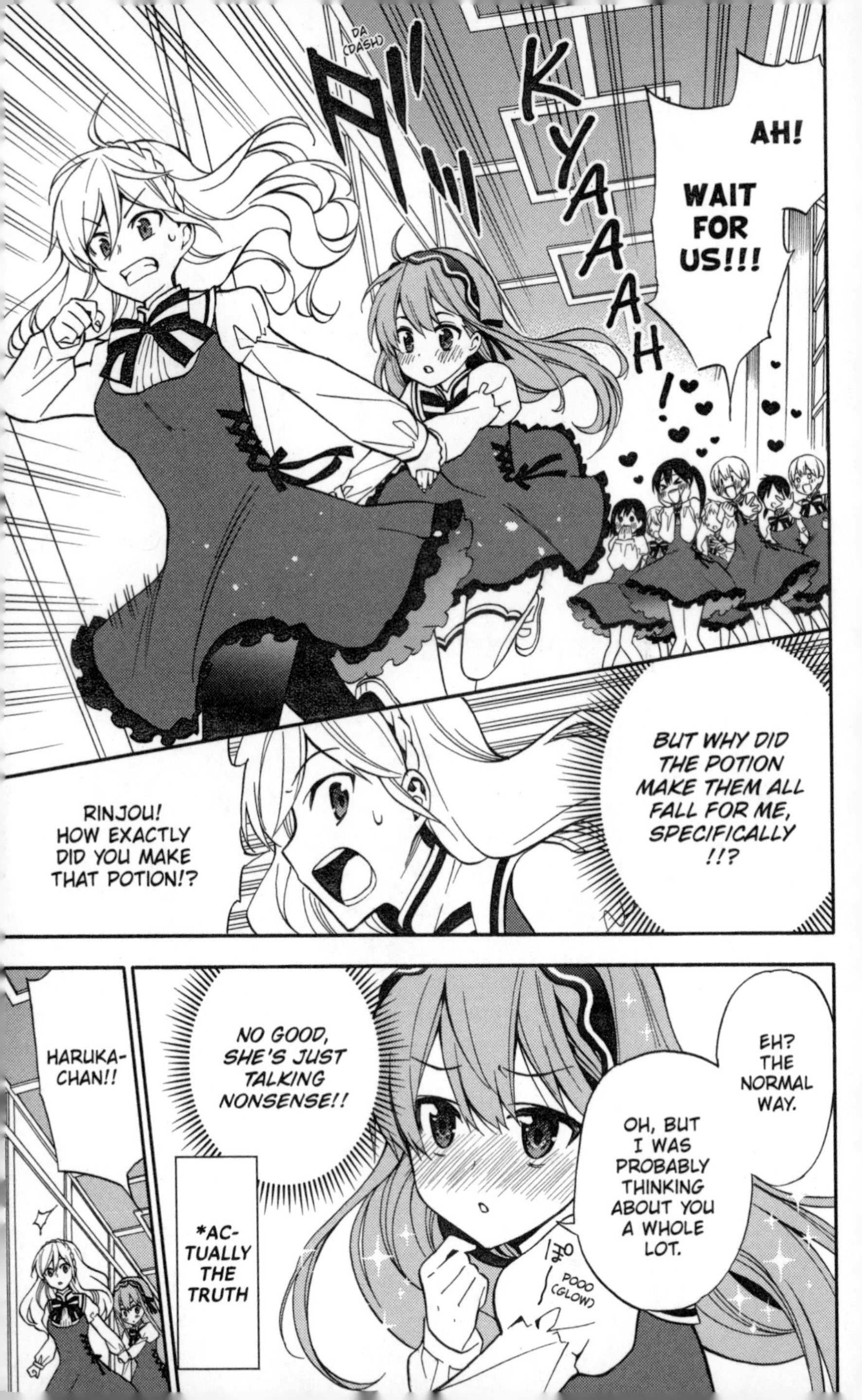
AH!
WAIT FOR US!!!
KYAAAH!
DA (DASH)
BUT WHY DID THE POTION MAKE THEM ALL FALL FOR ME, SPECIFICALLY !!?
RINJOU! HOW EXACTLY DID YOU MAKE THAT POTION!?
EH? THE NORMAL WAY.
OH, BUT I WAS PROBABLY THINKING ABOUT YOU A WHOLE LOT.
POOO (GLOW)
NO GOOD, SHE'S JUST TALKING NONSENSE!!
*AC-TUALLY THE TRUTH
HARUKA-CHAN!!

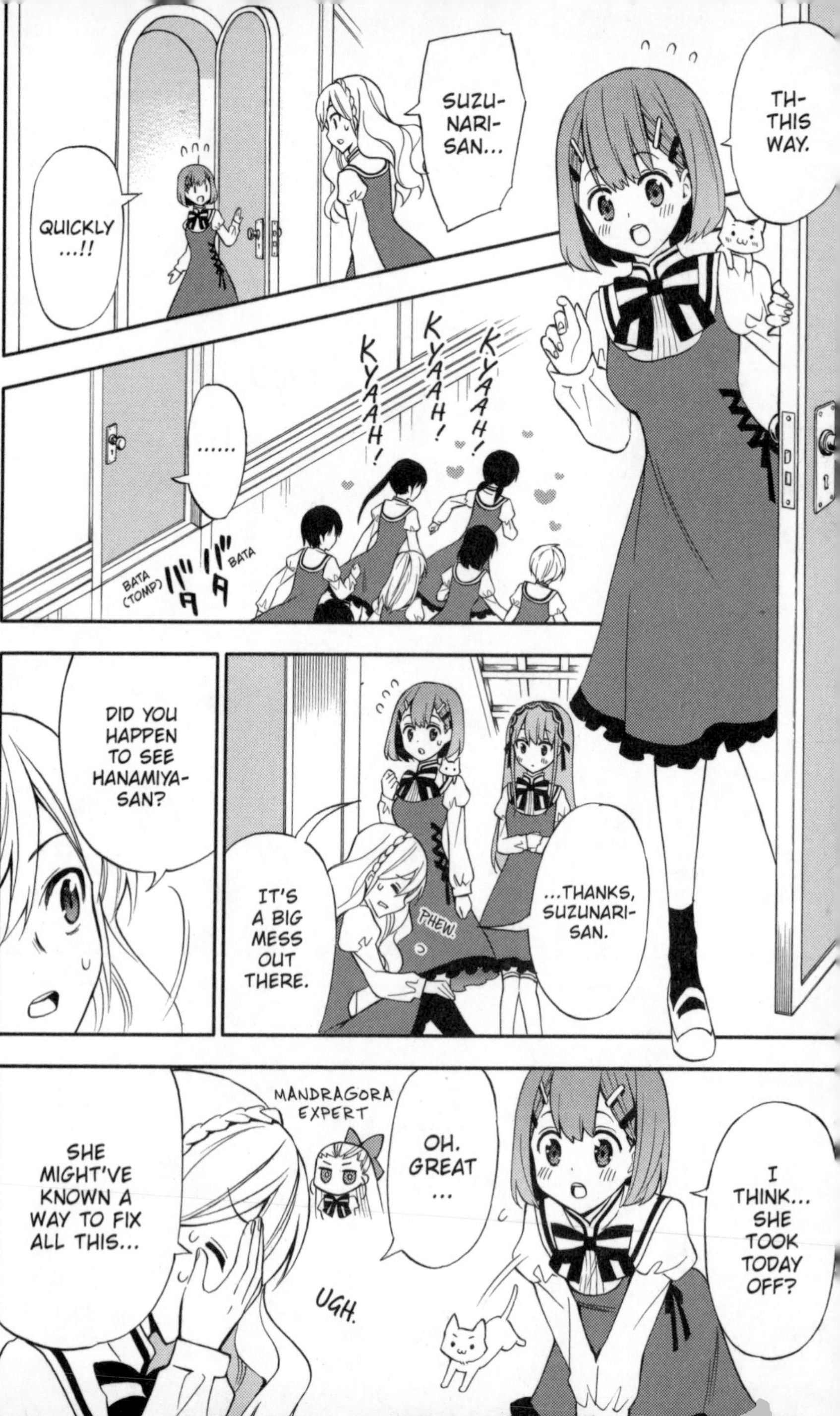
TH-THIS WAY.
SUZUNARI-SAN...
QUICKLY...!!
KYAAH!
KYAAH!
KYAAH!
......
BATA
BATA (TOMP)
...THANKS, SUZUNARI-SAN.
PHEW.
IT'S A BIG MESS OUT THERE.
DID YOU HAPPEN TO SEE HANAMIYA-SAN?
I THINK... SHE TOOK TODAY OFF?
OH. GREAT...
MANDRAGORA EXPERT
SHE MIGHT'VE KNOWN A WAY TO FIX ALL THIS...
UGH.

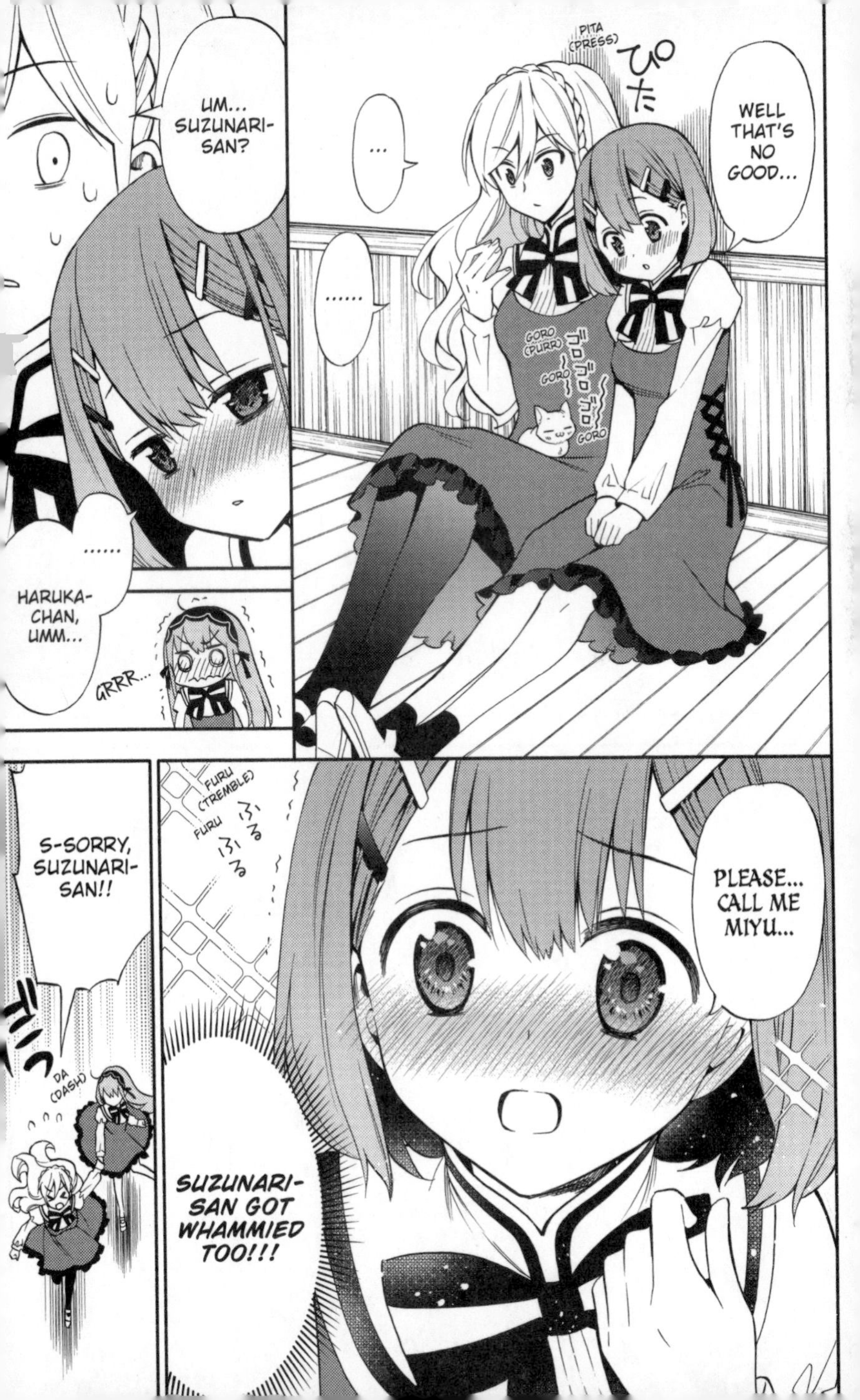

PITA (PRESS)
ぴた
WELL THAT'S NO GOOD...
...
......
GORO (PURR) ~GORO~ ~GORO
ゴロゴロゴロ
UM... SUZUNARI-SAN?
......
HARUKA-CHAN, UMM...
GRRR...
PLEASE... CALL ME MIYU...
FURU (TREMBLE) FURU
ふるふる
SUZUNARI-SAN GOT WHAMMIED TOO!!!
S-SORRY, SUZUNARI-SAN!!
DA (DASH)

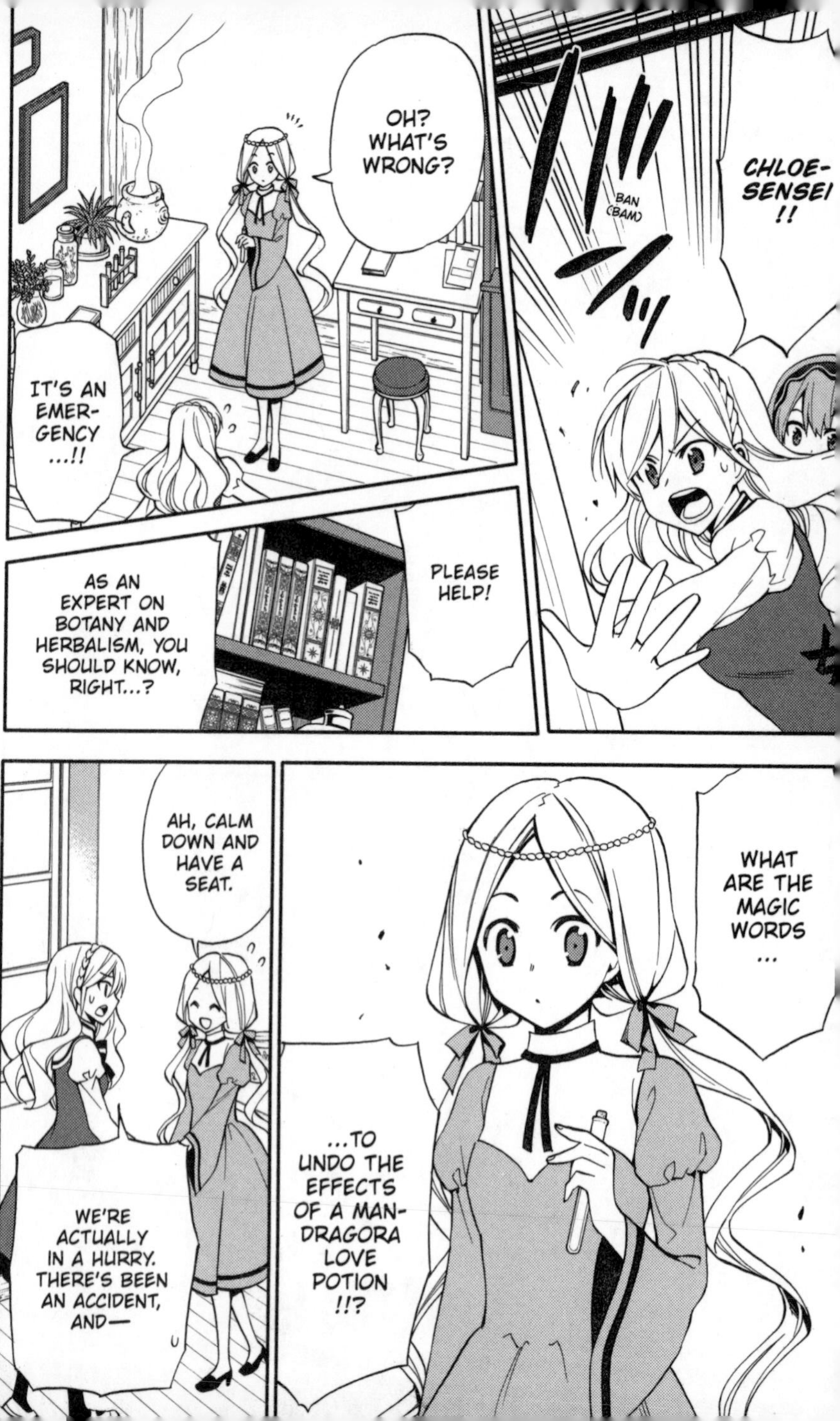
CHLOE-SENSEI!!
BAN (BAM)
OH? WHAT'S WRONG?
IT'S AN EMERGENCY...!!
PLEASE HELP!
AS AN EXPERT ON BOTANY AND HERBALISM, YOU SHOULD KNOW, RIGHT...?
WHAT ARE THE MAGIC WORDS...
...TO UNDO THE EFFECTS OF A MANDRAGORA LOVE POTION!!?
AH, CALM DOWN AND HAVE A SEAT.
WE'RE ACTUALLY IN A HURRY. THERE'S BEEN AN ACCIDENT, AND—

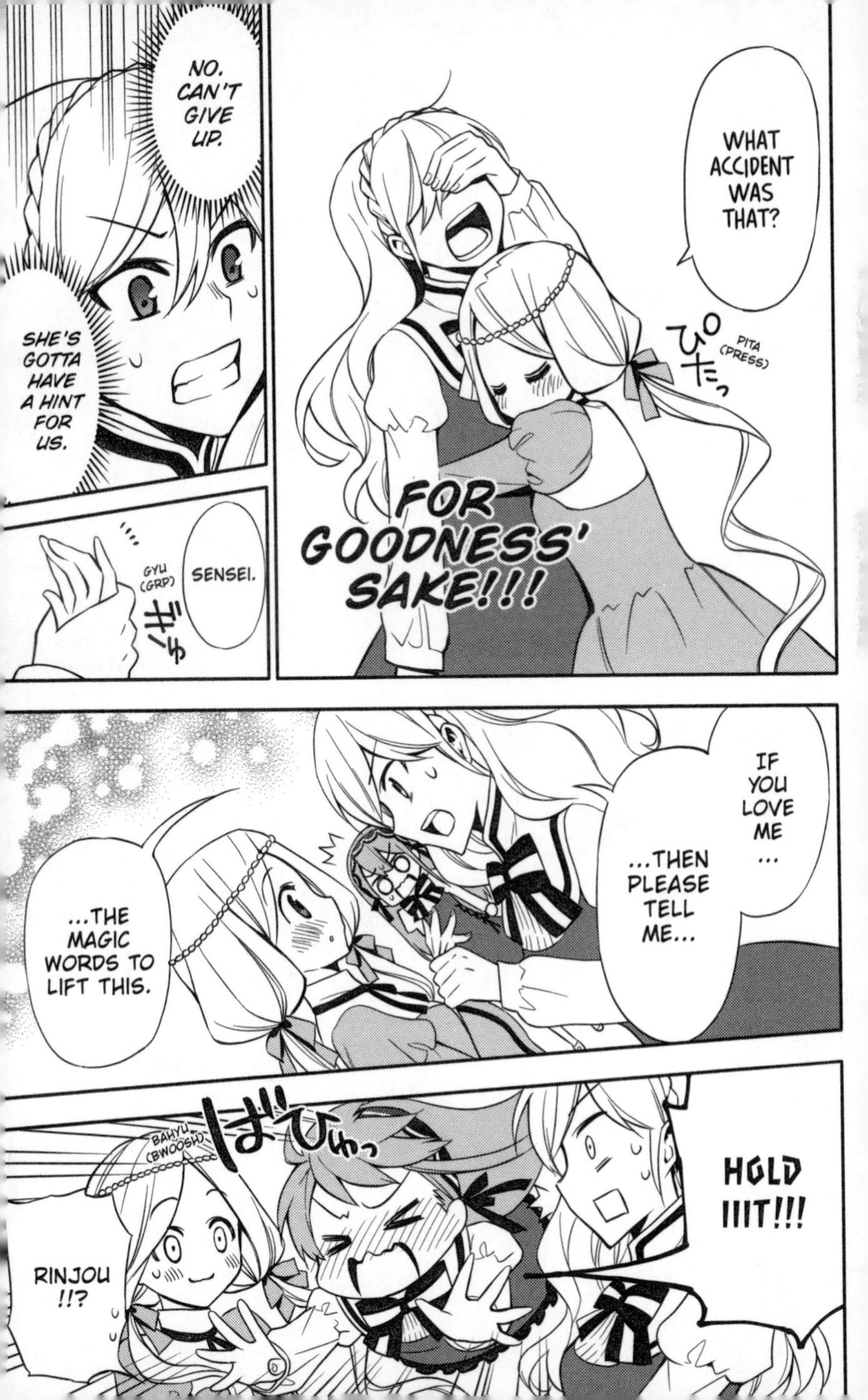
WHAT ACCIDENT WAS THAT?
ぴたっ
PITA (PRESS)
FOR GOODNESS' SAKE!!!
NO. CAN'T GIVE UP.
SHE'S GOTTA HAVE A HINT FOR US.
SENSEI.
GYU (GRP)
ぎゅ
IF YOU LOVE ME...
...THEN PLEASE TELL ME...
...THE MAGIC WORDS TO LIFT THIS.
HOLD IIIT!!!
ばひゅっ
BAHYU (BWOOSH)
RINJOU!!?

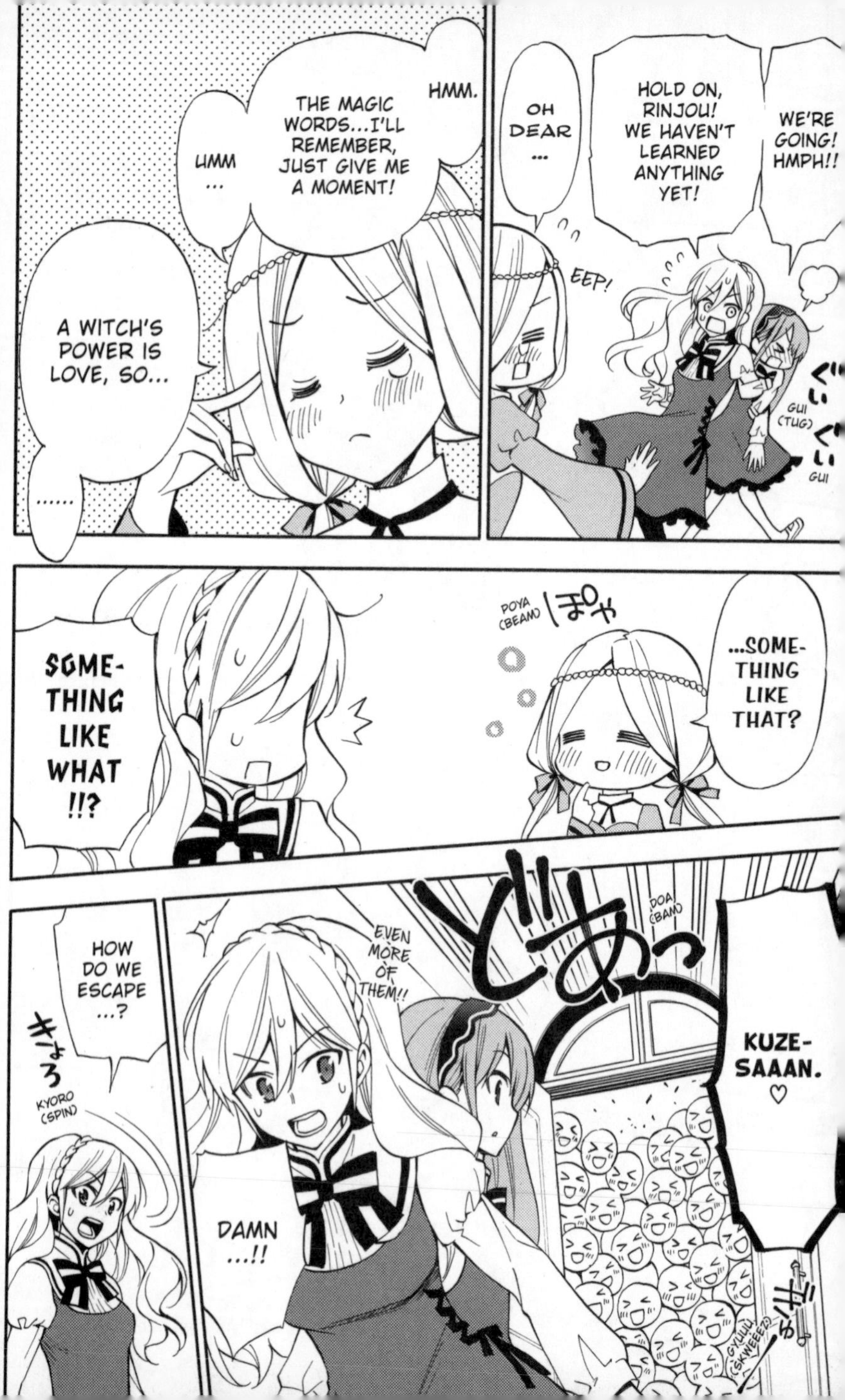
WE'RE GOING! HMPH!!
HOLD ON, RINJOU! WE HAVEN'T LEARNED ANYTHING YET!
OH DEAR ...
EEP!
GUI (TUG)
GUI
HMM.
THE MAGIC WORDS...I'LL REMEMBER, JUST GIVE ME A MOMENT!
UMM ...
A WITCH'S POWER IS LOVE, SO...
......
...SOME-THING LIKE THAT?
POYA (BEAM)
SOME-THING LIKE WHAT !!?
KUZE-SAAAN. ♡
DOA (BAM)
EVEN MORE OF THEM!!
DAMN ...!!
HOW DO WE ESCAPE ...?
KYORO (SPIN)

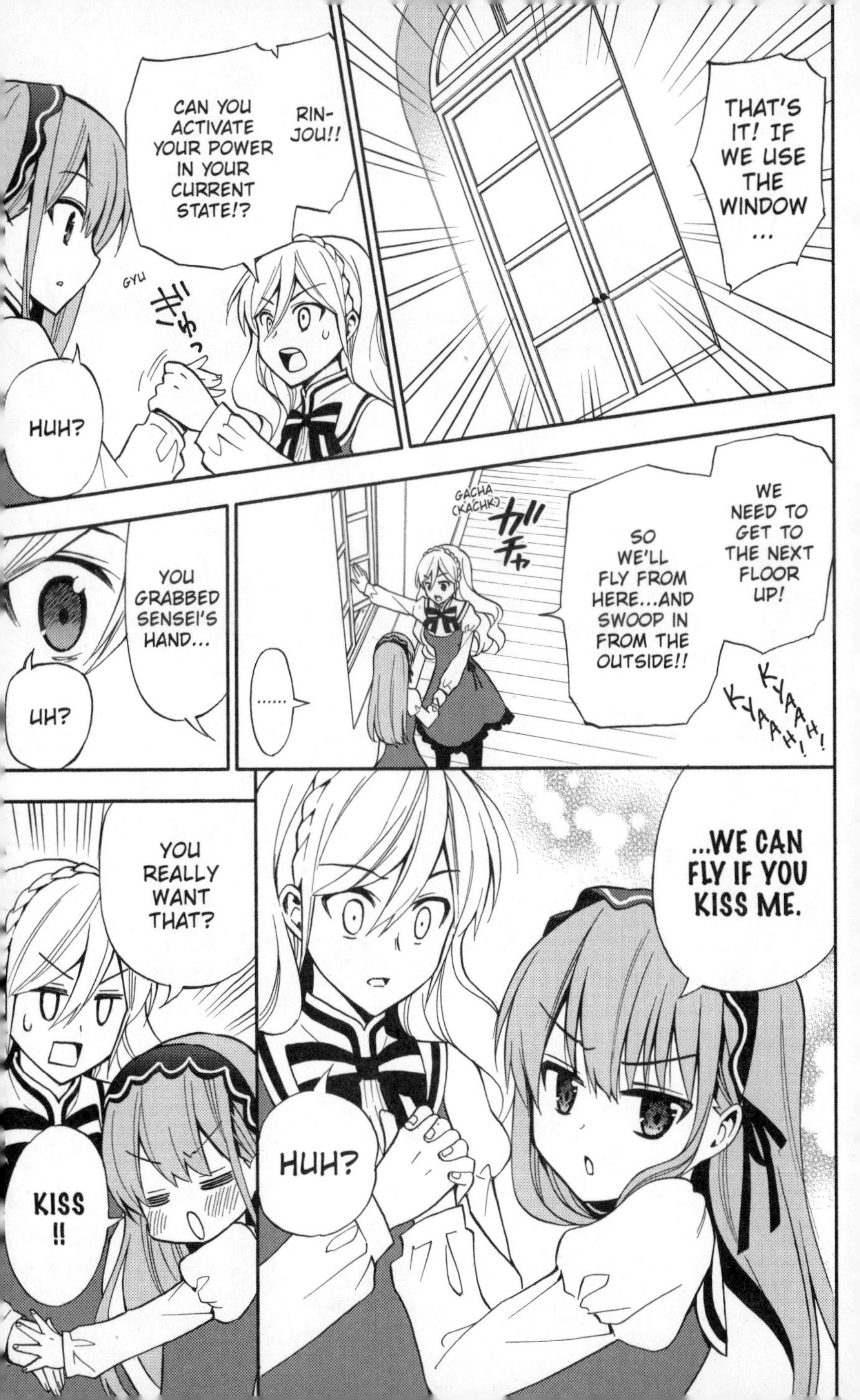
THAT'S IT! IF WE USE THE WINDOW...
RIN-JOU!!
CAN YOU ACTIVATE YOUR POWER IN YOUR CURRENT STATE!?
ぎゅっ
GYU
HUH?
WE NEED TO GET TO THE NEXT FLOOR UP!
SO WE'LL FLY FROM HERE...AND SWOOP IN FROM THE OUTSIDE!!
ガチャ
GACHA (KACHK)
......
KYAAAH! KYAAAH!
YOU GRABBED SENSEI'S HAND...
UH?
...WE CAN FLY IF YOU KISS ME.
HUH?
YOU REALLY WANT THAT?
KISS!!

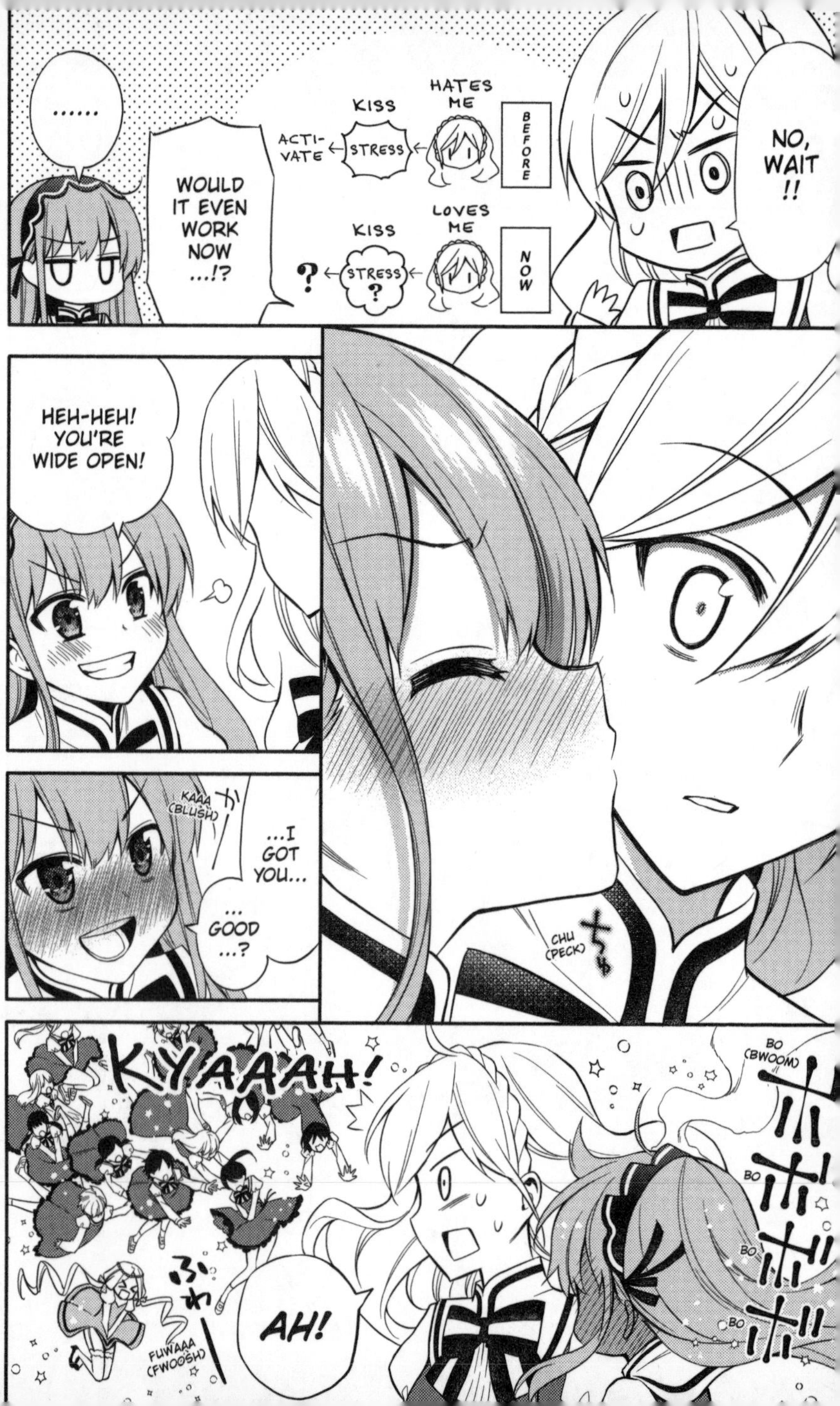
NO, WAIT!!
HATES ME
BEFORE
KISS
ACTI-VATE ← STRESS ←
LOVES ME
NOW
KISS
? ← STRESS ? ←
WOULD IT EVEN WORK NOW ...!?
......
CHU (PECK)
HEH-HEH! YOU'RE WIDE OPEN!
KAAA (BLUSH)
...I GOT YOU...
...GOOD...?
BO (BWOOM)
BO
BO
BO
AH!
KYAAAH!
FUWAAA (FWOOSH)

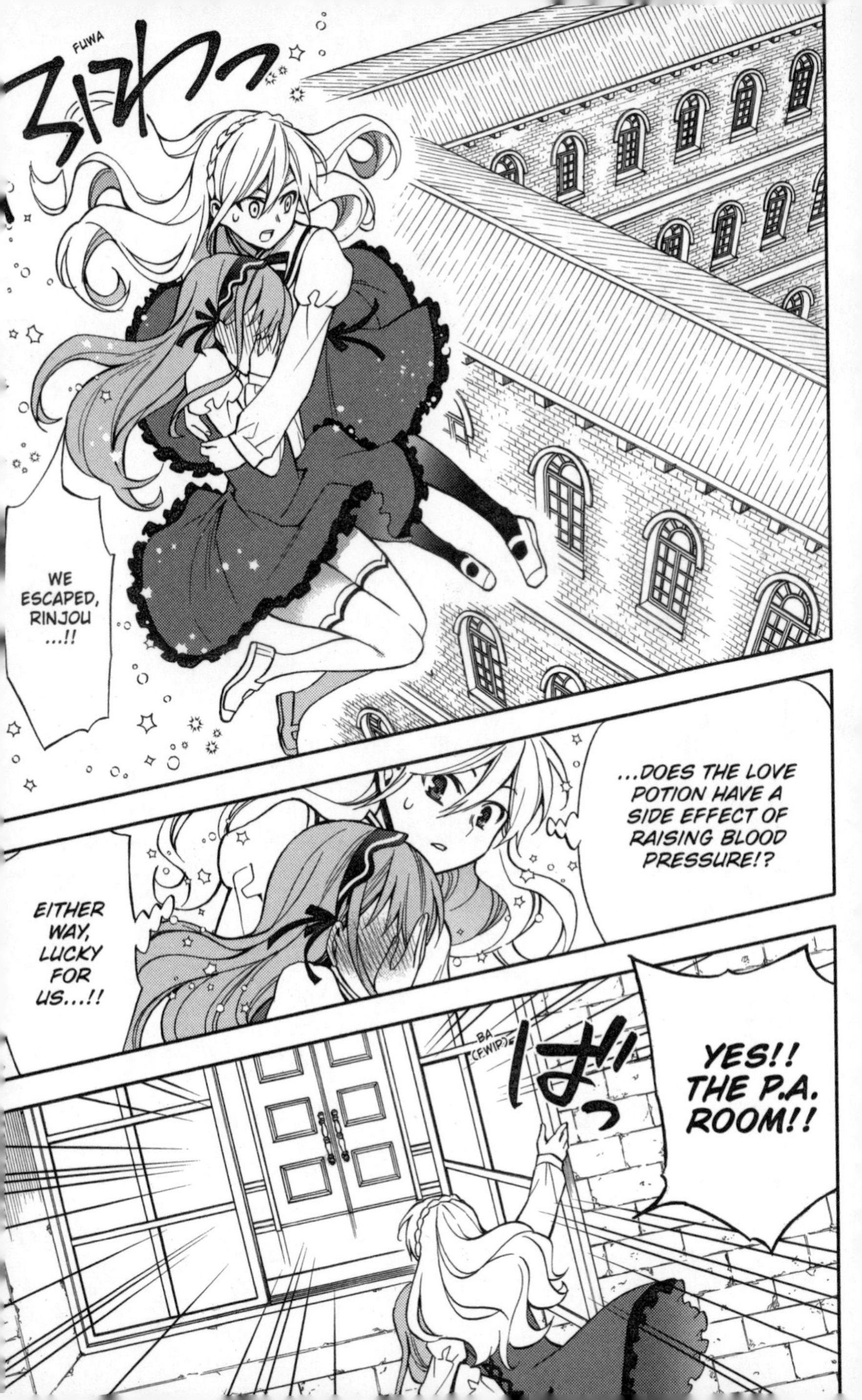
FUWA
WE ESCAPED, RINJOU ...!!
...DOES THE LOVE POTION HAVE A SIDE EFFECT OF RAISING BLOOD PRESSURE!?
EITHER WAY, LUCKY FOR US...!!
YES!! THE P.A. ROOM!!
BA (FWIP)

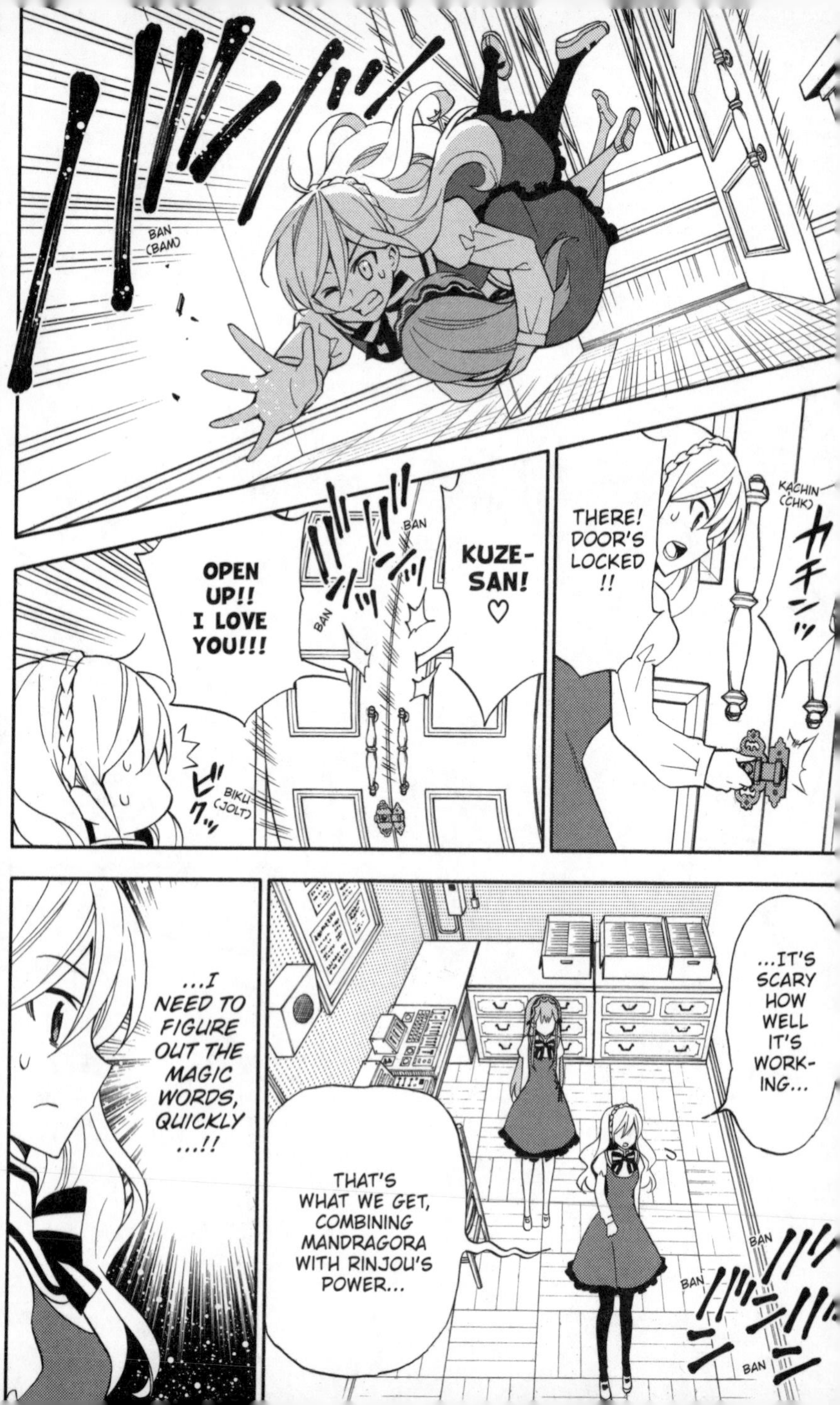
BAN (BAM)
KACHIN (CHK)
THERE! DOOR'S LOCKED!!
KUZE-SAN! ♡
BAN
BAN
OPEN UP!! I LOVE YOU!!!
BIKU (JOLT)
...IT'S SCARY HOW WELL IT'S WORKING...
THAT'S WHAT WE GET, COMBINING MANDRAGORA WITH RINJOU'S POWER...
BAN
BAN
BAN
...I NEED TO FIGURE OUT THE MAGIC WORDS, QUICKLY...!!

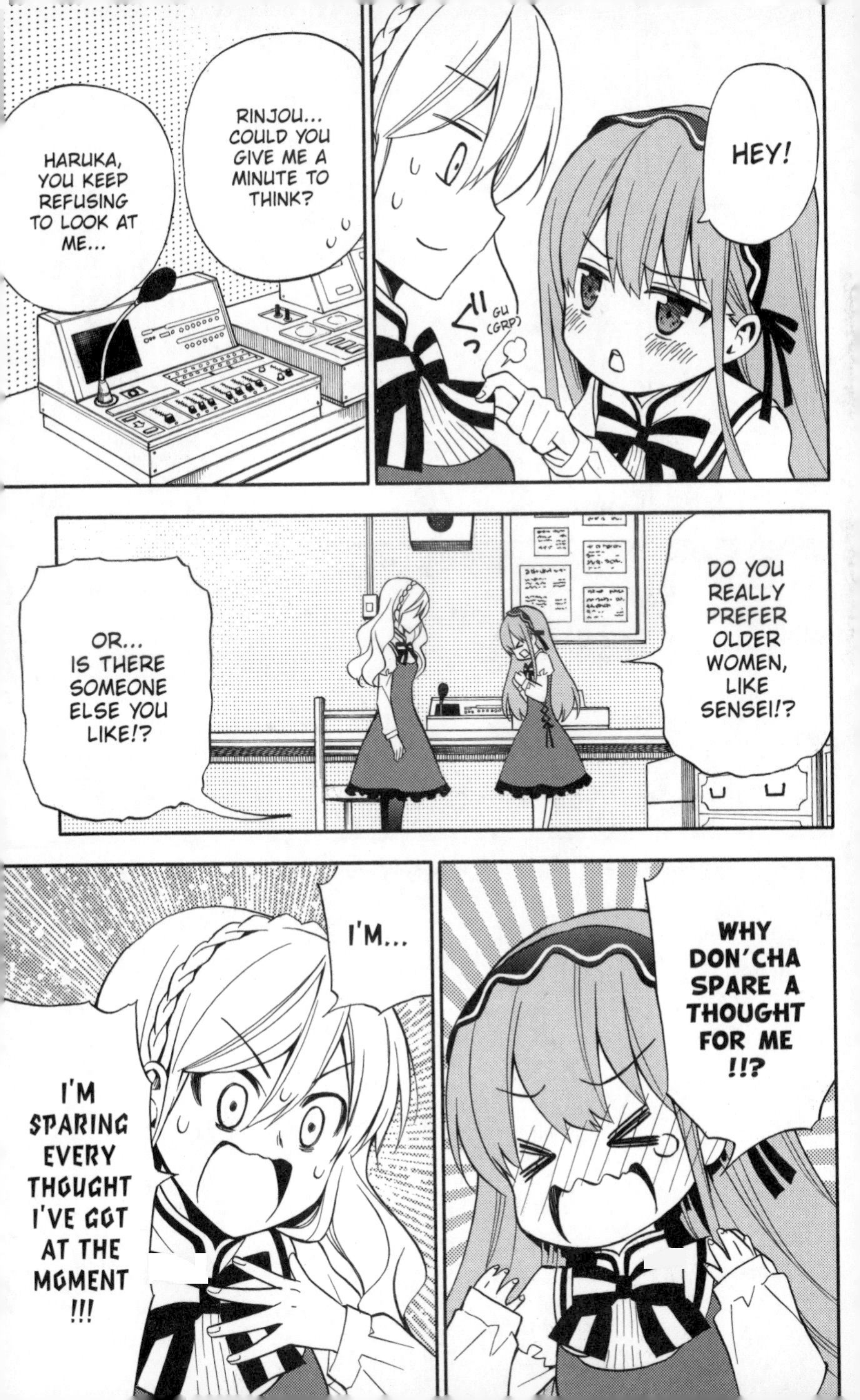
HEY!
GU (GRP)
RINJOU... COULD YOU GIVE ME A MINUTE TO THINK?
HARUKA, YOU KEEP REFUSING TO LOOK AT ME...
DO YOU REALLY PREFER OLDER WOMEN, LIKE SENSEI!?
OR... IS THERE SOMEONE ELSE YOU LIKE!?
WHY DON'CHA SPARE A THOUGHT FOR ME !!?
I'M...
I'M SPARING EVERY THOUGHT I'VE GOT AT THE MOMENT !!!

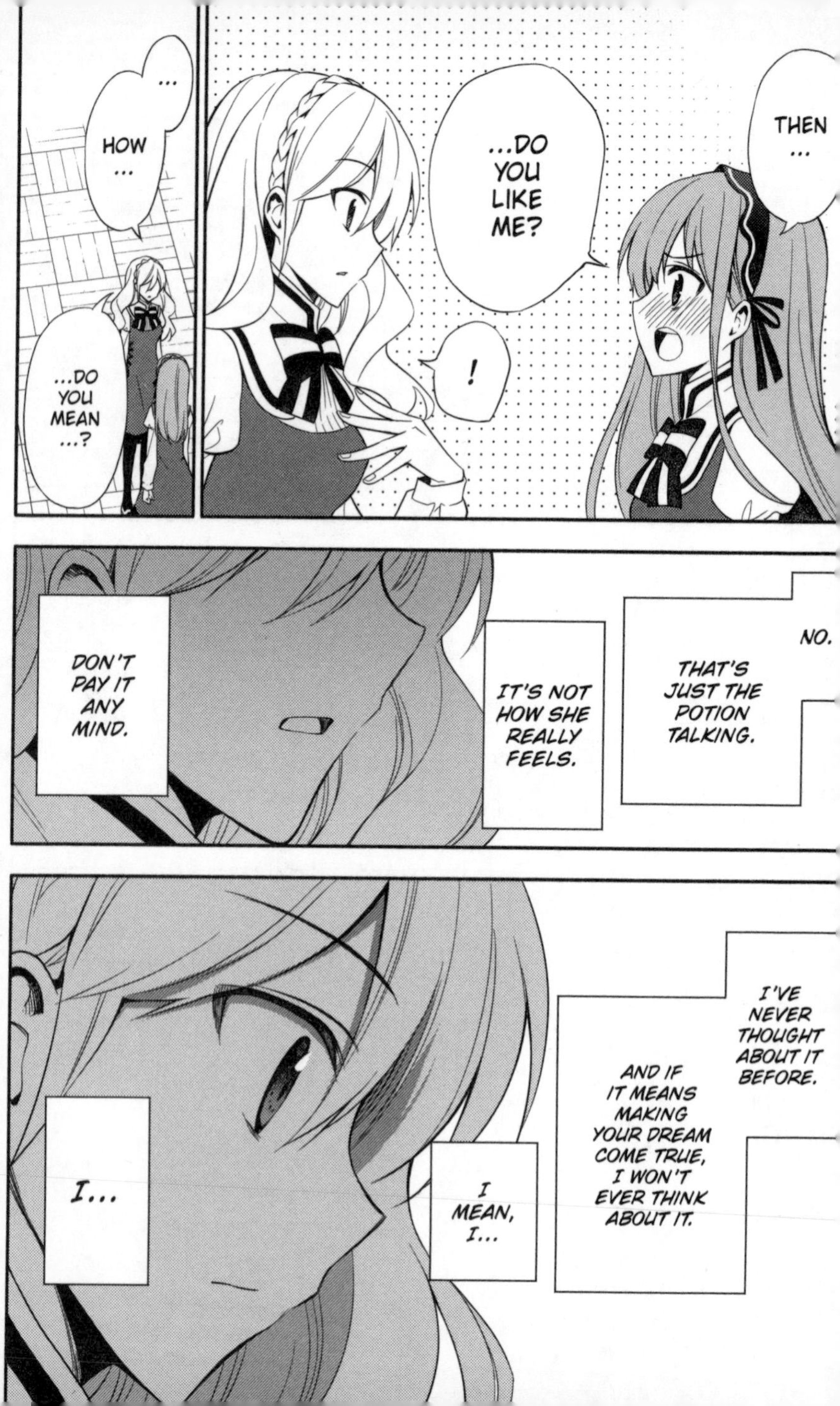
THEN...
...DO YOU LIKE ME?
!
...
HOW...
...DO YOU MEAN...?
NO.
THAT'S JUST THE POTION TALKING.
IT'S NOT HOW SHE REALLY FEELS.
DON'T PAY IT ANY MIND.
I'VE NEVER THOUGHT ABOUT IT BEFORE.
AND IF IT MEANS MAKING YOUR DREAM COME TRUE, I WON'T EVER THINK ABOUT IT.
I MEAN, I...
I...

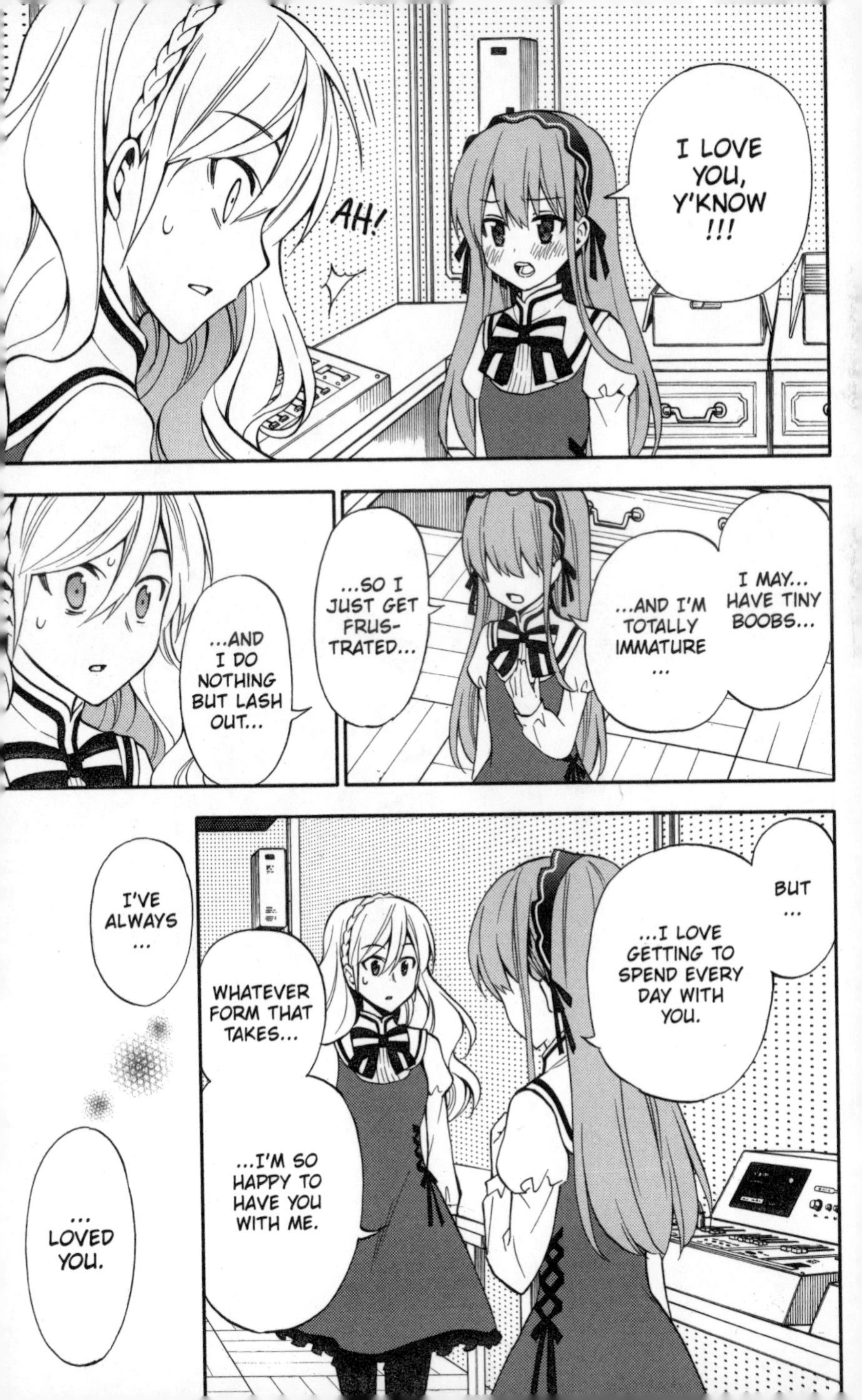
I LOVE YOU, Y'KNOW !!!
AH!
I MAY... HAVE TINY BOOBS...
...AND I'M TOTALLY IMMATURE ...
...SO I JUST GET FRUS-TRATED...
...AND I DO NOTHING BUT LASH OUT...
BUT ...
...I LOVE GETTING TO SPEND EVERY DAY WITH YOU.
WHATEVER FORM THAT TAKES...
...I'M SO HAPPY TO HAVE YOU WITH ME.
I'VE ALWAYS ...
... LOVED YOU.

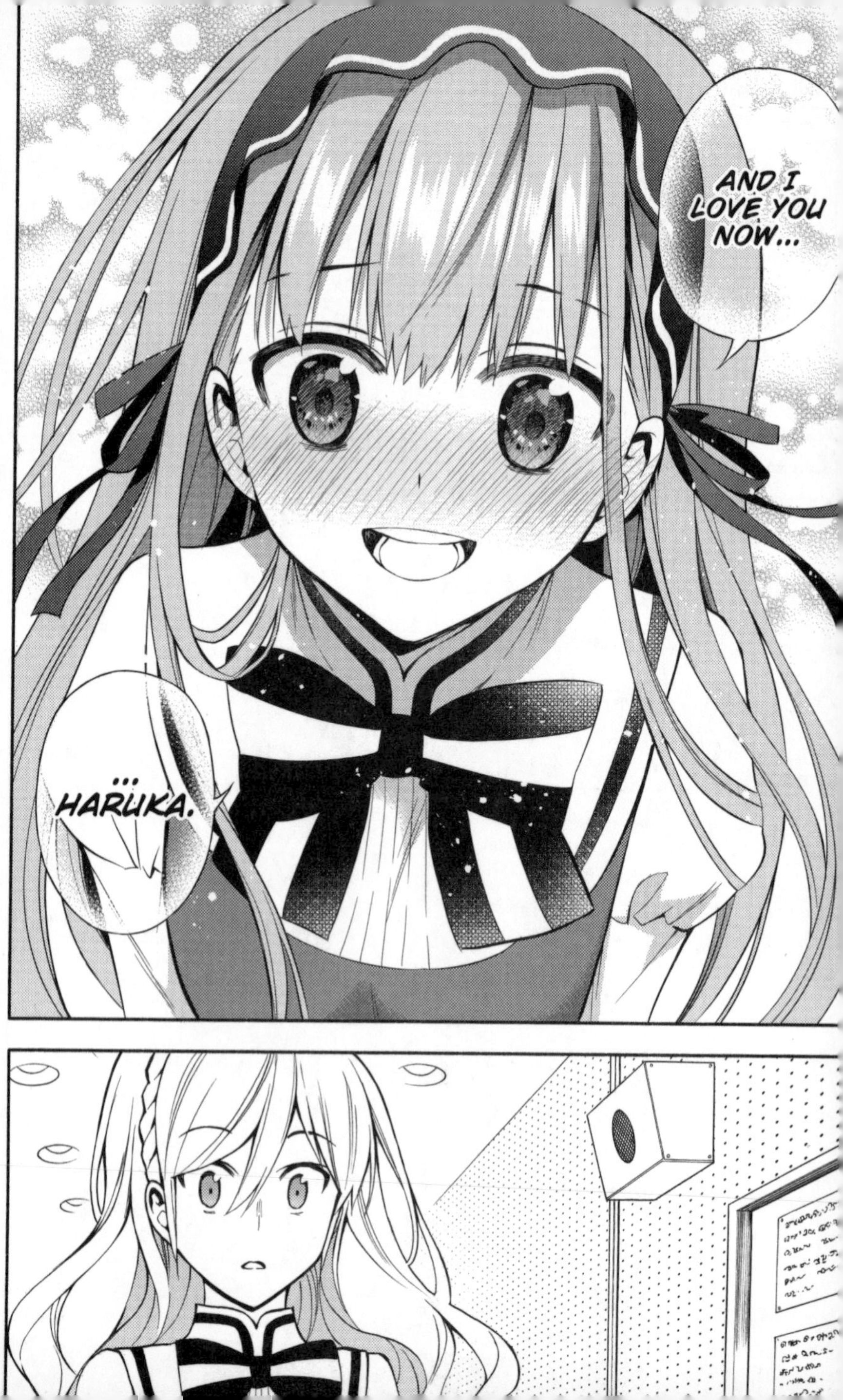
AND I LOVE YOU NOW...
...HARUKA.

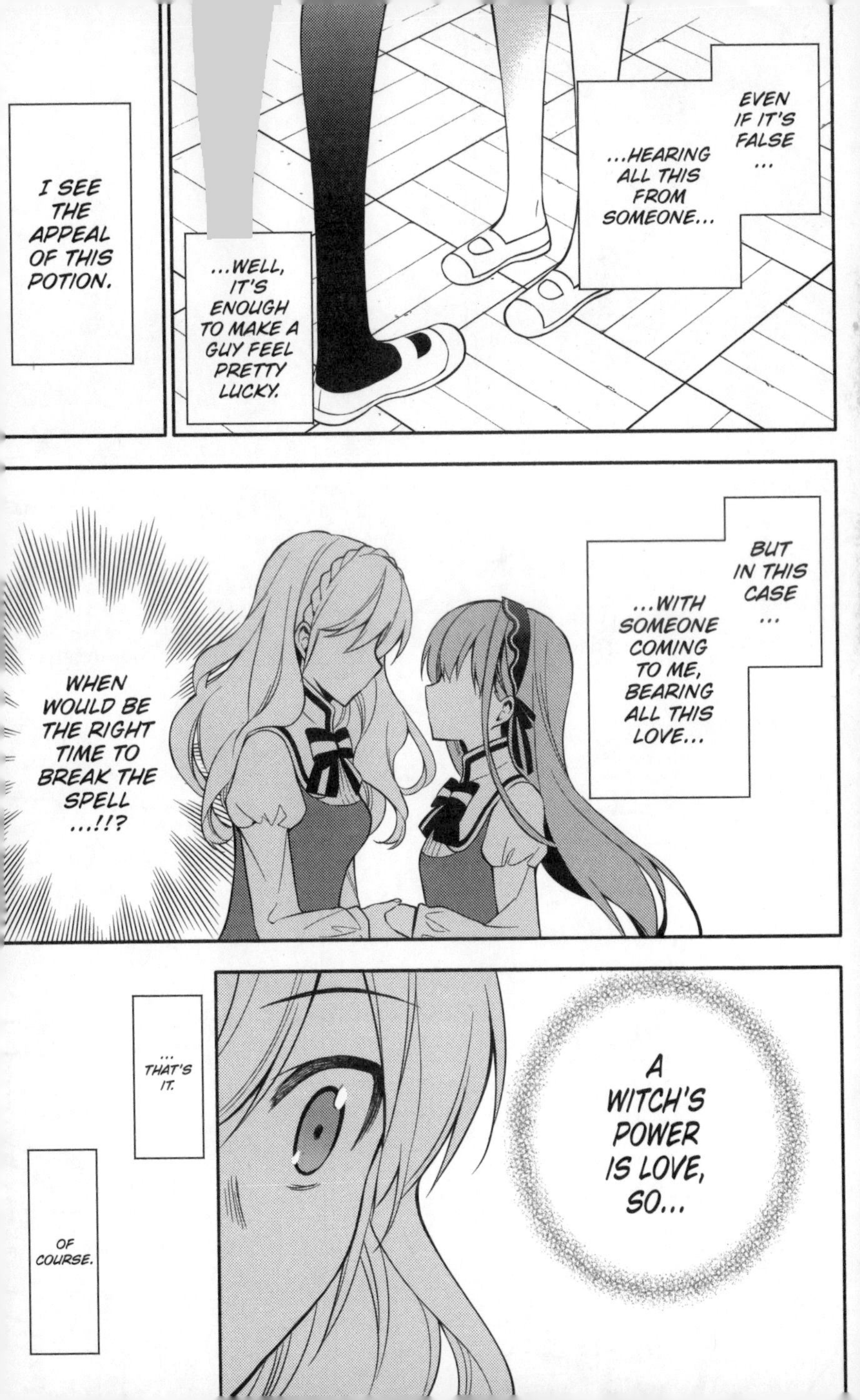
EVEN IF IT'S FALSE...
...HEARING ALL THIS FROM SOMEONE...
...WELL, IT'S ENOUGH TO MAKE A GUY FEEL PRETTY LUCKY.
I SEE THE APPEAL OF THIS POTION.
BUT IN THIS CASE...
...WITH SOMEONE COMING TO ME, BEARING ALL THIS LOVE...
WHEN WOULD BE THE RIGHT TIME TO BREAK THE SPELL...!!?
A WITCH'S POWER IS LOVE, SO...
...THAT'S IT.
OF COURSE.

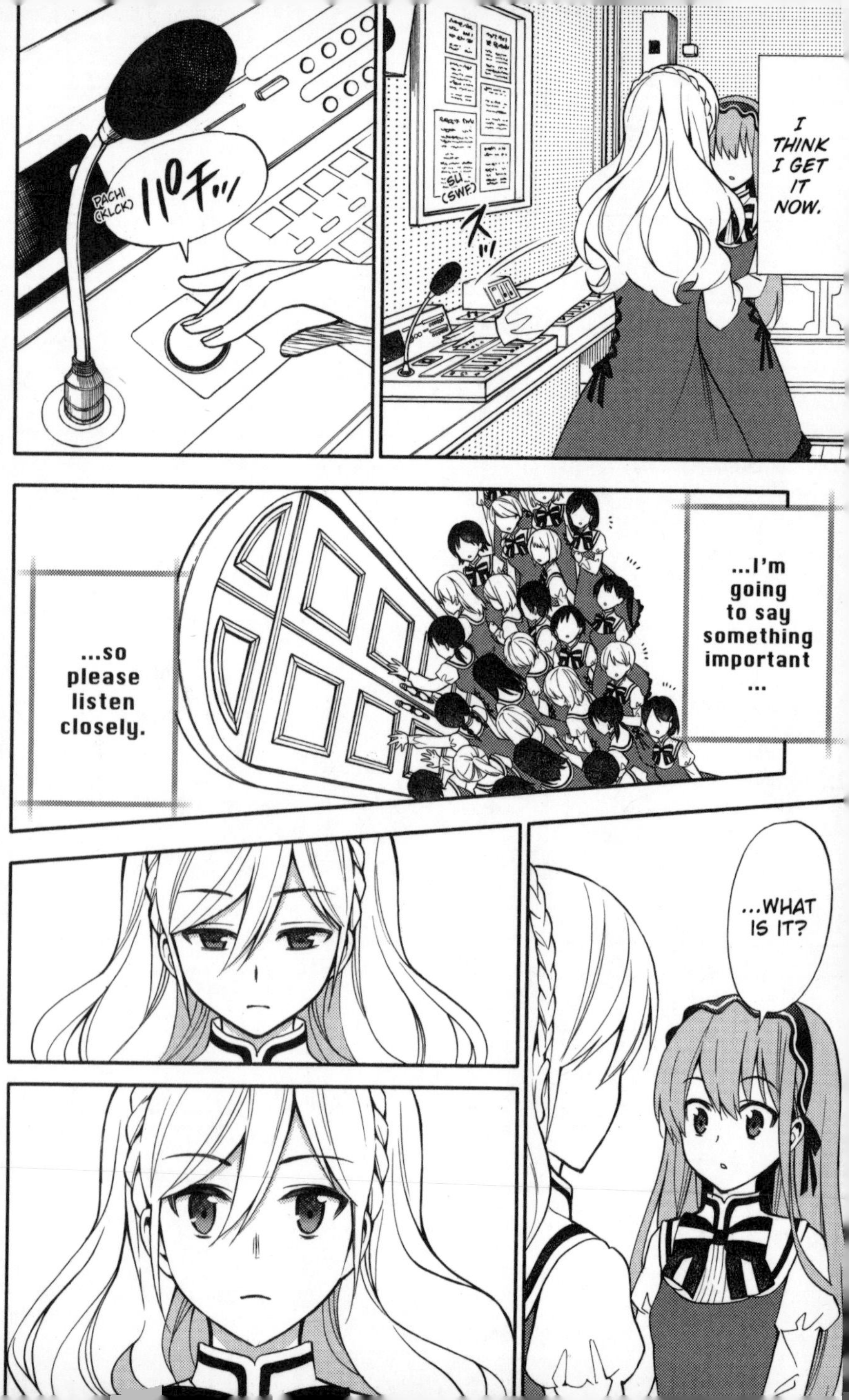

I THINK I GET IT NOW.
スッ
SU (SWF)
パチッ
PACHI (KLCK)
...I'm going to say something important...
...so please listen closely.
...WHAT IS IT?

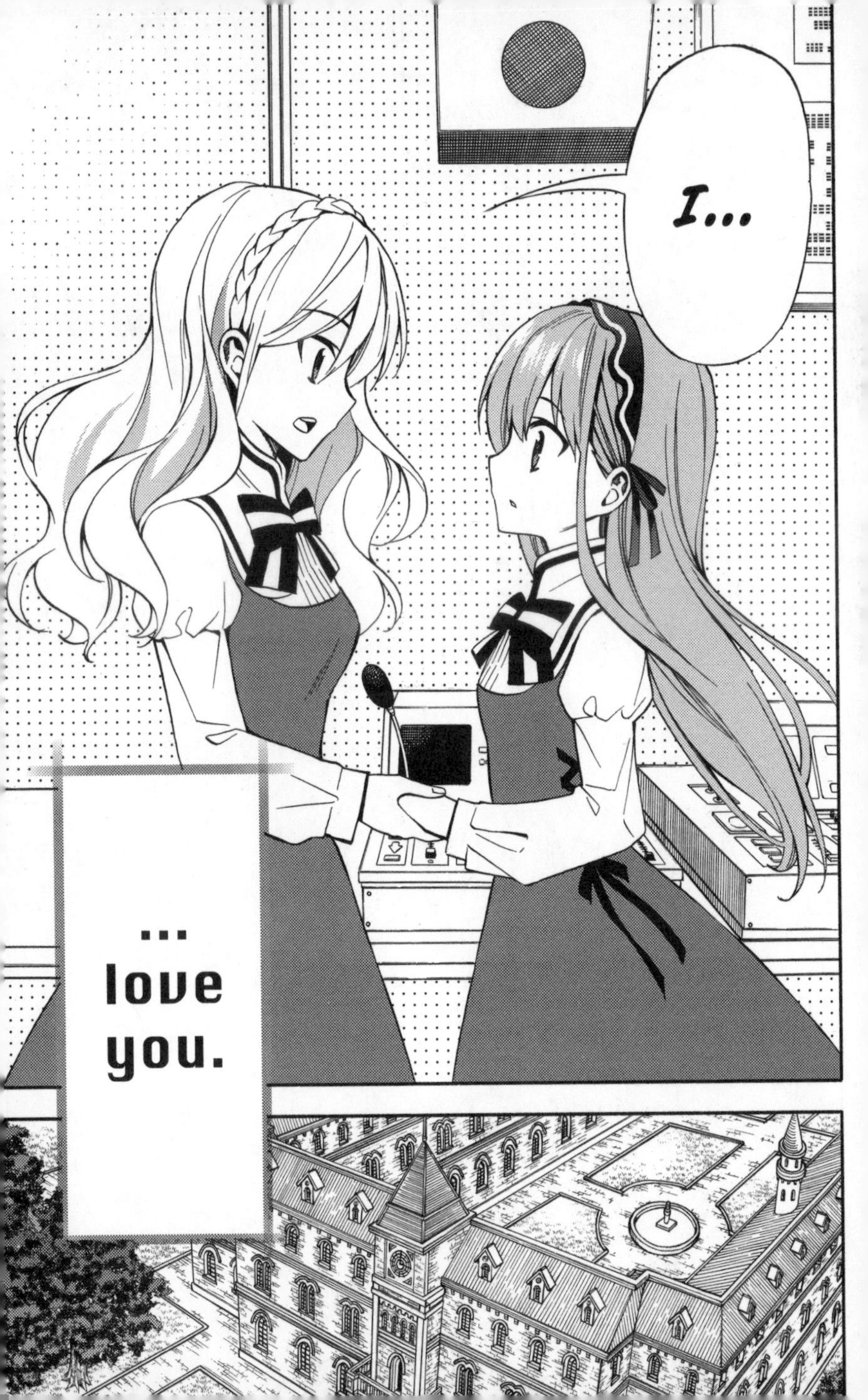
I...
...love you.

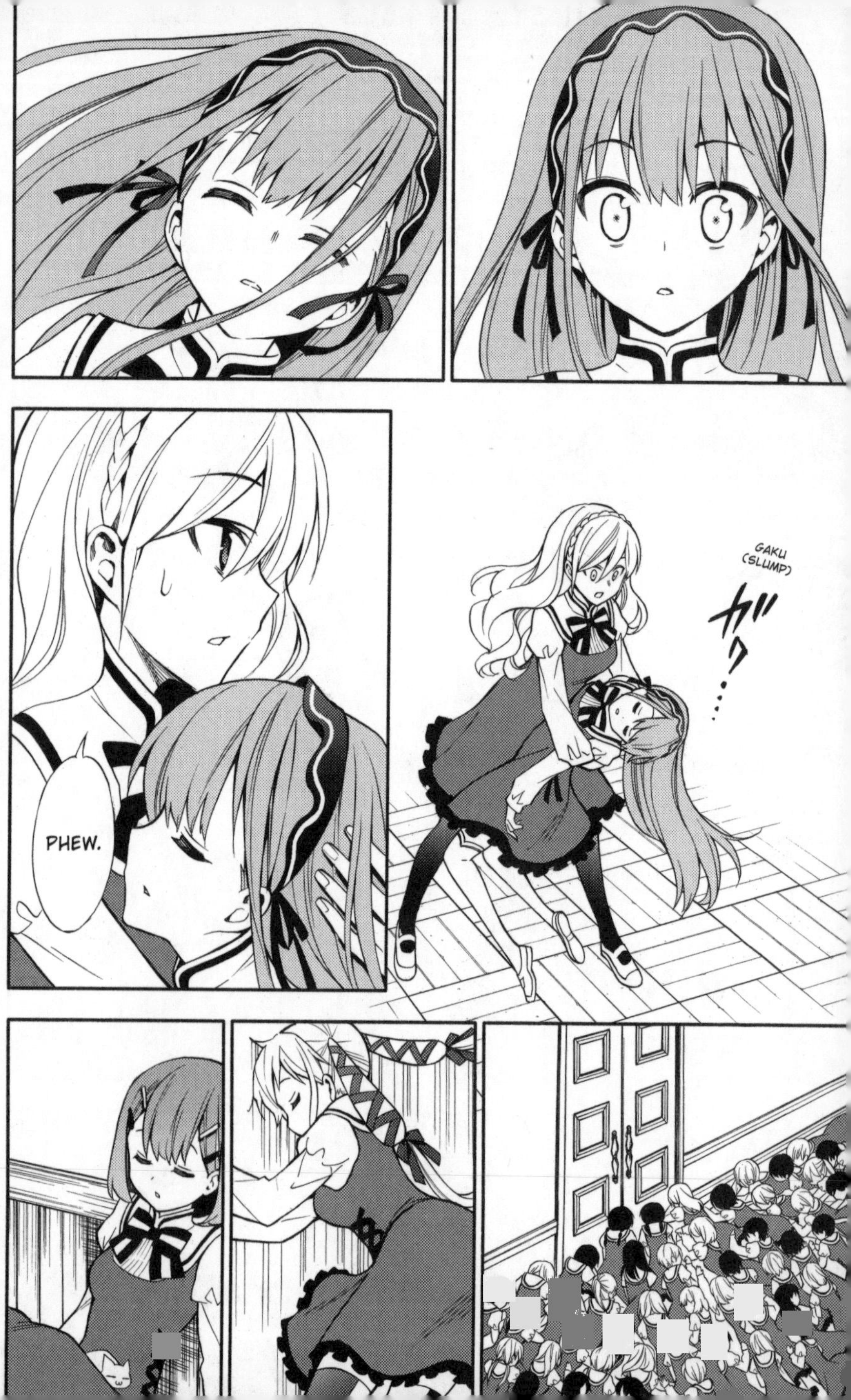
GAKU (SLUMP)
ガク…
PHEW.

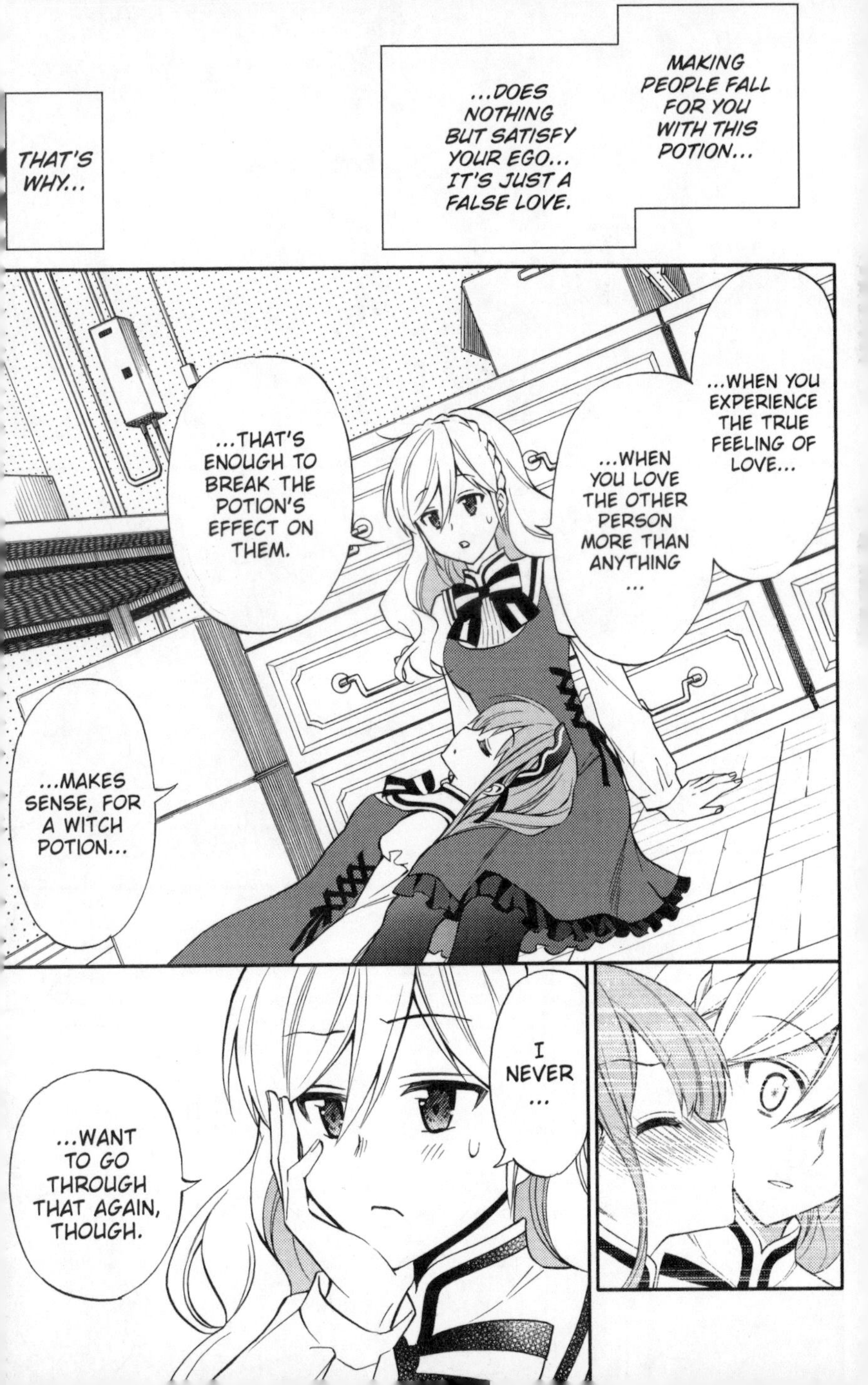
MAKING PEOPLE FALL FOR YOU WITH THIS POTION...
...DOES NOTHING BUT SATISFY YOUR EGO... IT'S JUST A FALSE LOVE.
THAT'S WHY...
...WHEN YOU EXPERIENCE THE TRUE FEELING OF LOVE...
...WHEN YOU LOVE THE OTHER PERSON MORE THAN ANYTHING ...
...THAT'S ENOUGH TO BREAK THE POTION'S EFFECT ON THEM.
...MAKES SENSE, FOR A WITCH POTION...
I NEVER ...
...WANT TO GO THROUGH THAT AGAIN, THOUGH.

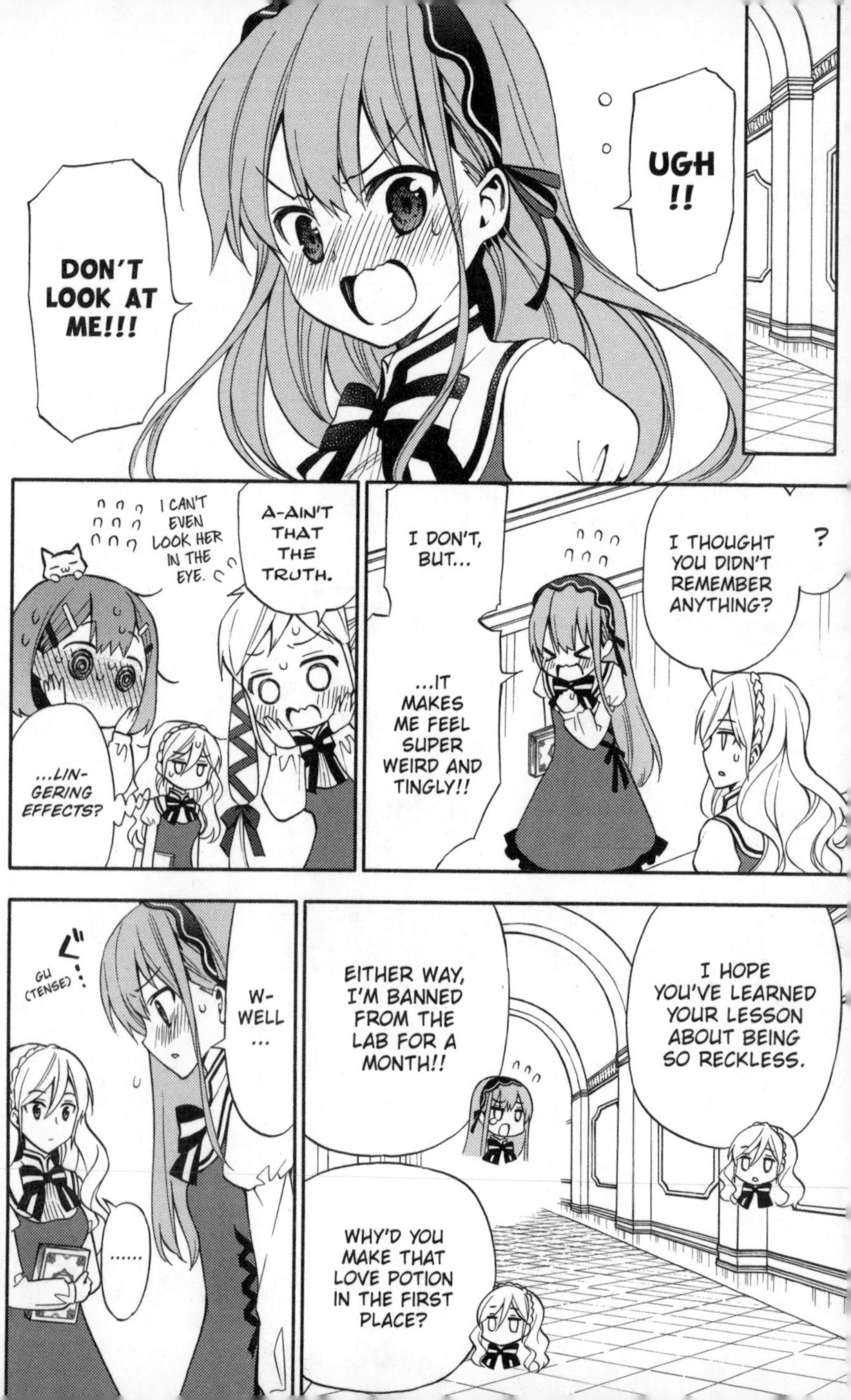
UGH!!
DON'T LOOK AT ME!!!
I THOUGHT YOU DIDN'T REMEMBER ANYTHING?
?
I DON'T, BUT...
...IT MAKES ME FEEL SUPER WEIRD AND TINGLY!!
A-AIN'T THAT THE TRUTH.
I CAN'T EVEN LOOK HER IN THE EYE.
...LINGERING EFFECTS?
I HOPE YOU'VE LEARNED YOUR LESSON ABOUT BEING SO RECKLESS.
EITHER WAY, I'M BANNED FROM THE LAB FOR A MONTH!!
WHY'D YOU MAKE THAT LOVE POTION IN THE FIRST PLACE?
W-WELL...
ぐ
GU (TENSE)
......

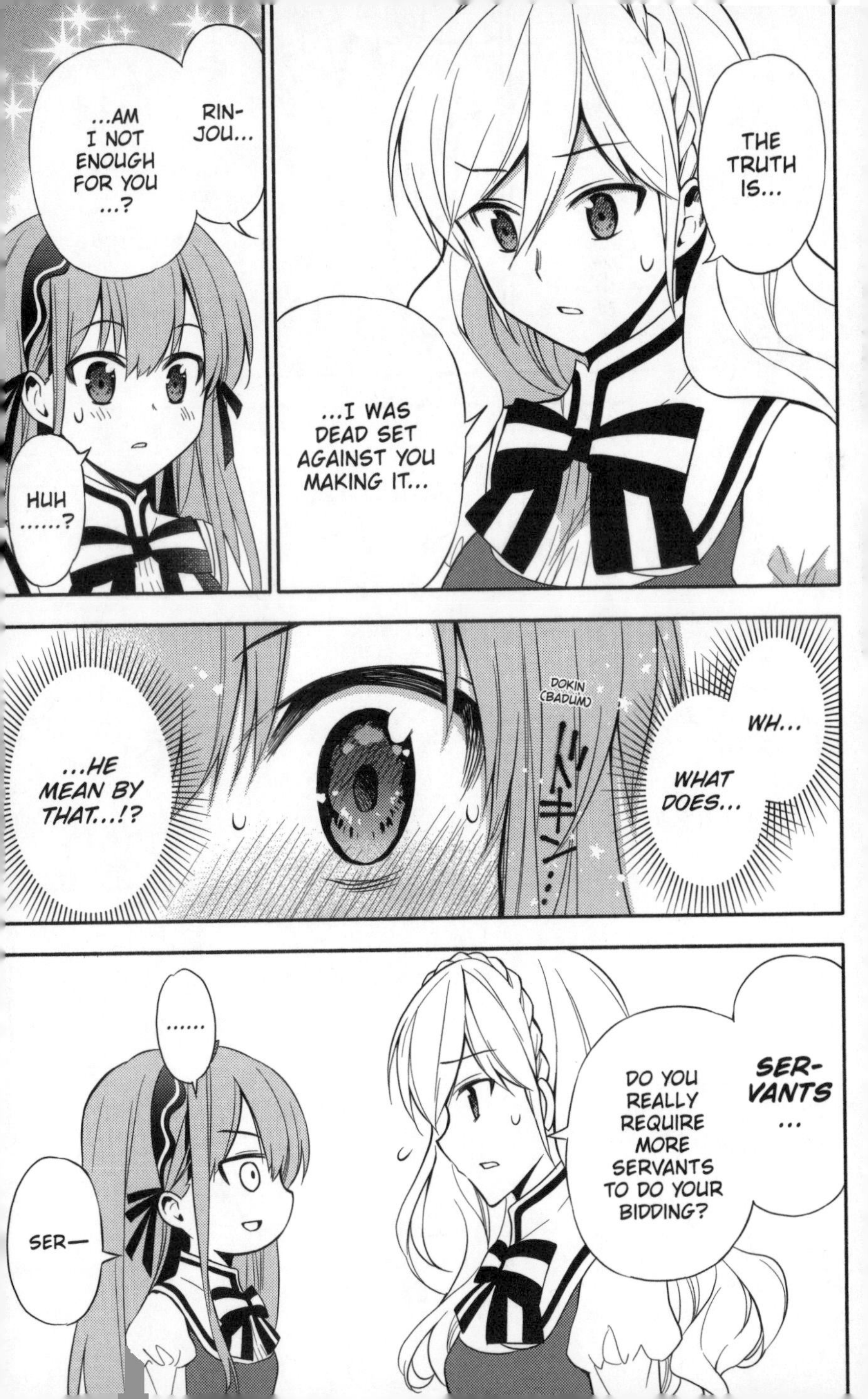
THE TRUTH IS...
...I WAS DEAD SET AGAINST YOU MAKING IT...
RIN-JOU...
...AM I NOT ENOUGH FOR YOU ...?
HUH ......?
WH...
WHAT DOES...
DOKIN (BADUM)
...HE MEAN BY THAT...!?
SER-VANTS ...
DO YOU REALLY REQUIRE MORE SERVANTS TO DO YOUR BIDDING?
......
SER—

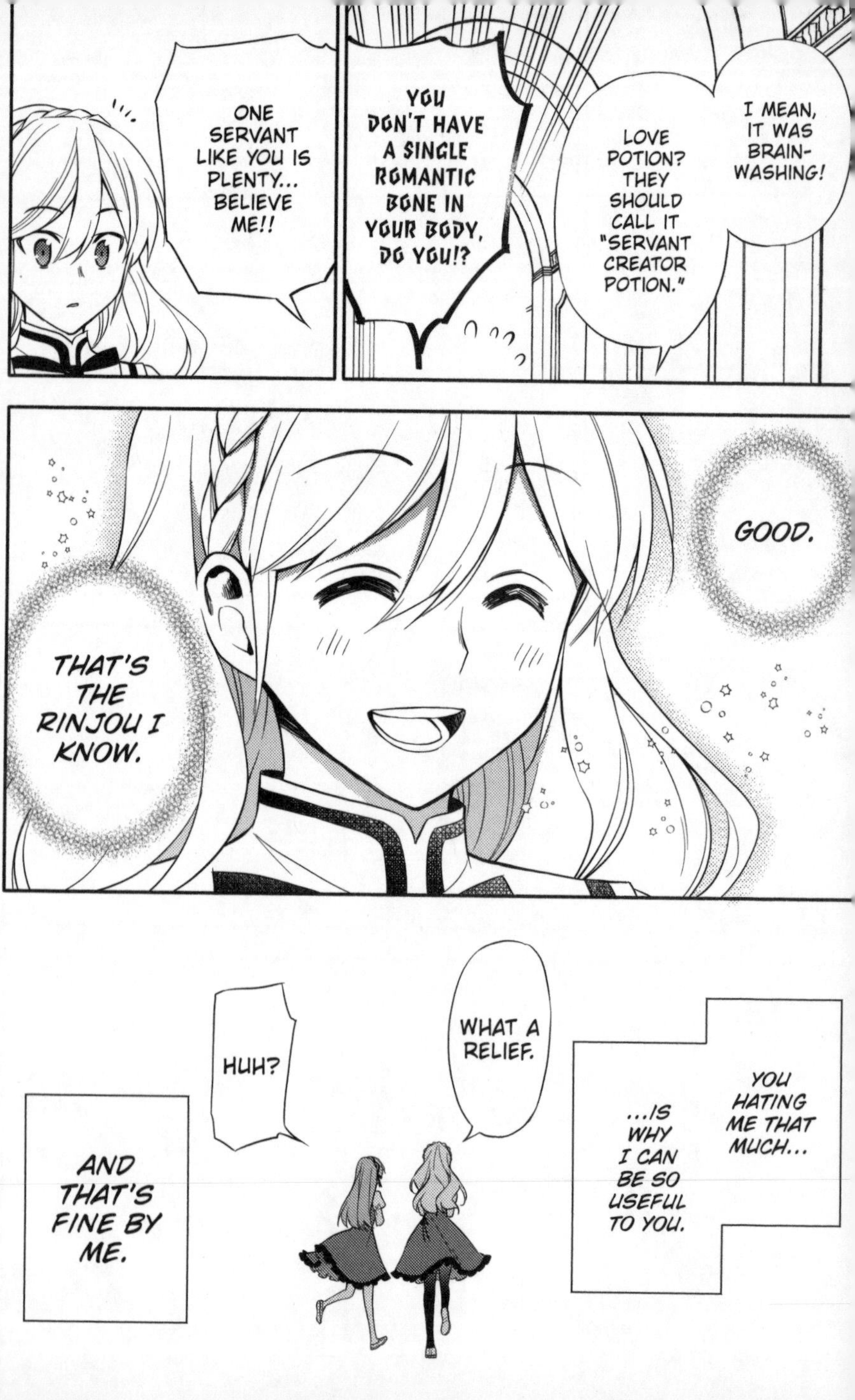

I MEAN, IT WAS BRAIN-WASHING!
LOVE POTION? THEY SHOULD CALL IT "SERVANT CREATOR POTION."
YOU DON'T HAVE A SINGLE ROMANTIC BONE IN YOUR BODY, DO YOU!?
ONE SERVANT LIKE YOU IS PLENTY... BELIEVE ME!!
GOOD.
THAT'S THE RINJOU I KNOW.
YOU HATING ME THAT MUCH...
...IS WHY I CAN BE SO USEFUL TO YOU.
WHAT A RELIEF.
HUH?
AND THAT'S FINE BY ME.

If Witch, Then Which?

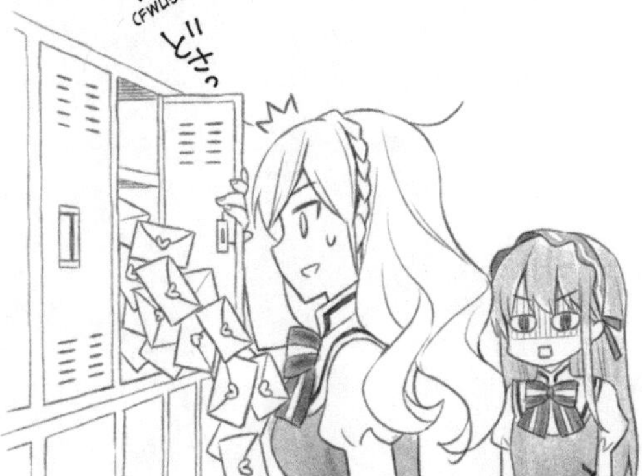
DOSA
(FWUSH)
どさっ

If Witch, then Which?

N-NO CLUE.

BUT WHY DID THE POTION'S EFFECTS CENTER AROUND ME?

HMM?

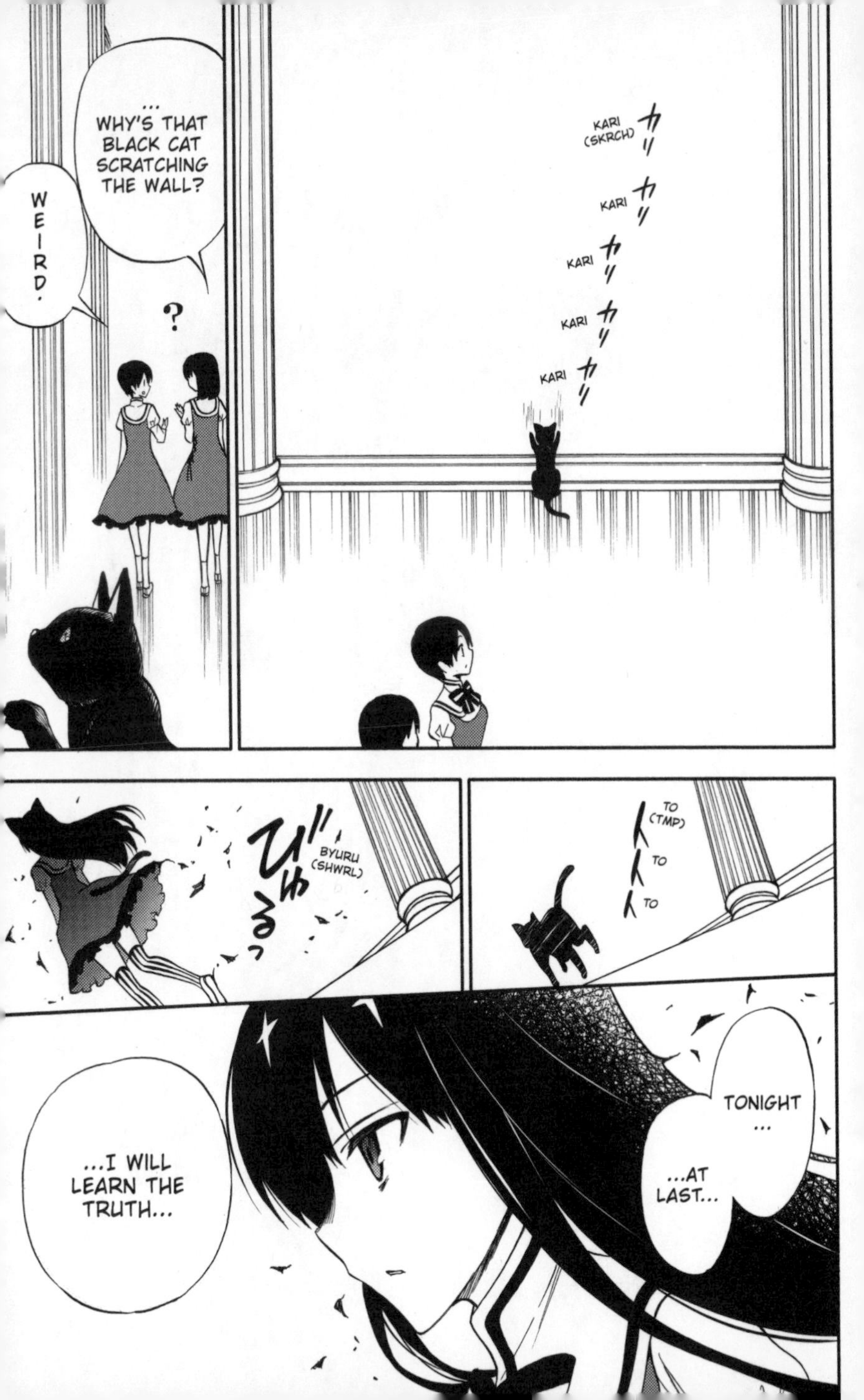
KARI (SKRCH) カリ
KARI カリ
KARI カリ
KARI カリ
KARI カリ
...WHY'S THAT BLACK CAT SCRATCHING THE WALL?
WEIRD.
?
TO (TMP) ト
TO ト
TO ト
BYURU (SHWRL) びゅるっ
TONIGHT...
...AT LAST...
...I WILL LEARN THE TRUTH...

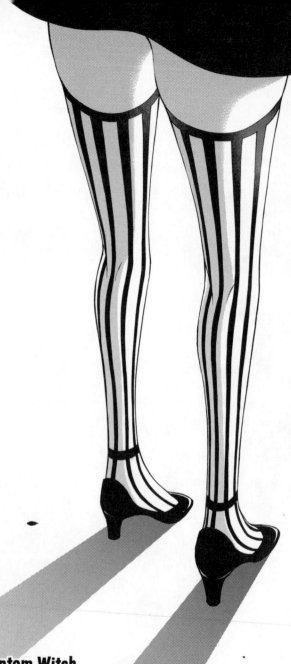

MAGIC.8 **The Phantom Witch**

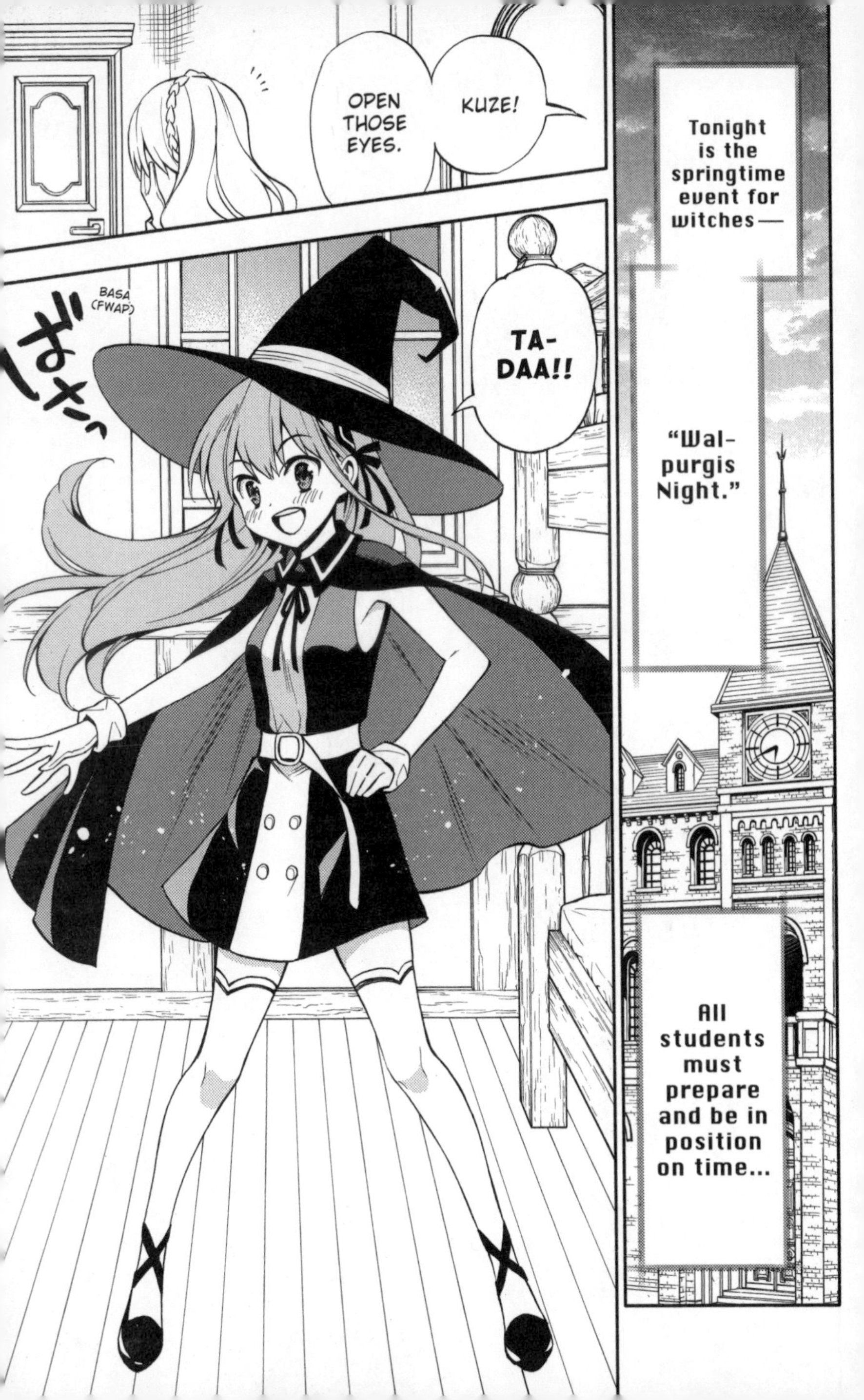

Tonight is the springtime event for witches—
"Wal-purgis Night."
All students must prepare and be in position on time...
KUZE!
OPEN THOSE EYES.
TA-DAA!!
BASA (FWAP)

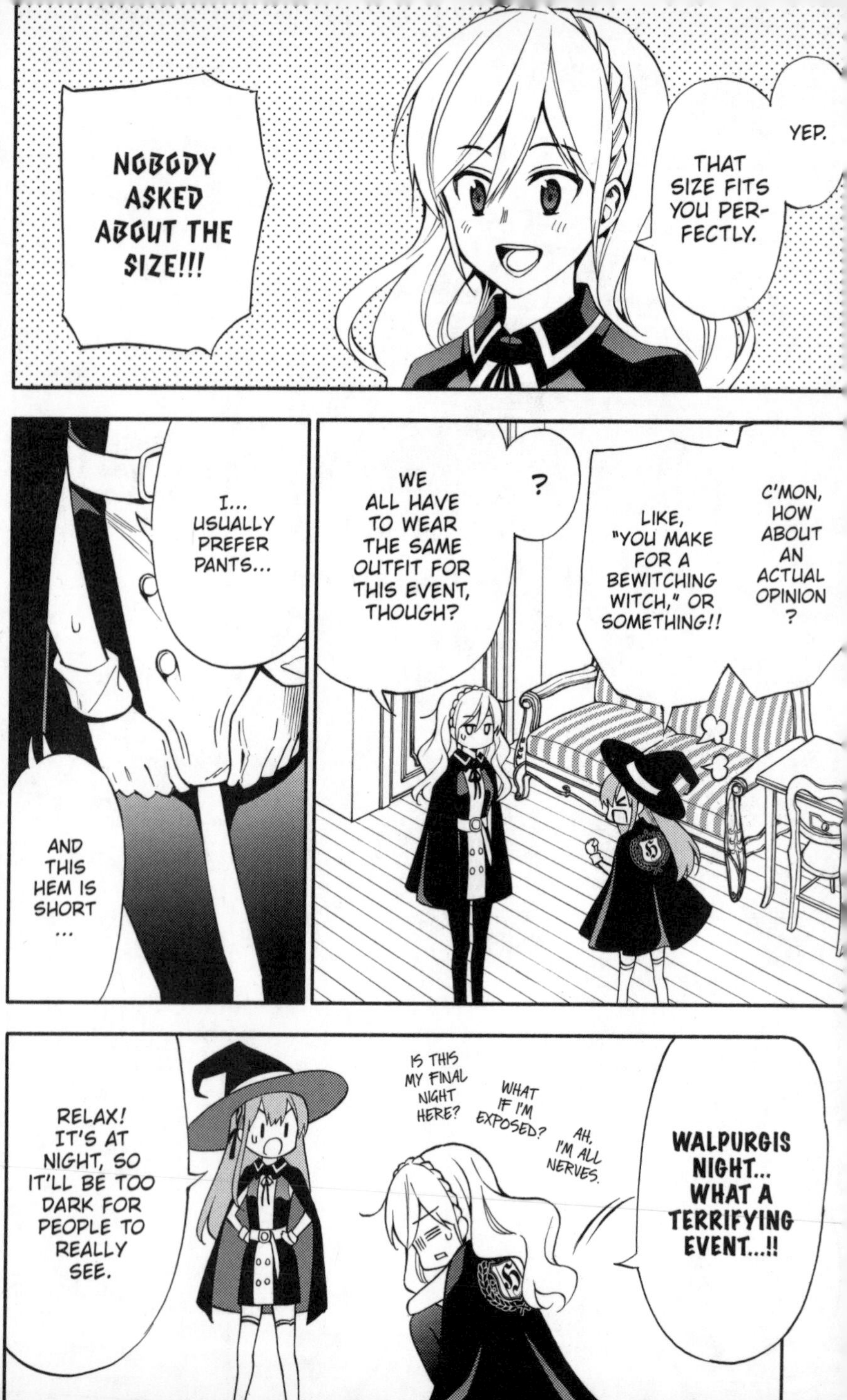
YEP.
THAT SIZE FITS YOU PER-FECTLY.
NOBODY ASKED ABOUT THE SIZE!!!
C'MON, HOW ABOUT AN ACTUAL OPINION?
LIKE, "YOU MAKE FOR A BEWITCHING WITCH," OR SOMETHING!!
?
WE ALL HAVE TO WEAR THE SAME OUTFIT FOR THIS EVENT, THOUGH?
I... USUALLY PREFER PANTS...
AND THIS HEM IS SHORT...
WALPURGIS NIGHT... WHAT A TERRIFYING EVENT...!!
AH, I'M ALL NERVES.
WHAT IF I'M EXPOSED?
IS THIS MY FINAL NIGHT HERE?
RELAX! IT'S AT NIGHT, SO IT'LL BE TOO DARK FOR PEOPLE TO REALLY SEE.

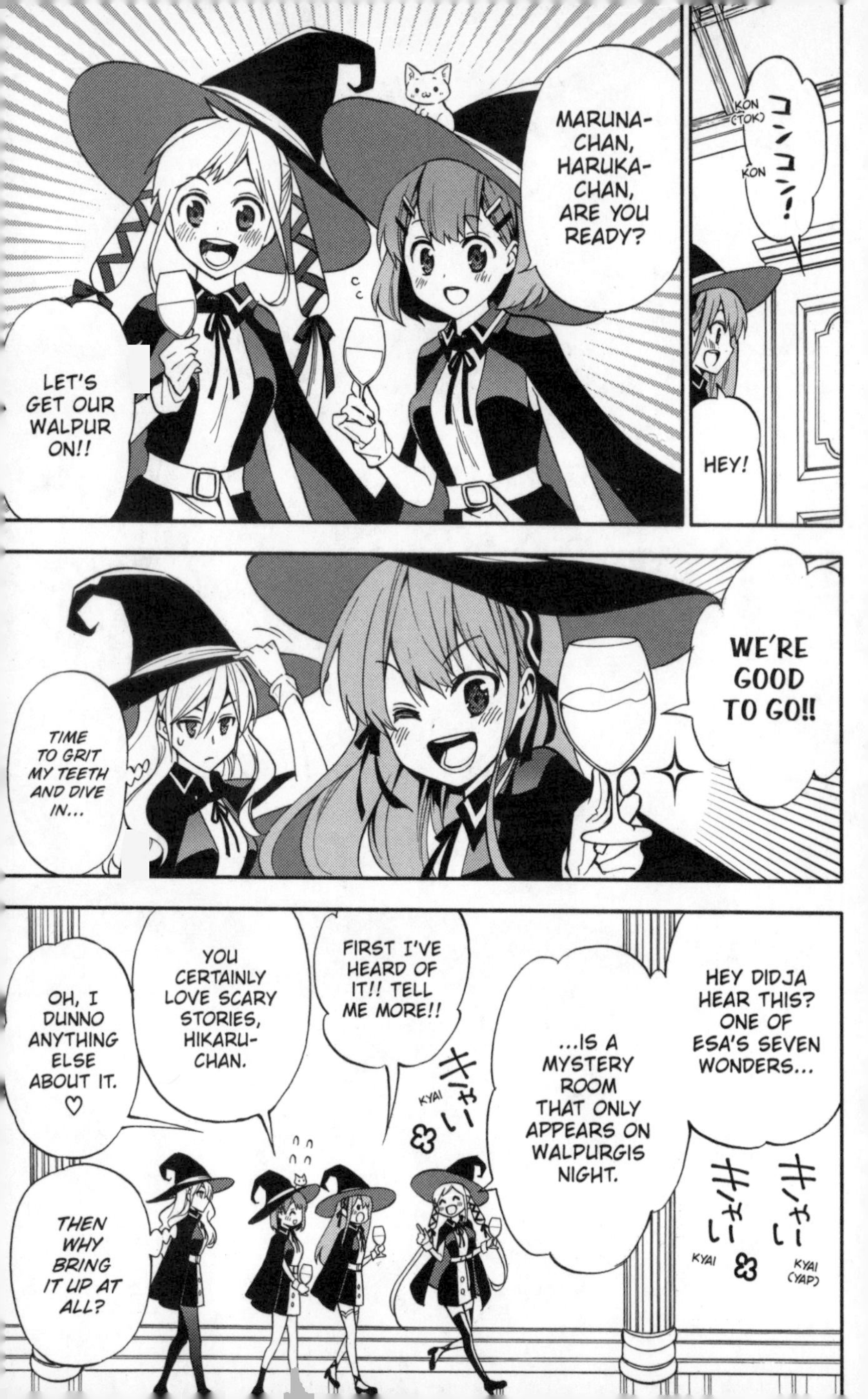
コンコン!
KON (TOK)
KON
HEY!
MARUNA-CHAN, HARUKA-CHAN, ARE YOU READY?
LET'S GET OUR WALPUR ON!!
WE'RE GOOD TO GO!!
TIME TO GRIT MY TEETH AND DIVE IN...
HEY DIDJA HEAR THIS? ONE OF ESA'S SEVEN WONDERS...
キャーキャー
KYAI (YAP)
KYAI
...IS A MYSTERY ROOM THAT ONLY APPEARS ON WALPURGIS NIGHT.
キャー
KYAI
FIRST I'VE HEARD OF IT!! TELL ME MORE!!
YOU CERTAINLY LOVE SCARY STORIES, HIKARU-CHAN.
OH, I DUNNO ANYTHING ELSE ABOUT IT. ♡
THEN WHY BRING IT UP AT ALL?

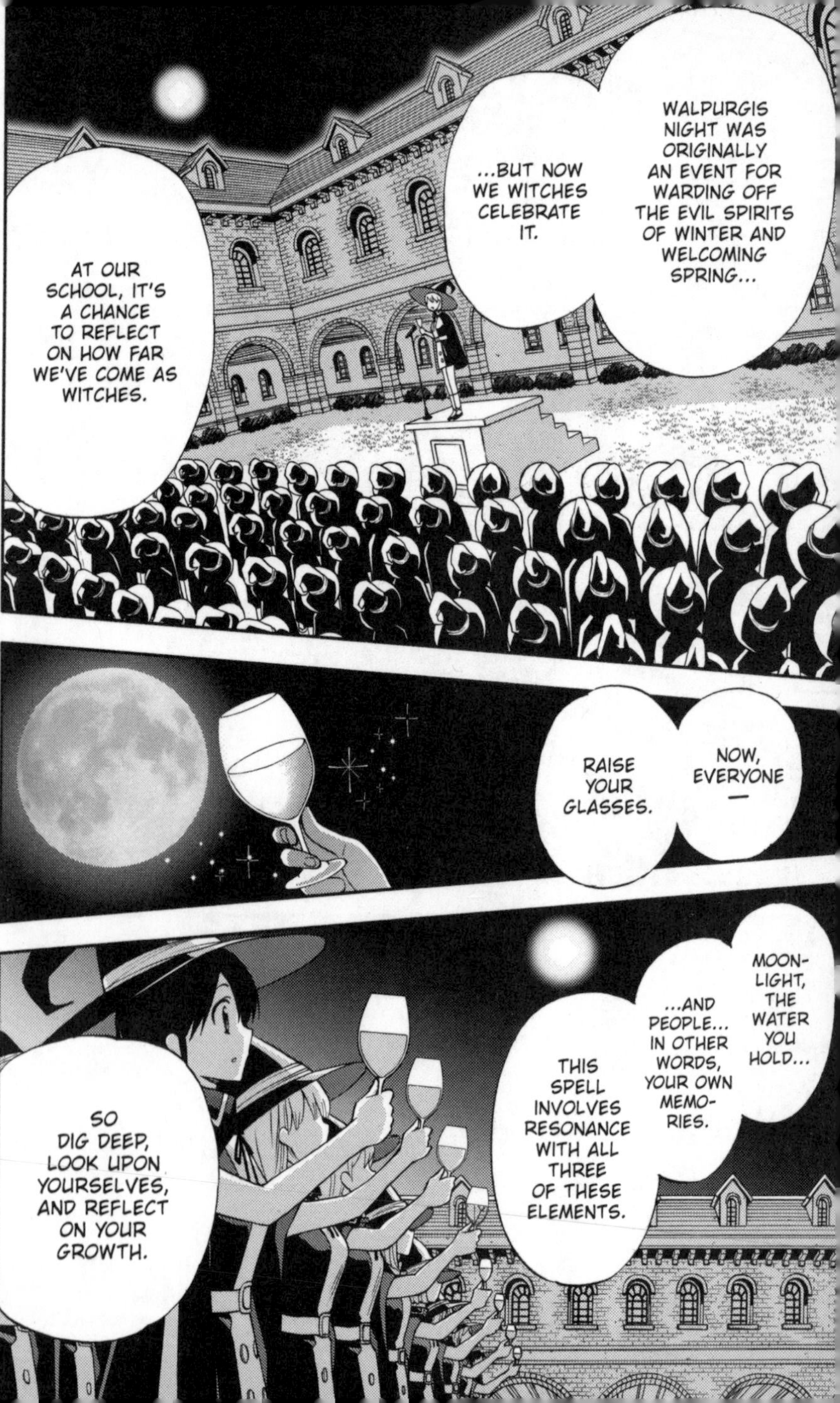
WALPURGIS NIGHT WAS ORIGINALLY AN EVENT FOR WARDING OFF THE EVIL SPIRITS OF WINTER AND WELCOMING SPRING...
...BUT NOW WE WITCHES CELEBRATE IT.
AT OUR SCHOOL, IT'S A CHANCE TO REFLECT ON HOW FAR WE'VE COME AS WITCHES.
NOW, EVERYONE—
RAISE YOUR GLASSES.
MOONLIGHT, THE WATER YOU HOLD...
...AND PEOPLE... IN OTHER WORDS, YOUR OWN MEMORIES.
THIS SPELL INVOLVES RESONANCE WITH ALL THREE OF THESE ELEMENTS.
SO DIG DEEP, LOOK UPON YOURSELVES, AND REFLECT ON YOUR GROWTH.

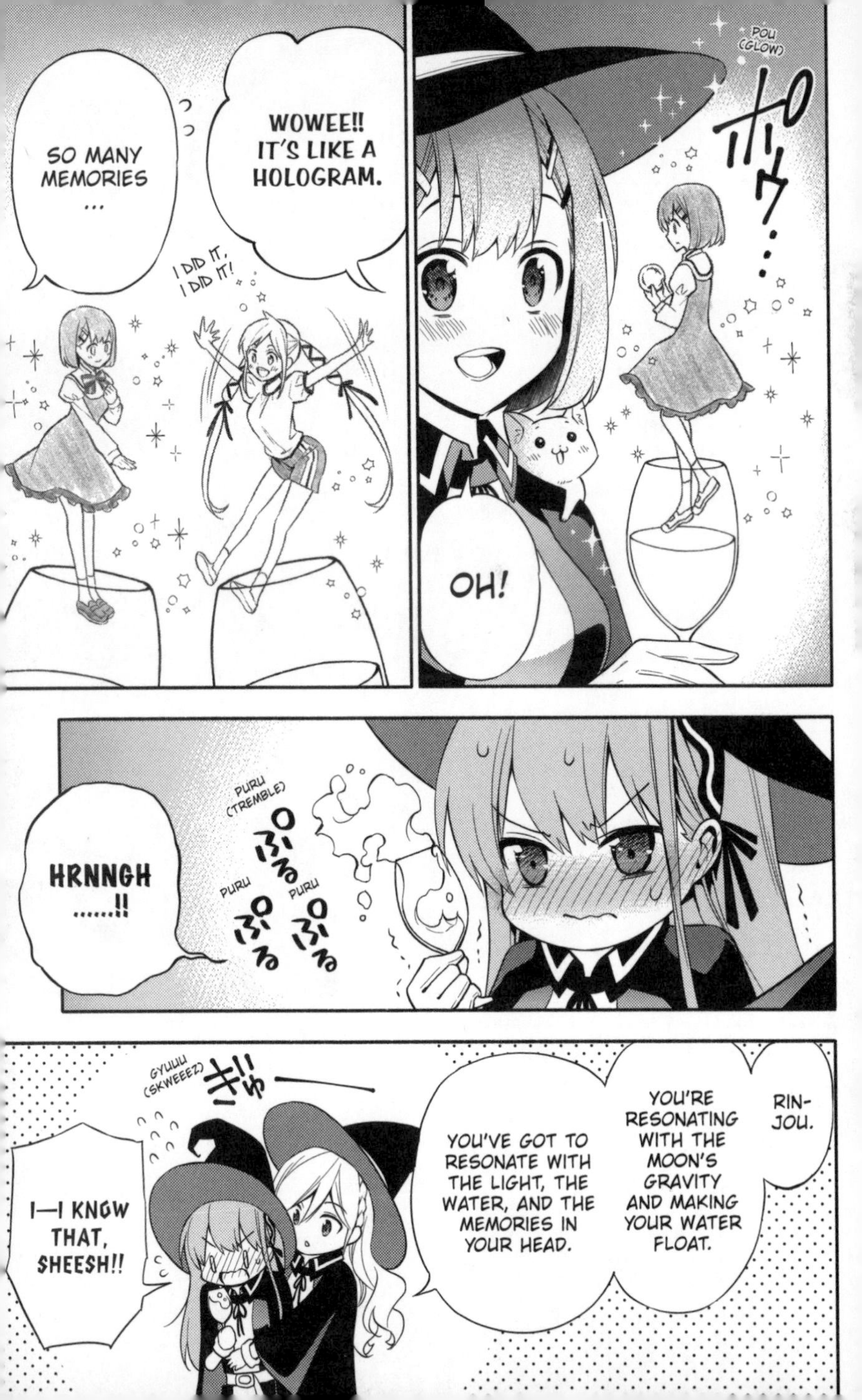

POU (GLOW)
ポウ・・・
OH!
WOWEE!! IT'S LIKE A HOLOGRAM.
SO MANY MEMORIES ...
I DID IT, I DID IT!
PURU (TREMBLE)
ぷる
PURU
ぷる
PURU
ぷる
HRNNGH ......!!
RIN-JOU.
YOU'RE RESONATING WITH THE MOON'S GRAVITY AND MAKING YOUR WATER FLOAT.
YOU'VE GOT TO RESONATE WITH THE LIGHT, THE WATER, AND THE MEMORIES IN YOUR HEAD.
GYUUU (SKWEEEZ)
ぎゅー
I—I KNOW THAT, SHEESH!!

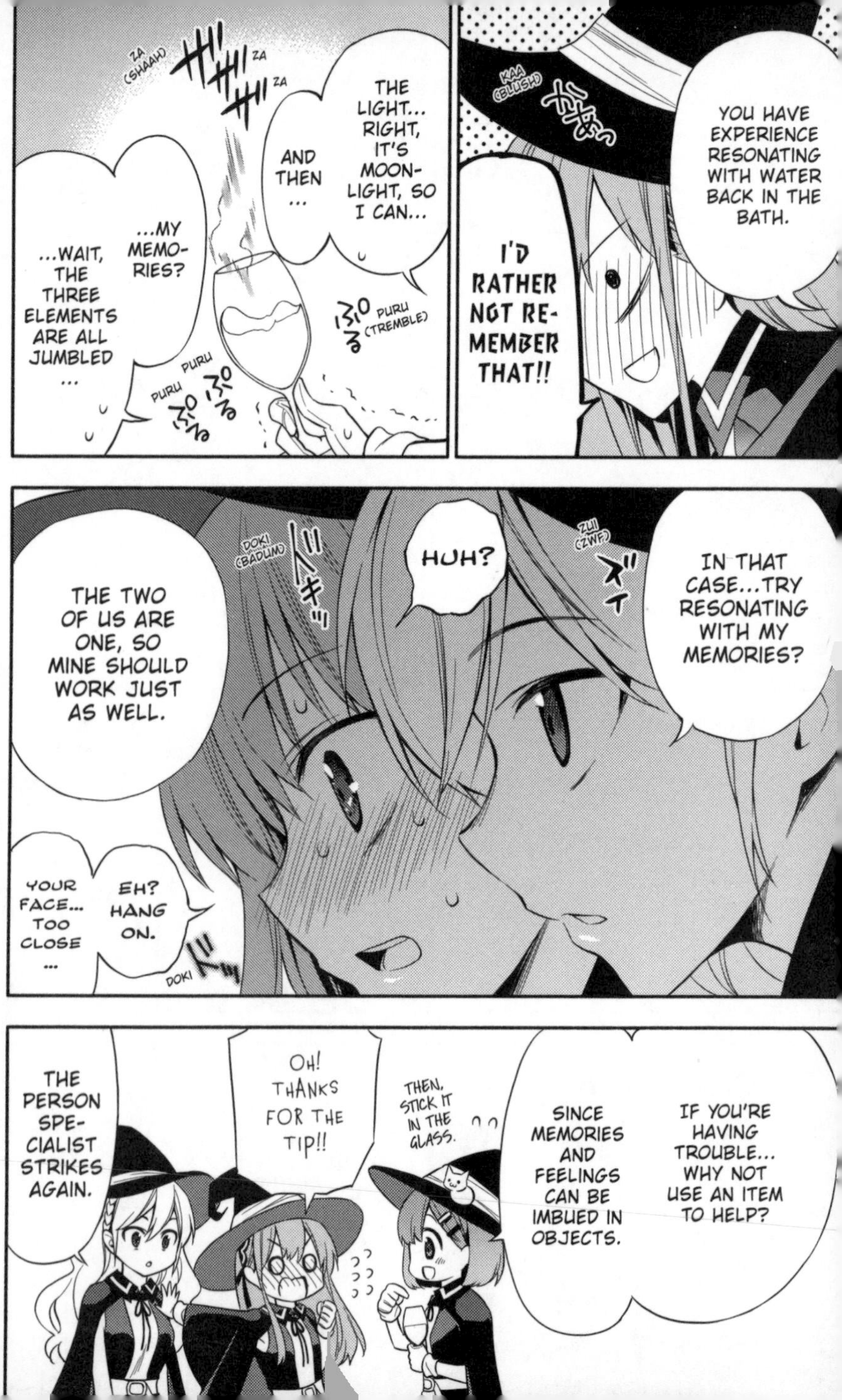
YOU HAVE EXPERIENCE RESONATING WITH WATER BACK IN THE BATH.
KAA (BLUSH)
I'D RATHER NOT RE-MEMBER THAT!!
THE LIGHT... RIGHT, IT'S MOON-LIGHT, SO I CAN...
AND THEN ...
ZA (SHAAH)
ZA
ZA
...MY MEMO-RIES?
...WAIT, THE THREE ELEMENTS ARE ALL JUMBLED ...
PURU (TREMBLE)
PURU
PURU
ZUI (ZWF)
IN THAT CASE...TRY RESONATING WITH MY MEMORIES?
HUH?
DOKI (BADUM)
THE TWO OF US ARE ONE, SO MINE SHOULD WORK JUST AS WELL.
EH? HANG ON.
YOUR FACE... TOO CLOSE ...
DOKI
IF YOU'RE HAVING TROUBLE... WHY NOT USE AN ITEM TO HELP?
SINCE MEMORIES AND FEELINGS CAN BE IMBUED IN OBJECTS.
THEN, STICK IT IN THE GLASS.
OH! THANKS FOR THE TIP!!
THE PERSON SPE-CIALIST STRIKES AGAIN.

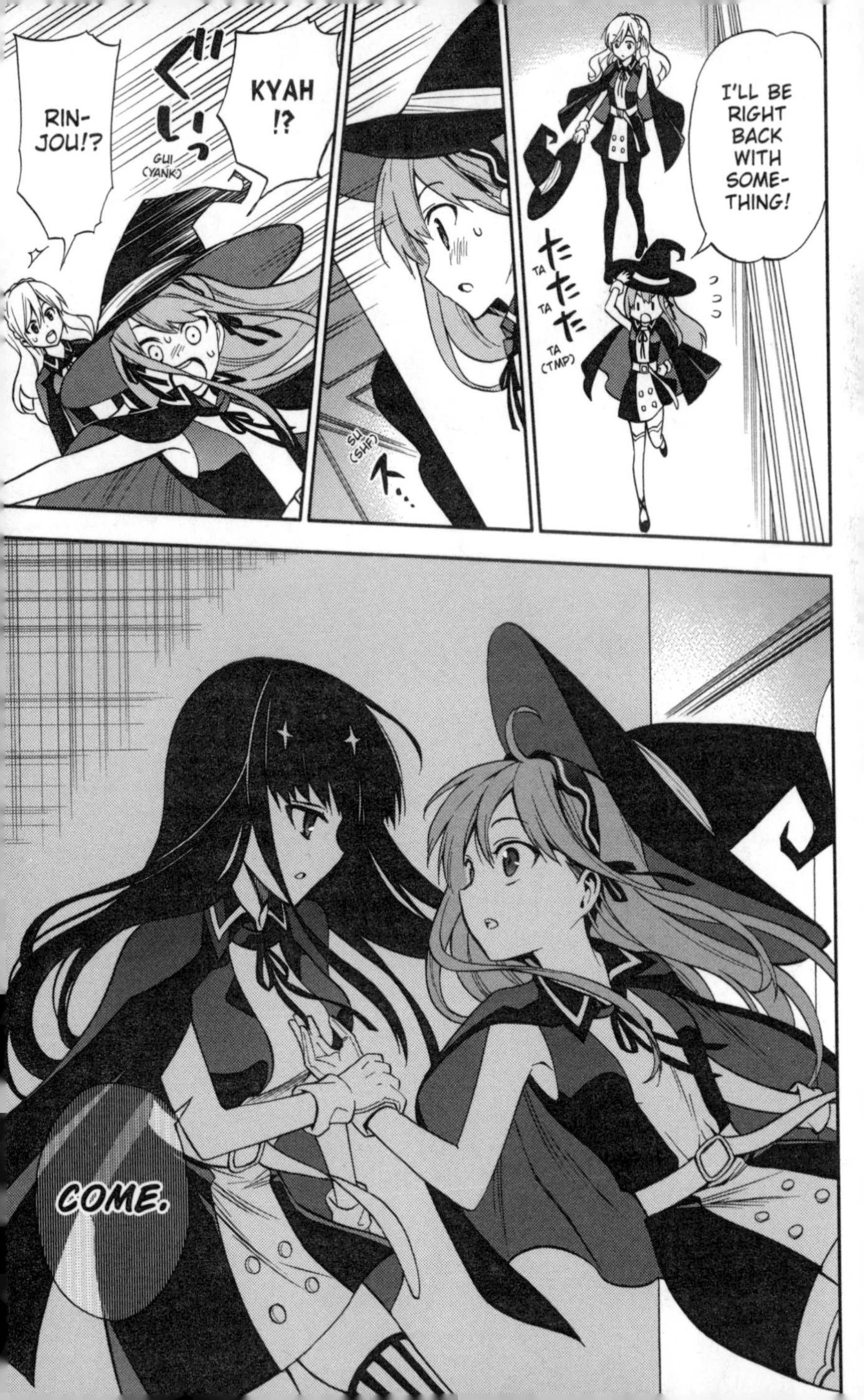
I'LL BE RIGHT BACK WITH SOMETHING!
たたた
TA TA TA (TMP)
SU (SHF)
KYAH!?
ぐいっ
GUI (YANK)
RIN-JOU!?
COME.

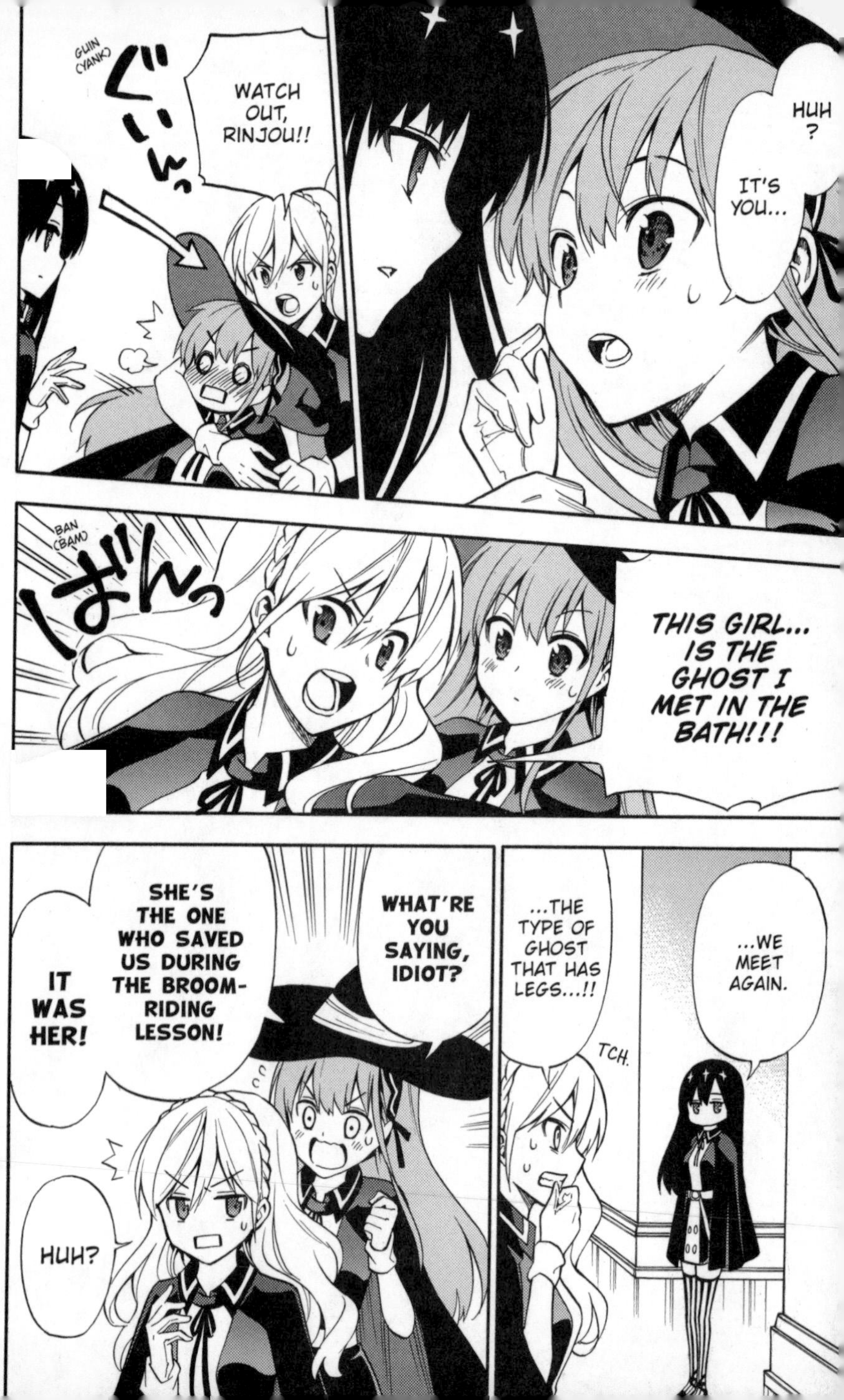
HUH?
IT'S YOU...
GUIN (YANK)
ぐいんっ
WATCH OUT, RINJOU!!
THIS GIRL... IS THE GHOST I MET IN THE BATH!!!
BAN (BAM)
ばんっ
...WE MEET AGAIN.
...THE TYPE OF GHOST THAT HAS LEGS...!!
TCH.
WHAT'RE YOU SAYING, IDIOT?
SHE'S THE ONE WHO SAVED US DURING THE BROOM-RIDING LESSON!
IT WAS HER!
HUH?

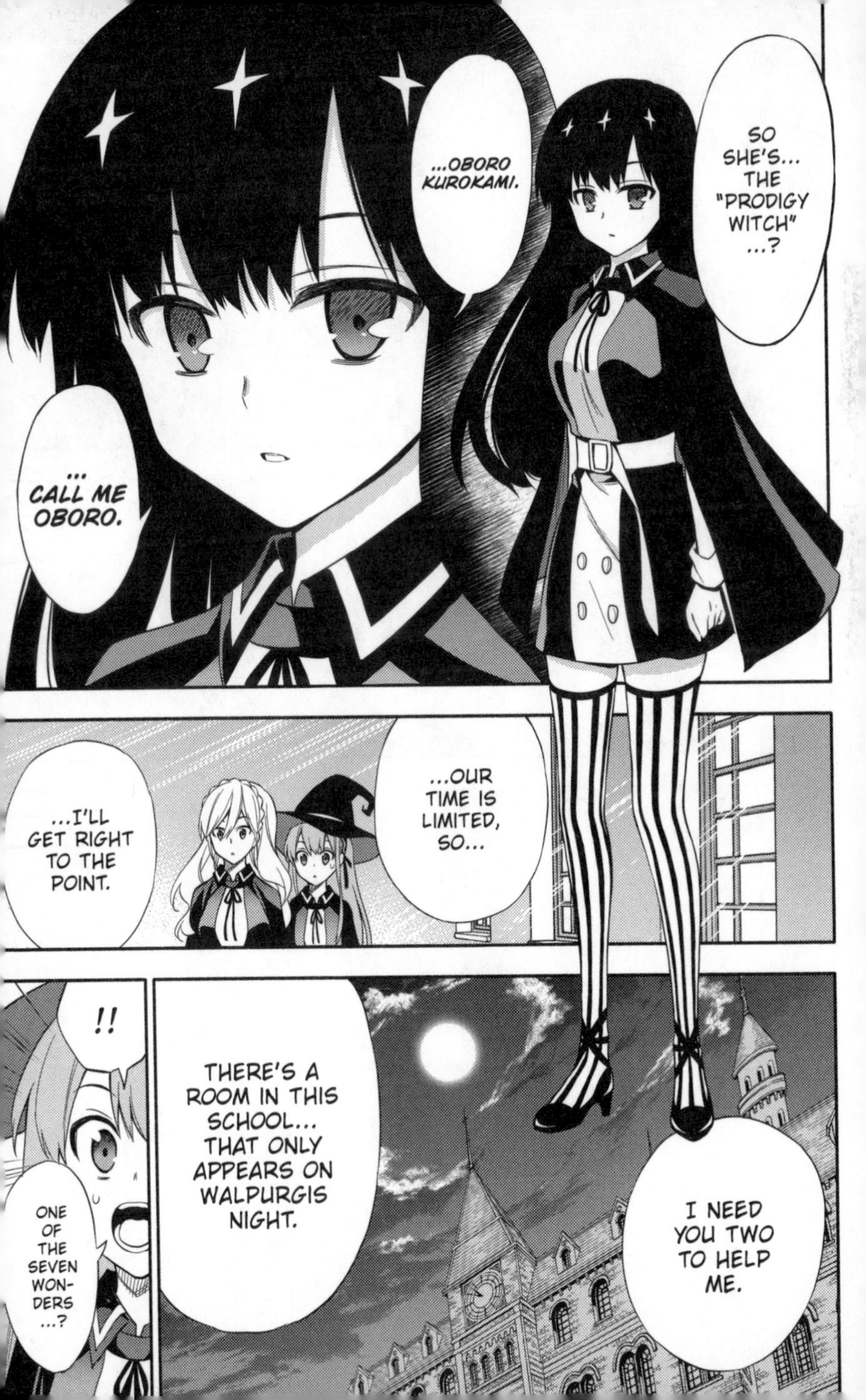
SO SHE'S... THE "PRODIGY WITCH" ...?
...OBORO KUROKAMI.
... CALL ME OBORO.
...OUR TIME IS LIMITED, SO...
...I'LL GET RIGHT TO THE POINT.
THERE'S A ROOM IN THIS SCHOOL... THAT ONLY APPEARS ON WALPURGIS NIGHT.
I NEED YOU TWO TO HELP ME.
!!
ONE OF THE SEVEN WON-DERS ...?

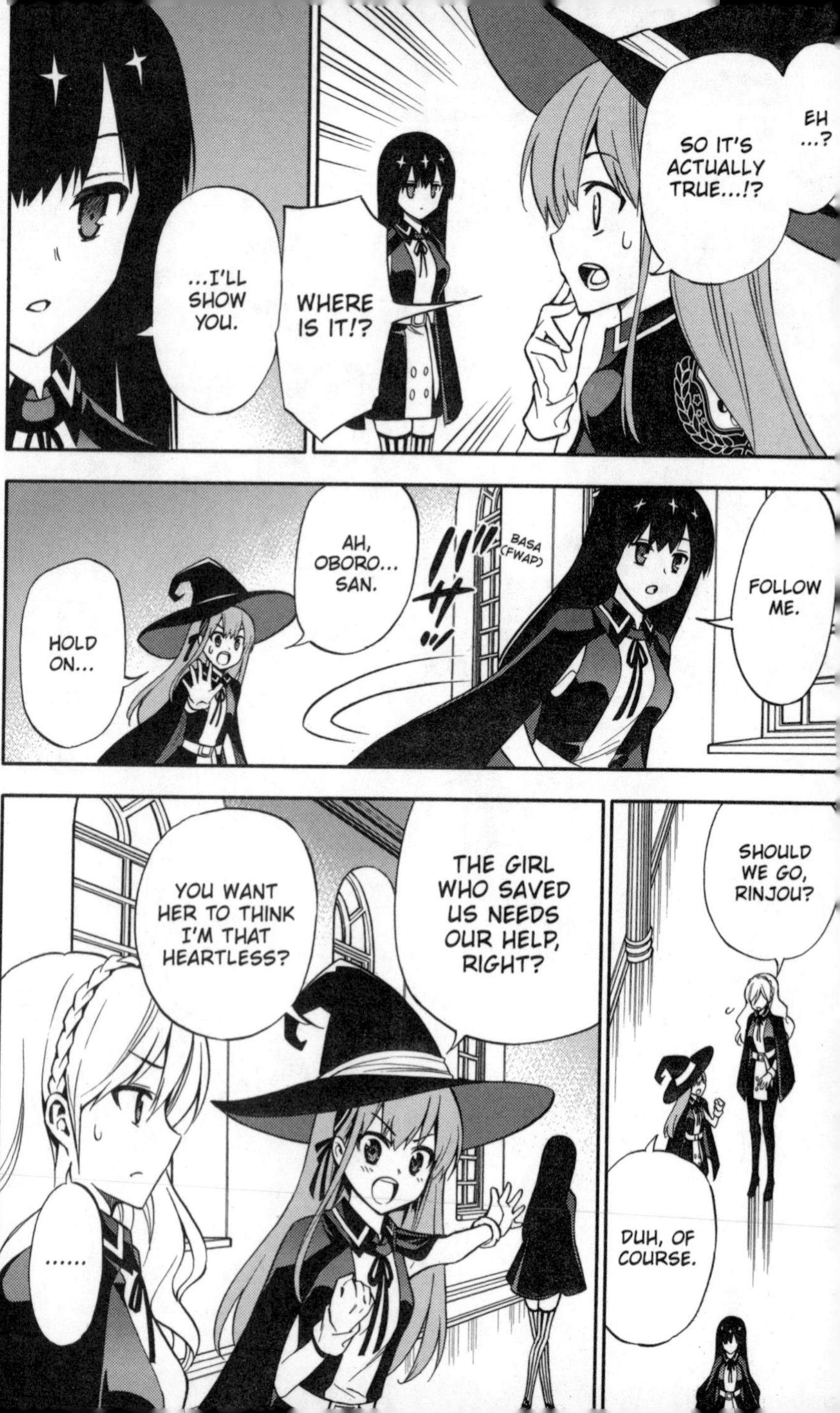
EH ...?
SO IT'S ACTUALLY TRUE...!?
WHERE IS IT!?
...I'LL SHOW YOU.
FOLLOW ME.
BASA (FWAP)
AH, OBORO... SAN.
HOLD ON...
SHOULD WE GO, RINJOU?
DUH, OF COURSE.
THE GIRL WHO SAVED US NEEDS OUR HELP, RIGHT?
YOU WANT HER TO THINK I'M THAT HEARTLESS?
......

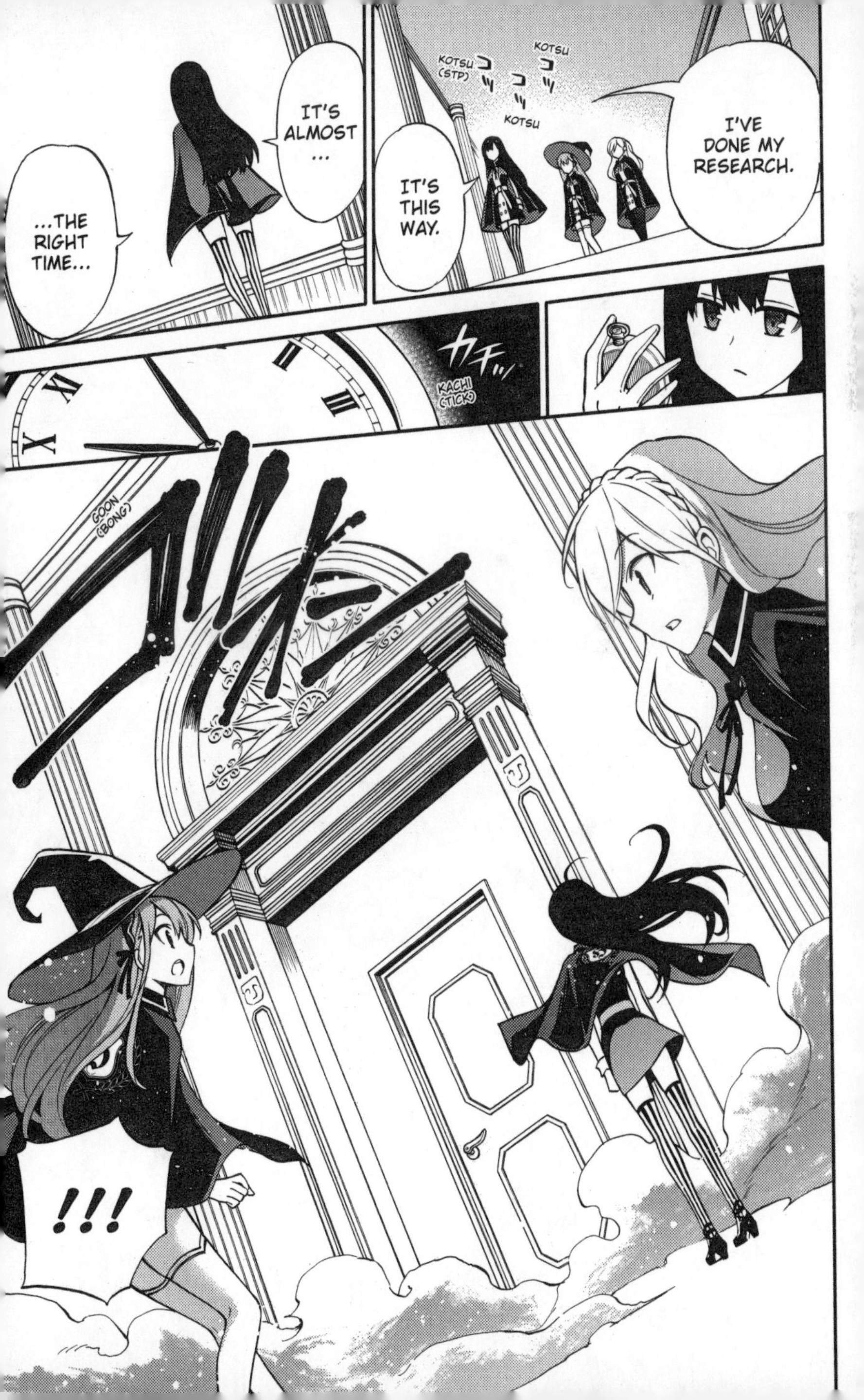
KOTSU
KOTSU (STP)
コツ
コツ
コツ
KOTSU
I'VE DONE MY RESEARCH.
IT'S THIS WAY.
IT'S ALMOST...
...THE RIGHT TIME...
カチッ
KACHI (TICK)
GOON (BONG)
!!!

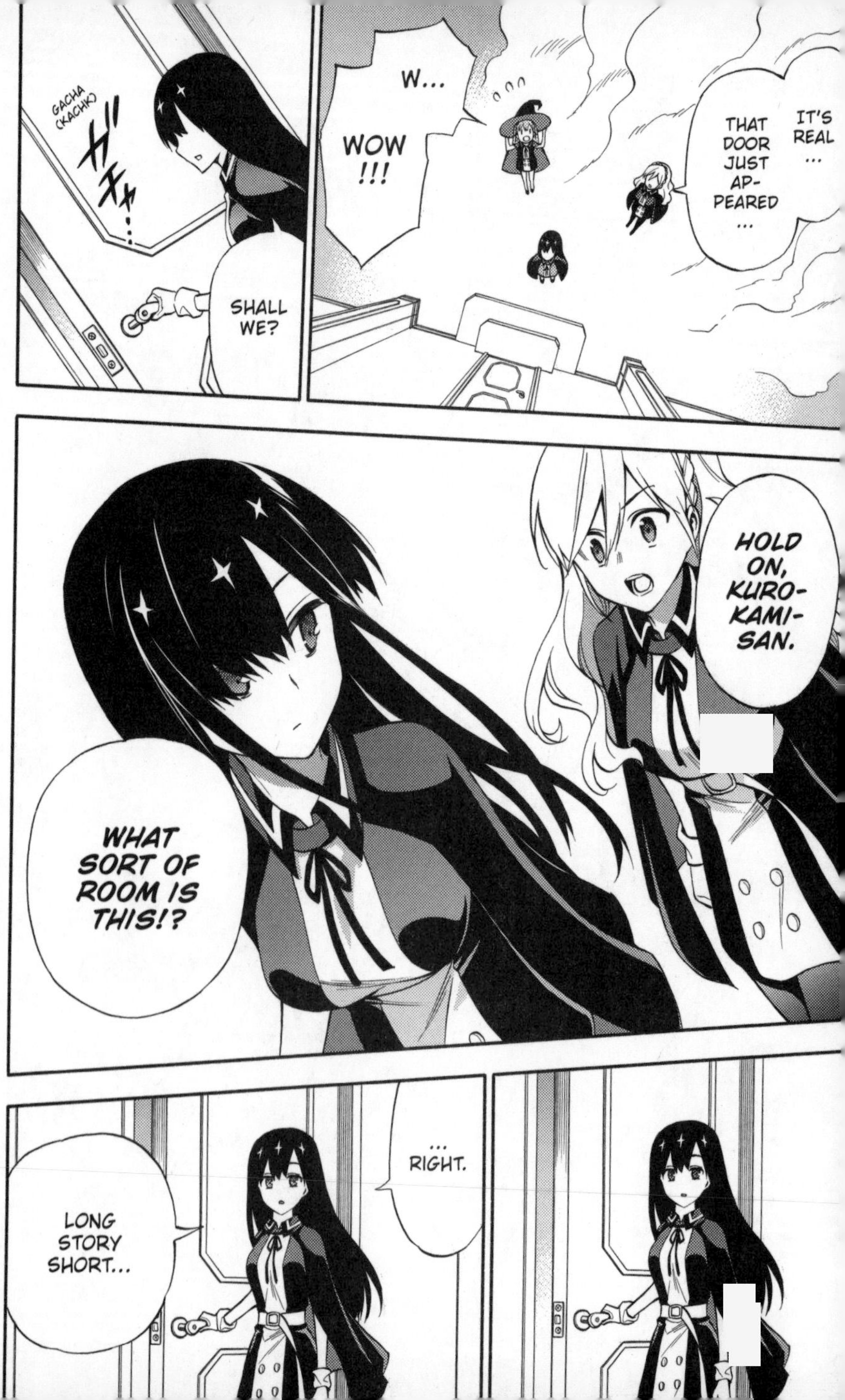
IT'S REAL ...
THAT DOOR JUST AP-PEARED ...
W...
WOW !!!
GACHA (KACHK)
ガチャ…
SHALL WE?
HOLD ON, KURO-KAMI-SAN.
WHAT SORT OF ROOM IS THIS!?
... RIGHT.
LONG STORY SHORT...

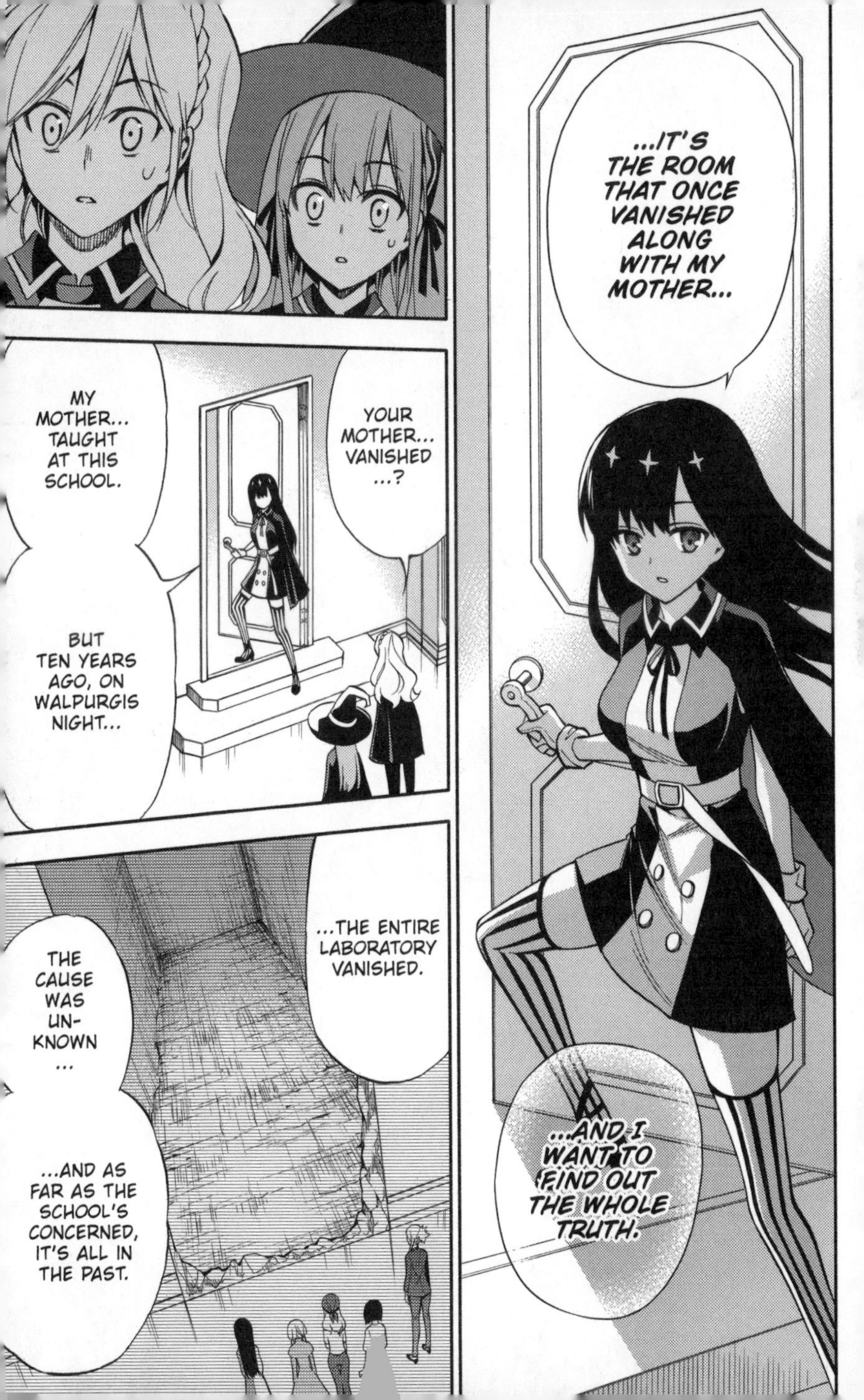
...IT'S THE ROOM THAT ONCE VANISHED ALONG WITH MY MOTHER...
...AND I WANT TO FIND OUT THE WHOLE TRUTH.
YOUR MOTHER... VANISHED ...?
MY MOTHER... TAUGHT AT THIS SCHOOL.
BUT TEN YEARS AGO, ON WALPURGIS NIGHT...
...THE ENTIRE LABORATORY VANISHED.
THE CAUSE WAS UN-KNOWN ...
...AND AS FAR AS THE SCHOOL'S CONCERNED, IT'S ALL IN THE PAST.

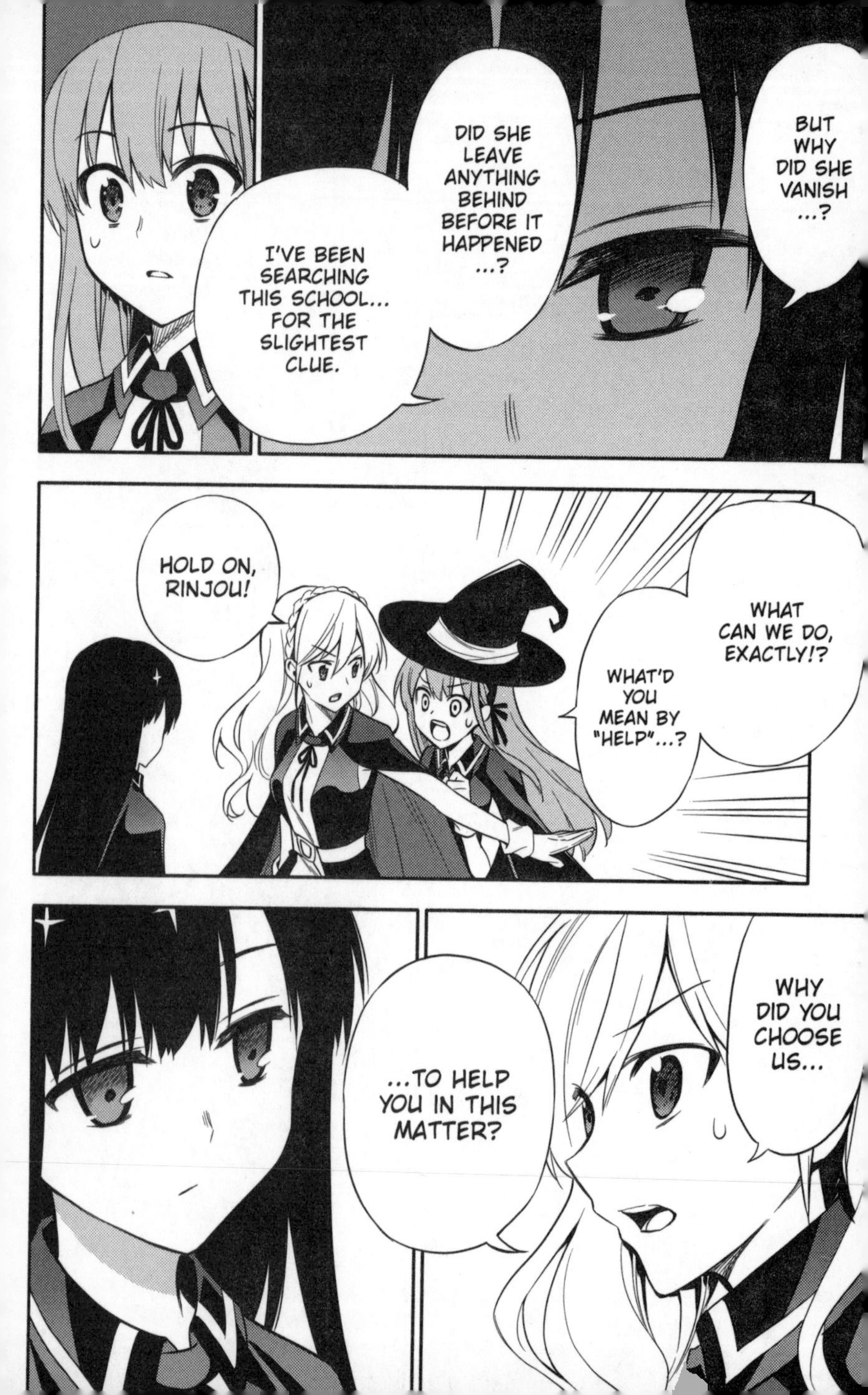
BUT WHY DID SHE VANISH ...?
DID SHE LEAVE ANYTHING BEHIND BEFORE IT HAPPENED ...?
I'VE BEEN SEARCHING THIS SCHOOL... FOR THE SLIGHTEST CLUE.
WHAT CAN WE DO, EXACTLY!?
WHAT'D YOU MEAN BY "HELP"...?
HOLD ON, RINJOU!
WHY DID YOU CHOOSE US...
...TO HELP YOU IN THIS MATTER?

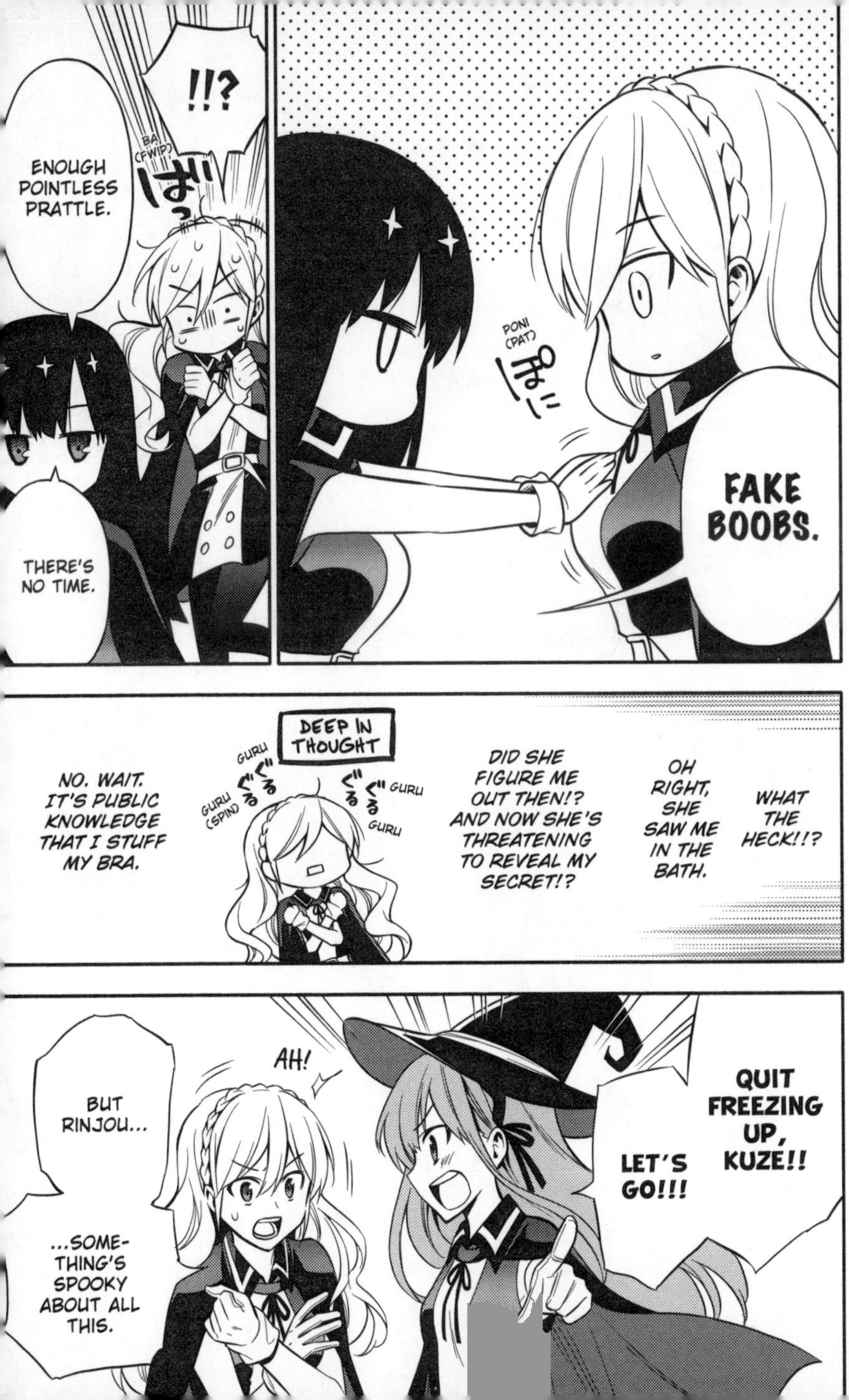
PONI (PAT) ぽに
FAKE BOOBS.
!!?
BA (FWIP) ばっ
ENOUGH POINTLESS PRATTLE.
THERE'S NO TIME.
WHAT THE HECK!!?
OH RIGHT, SHE SAW ME IN THE BATH.
DID SHE FIGURE ME OUT THEN!? AND NOW SHE'S THREATENING TO REVEAL MY SECRET!?
GURU ぐる GURU ぐる
DEEP IN THOUGHT
GURU ぐる GURU (SPIN) ぐる
NO. WAIT. IT'S PUBLIC KNOWLEDGE THAT I STUFF MY BRA.
QUIT FREEZING UP, KUZE!!
LET'S GO!!!
AH!
BUT RINJOU...
...SOME-THING'S SPOOKY ABOUT ALL THIS.

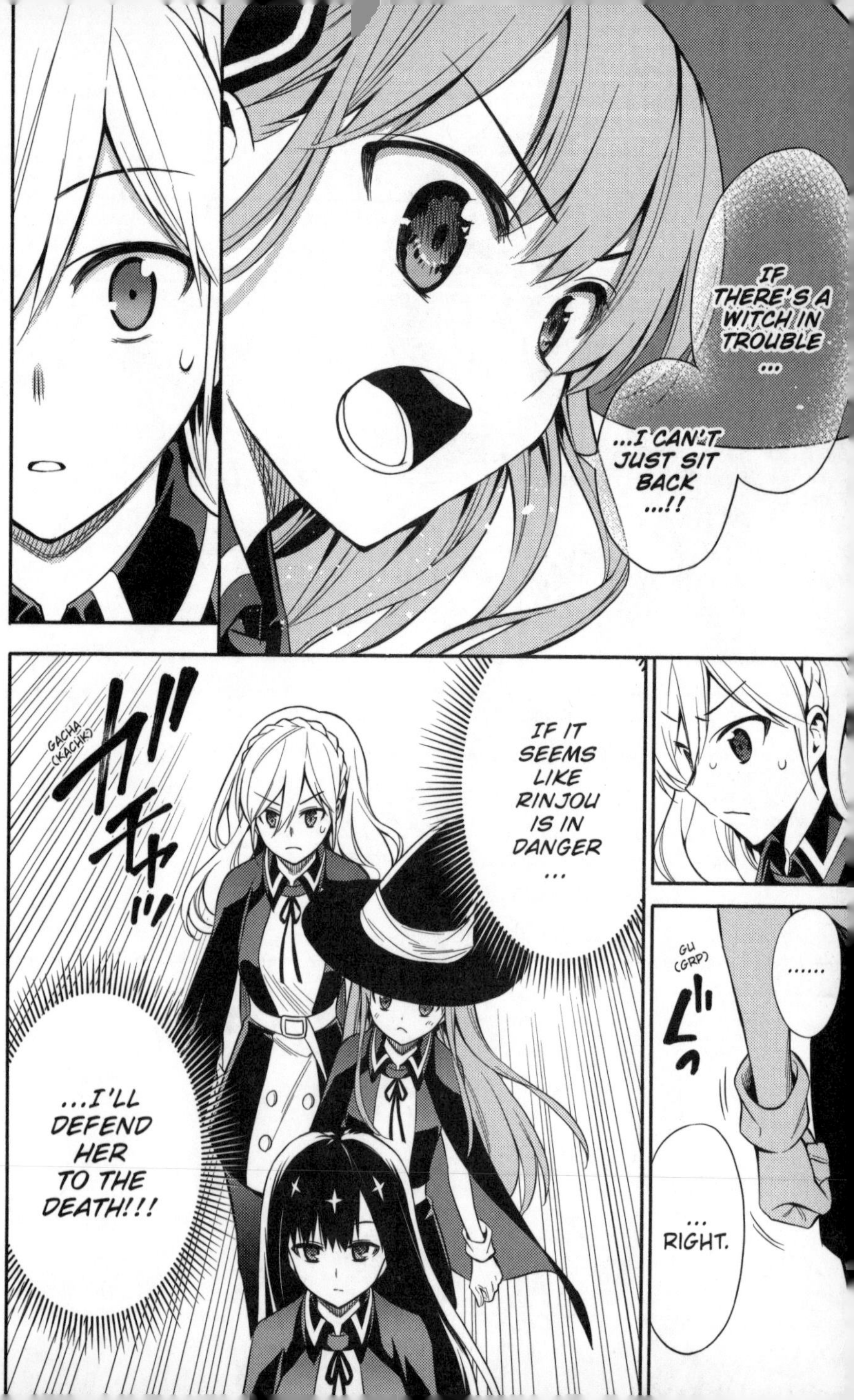
IF THERE'S A WITCH IN TROUBLE ...
...I CAN'T JUST SIT BACK ...!!
GU (GRP)
......
... RIGHT.
GACHA (KACHK)
IF IT SEEMS LIKE RINJOU IS IN DANGER ...
...I'LL DEFEND HER TO THE DEATH!!!

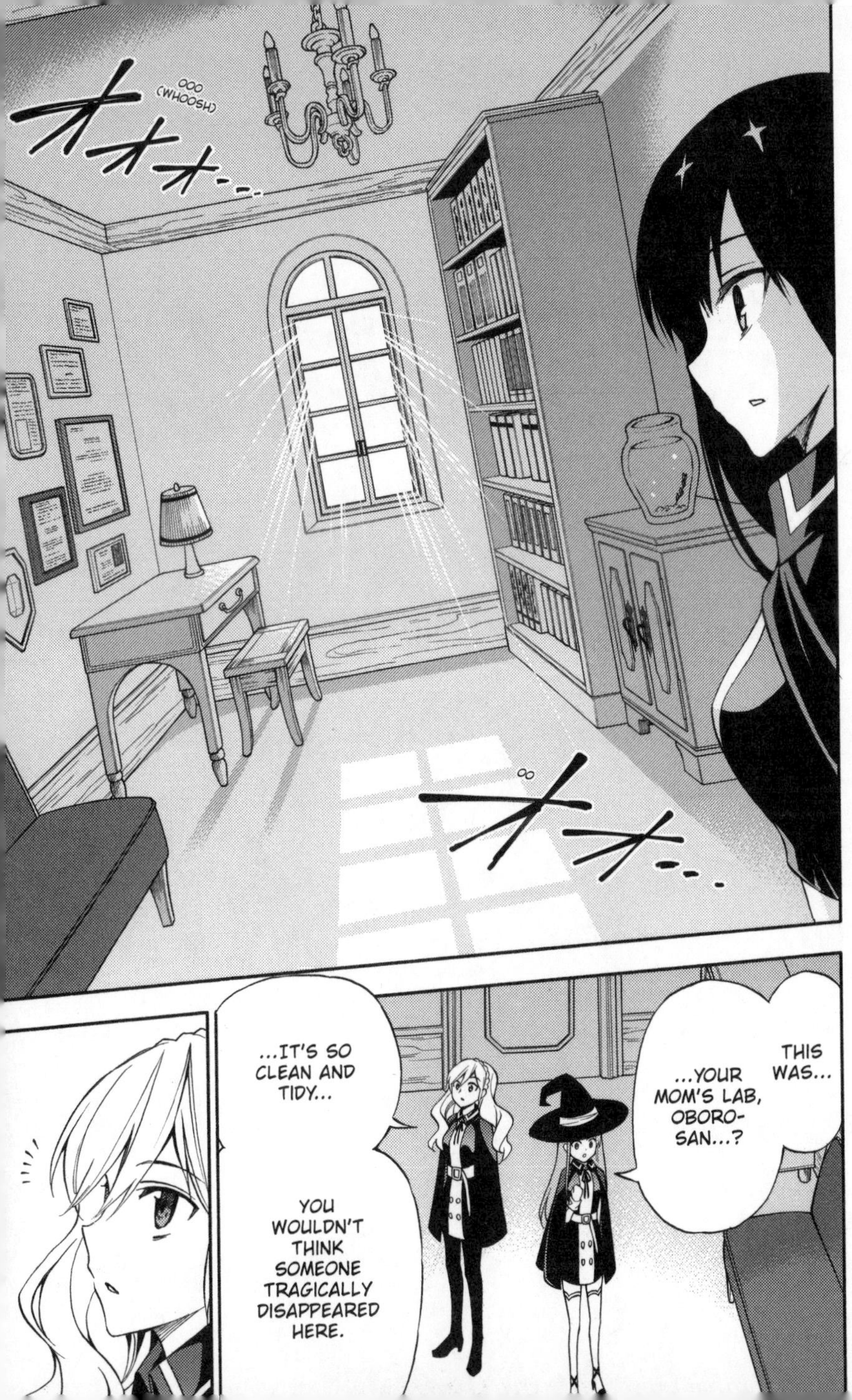
オオオ…
OOO (WHOOSH)
オオ…
OO
THIS WAS...
...YOUR MOM'S LAB, OBORO-SAN...?
...IT'S SO CLEAN AND TIDY...
YOU WOULDN'T THINK SOMEONE TRAGICALLY DISAPPEARED HERE.

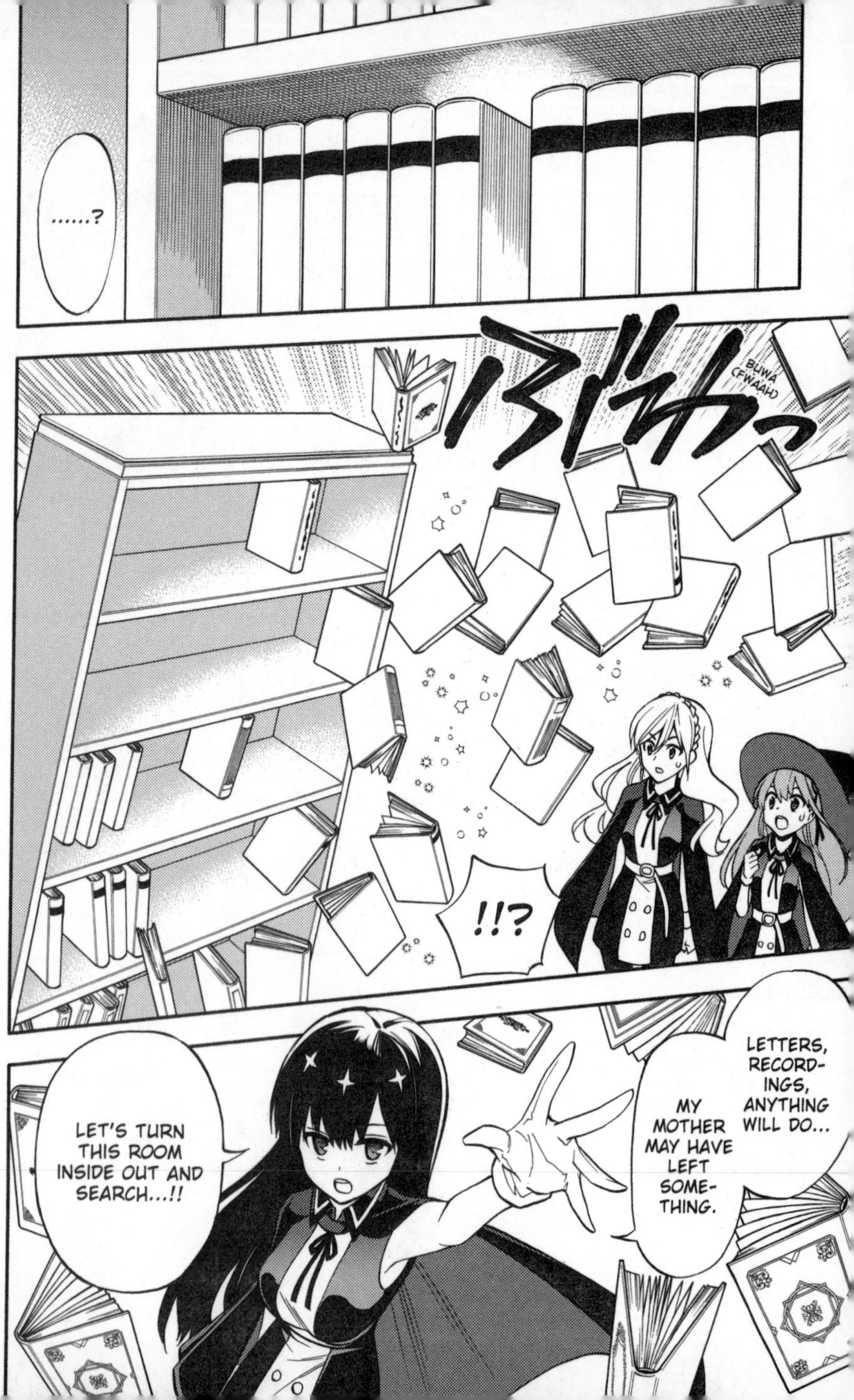
......?
ぶわっ
BUWA (FWAAH)
!!?
LETTERS, RECORD-INGS, ANYTHING WILL DO...
MY MOTHER MAY HAVE LEFT SOME-THING.
LET'S TURN THIS ROOM INSIDE OUT AND SEARCH...!!

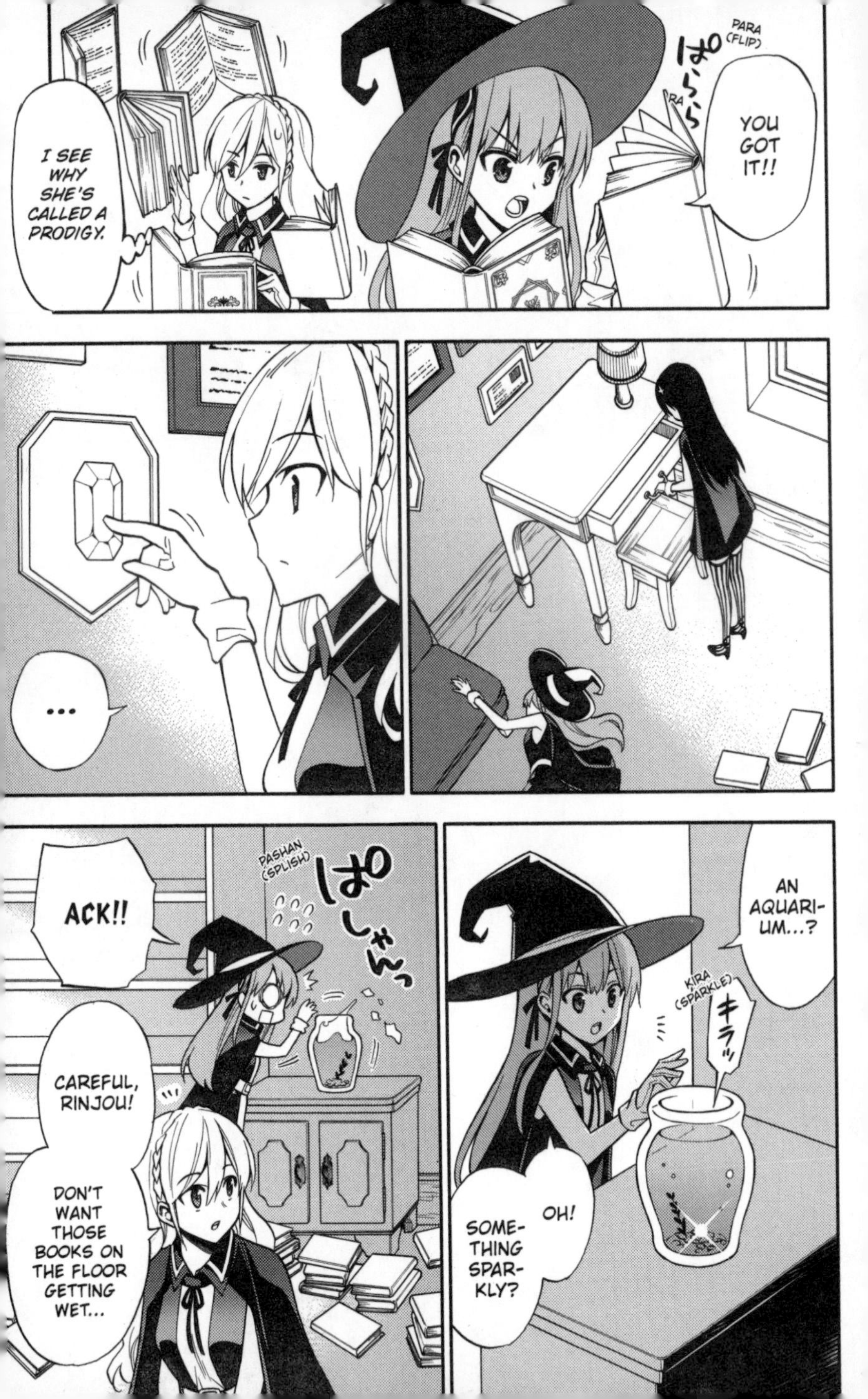
PARA (FLIP)
ぱららら
RA
YOU GOT IT!!
I SEE WHY SHE'S CALLED A PRODIGY.
...
AN AQUARI-UM...?
KIRA (SPARKLE)
キラッ
OH!
SOME-THING SPAR-KLY?
PASHAN (SPLISH)
ぱしゃんっ
ACK!!
CAREFUL, RINJOU!
DON'T WANT THOSE BOOKS ON THE FLOOR GETTING WET...

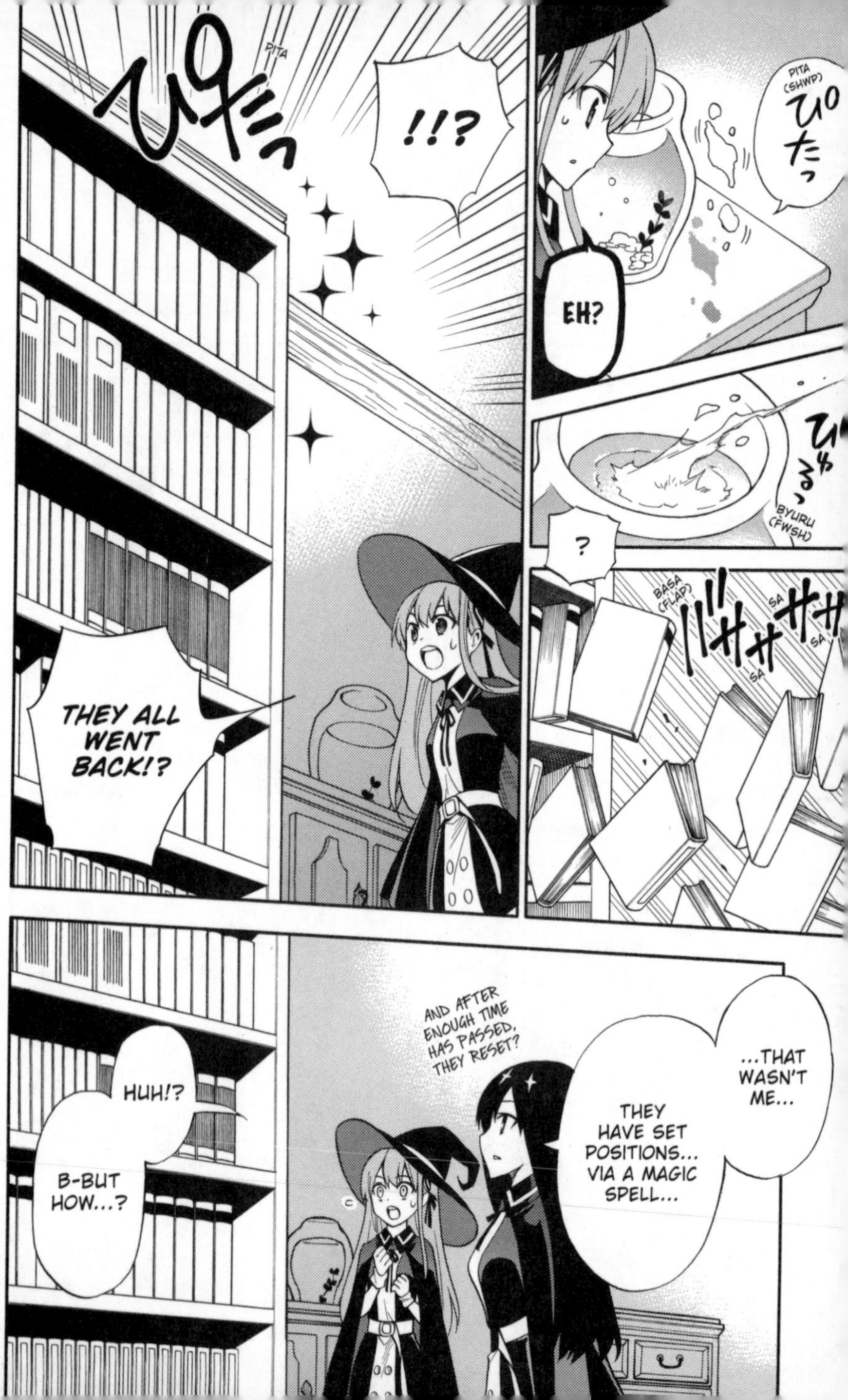

PITA (SHWP)
ぴたっ
EH?
ひゅるっ
BYURU (FWSH)
?
BASA (FLAP)
SA
SA
SA
PITA
!!?
THEY ALL WENT BACK!?
...THAT WASN'T ME...
THEY HAVE SET POSITIONS... VIA A MAGIC SPELL...
AND AFTER ENOUGH TIME HAS PASSED, THEY RESET?
HUH!?
B-BUT HOW...?

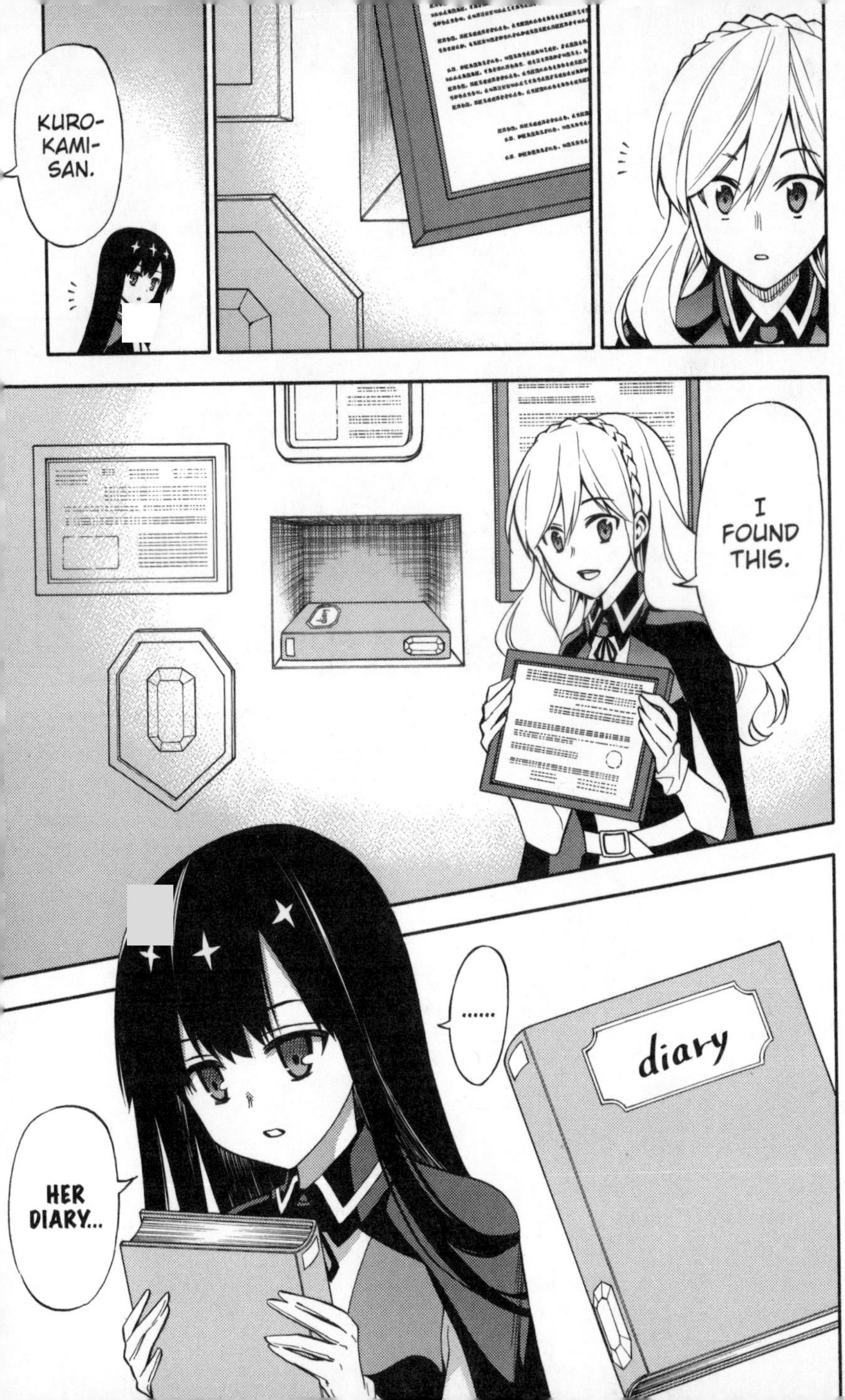
KURO-KAMI-SAN.
I FOUND THIS.
......
diary
HER DIARY...

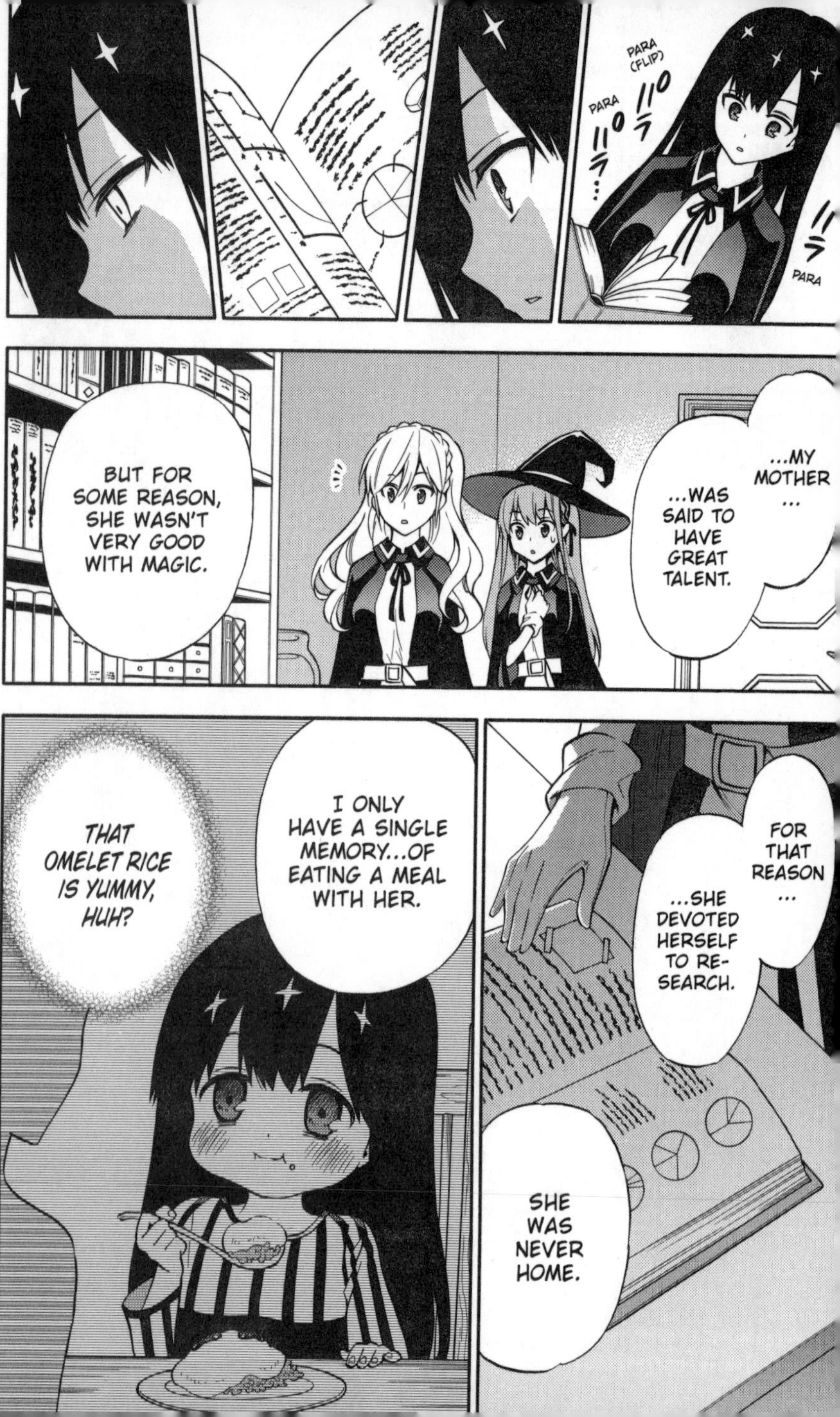

PARA (FLIP)
PARA
PARA
...MY MOTHER ...
...WAS SAID TO HAVE GREAT TALENT.
BUT FOR SOME REASON, SHE WASN'T VERY GOOD WITH MAGIC.
FOR THAT REASON ...
...SHE DEVOTED HERSELF TO RE-SEARCH.
SHE WAS NEVER HOME.
I ONLY HAVE A SINGLE MEMORY...OF EATING A MEAL WITH HER.
THAT OMELET RICE IS YUMMY, HUH?

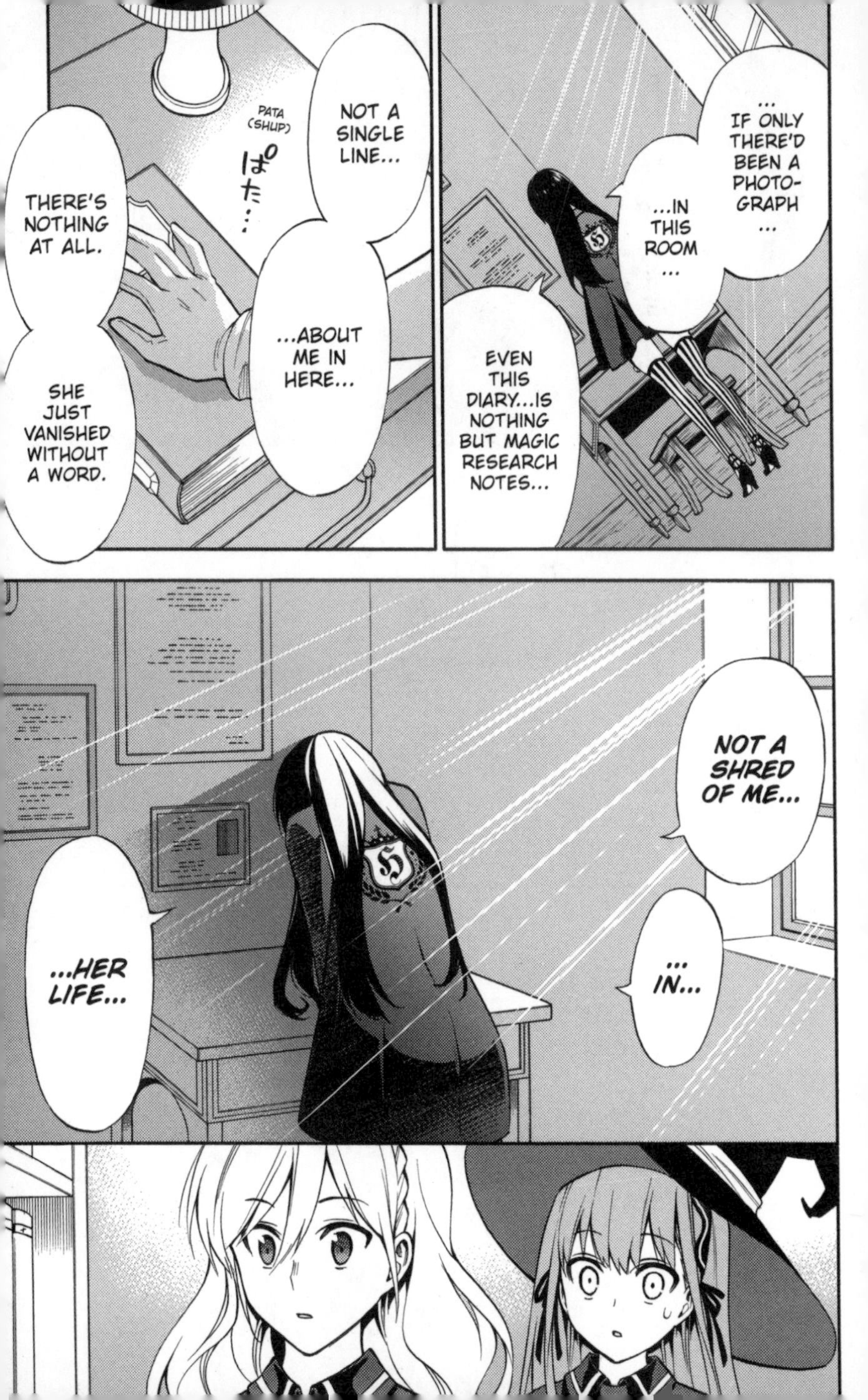
...IF ONLY THERE'D BEEN A PHOTOGRAPH...
...IN THIS ROOM...
EVEN THIS DIARY...IS NOTHING BUT MAGIC RESEARCH NOTES...
NOT A SINGLE LINE...
...ABOUT ME IN HERE...
ぱた…
PATA (SHUP)
THERE'S NOTHING AT ALL.
SHE JUST VANISHED WITHOUT A WORD.
NOT A SHRED OF ME...
...IN...
...HER LIFE...

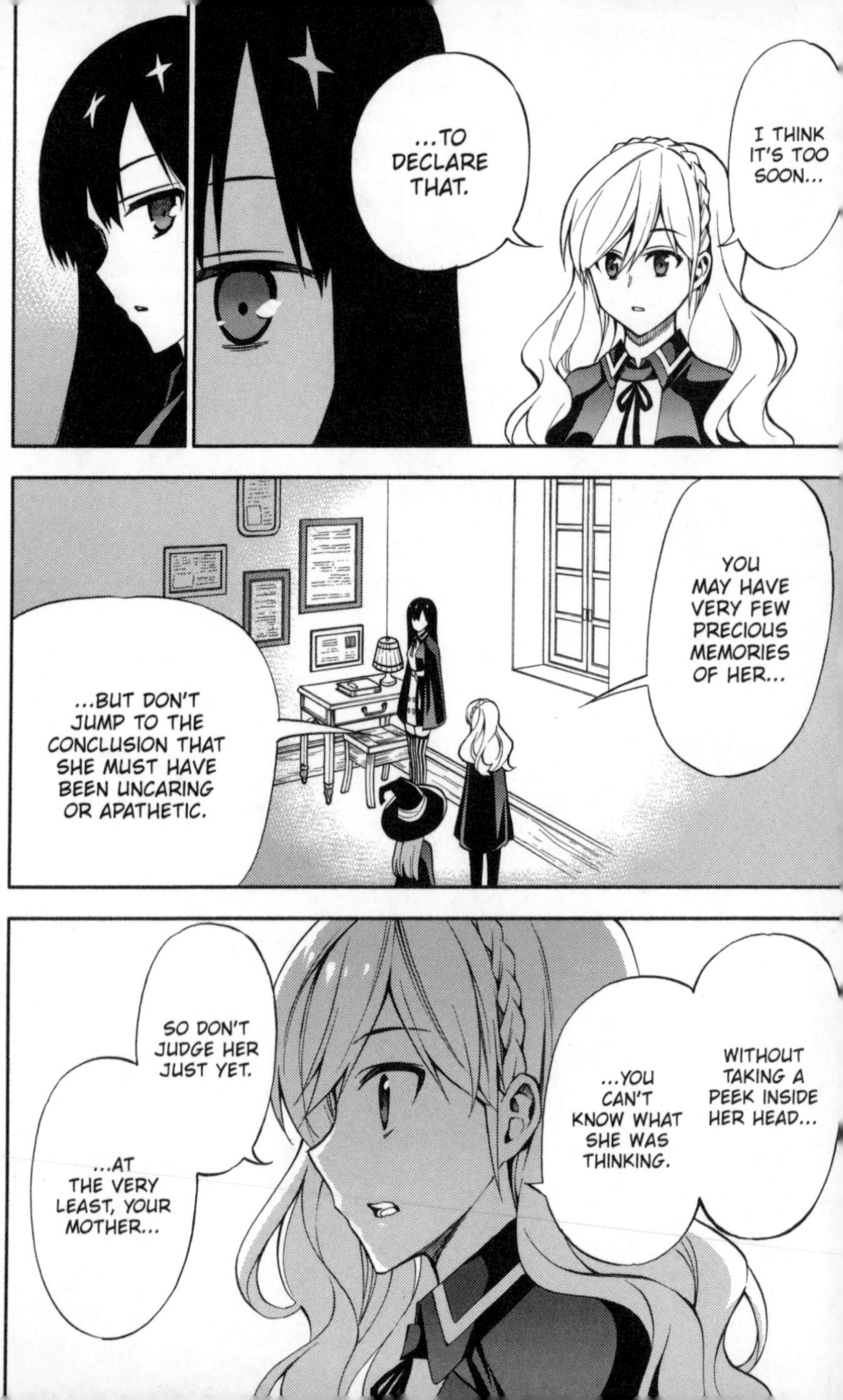
I THINK IT'S TOO SOON...
...TO DECLARE THAT.
YOU MAY HAVE VERY FEW PRECIOUS MEMORIES OF HER...
...BUT DON'T JUMP TO THE CONCLUSION THAT SHE MUST HAVE BEEN UNCARING OR APATHETIC.
WITHOUT TAKING A PEEK INSIDE HER HEAD...
...YOU CAN'T KNOW WHAT SHE WAS THINKING.
SO DON'T JUDGE HER JUST YET.
...AT THE VERY LEAST, YOUR MOTHER...

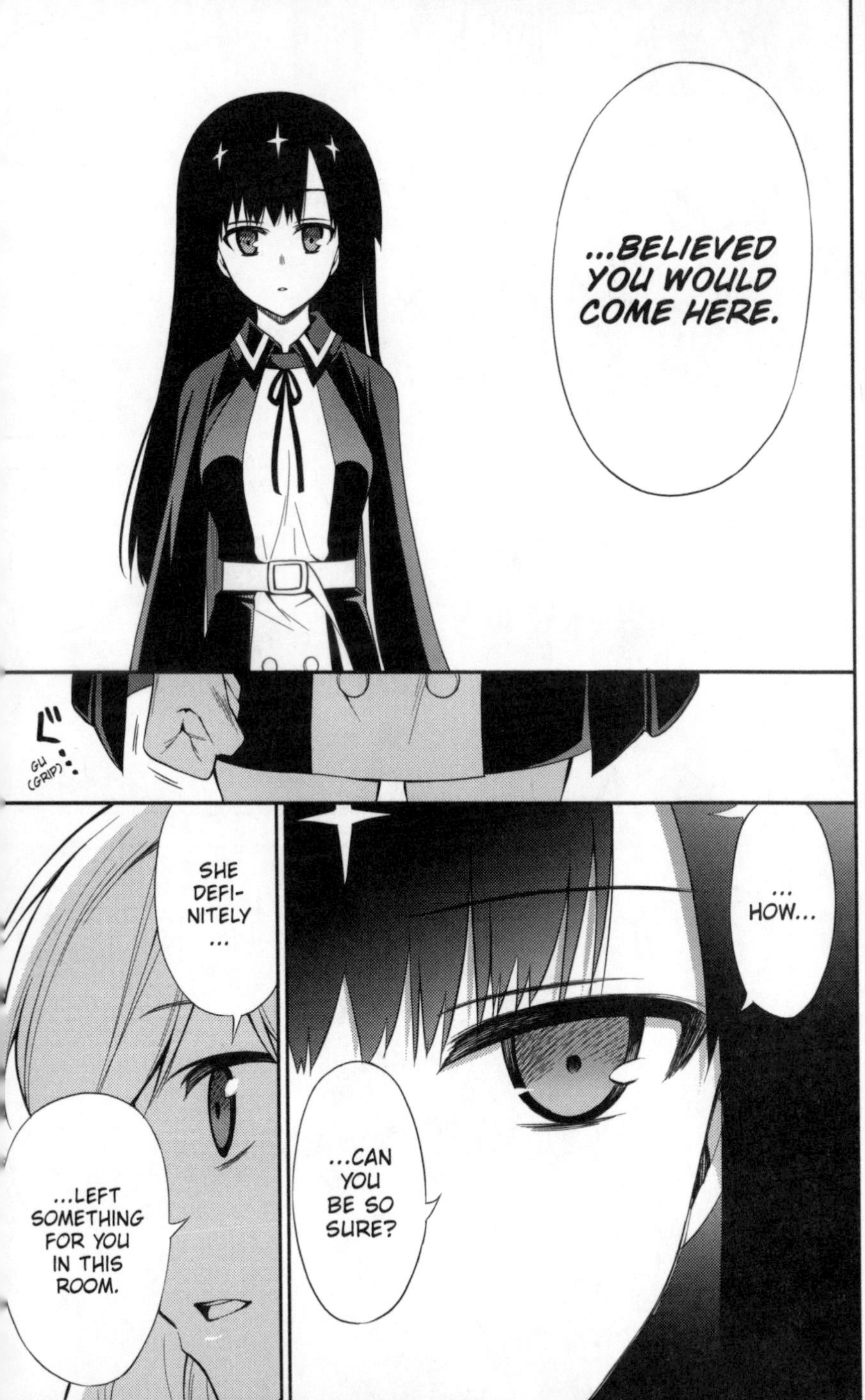
...BELIEVED YOU WOULD COME HERE.
ぐ
GU (GRIP)
...HOW...
...CAN YOU BE SO SURE?
SHE DEFI-NITELY...
...LEFT SOMETHING FOR YOU IN THIS ROOM.

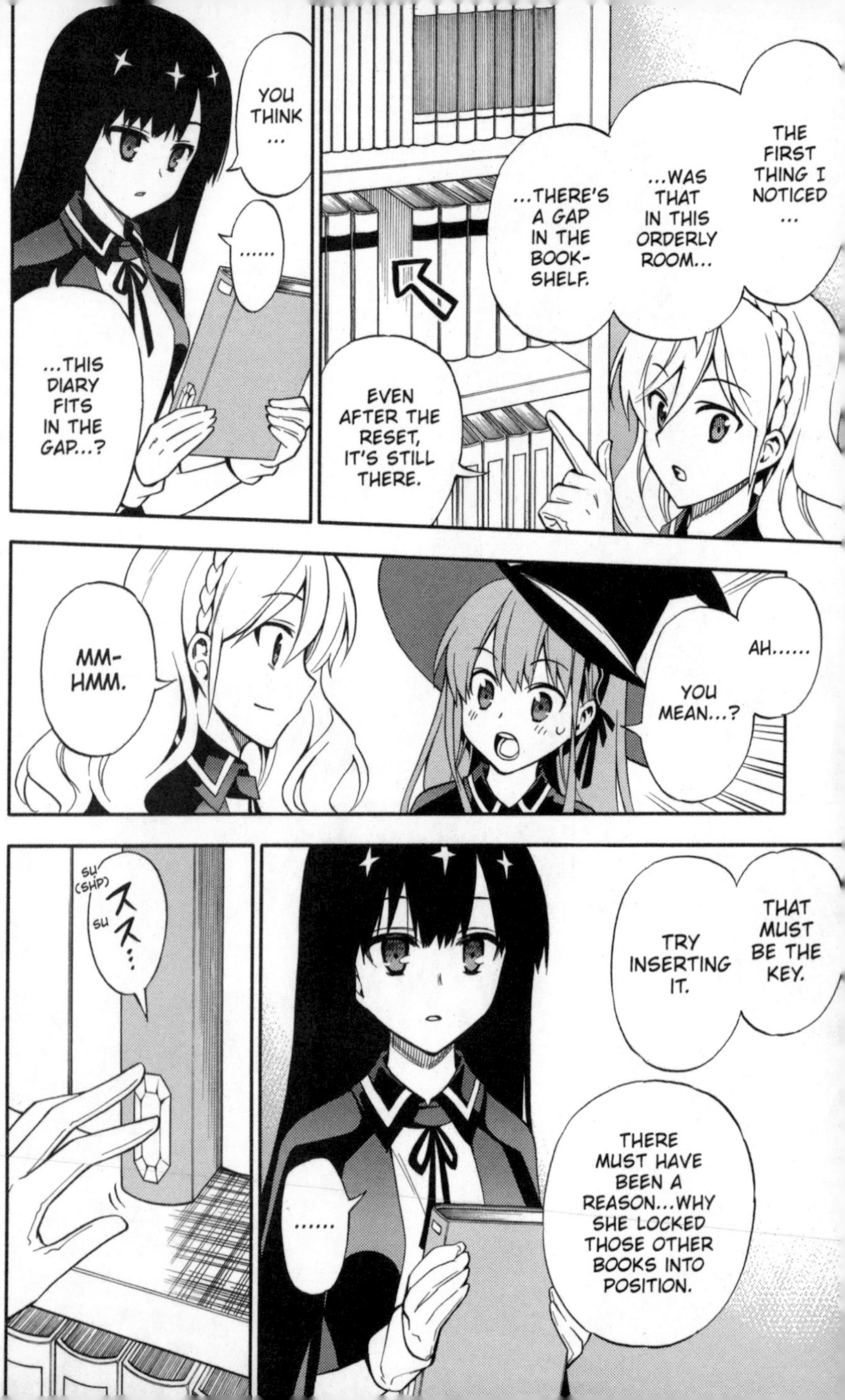
THE FIRST THING I NOTICED ...
...WAS THAT IN THIS ORDERLY ROOM...
...THERE'S A GAP IN THE BOOK-SHELF.
EVEN AFTER THE RESET, IT'S STILL THERE.
YOU THINK ...
......
...THIS DIARY FITS IN THE GAP...?
AH......
YOU MEAN...?
MM-HMM.
THAT MUST BE THE KEY.
TRY INSERTING IT.
THERE MUST HAVE BEEN A REASON...WHY SHE LOCKED THOSE OTHER BOOKS INTO POSITION.
......
スス…
SU SU (SHP)

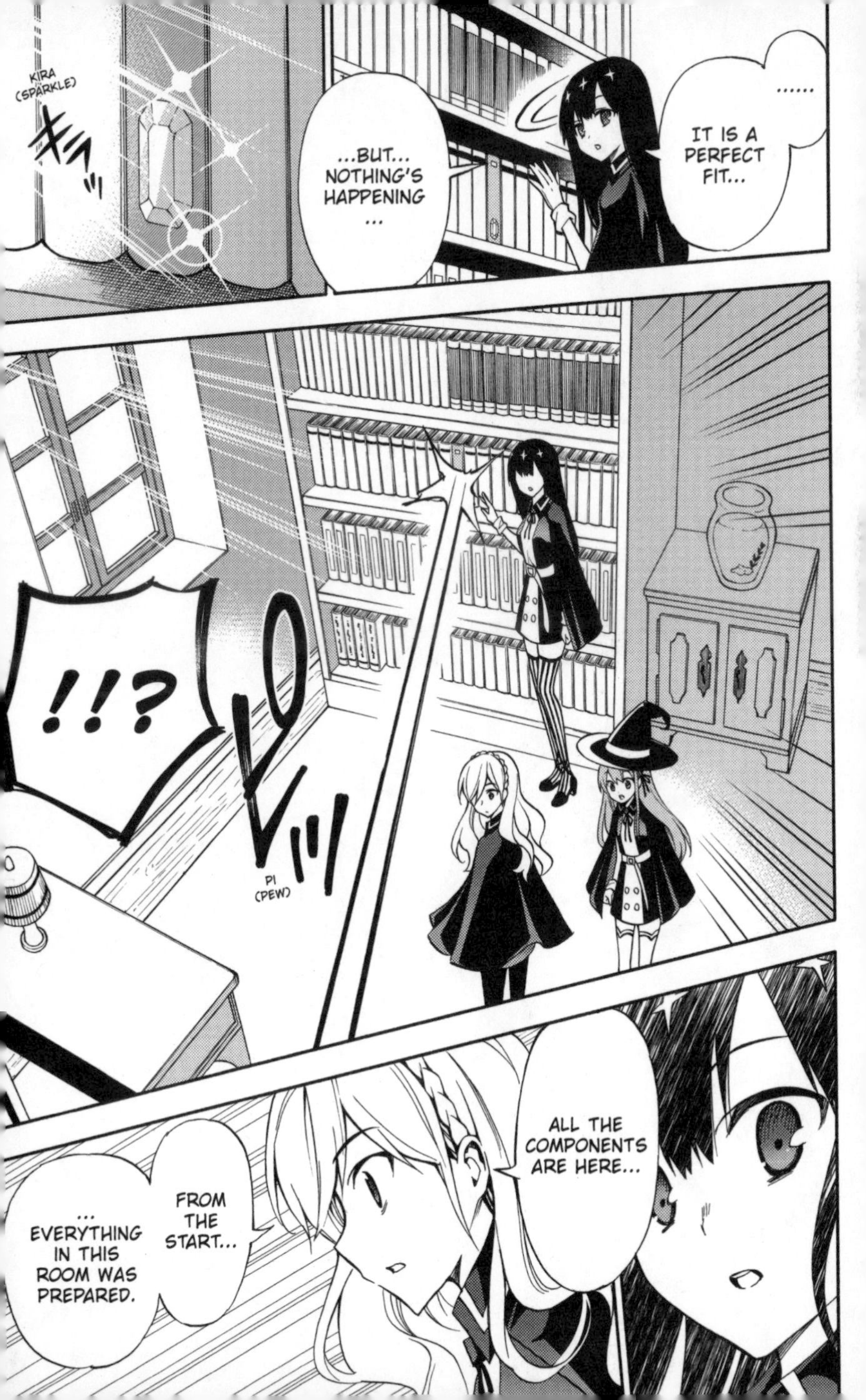
......
IT IS A PERFECT FIT...
...BUT... NOTHING'S HAPPENING ...
KIRA (SPÄRKLE)
!!?
PI (PEW)
ALL THE COMPONENTS ARE HERE...
FROM THE START...
... EVERYTHING IN THIS ROOM WAS PREPARED.

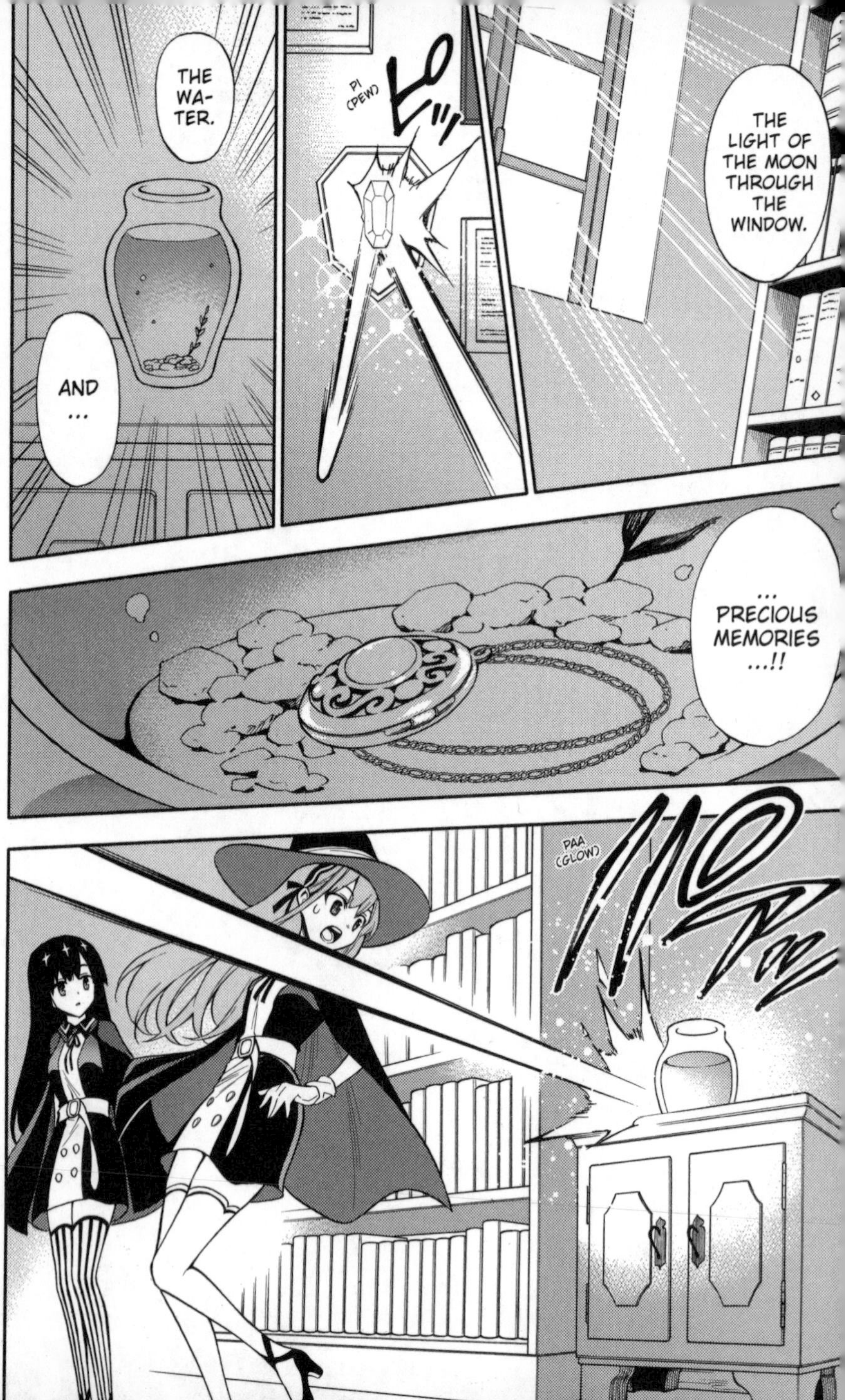
THE LIGHT OF THE MOON THROUGH THE WINDOW.
PI (PEW)
THE WA-TER.
AND ...
... PRECIOUS MEMORIES ...!!
PAA (GLOW)

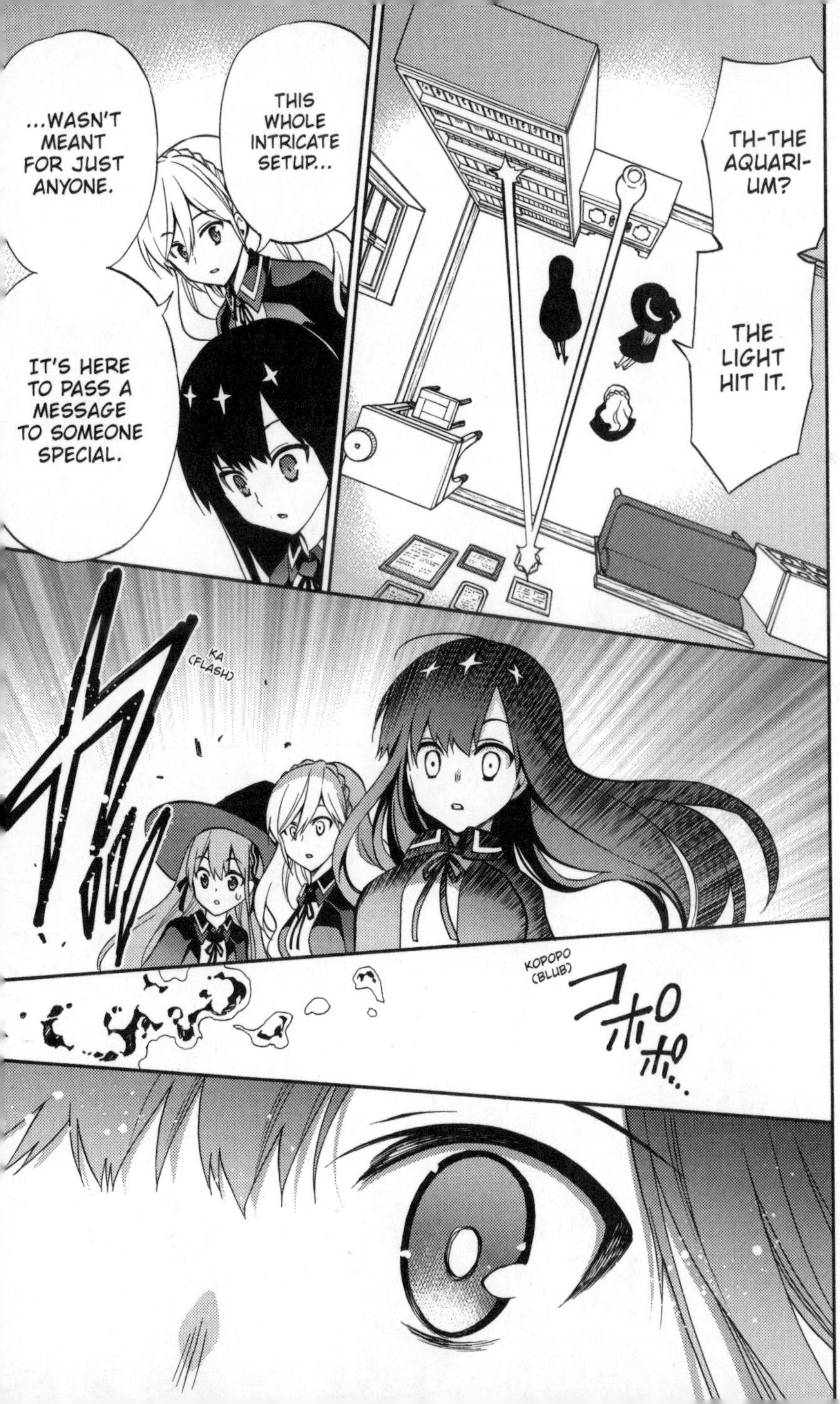
TH-THE AQUARI-UM?
THE LIGHT HIT IT.
THIS WHOLE INTRICATE SETUP...
...WASN'T MEANT FOR JUST ANYONE.
IT'S HERE TO PASS A MESSAGE TO SOMEONE SPECIAL.
KA (FLASH)
KOPOPO (BLUB)
コポポ...

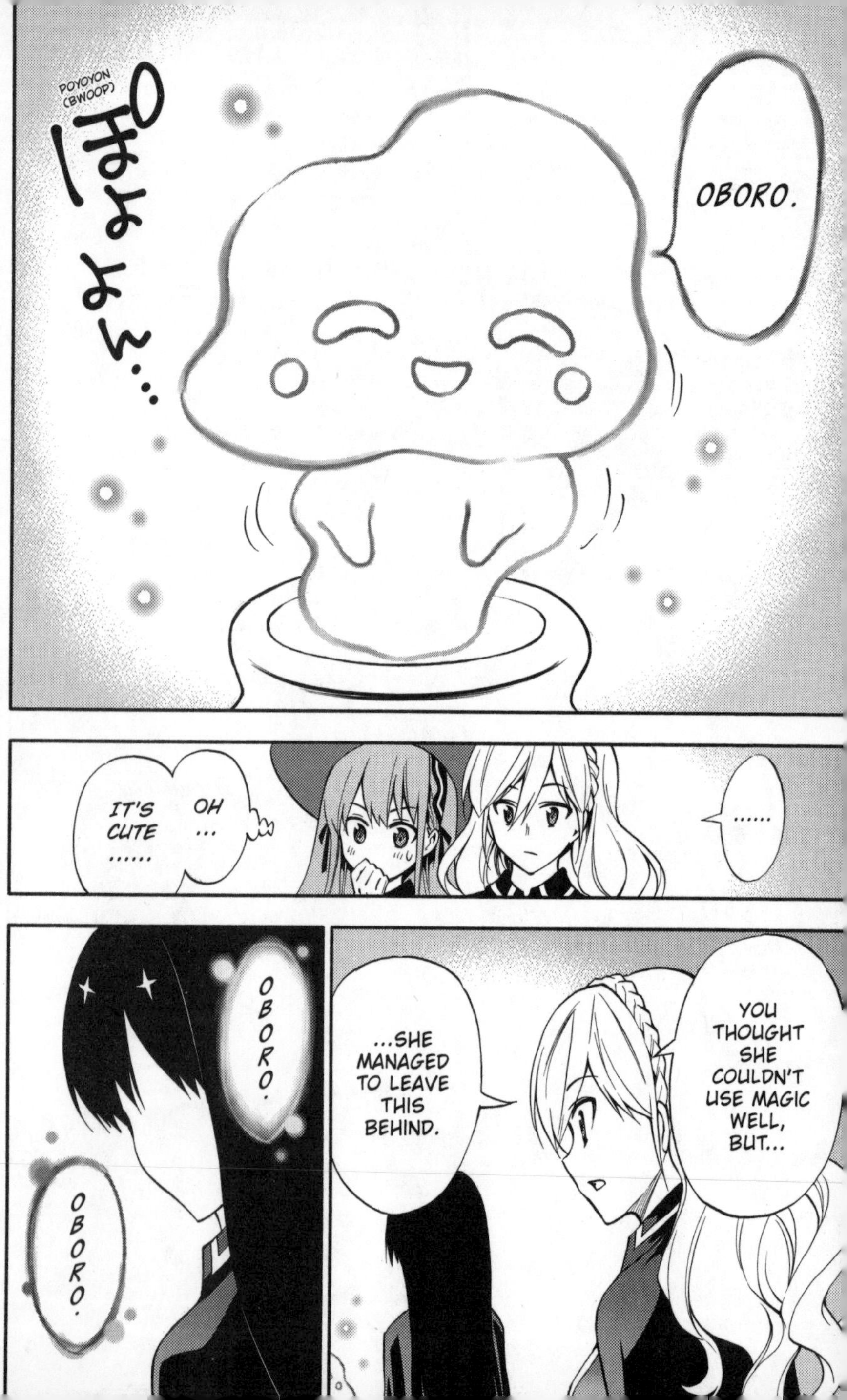
OBORO.
POYOYON (BWOOP)
ぽよよん…
......
OH ...
IT'S CUTE ......
YOU THOUGHT SHE COULDN'T USE MAGIC WELL, BUT...
...SHE MANAGED TO LEAVE THIS BEHIND.
OBORO.
OBORO.

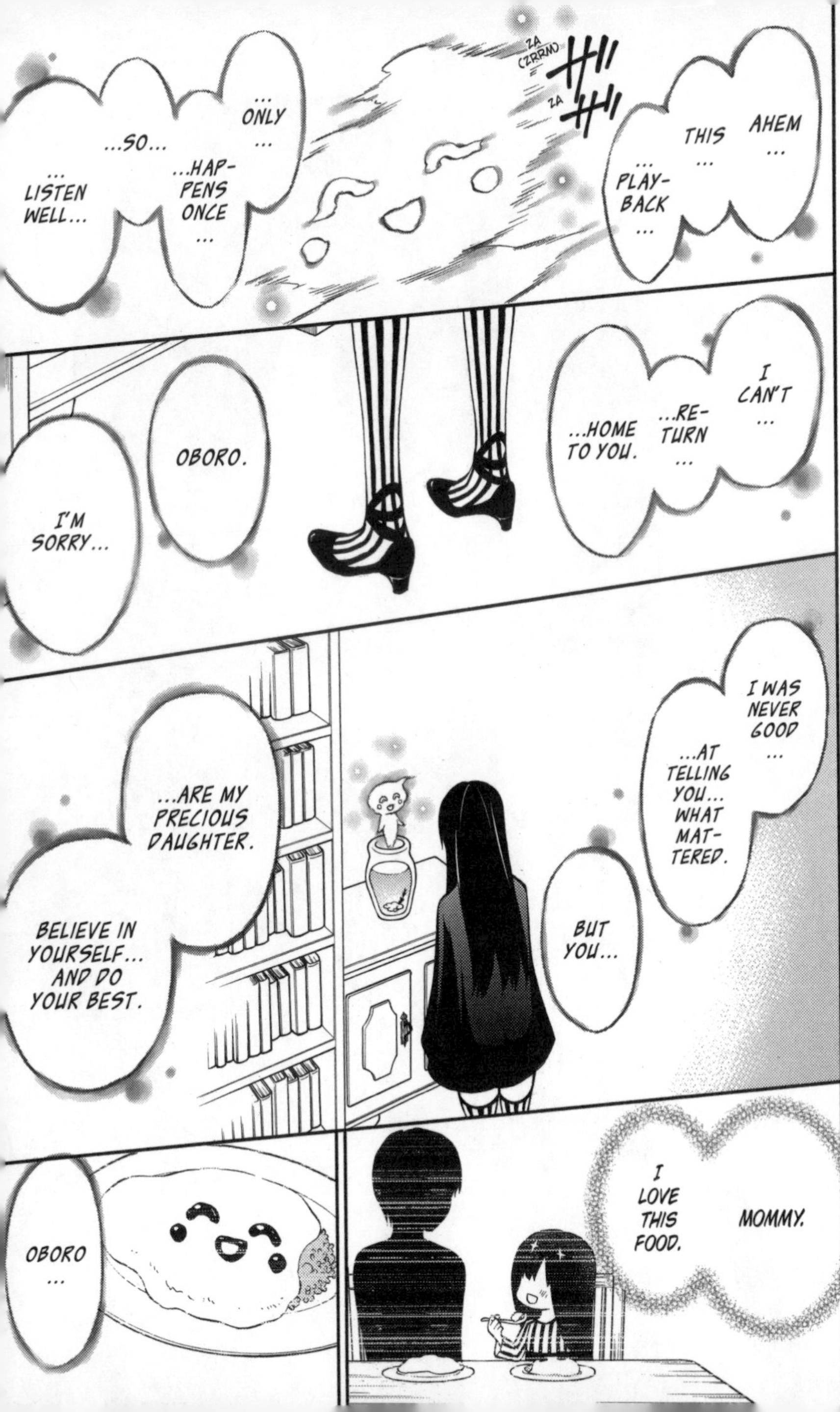
AHEM...
THIS...
...PLAYBACK...
ZA (ZRRM)
ZA
...ONLY...
...HAPPENS ONCE...
...SO...
...LISTEN WELL...
I CAN'T...
...RETURN...
...HOME TO YOU.
OBORO.
I'M SORRY...
I WAS NEVER GOOD...
...AT TELLING YOU... WHAT MATTERED.
BUT YOU...
...ARE MY PRECIOUS DAUGHTER.
BELIEVE IN YOURSELF... AND DO YOUR BEST.
MOMMY.
I LOVE THIS FOOD.
OBORO...

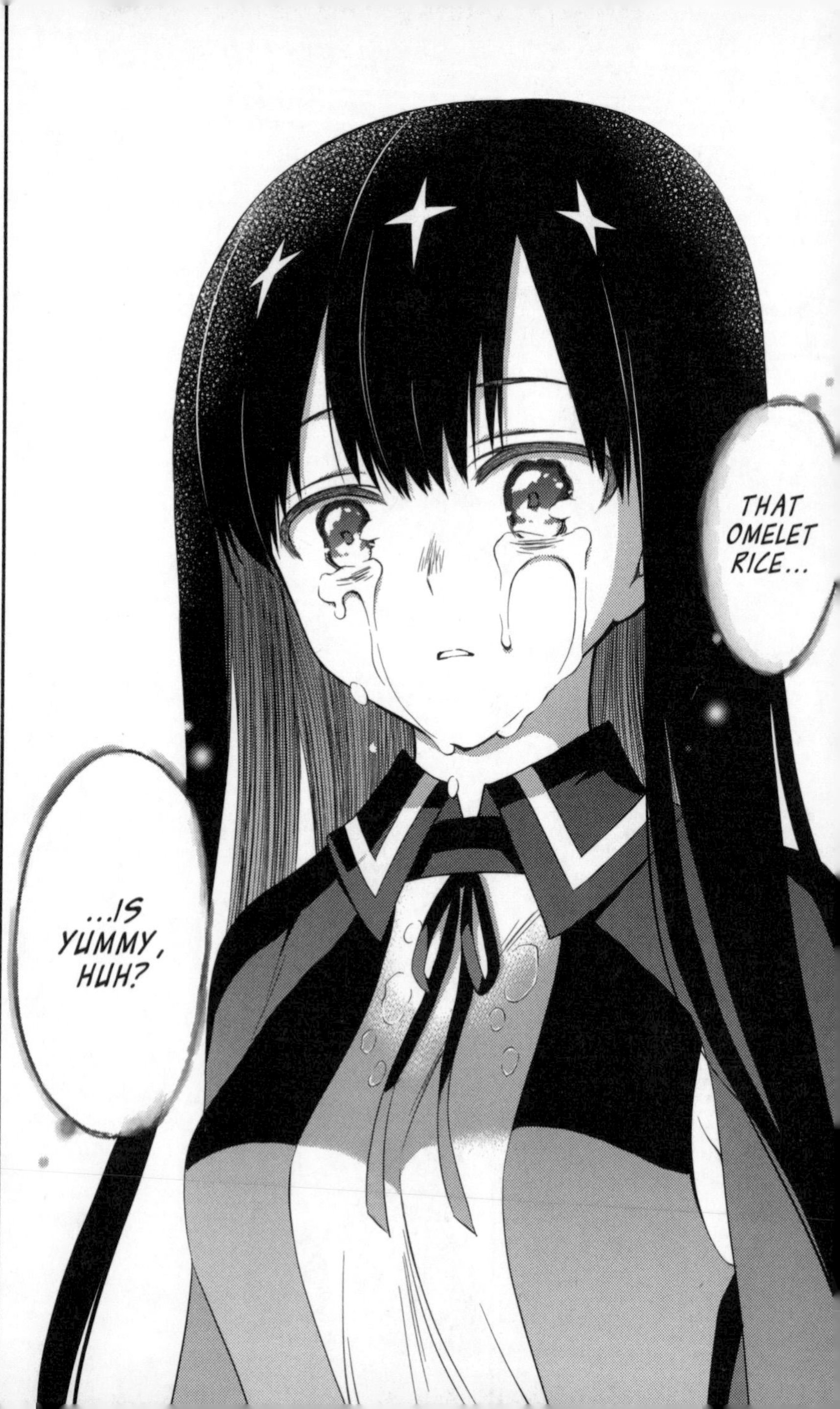
THAT OMELET RICE...
...IS YUMMY, HUH?

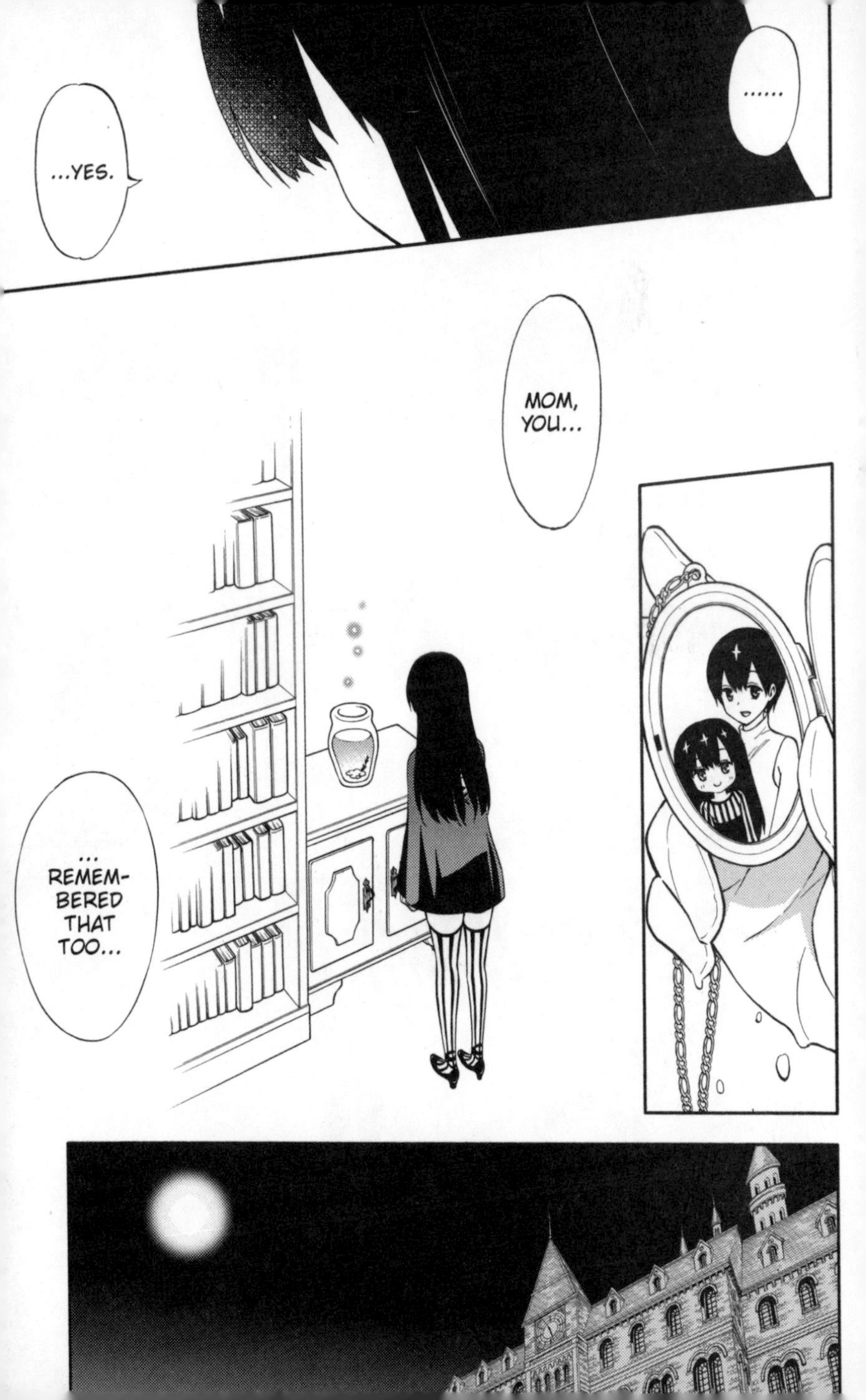
......
...YES.
MOM, YOU...
...REMEM-BERED THAT TOO...

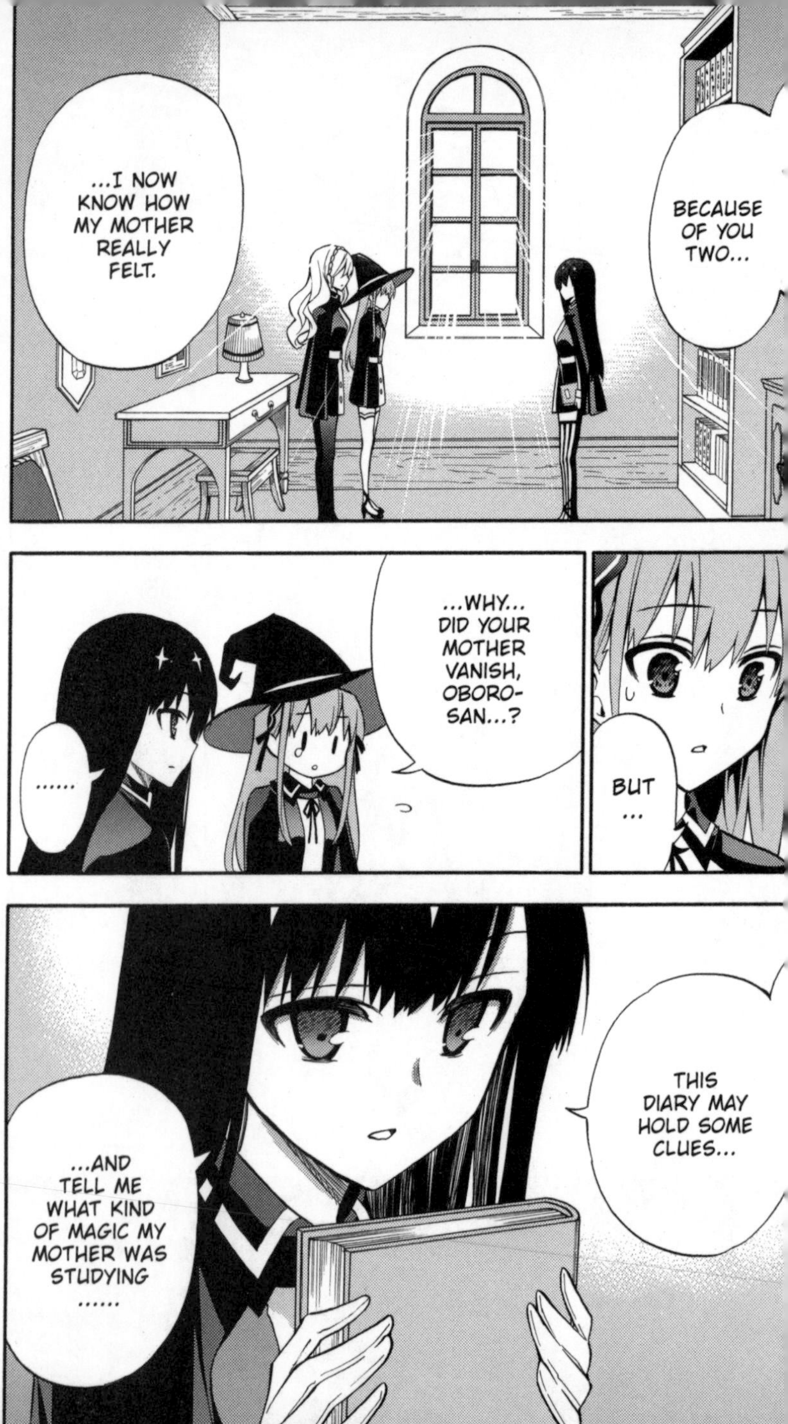
BECAUSE OF YOU TWO...
...I NOW KNOW HOW MY MOTHER REALLY FELT.
BUT ...
...WHY... DID YOUR MOTHER VANISH, OBORO-SAN...?
......
THIS DIARY MAY HOLD SOME CLUES...
...AND TELL ME WHAT KIND OF MAGIC MY MOTHER WAS STUDYING ......

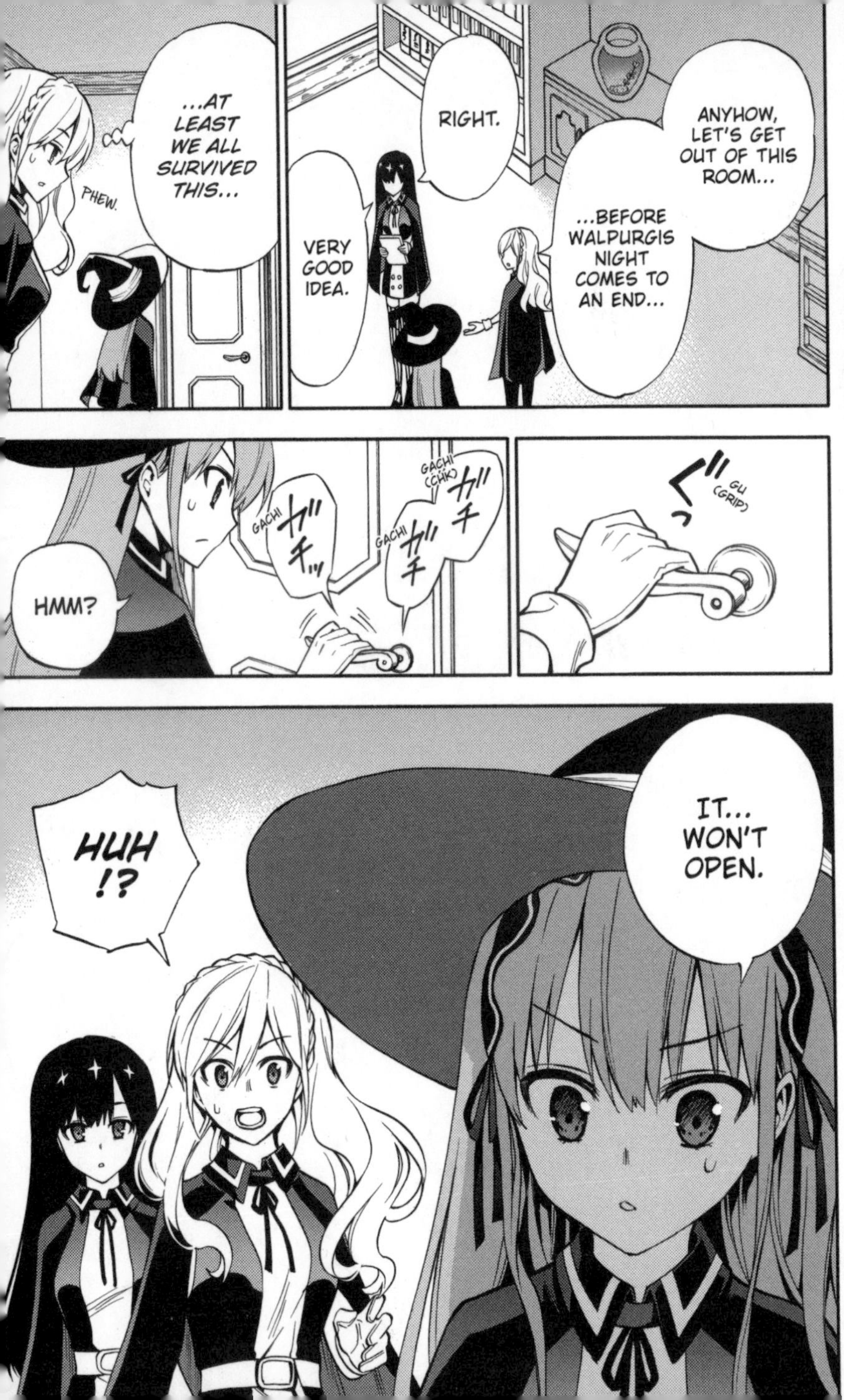
ANYHOW, LET'S GET OUT OF THIS ROOM...
...BEFORE WALPURGIS NIGHT COMES TO AN END...
RIGHT.
VERY GOOD IDEA.
...AT LEAST WE ALL SURVIVED THIS...
PHEW.
ぐっ
GU (GRIP)
ガチ
GACHI (CHK)
ガチ
GACHI
ガチッ
GACHI
HMM?
IT... WON'T OPEN.
HUH!?

If Witch, Then Which?

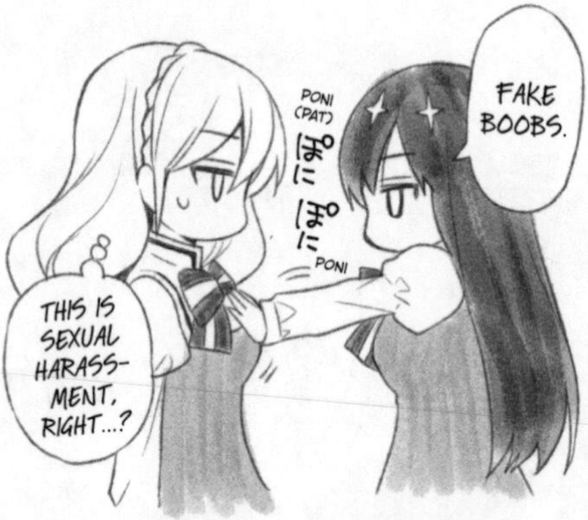
FAKE BOOBS.
PONI (PAT)
ぽに ぽに
PONI
THIS IS SEXUAL HARASS-MENT, RIGHT...?

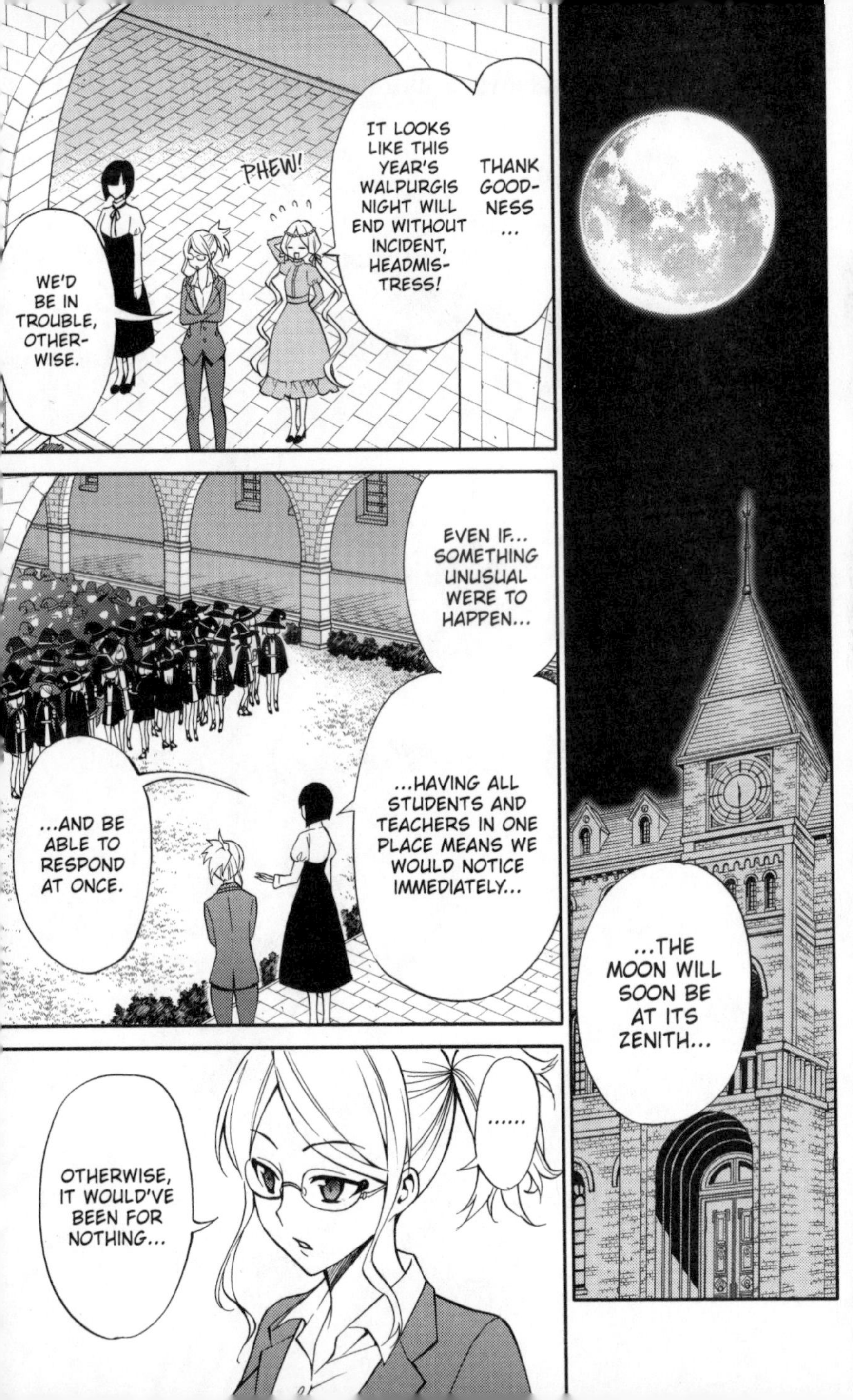
...THE MOON WILL SOON BE AT ITS ZENITH...
THANK GOODNESS...
IT LOOKS LIKE THIS YEAR'S WALPURGIS NIGHT WILL END WITHOUT INCIDENT, HEADMISTRESS!
PHEW!
WE'D BE IN TROUBLE, OTHERWISE.
EVEN IF... SOMETHING UNUSUAL WERE TO HAPPEN...
...HAVING ALL STUDENTS AND TEACHERS IN ONE PLACE MEANS WE WOULD NOTICE IMMEDIATELY...
...AND BE ABLE TO RESPOND AT ONCE.
......
OTHERWISE, IT WOULD'VE BEEN FOR NOTHING...

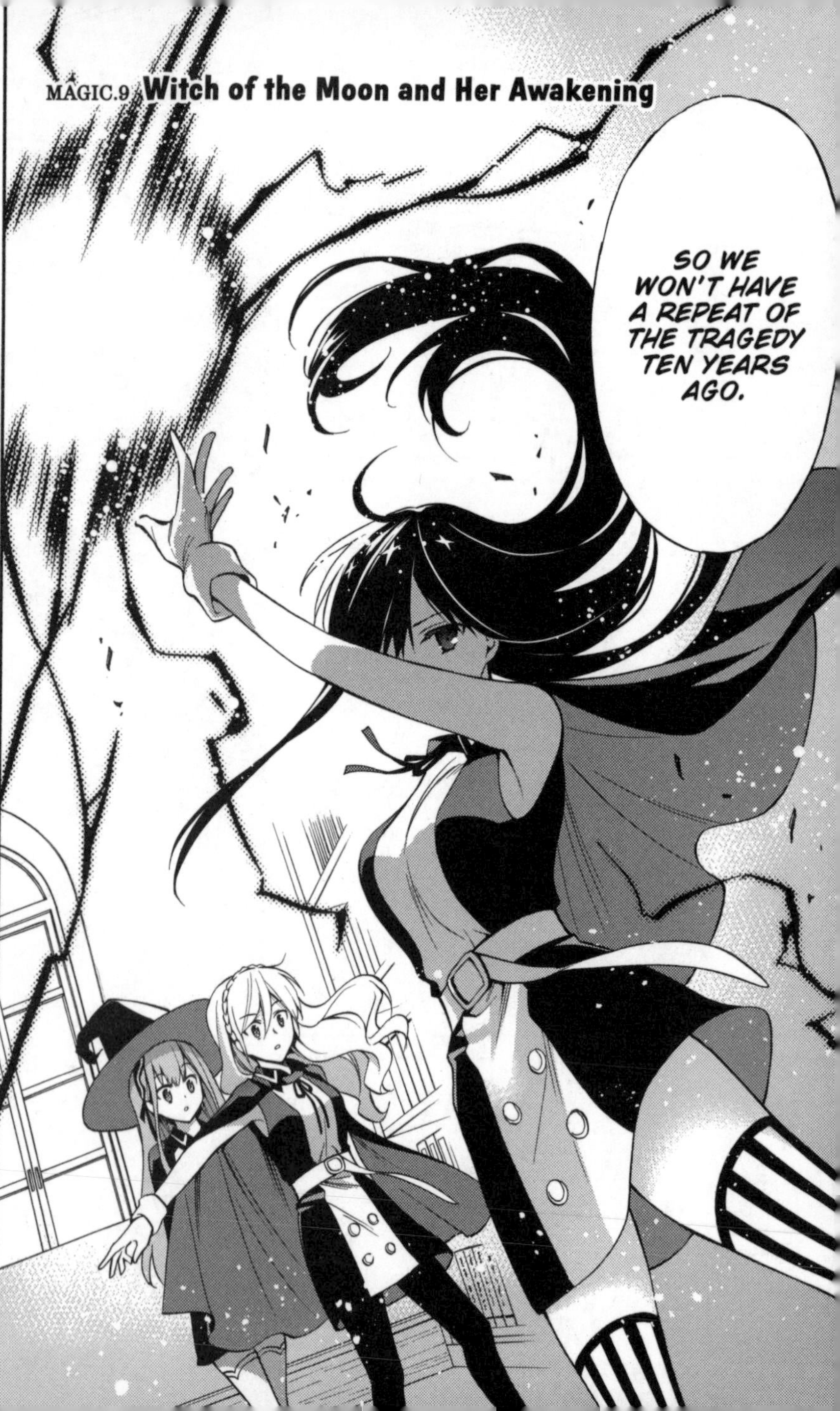
MAGIC.9 Witch of the Moon and Her Awakening
SO WE WON'T HAVE A REPEAT OF THE TRAGEDY TEN YEARS AGO.

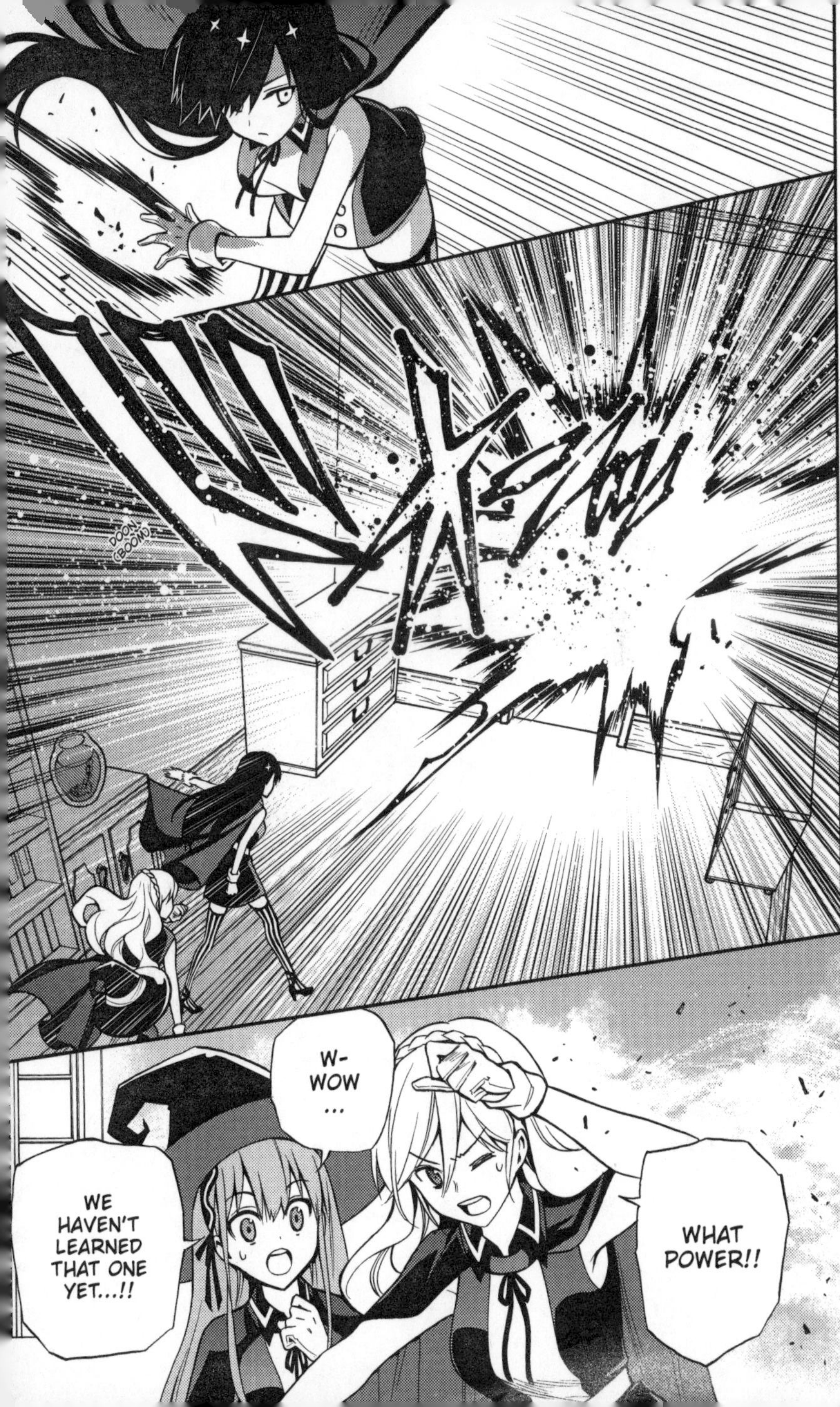
DOON (BOOM)
W-WOW...
WHAT POWER!!
WE HAVEN'T LEARNED THAT ONE YET...!!

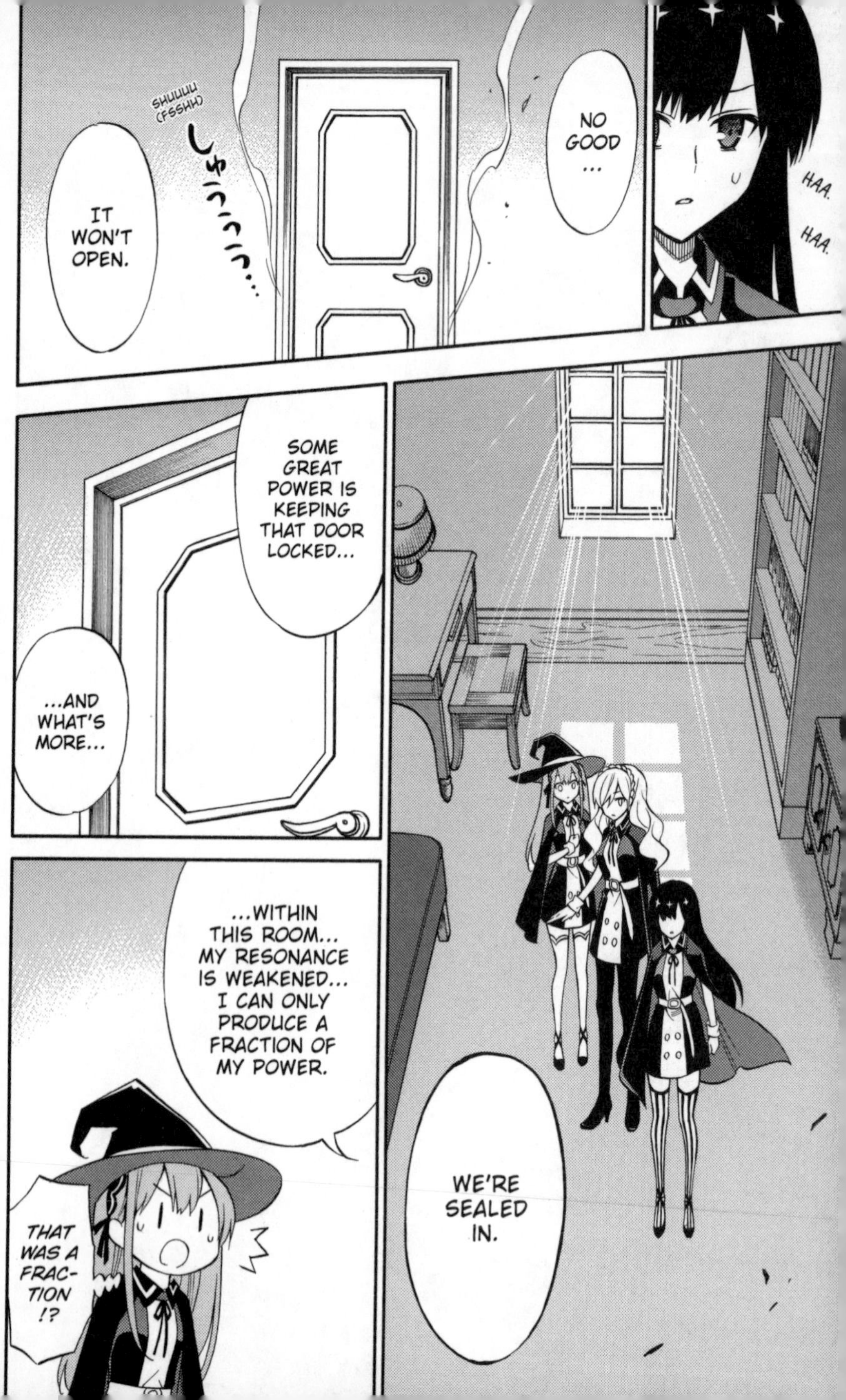
NO GOOD...
HAA. HAA.
SHUUUU (FSSHH)
しゅ〜〜〜〜…
IT WON'T OPEN.
WE'RE SEALED IN.
SOME GREAT POWER IS KEEPING THAT DOOR LOCKED...
...AND WHAT'S MORE...
...WITHIN THIS ROOM... MY RESONANCE IS WEAKENED... I CAN ONLY PRODUCE A FRACTION OF MY POWER.
THAT WAS A FRACTION!?

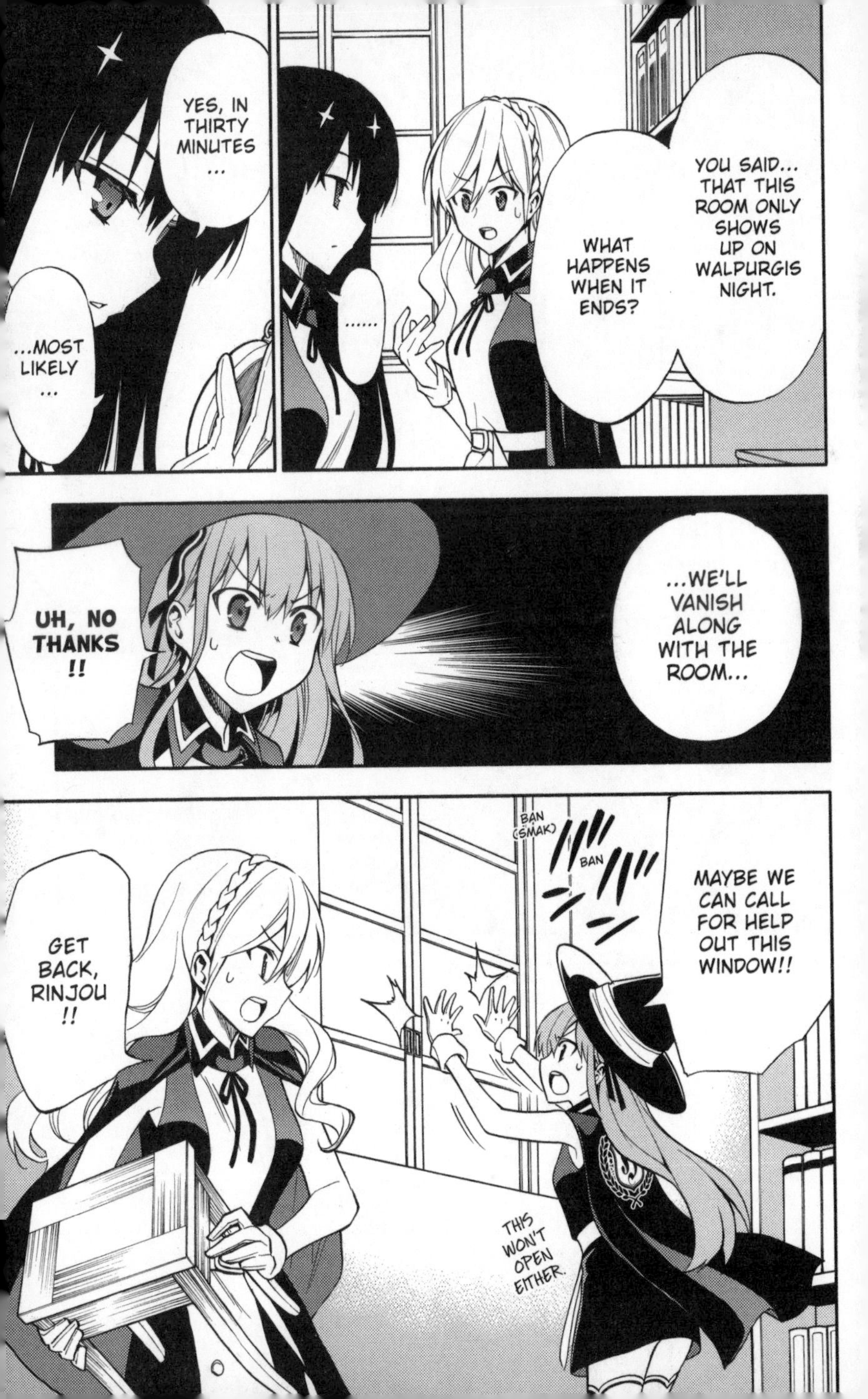
YOU SAID... THAT THIS ROOM ONLY SHOWS UP ON WALPURGIS NIGHT.
WHAT HAPPENS WHEN IT ENDS?
......
YES, IN THIRTY MINUTES ...
...MOST LIKELY ...
...WE'LL VANISH ALONG WITH THE ROOM...
UH, NO THANKS!!
MAYBE WE CAN CALL FOR HELP OUT THIS WINDOW!!
BAN (SMAK)
BAN
THIS WON'T OPEN EITHER.
GET BACK, RINJOU!!

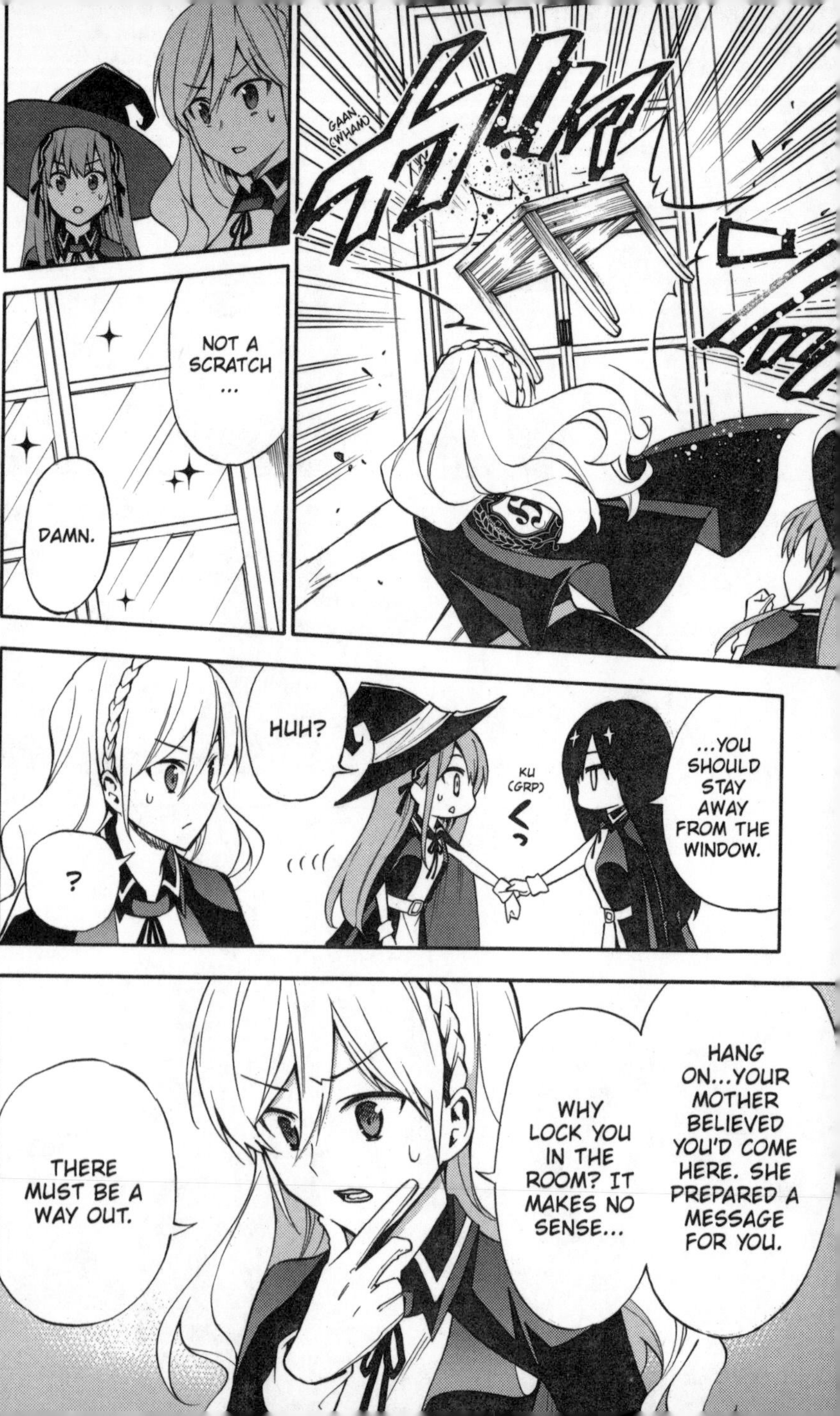
GAAN (WHAM)
NOT A SCRATCH ...
DAMN.
...YOU SHOULD STAY AWAY FROM THE WINDOW.
KU (GRP)
HUH?
?
HANG ON...YOUR MOTHER BELIEVED YOU'D COME HERE. SHE PREPARED A MESSAGE FOR YOU.
WHY LOCK YOU IN THE ROOM? IT MAKES NO SENSE...
THERE MUST BE A WAY OUT.

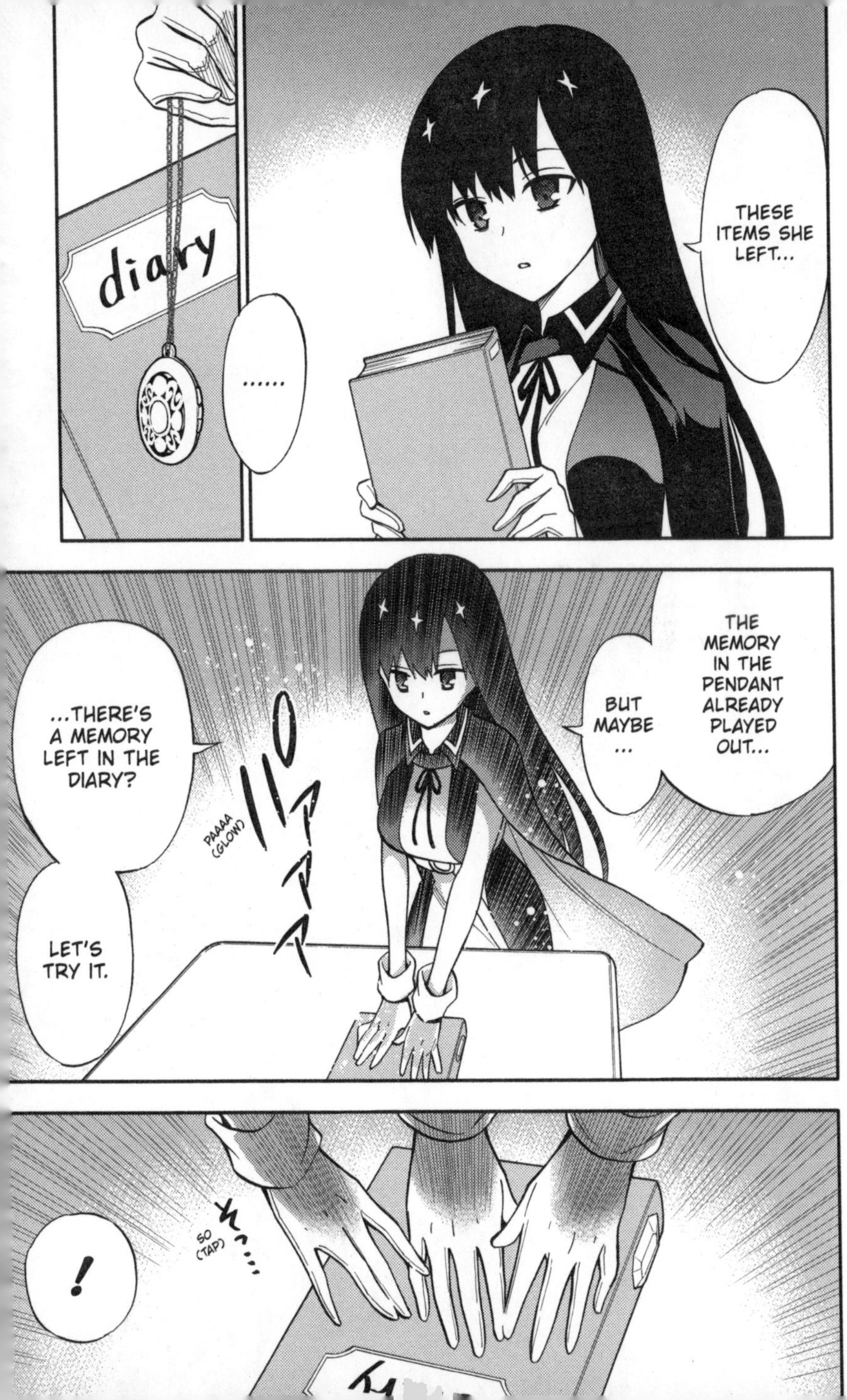
THESE ITEMS SHE LEFT...
......
diary
THE MEMORY IN THE PENDANT ALREADY PLAYED OUT...
BUT MAYBE ...
...THERE'S A MEMORY LEFT IN THE DIARY?
PAAAA (GLOW)
LET'S TRY IT.
SO (TAP)
!

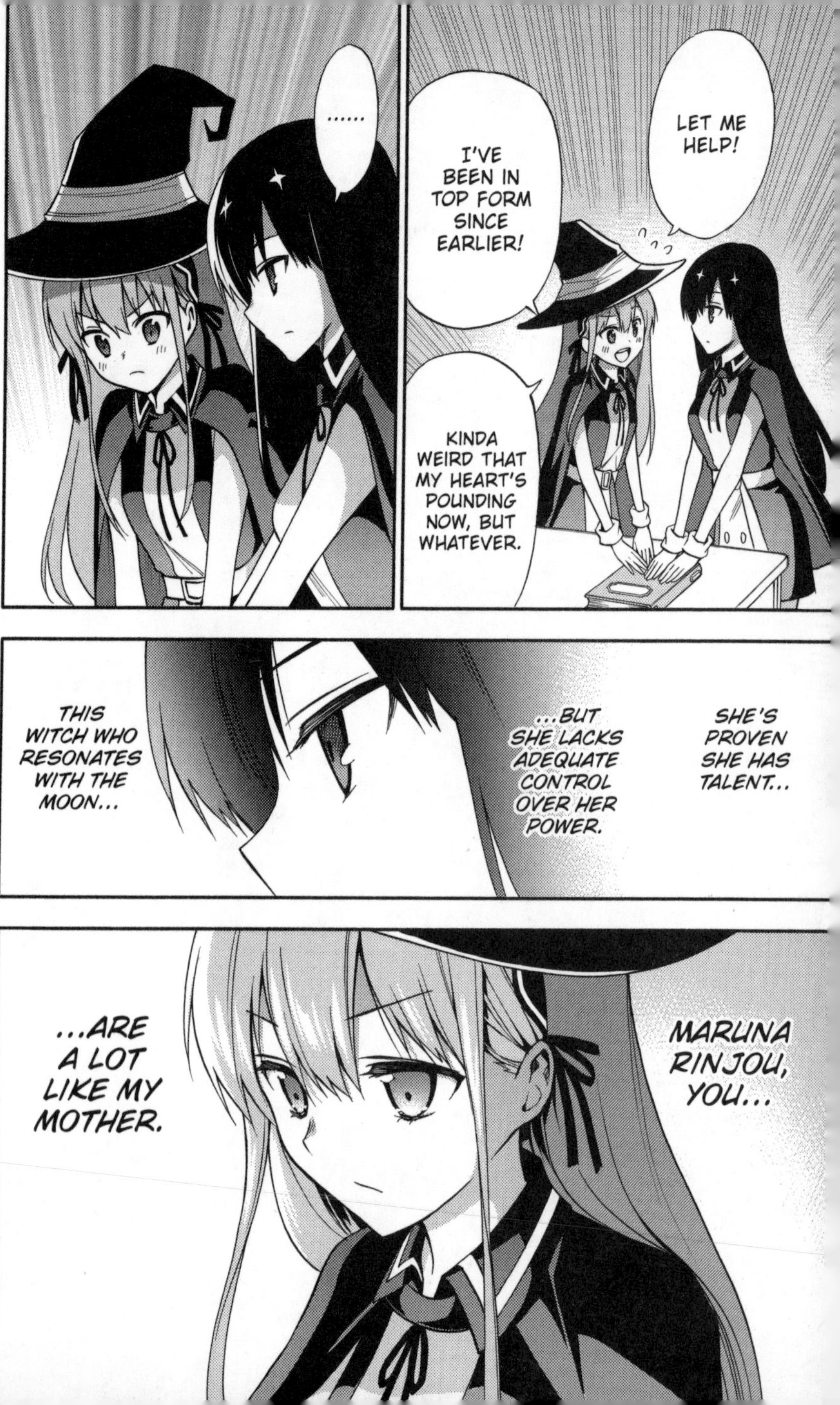
LET ME HELP!
I'VE BEEN IN TOP FORM SINCE EARLIER!
KINDA WEIRD THAT MY HEART'S POUNDING NOW, BUT WHATEVER.
......
SHE'S PROVEN SHE HAS TALENT...
...BUT SHE LACKS ADEQUATE CONTROL OVER HER POWER.
THIS WITCH WHO RESONATES WITH THE MOON...
MARUNA RINJOU, YOU...
...ARE A LOT LIKE MY MOTHER.

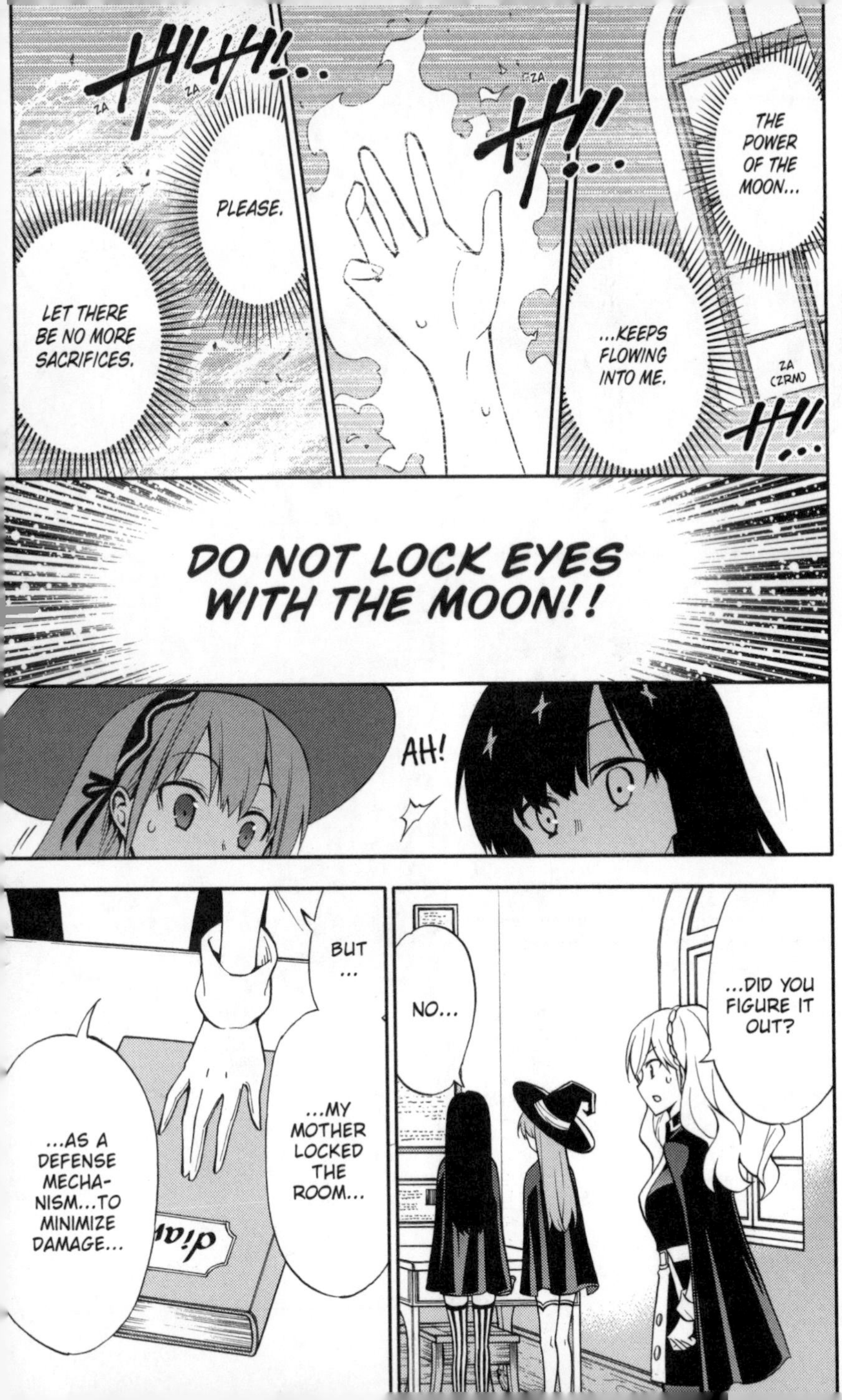
THE POWER OF THE MOON...
...KEEPS FLOWING INTO ME.
ZA (ZRM)
ZA
PLEASE.
LET THERE BE NO MORE SACRIFICES.
ZA
ZA
DO NOT LOCK EYES WITH THE MOON!!
AH!
...DID YOU FIGURE IT OUT?
NO...
BUT ...
...MY MOTHER LOCKED THE ROOM...
...AS A DEFENSE MECHANISM...TO MINIMIZE DAMAGE...

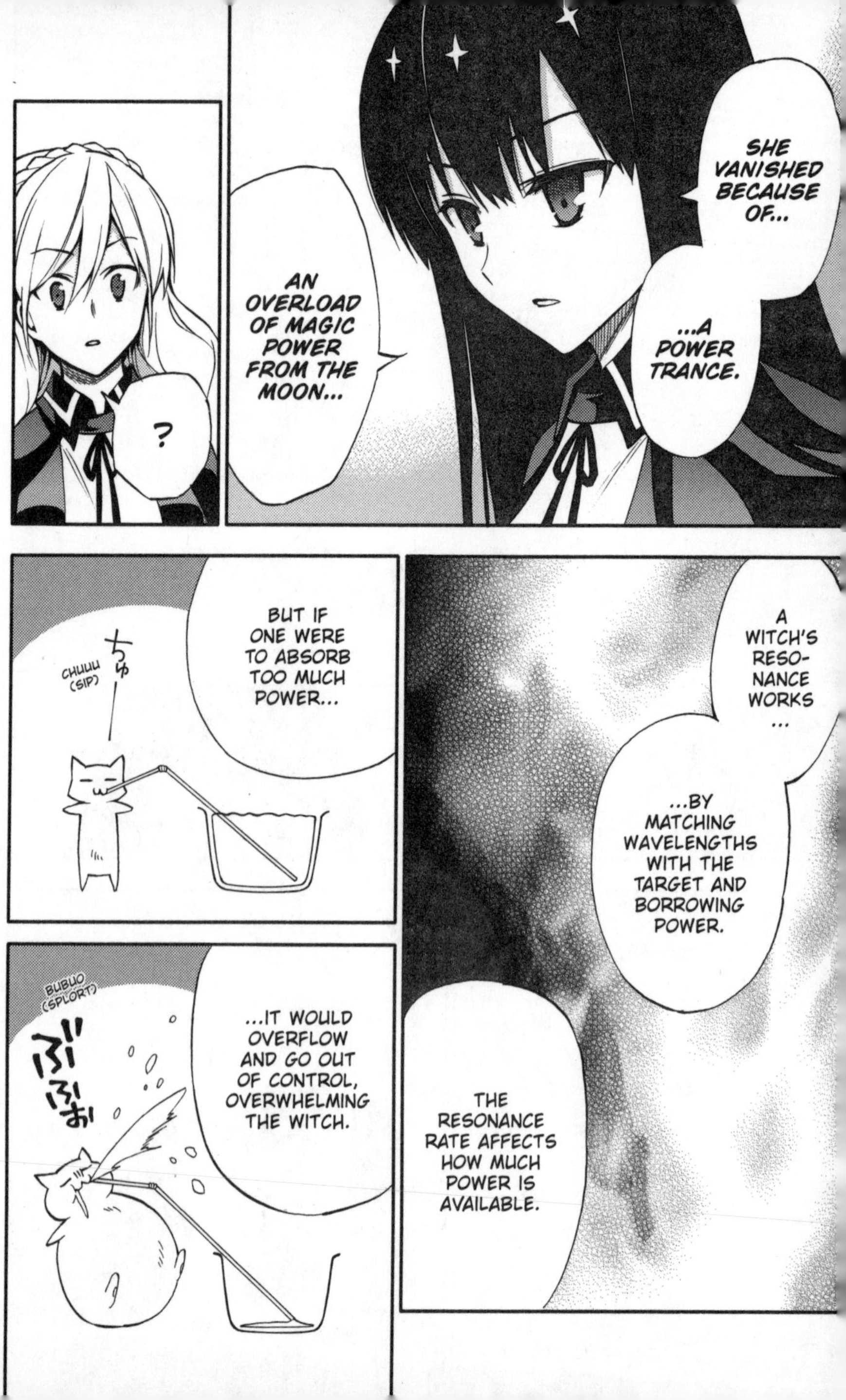
SHE VANISHED BECAUSE OF...
...A POWER TRANCE.
AN OVERLOAD OF MAGIC POWER FROM THE MOON...
?
A WITCH'S RESO-NANCE WORKS ...
...BY MATCHING WAVELENGTHS WITH THE TARGET AND BORROWING POWER.
THE RESONANCE RATE AFFECTS HOW MUCH POWER IS AVAILABLE.
BUT IF ONE WERE TO ABSORB TOO MUCH POWER...
ちゅー
CHUUU (SIP)
...IT WOULD OVERFLOW AND GO OUT OF CONTROL, OVERWHELMING THE WITCH.
ぶふぉ
BUBUO (SPLORT)

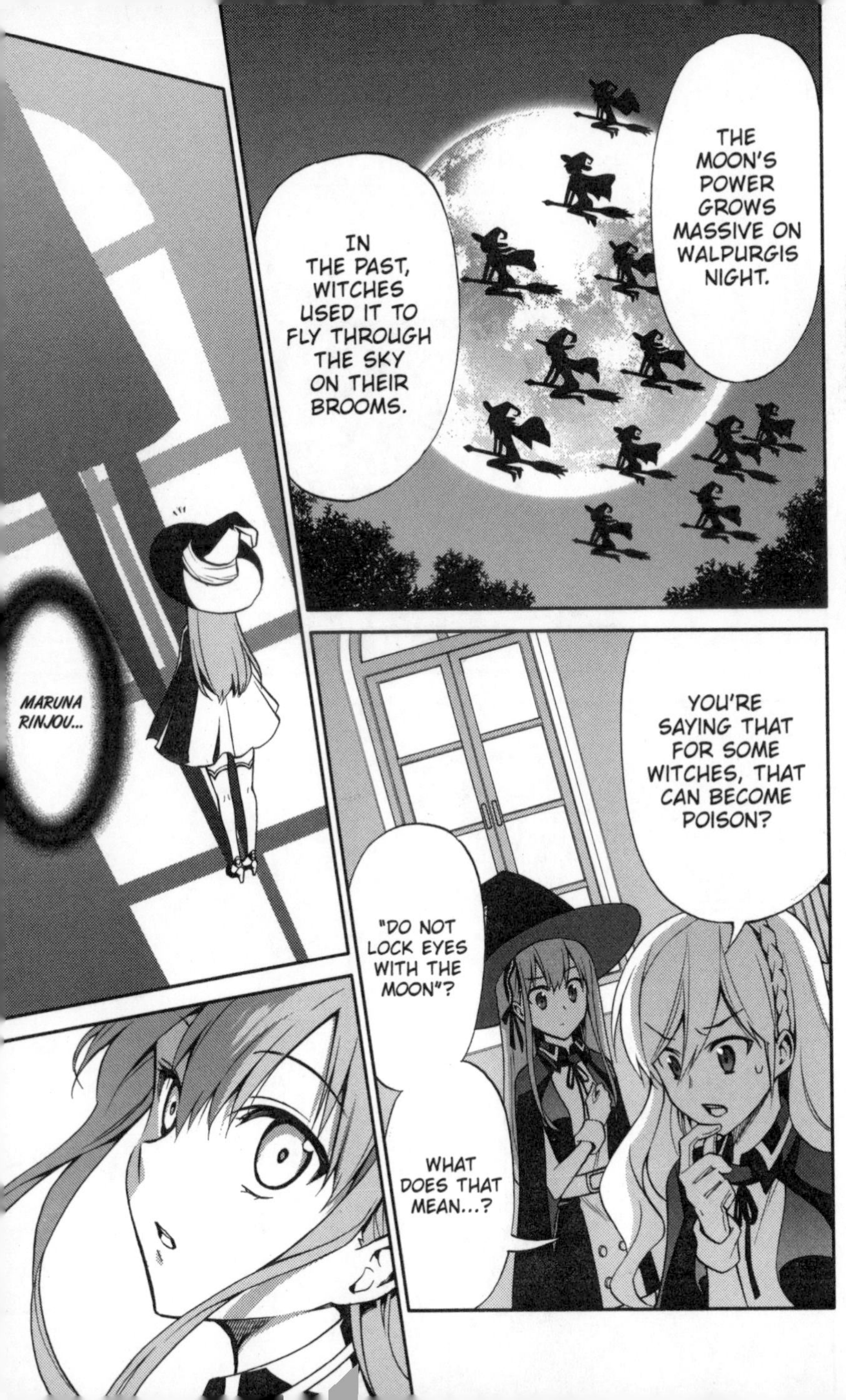
THE MOON'S POWER GROWS MASSIVE ON WALPURGIS NIGHT.
IN THE PAST, WITCHES USED IT TO FLY THROUGH THE SKY ON THEIR BROOMS.
YOU'RE SAYING THAT FOR SOME WITCHES, THAT CAN BECOME POISON?
"DO NOT LOCK EYES WITH THE MOON"?
WHAT DOES THAT MEAN...?
MARUNA RINJOU...

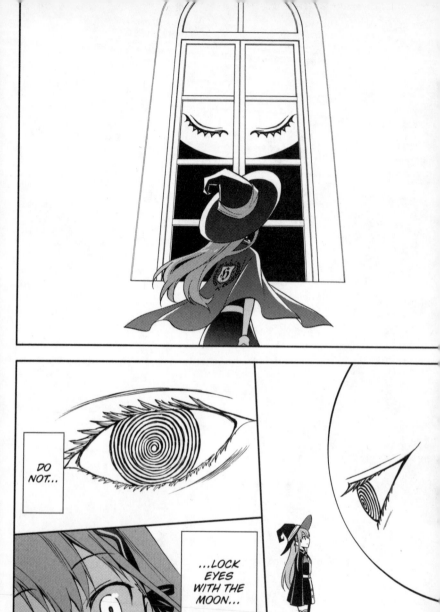

DO NOT...

...LOCK EYES WITH THE MOON...

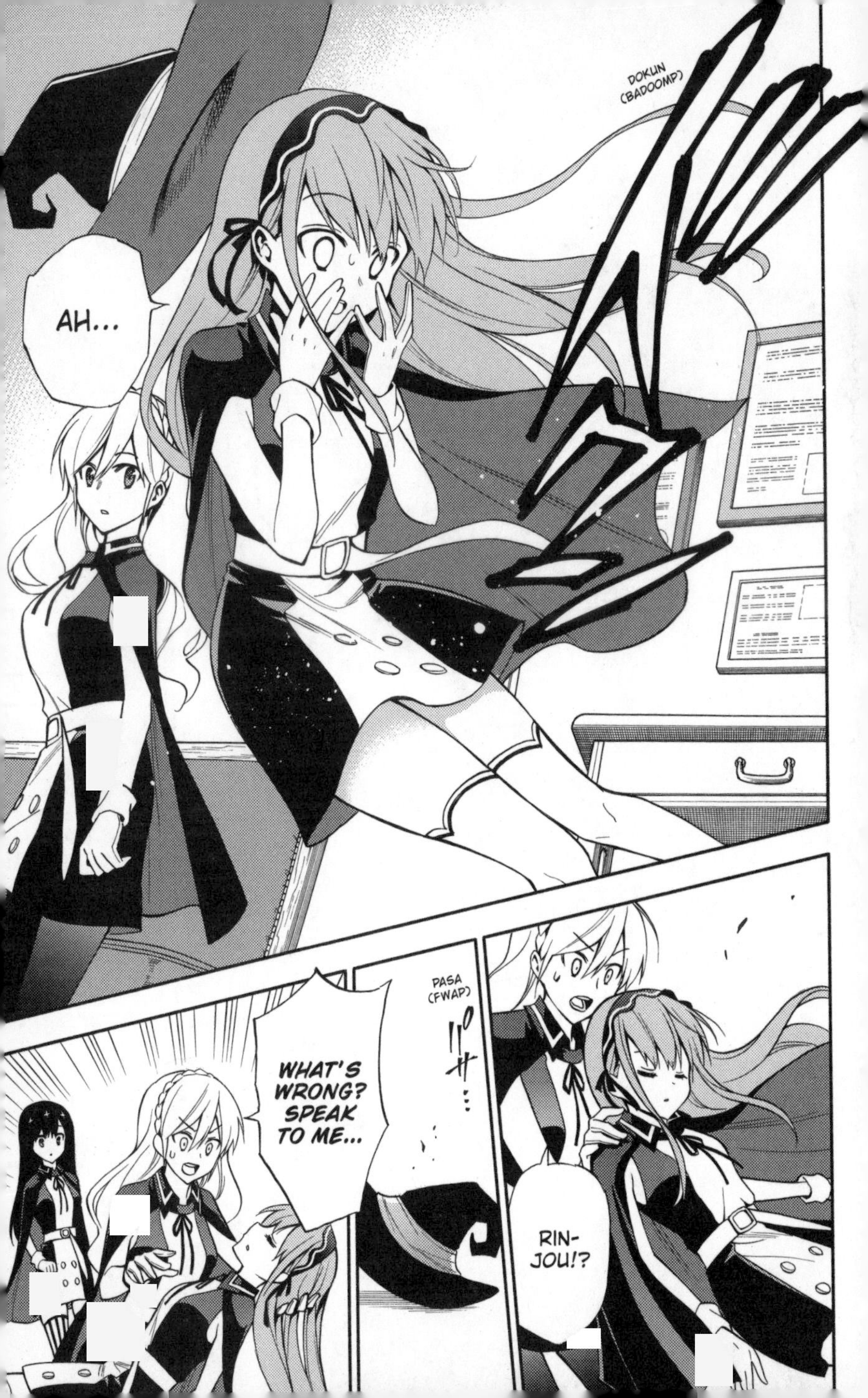
DOKUN (BADOOMP)
AH...
RIN-JOU!?
PASA (FWAP)
WHAT'S WRONG? SPEAK TO ME...

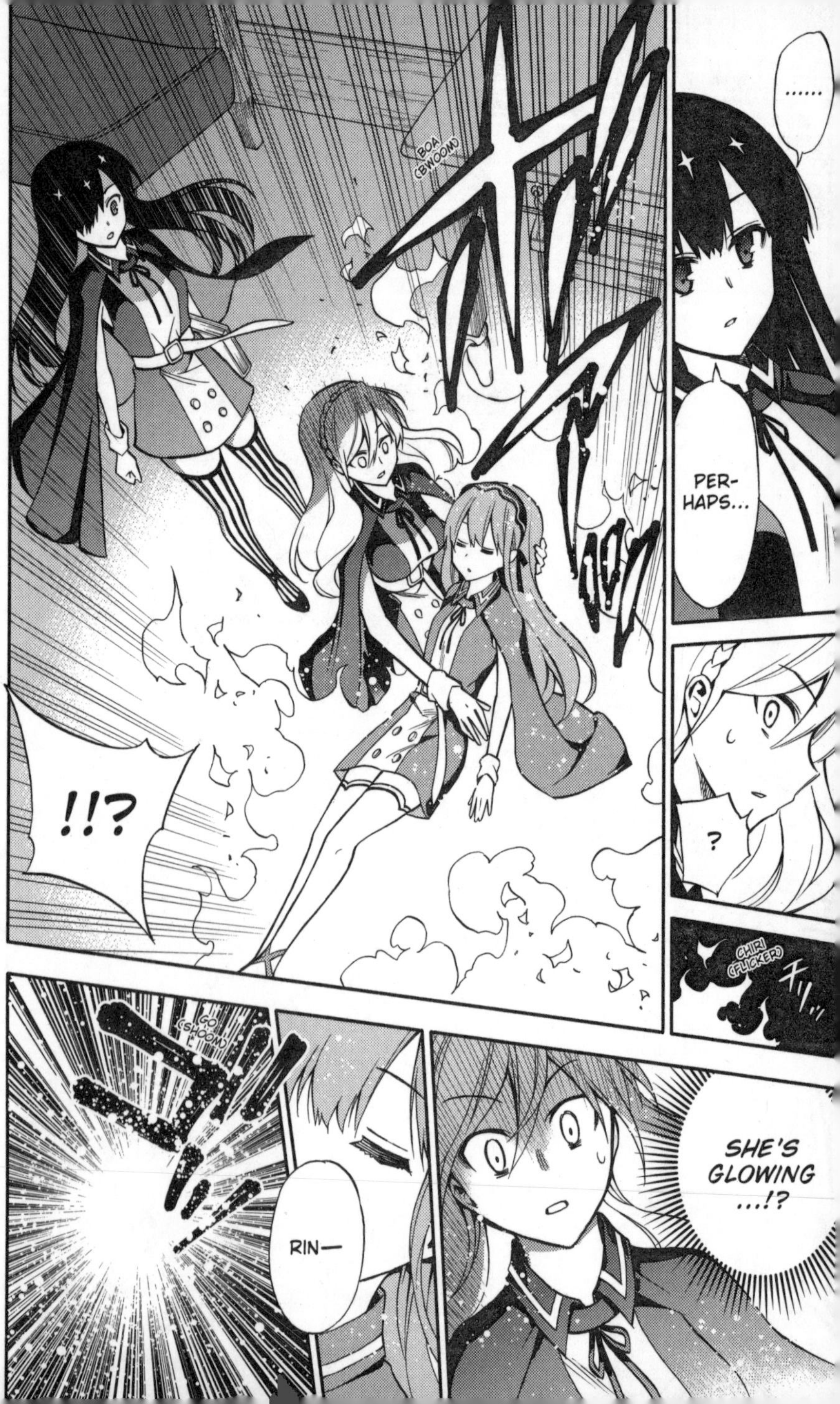
......
PER-HAPS...
?
CHIRI (FLICKER)
チリッ
BOA (BWOOM)
!!?
SHE'S GLOWING ...!?
RIN—
GO (SHOOM)

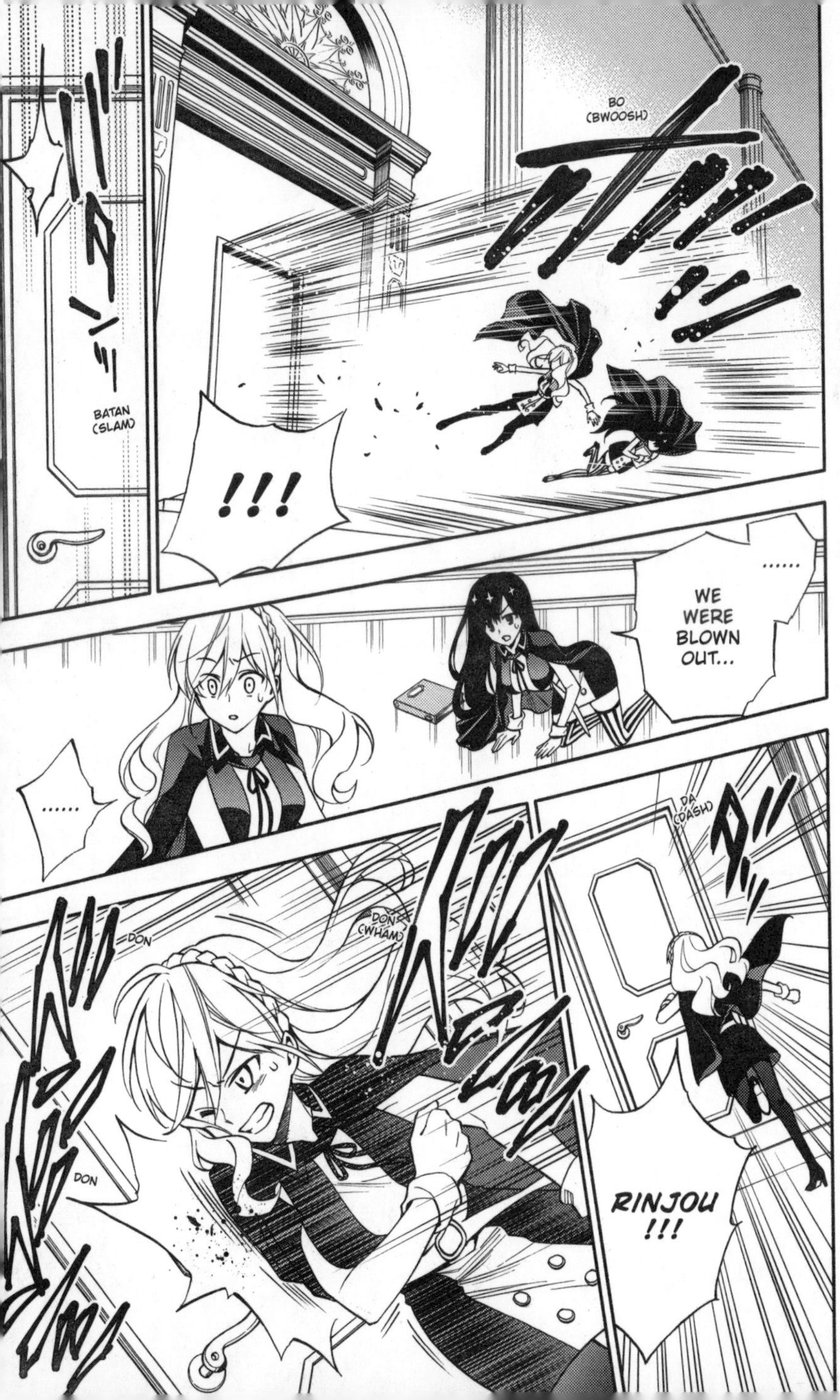
BO (BWOOSH)
!!!
BATAN (SLAM)
......
WE WERE BLOWN OUT...
......
DA (DASH)
RINJOU !!!
DON (WHAM)
DON
DON

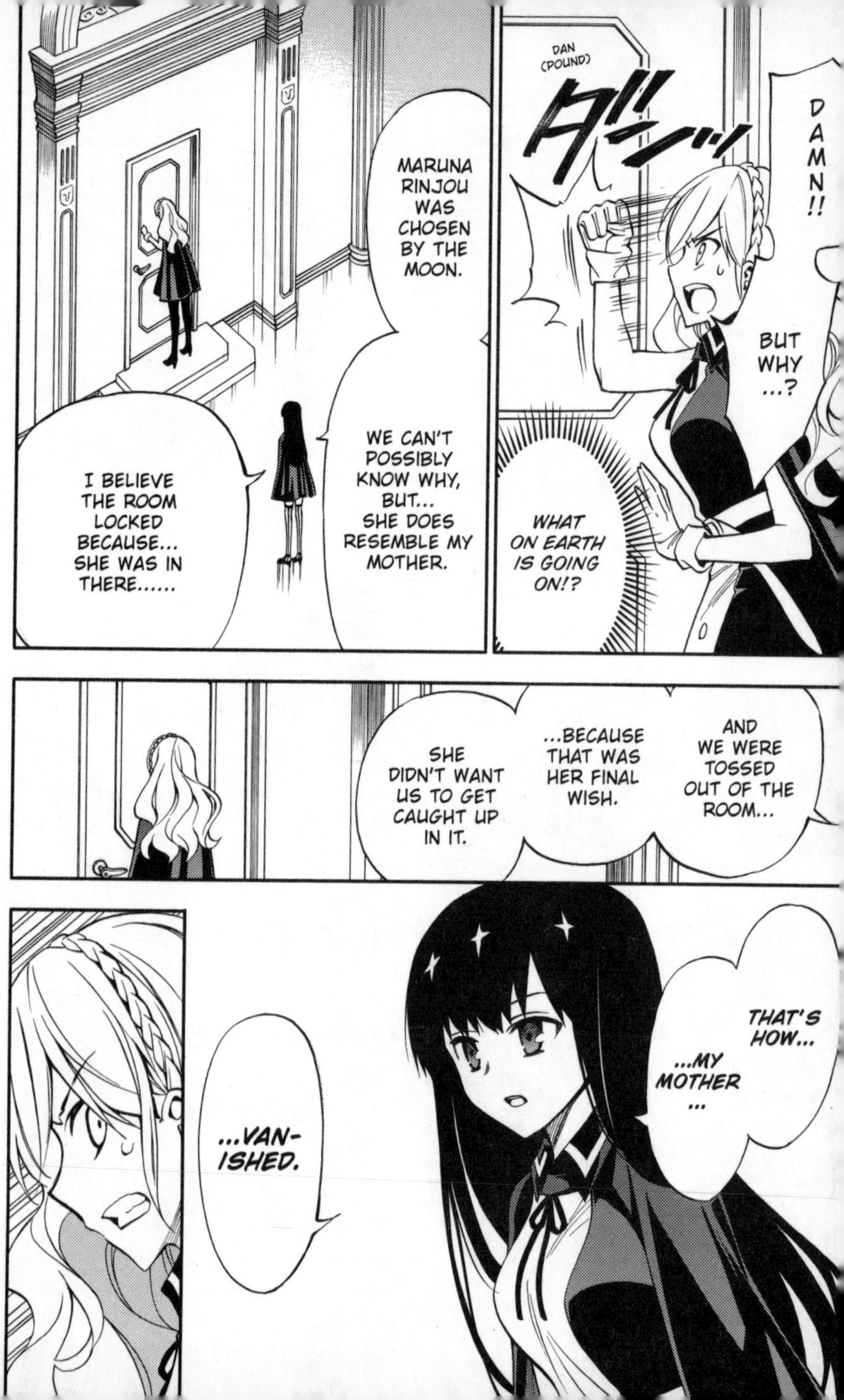
DAN (POUND)
DAMN!!
BUT WHY ...?
WHAT ON EARTH IS GOING ON!?
MARUNA RINJOU WAS CHOSEN BY THE MOON.
WE CAN'T POSSIBLY KNOW WHY, BUT... SHE DOES RESEMBLE MY MOTHER.
I BELIEVE THE ROOM LOCKED BECAUSE... SHE WAS IN THERE......
AND WE WERE TOSSED OUT OF THE ROOM...
...BECAUSE THAT WAS HER FINAL WISH.
SHE DIDN'T WANT US TO GET CAUGHT UP IN IT.
THAT'S HOW...
...MY MOTHER ...
...VAN-ISHED.

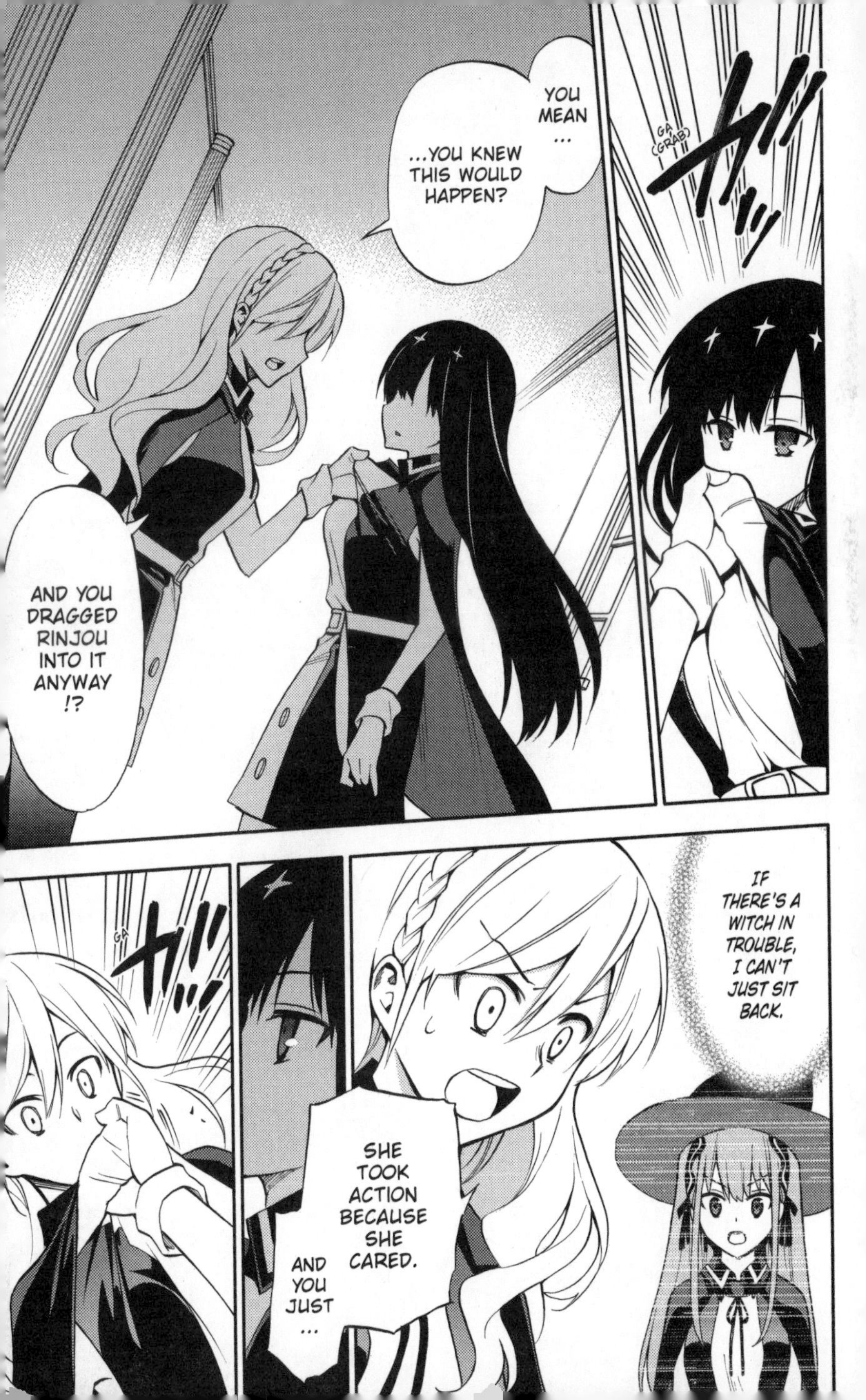
GA (GRAB)
YOU MEAN ...
...YOU KNEW THIS WOULD HAPPEN?
AND YOU DRAGGED RINJOU INTO IT ANYWAY !?
IF THERE'S A WITCH IN TROUBLE, I CAN'T JUST SIT BACK.
SHE TOOK ACTION BECAUSE SHE CARED.
AND YOU JUST ...
GA

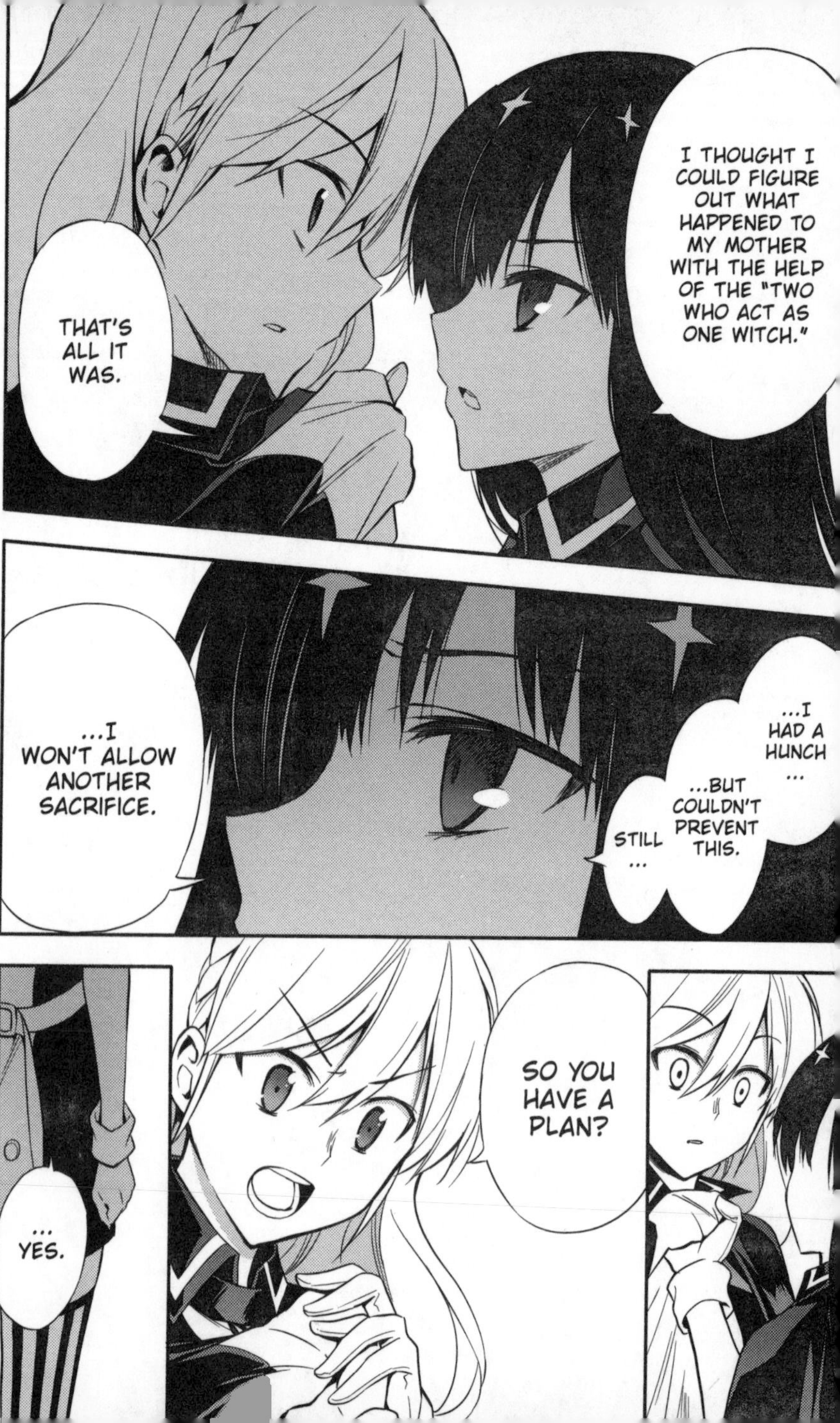
I THOUGHT I COULD FIGURE OUT WHAT HAPPENED TO MY MOTHER WITH THE HELP OF THE "TWO WHO ACT AS ONE WITCH."
THAT'S ALL IT WAS.
...I HAD A HUNCH...
...BUT COULDN'T PREVENT THIS.
STILL...
...I WON'T ALLOW ANOTHER SACRIFICE.
SO YOU HAVE A PLAN?
...YES.

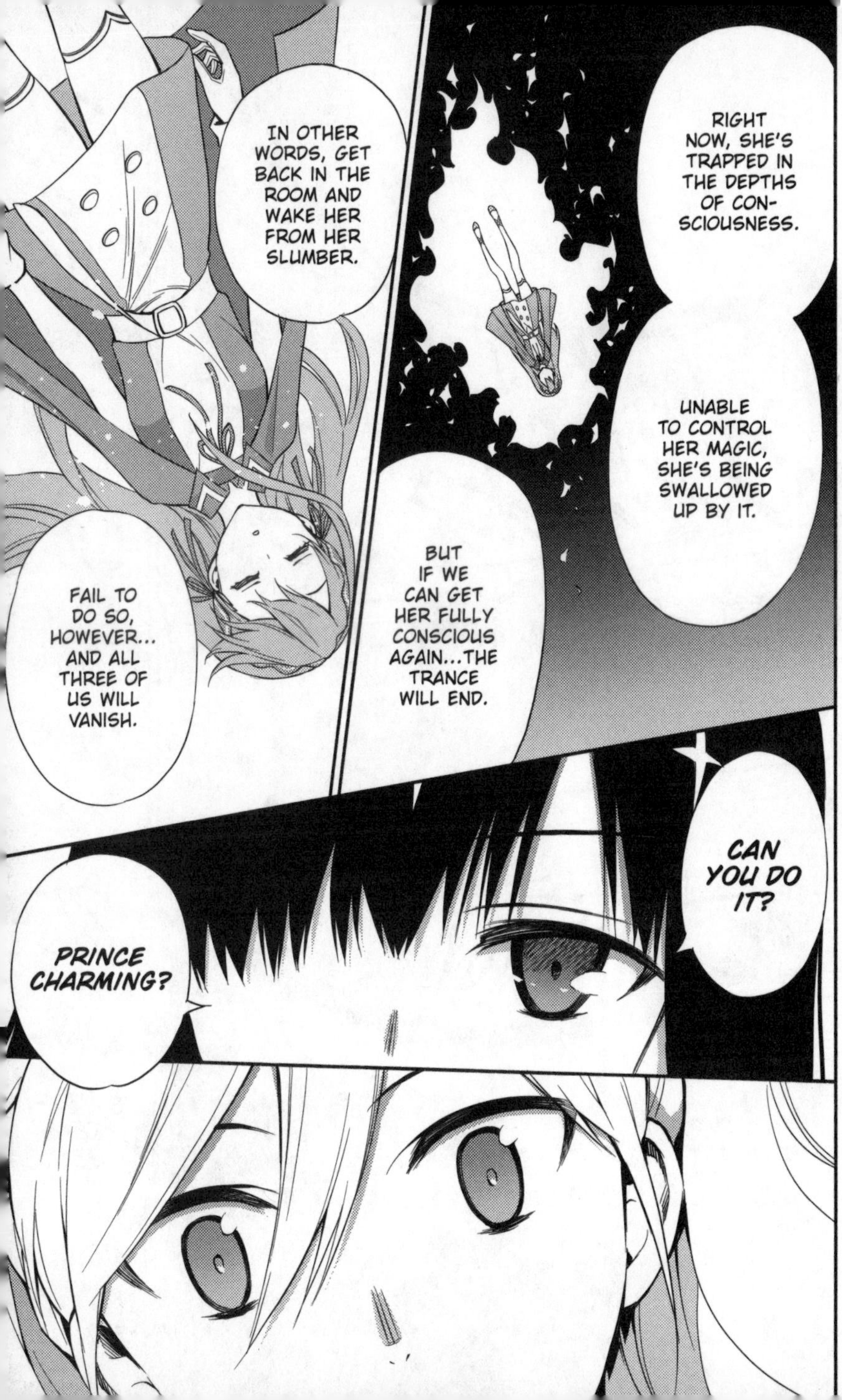
RIGHT NOW, SHE'S TRAPPED IN THE DEPTHS OF CON-SCIOUSNESS.
UNABLE TO CONTROL HER MAGIC, SHE'S BEING SWALLOWED UP BY IT.
BUT IF WE CAN GET HER FULLY CONSCIOUS AGAIN...THE TRANCE WILL END.
IN OTHER WORDS, GET BACK IN THE ROOM AND WAKE HER FROM HER SLUMBER.
FAIL TO DO SO, HOWEVER... AND ALL THREE OF US WILL VANISH.
CAN YOU DO IT?
PRINCE CHARMING?

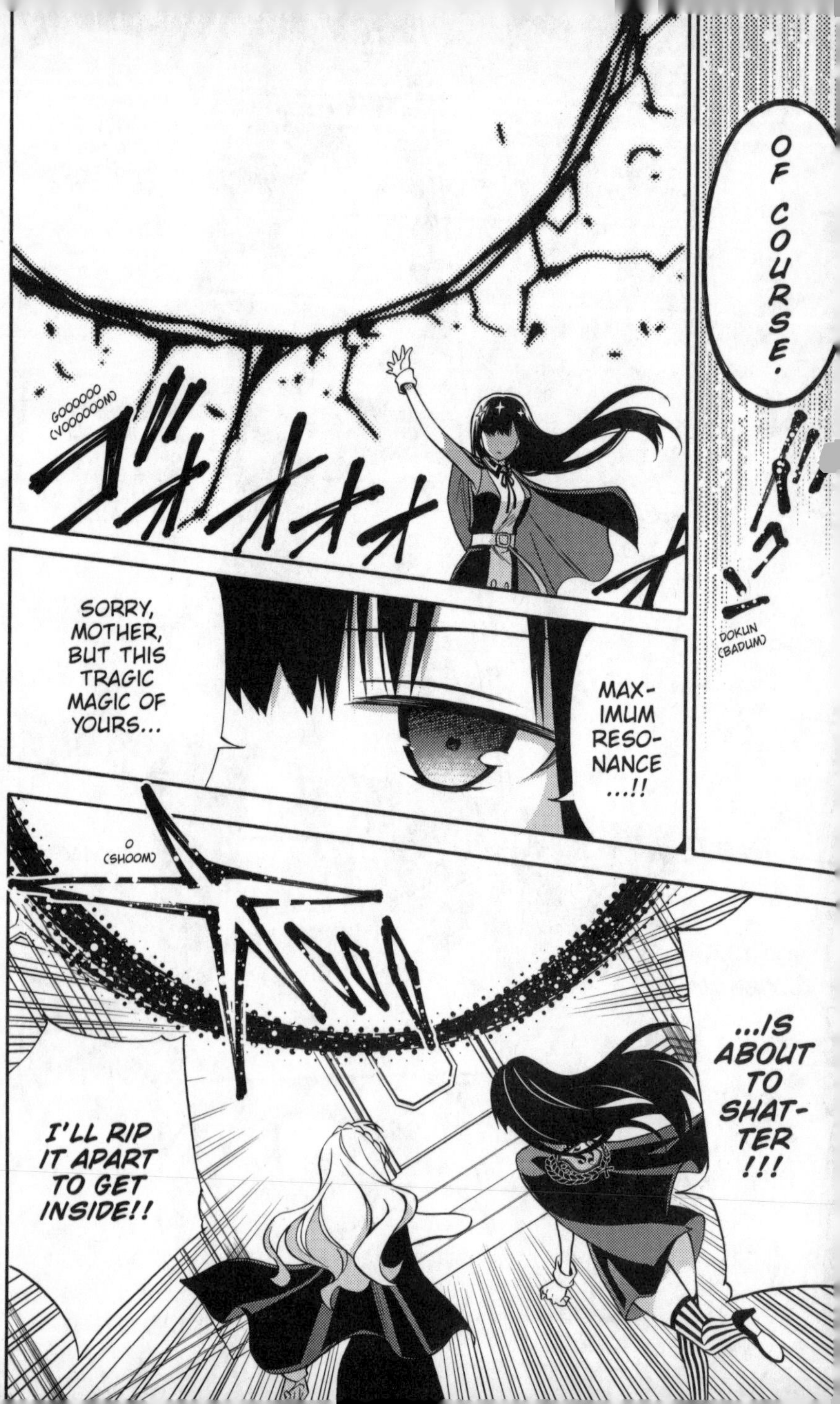
OF COURSE.
DOKUN (BADUM)
GOOOOOO (VOOOOOOM)
MAX-IMUM RESO-NANCE ...!!
SORRY, MOTHER, BUT THIS TRAGIC MAGIC OF YOURS...
O (SHOOM)
...IS ABOUT TO SHAT-TER!!!
I'LL RIP IT APART TO GET INSIDE!!

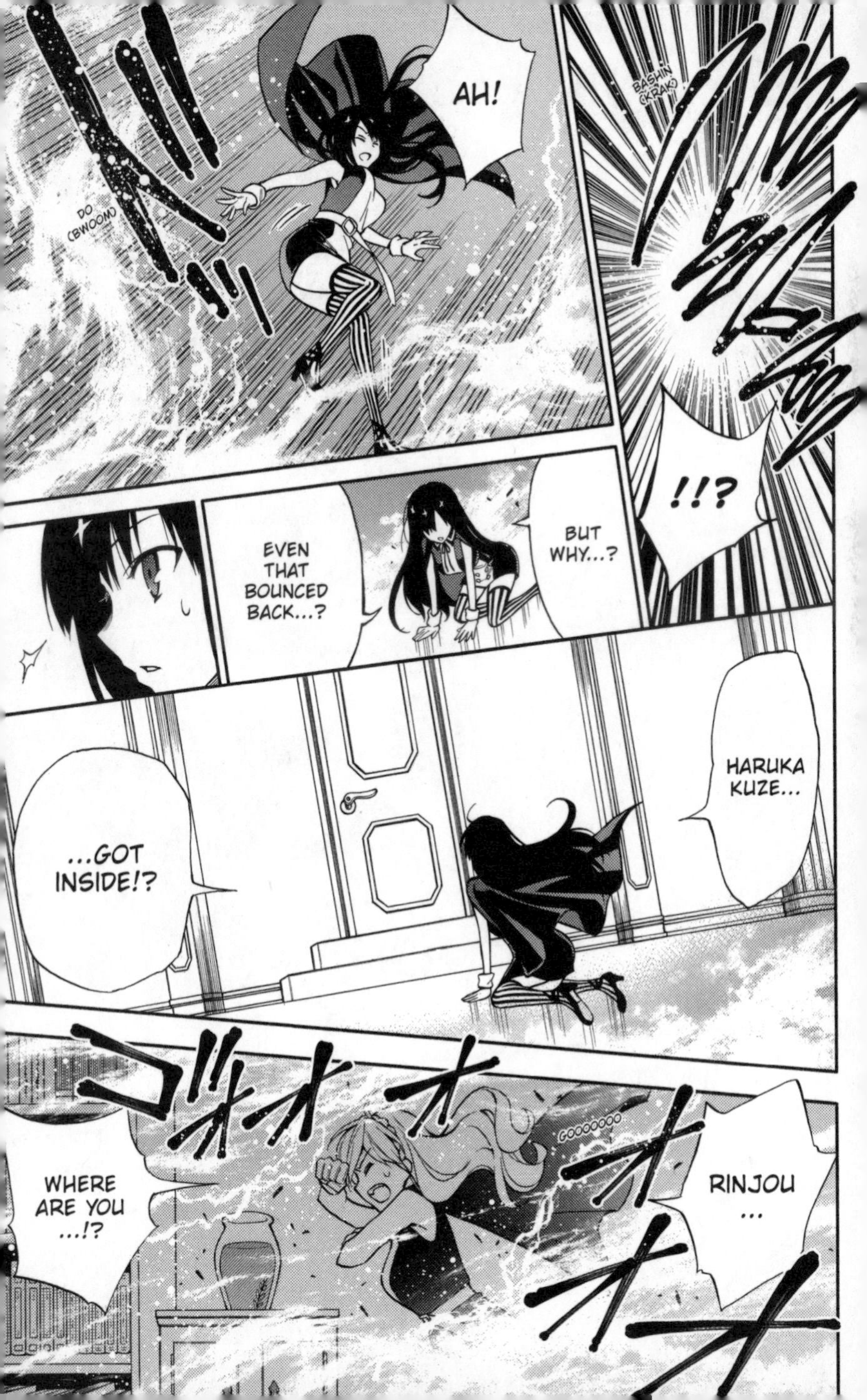
BASHIN (KRAK)
!!?
AH!
DO (BWOOM)
BUT WHY...?
EVEN THAT BOUNCED BACK...?
HARUKA KUZE...
...GOT INSIDE!?
GOOOOOOO
RINJOU ...
WHERE ARE YOU ...!?

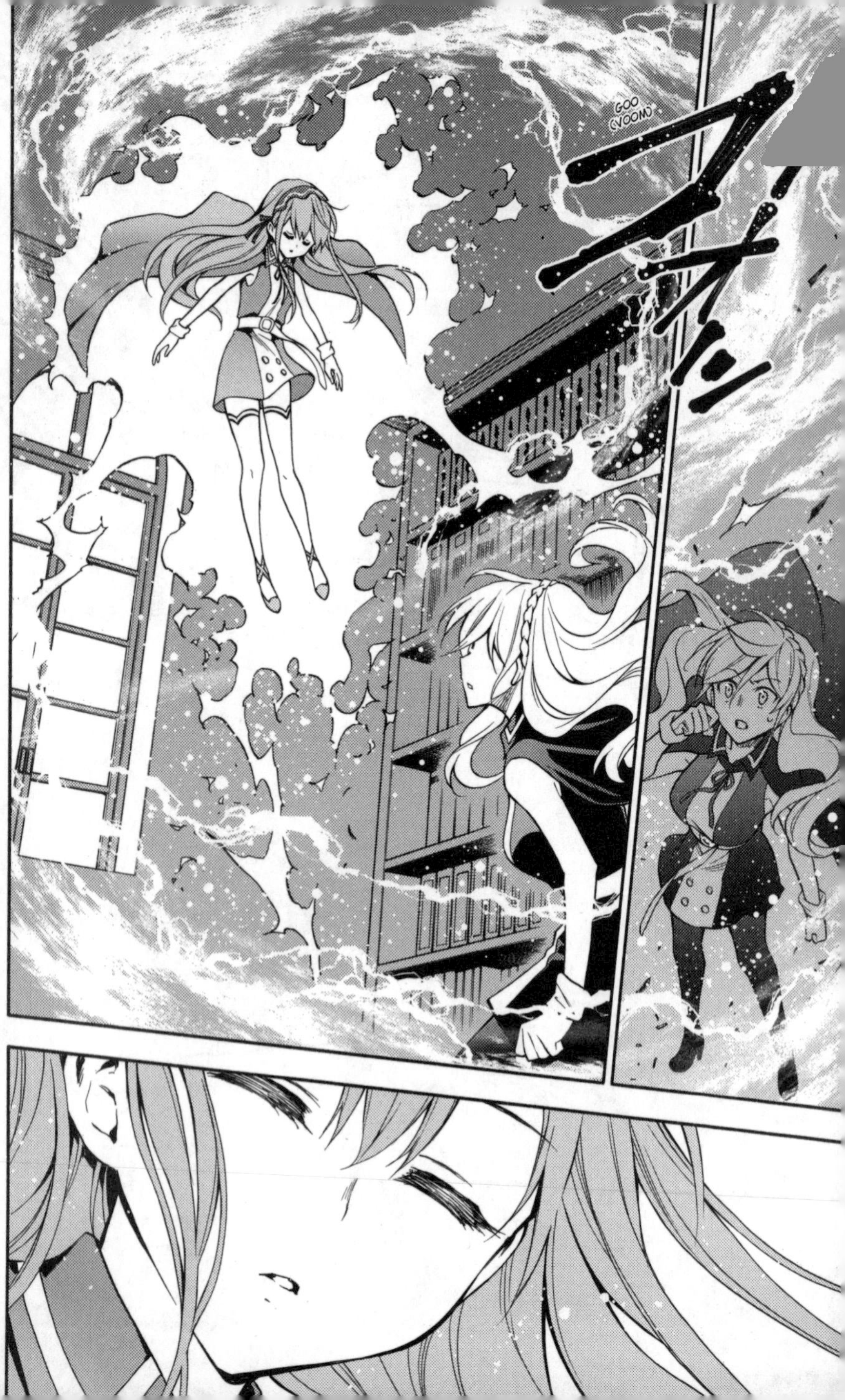
GOO
(VOOM)

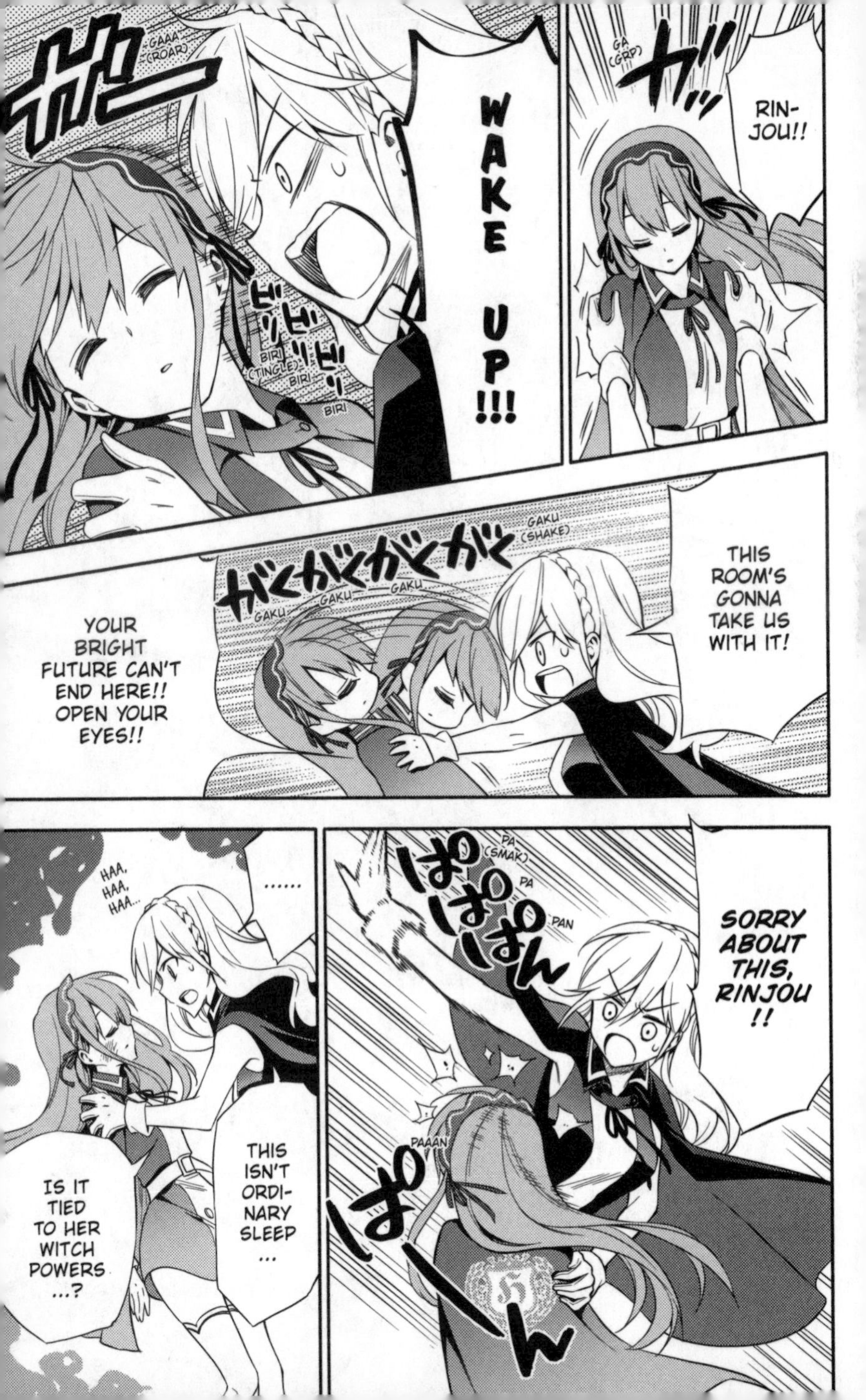
GA (GRP)
RIN-JOU!!
GAAA (ROAR)
WAKE UP!!!
BIRI (TINGLE) BIRI BIRI
THIS ROOM'S GONNA TAKE US WITH IT!
GAKU (SHAKE) GAKU GAKU GAKU
YOUR BRIGHT FUTURE CAN'T END HERE!! OPEN YOUR EYES!!
SORRY ABOUT THIS, RINJOU!!
PA (SMAK) PA PAN
PAAAN
......
HAA, HAA, HAA...
THIS ISN'T ORDINARY SLEEP...
IS IT TIED TO HER WITCH POWERS...?

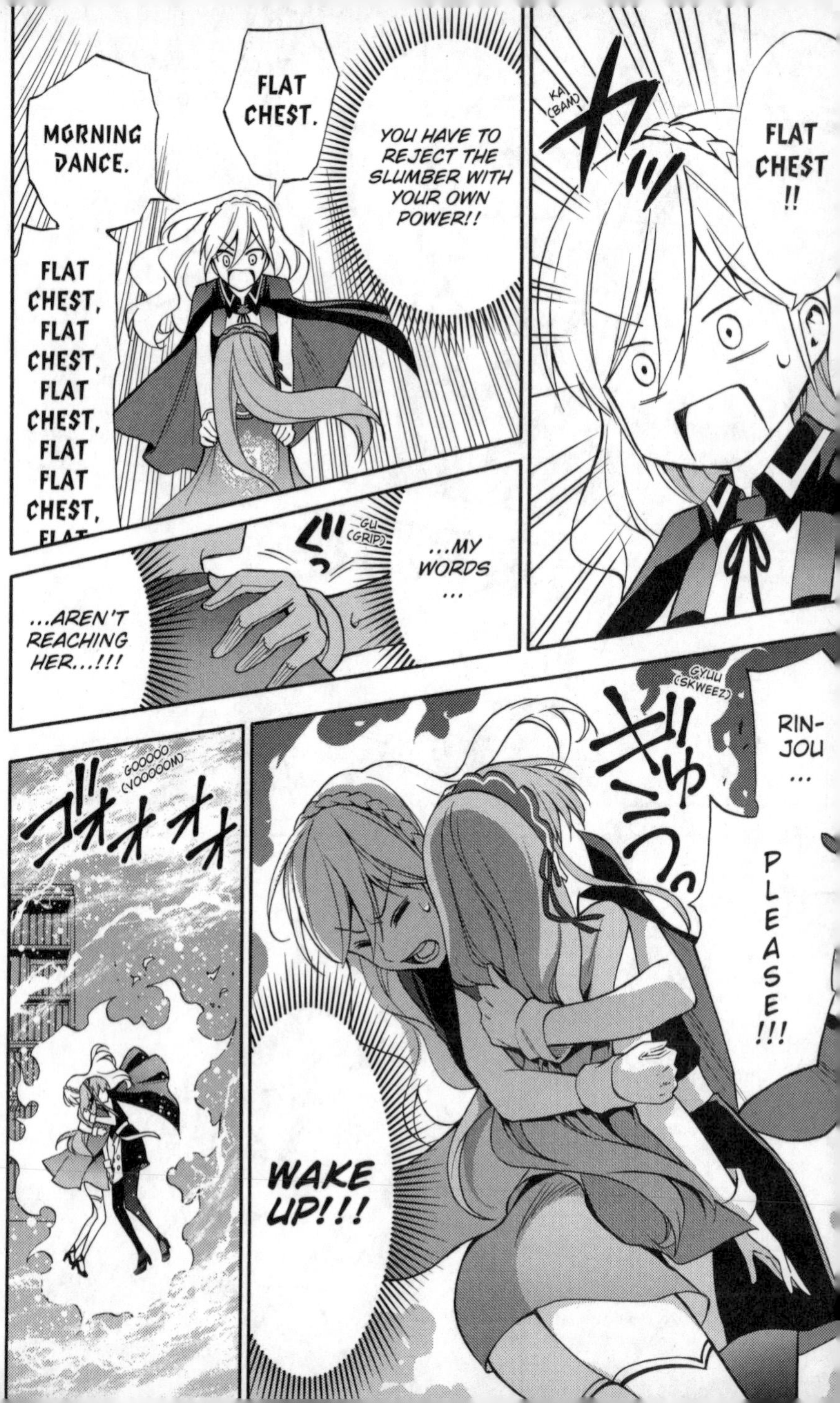

KA (BAM)
FLAT CHEST!!
YOU HAVE TO REJECT THE SLUMBER WITH YOUR OWN POWER!!
FLAT CHEST.
MORNING DANCE.
FLAT CHEST, FLAT CHEST, FLAT CHEST, FLAT FLAT CHEST, FLAT
GU (GRIP)
...MY WORDS...
...AREN'T REACHING HER...!!!
GYUU (SKWEEZ)
RIN-JOU... PLEASE!!!
WAKE UP!!!
GOOOOOO (VOOOOOM)

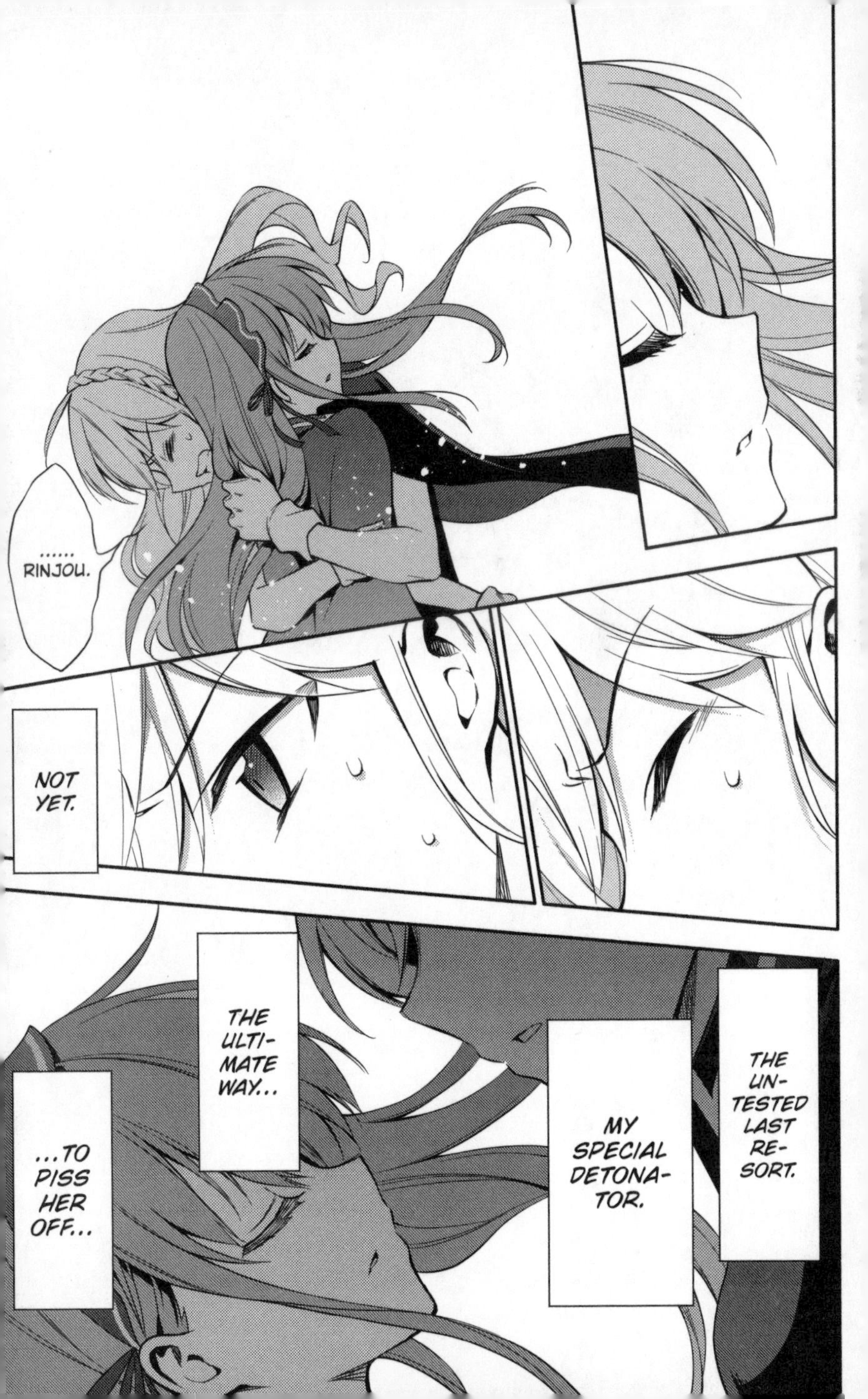

......
RINJOU.
NOT YET.
THE UNTESTED LAST RESORT.
MY SPECIAL DETONATOR.
THE ULTIMATE WAY...
...TO PISS HER OFF...

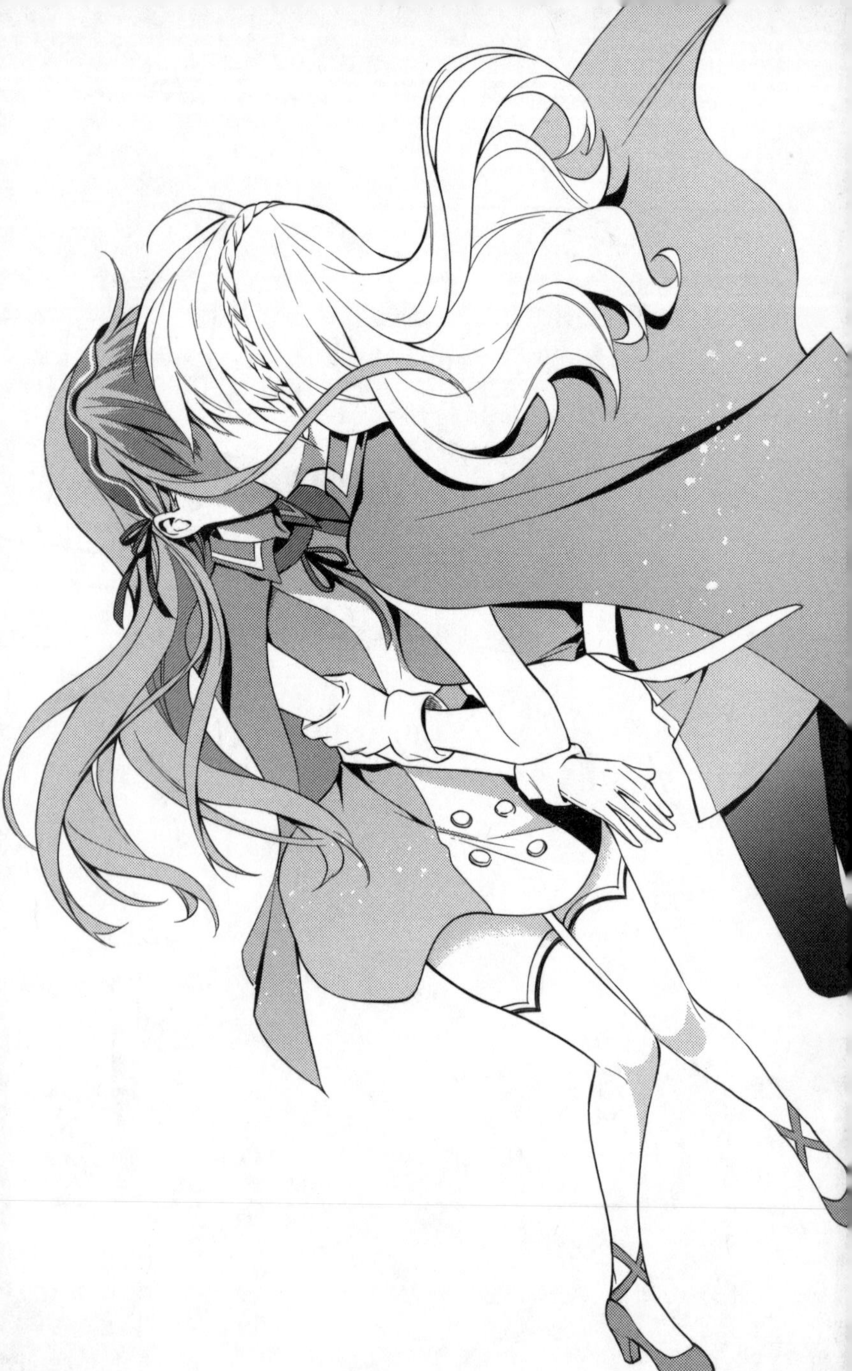

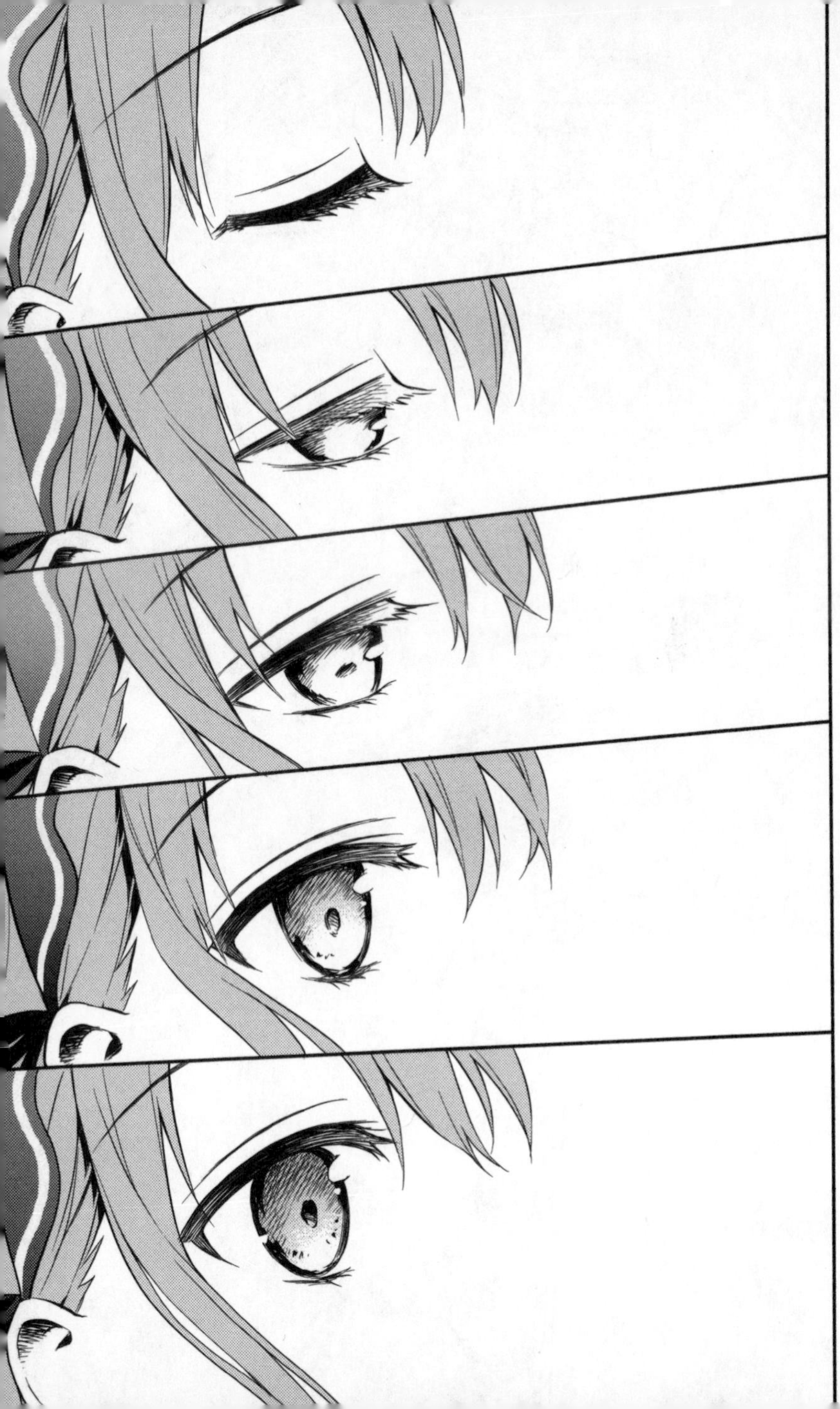

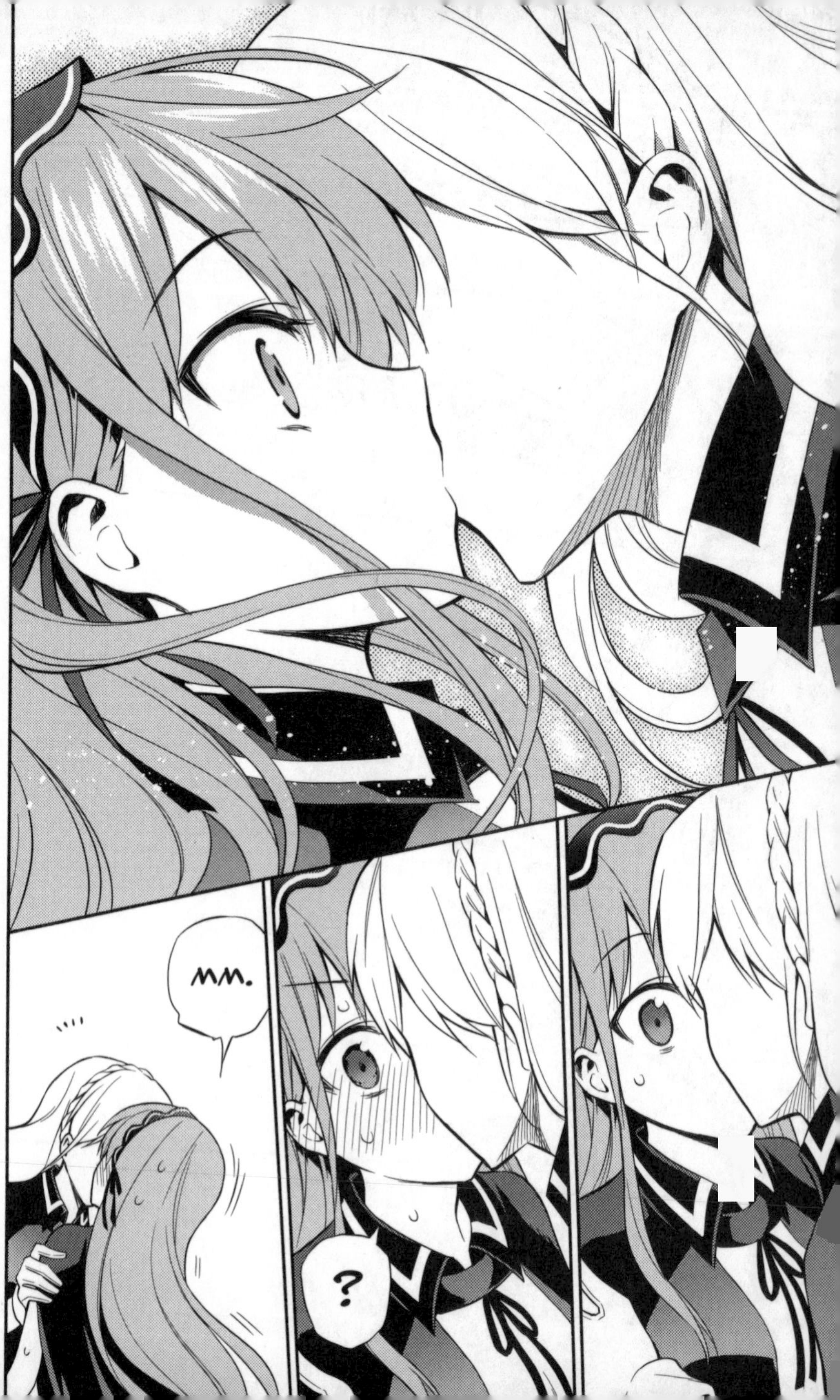
?
MM.

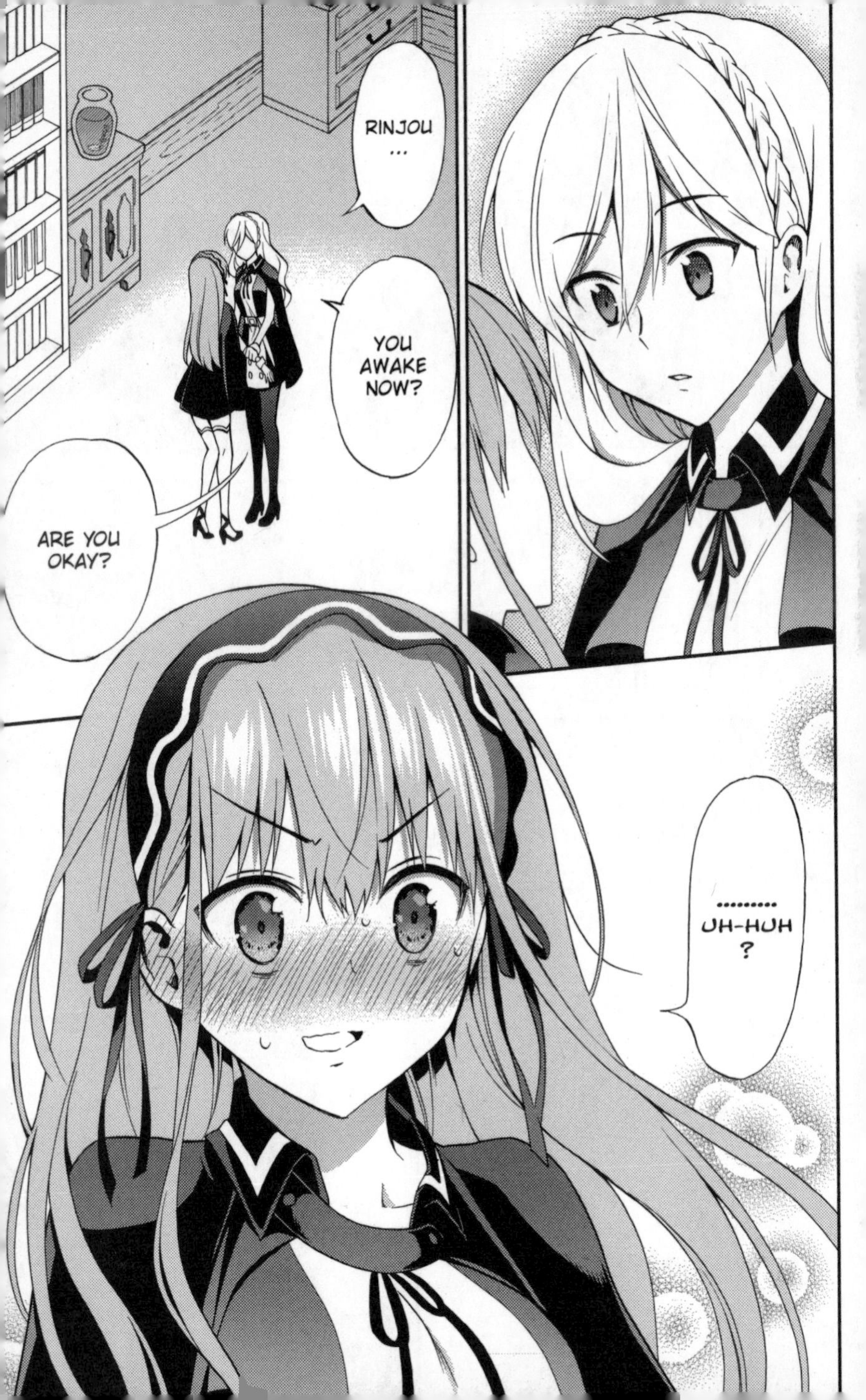
RINJOU ...
YOU AWAKE NOW?
ARE YOU OKAY?
.... UH-HUH ?

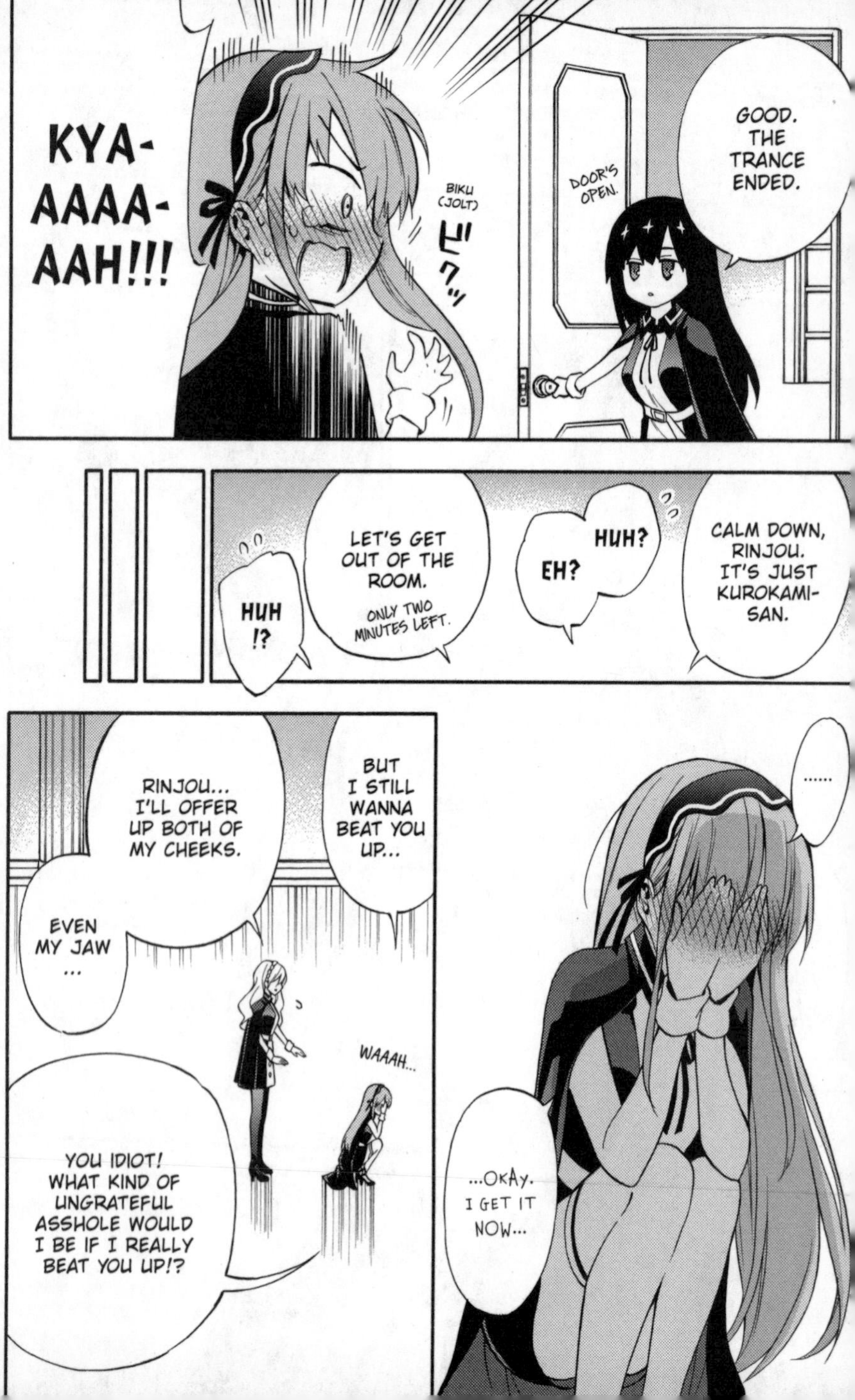
GOOD. THE TRANCE ENDED.
DOOR'S OPEN.
BIKU (JOLT)
ビクッ
KYA-AAAA-AAH!!!
CALM DOWN, RINJOU. IT'S JUST KUROKAMI-SAN.
HUH?
EH?
LET'S GET OUT OF THE ROOM.
ONLY TWO MINUTES LEFT.
HUH!?
......
...OKAY. I GET IT NOW...
BUT I STILL WANNA BEAT YOU UP...
RINJOU... I'LL OFFER UP BOTH OF MY CHEEKS.
EVEN MY JAW...
WAAAH...
YOU IDIOT! WHAT KIND OF UNGRATEFUL ASSHOLE WOULD I BE IF I REALLY BEAT YOU UP!?

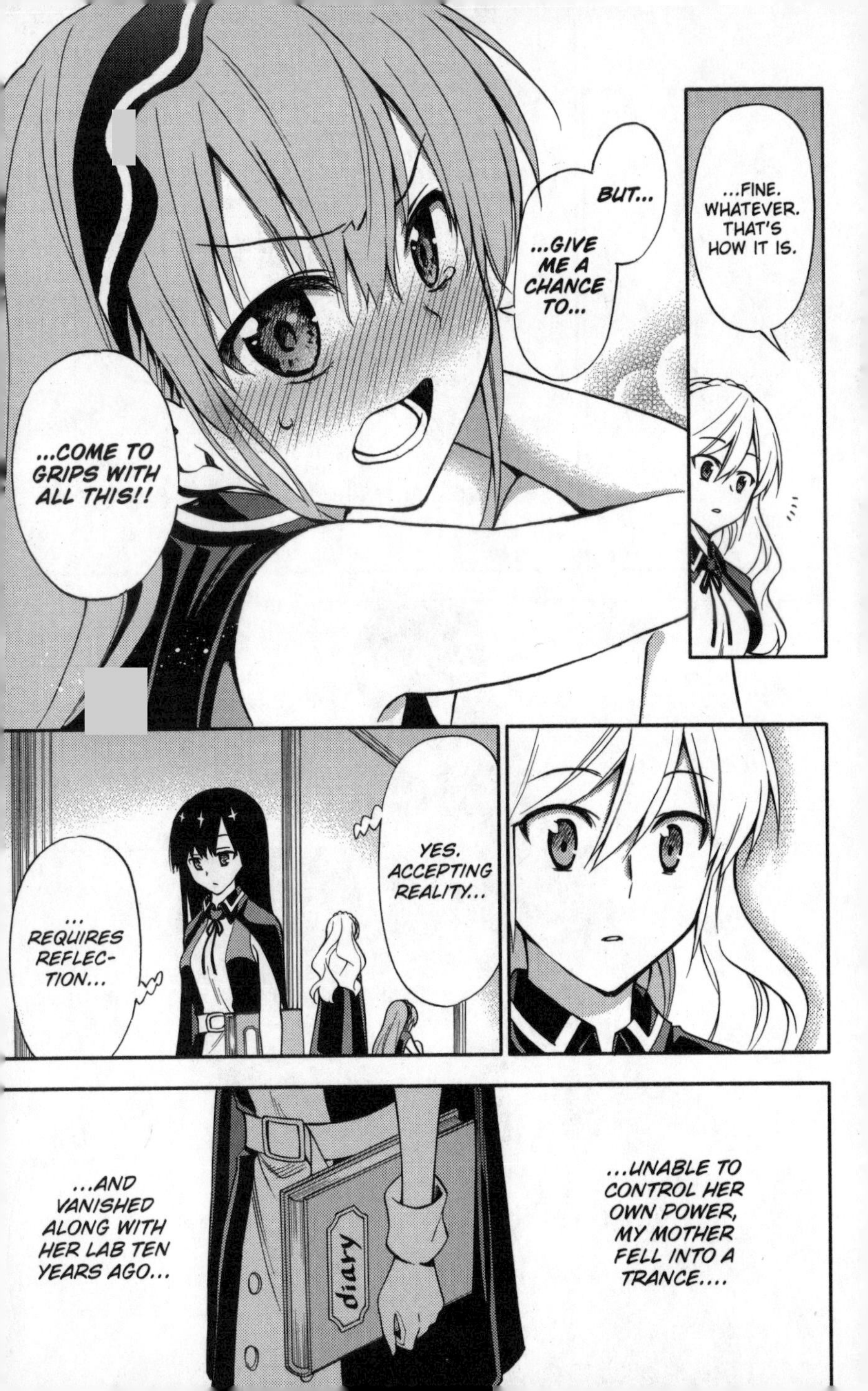
...FINE. WHATEVER. THAT'S HOW IT IS.
BUT...
...GIVE ME A CHANCE TO...
...COME TO GRIPS WITH ALL THIS!!
YES. ACCEPTING REALITY...
...REQUIRES REFLECTION...
...UNABLE TO CONTROL HER OWN POWER, MY MOTHER FELL INTO A TRANCE....
diary
...AND VANISHED ALONG WITH HER LAB TEN YEARS AGO...

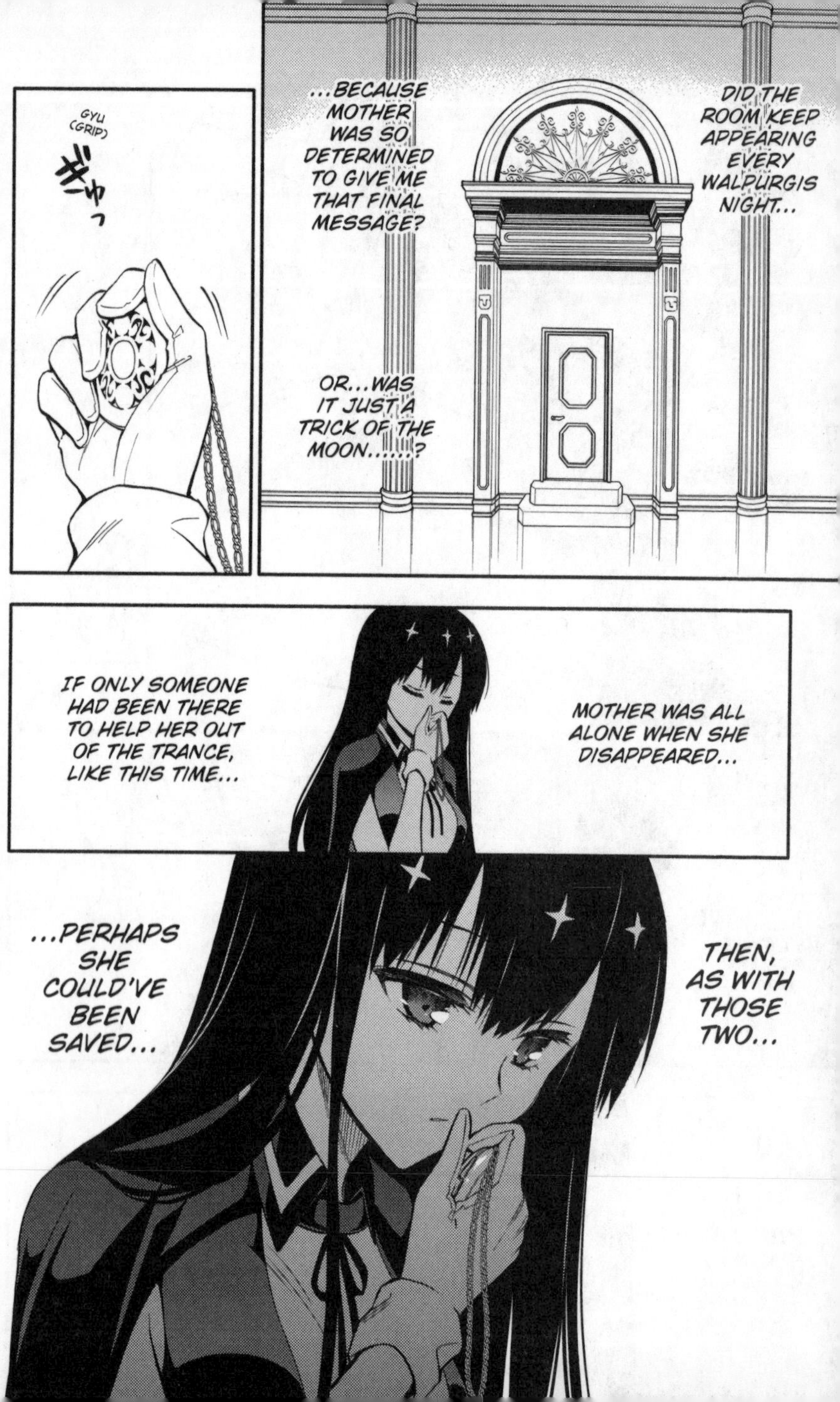
DID THE ROOM KEEP APPEARING EVERY WALPURGIS NIGHT...
...BECAUSE MOTHER WAS SO DETERMINED TO GIVE ME THAT FINAL MESSAGE?
OR...WAS IT JUST A TRICK OF THE MOON......?
GYU (GRIP)
ぎゅっ
MOTHER WAS ALL ALONE WHEN SHE DISAPPEARED...
IF ONLY SOMEONE HAD BEEN THERE TO HELP HER OUT OF THE TRANCE, LIKE THIS TIME...
THEN, AS WITH THOSE TWO...
...PERHAPS SHE COULD'VE BEEN SAVED...

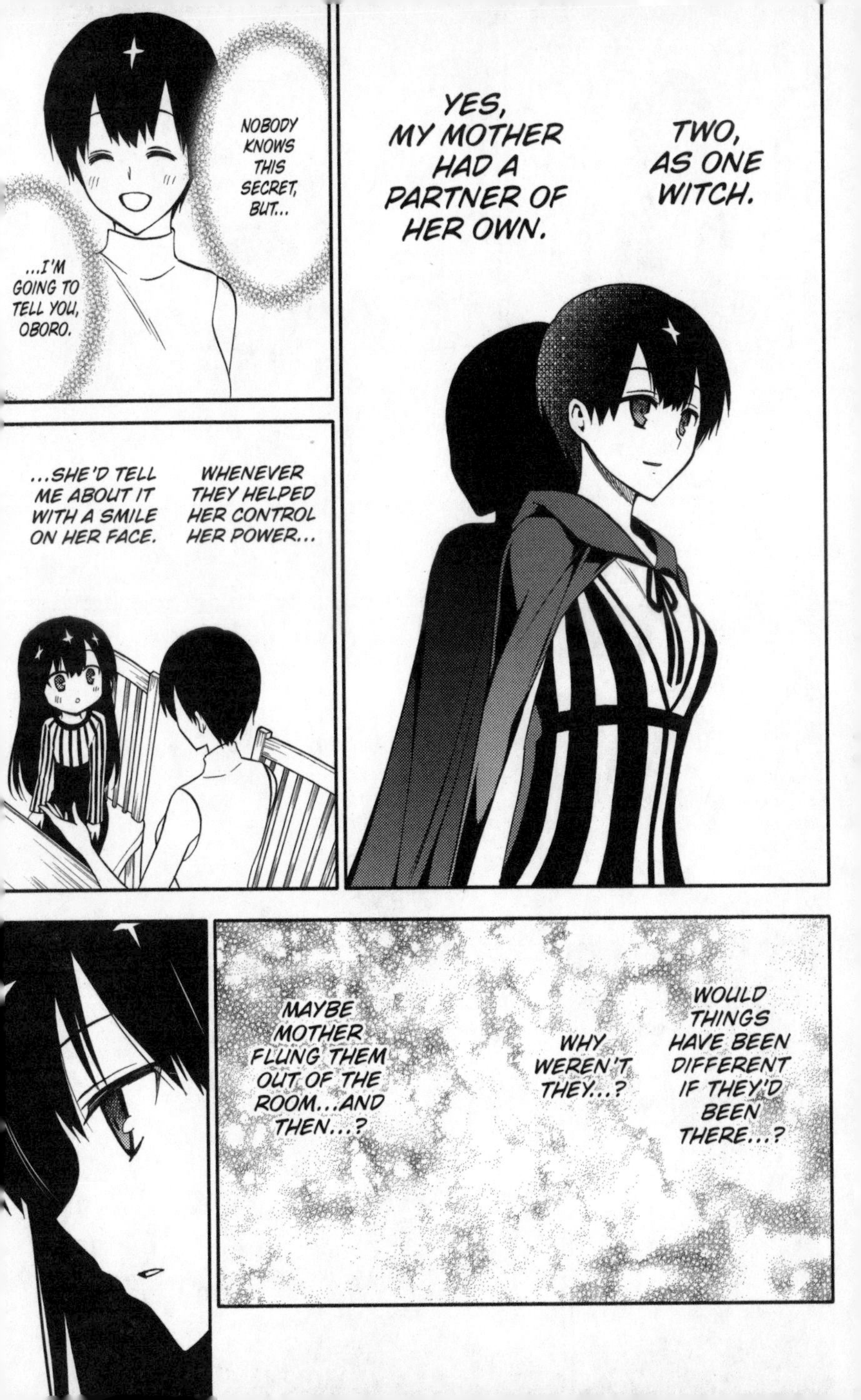
YES, MY MOTHER HAD A PARTNER OF HER OWN.
TWO, AS ONE WITCH.
NOBODY KNOWS THIS SECRET, BUT...
...I'M GOING TO TELL YOU, OBORO.
WHENEVER THEY HELPED HER CONTROL HER POWER...
...SHE'D TELL ME ABOUT IT WITH A SMILE ON HER FACE.
WOULD THINGS HAVE BEEN DIFFERENT IF THEY'D BEEN THERE...?
WHY WEREN'T THEY...?
MAYBE MOTHER FLUNG THEM OUT OF THE ROOM...AND THEN...?

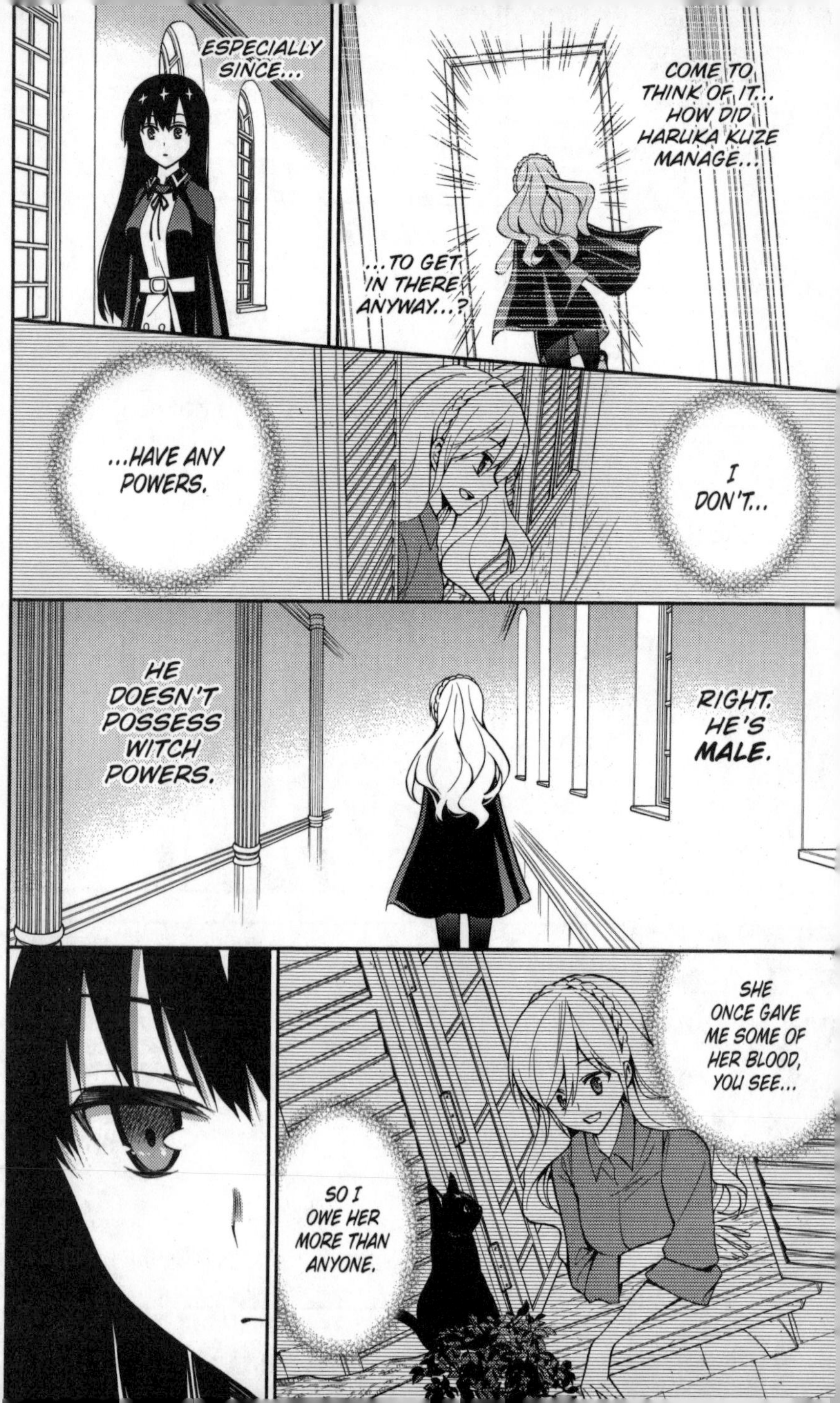
COME TO THINK OF IT... HOW DID HARUKA KUZE MANAGE...
...TO GET IN THERE ANYWAY...?
ESPECIALLY SINCE...
I DON'T...
...HAVE ANY POWERS.
RIGHT. HE'S **MALE**.
HE DOESN'T POSSESS WITCH POWERS.
SHE ONCE GAVE ME SOME OF HER BLOOD, YOU SEE...
SO I OWE HER MORE THAN ANYONE.

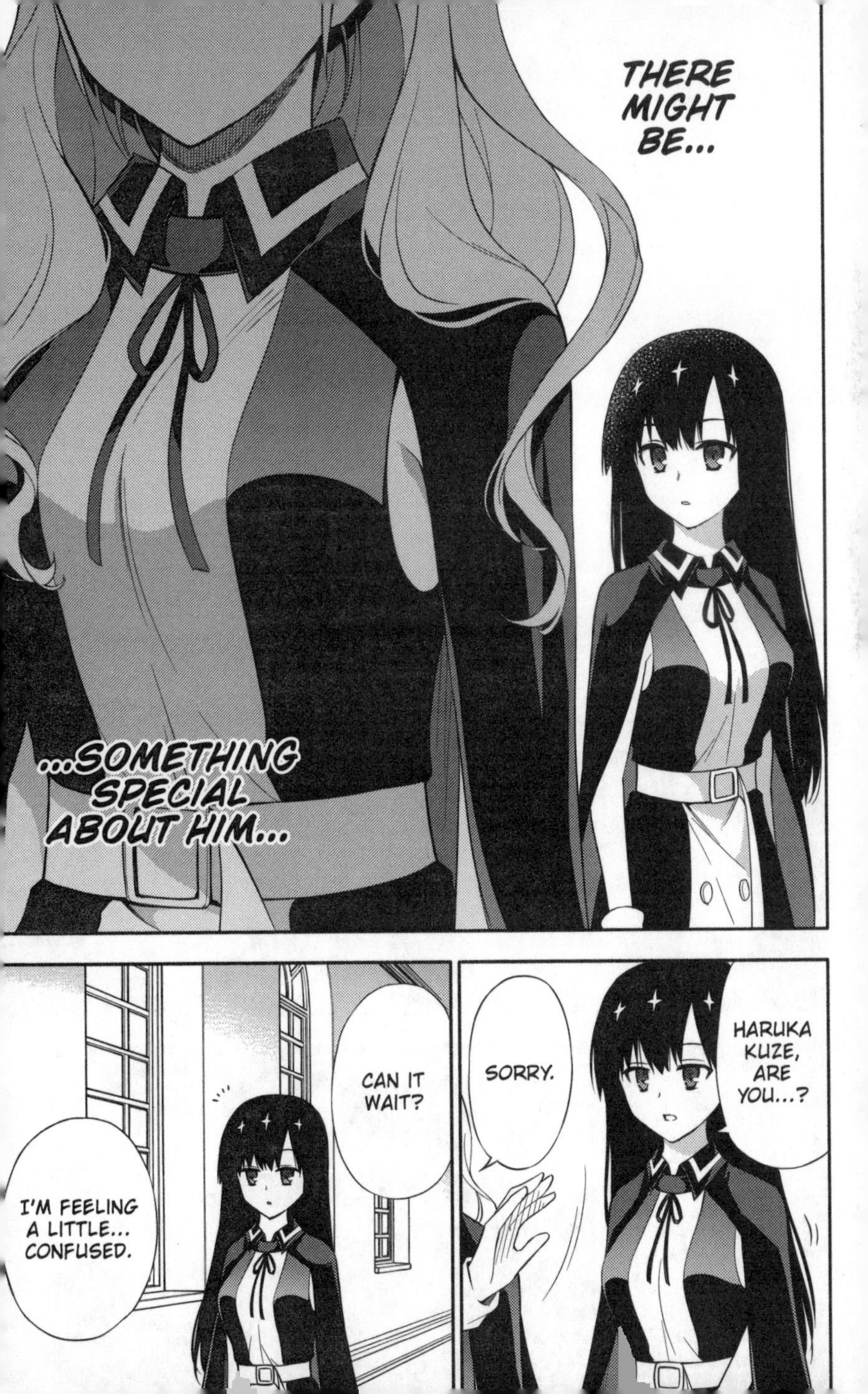
THERE MIGHT BE...
...SOMETHING SPECIAL ABOUT HIM...
HARUKA KUZE, ARE YOU...?
SORRY.
CAN IT WAIT?
I'M FEELING A LITTLE... CONFUSED.

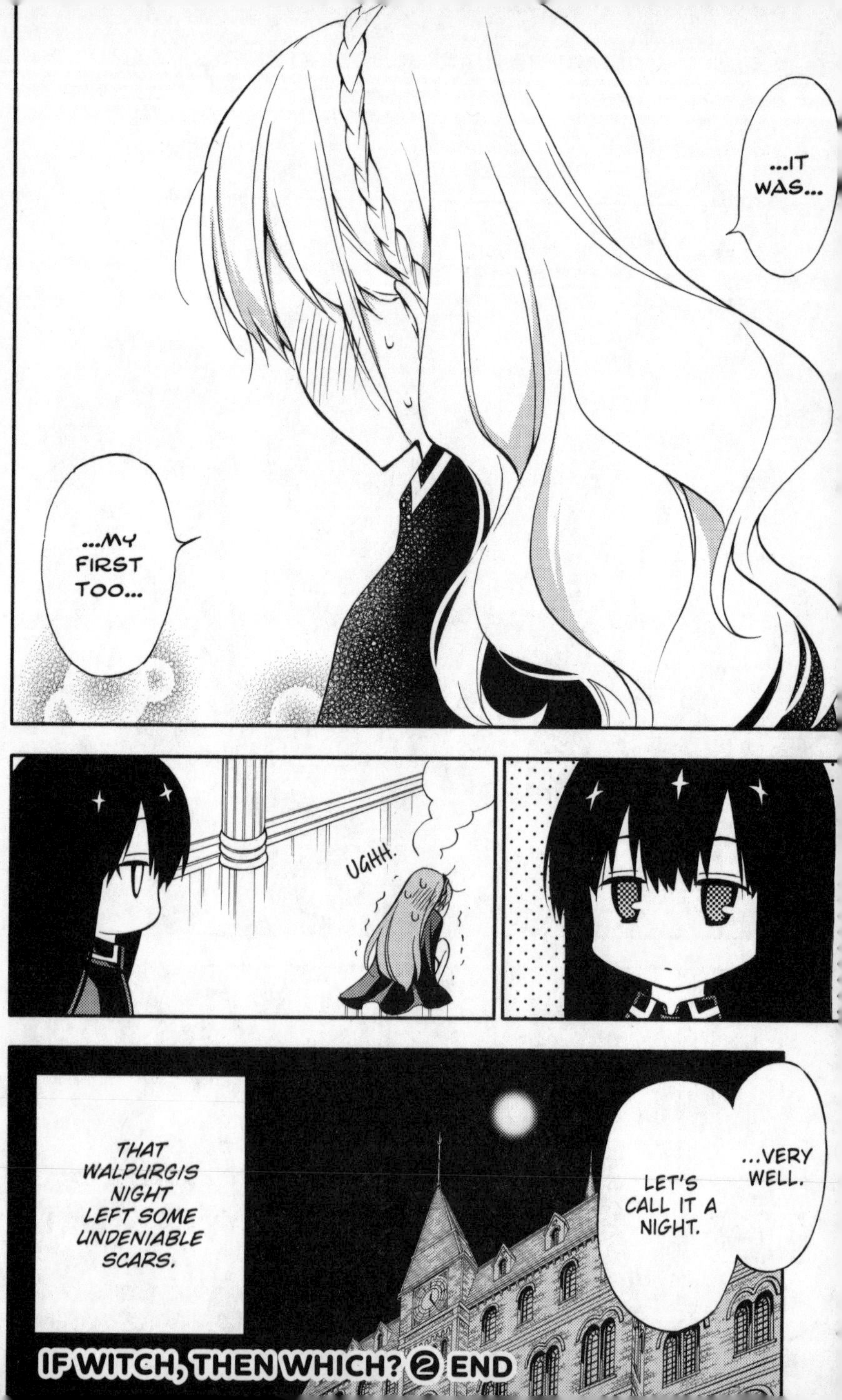
...IT WAS...
...MY FIRST TOO...
UGHH.
...VERY WELL.
LET'S CALL IT A NIGHT.
THAT WALPURGIS NIGHT LEFT SOME UNDENIABLE SCARS.
IF WITCH, THEN WHICH? ② END

BONUS COMIC **The Two's Night, After Walpurgis**

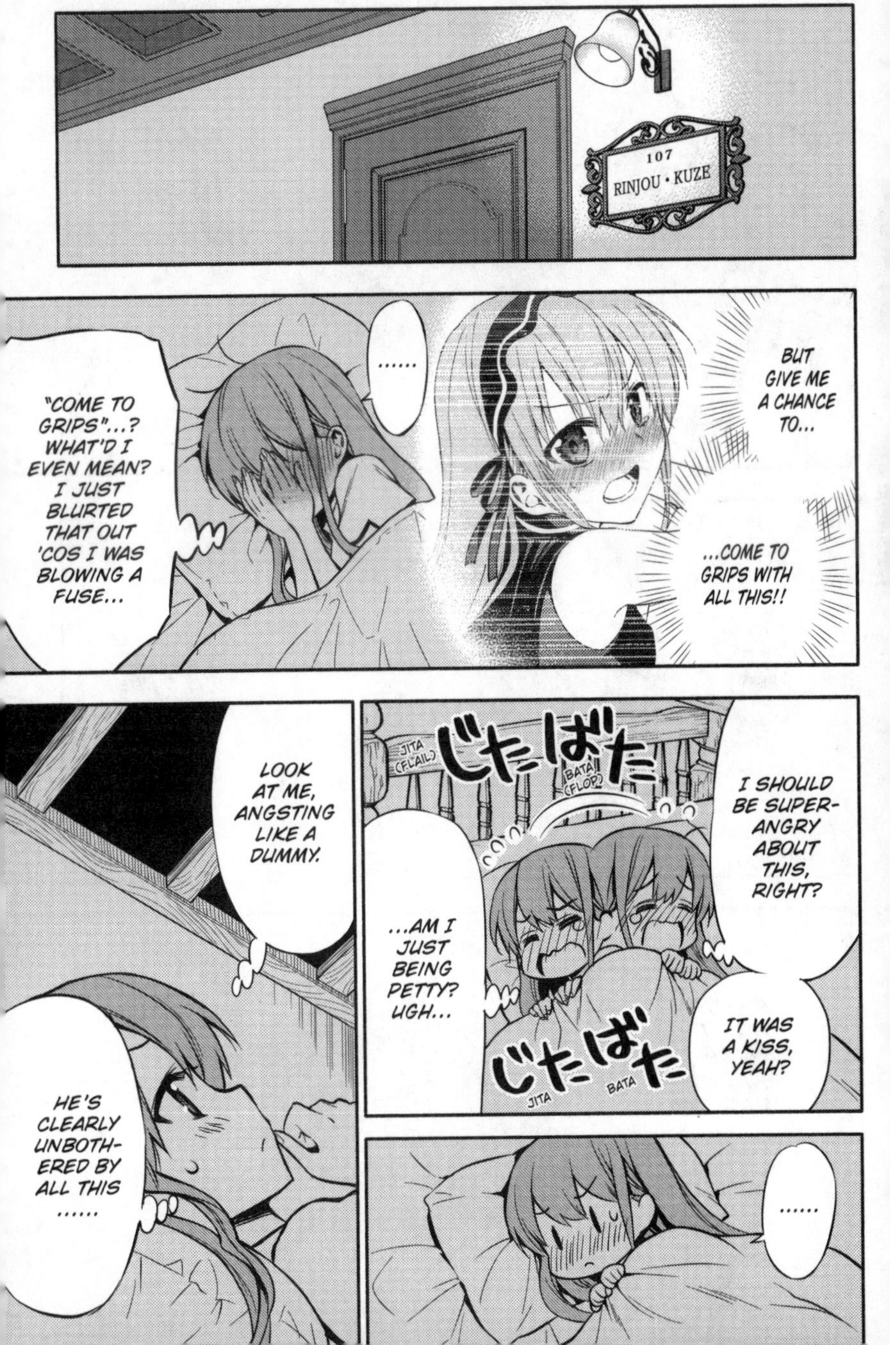
107
RINJOU • KUZE
BUT GIVE ME A CHANCE TO...
...COME TO GRIPS WITH ALL THIS!!
......
"COME TO GRIPS"...? WHAT'D I EVEN MEAN? I JUST BLURTED THAT OUT 'COS I WAS BLOWING A FUSE...
I SHOULD BE SUPER-ANGRY ABOUT THIS, RIGHT?
JITA (FLAIL) BATA (FLOP)
IT WAS A KISS, YEAH?
...AM I JUST BEING PETTY? UGH...
JITA BATA
......
LOOK AT ME, ANGSTING LIKE A DUMMY.
HE'S CLEARLY UNBOTHERED BY ALL THIS ......

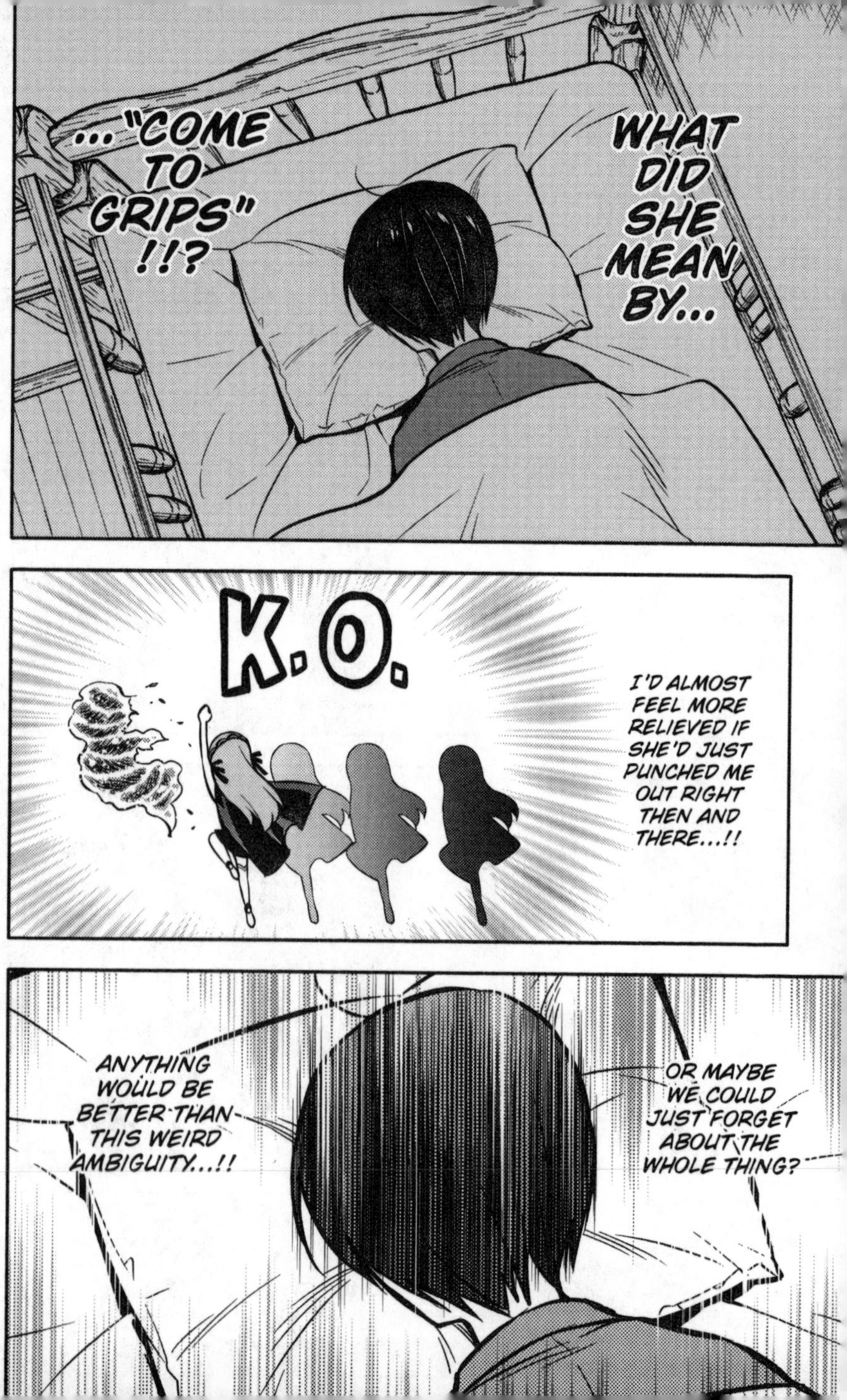
WHAT DID SHE MEAN BY...
..."COME TO GRIPS"!!?
I'D ALMOST FEEL MORE RELIEVED IF SHE'D JUST PUNCHED ME OUT RIGHT THEN AND THERE...!!
K.O.
OR MAYBE WE COULD JUST FORGET ABOUT THE WHOLE THING?
ANYTHING WOULD BE BETTER THAN THIS WEIRD AMBIGUITY...!!

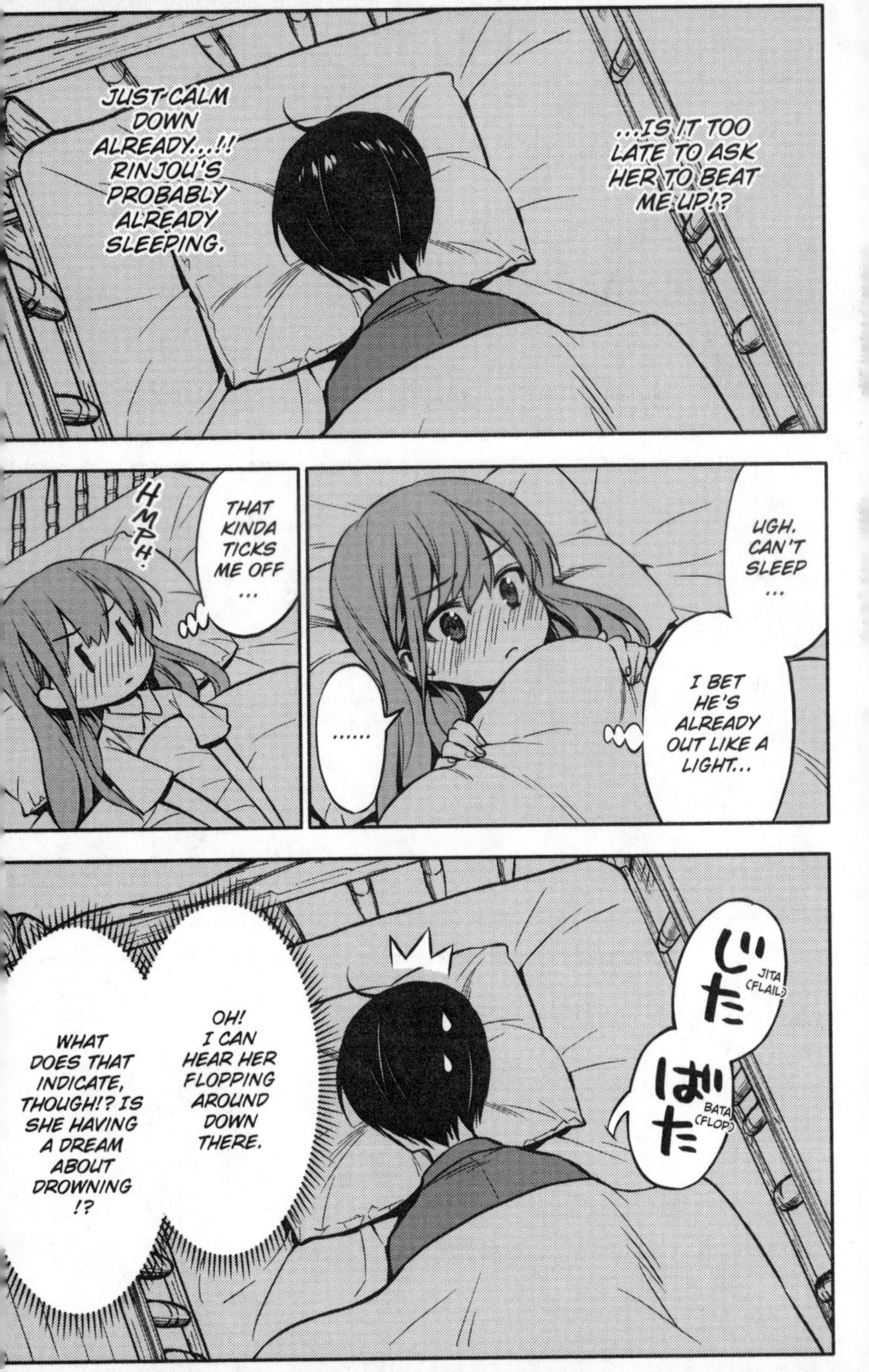
JUST CALM DOWN ALREADY...!! RINJOU'S PROBABLY ALREADY SLEEPING.
...IS IT TOO LATE TO ASK HER TO BEAT ME UP!?
UGH. CAN'T SLEEP ...
I BET HE'S ALREADY OUT LIKE A LIGHT...
......
HMPH.
THAT KINDA TICKS ME OFF ...
じたばた
JITA (FLAIL)
BATA (FLOP)
OH! I CAN HEAR HER FLOPPING AROUND DOWN THERE.
WHAT DOES THAT INDICATE, THOUGH!? IS SHE HAVING A DREAM ABOUT DROWNING !?

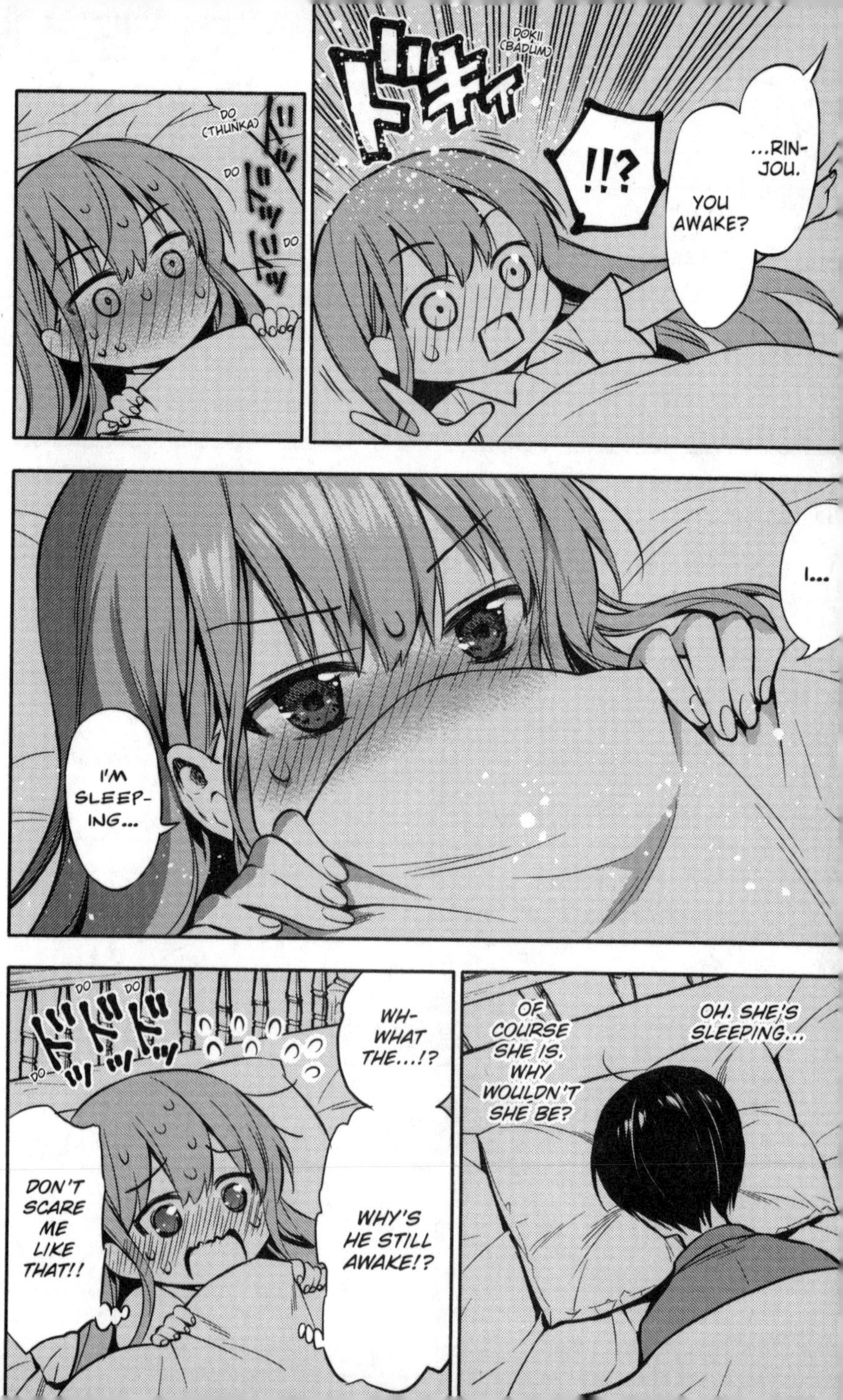
...RIN-JOU.
YOU AWAKE?
!!?
DOKII (BADUM)
DO (THUNKA)
DO
DO
I...
I'M SLEEPING...
OH. SHE'S SLEEPING...
OF COURSE SHE IS. WHY WOULDN'T SHE BE?
WH-WHAT THE...!?
WHY'S HE STILL AWAKE!?
DON'T SCARE ME LIKE THAT!!
DO
DO
DO

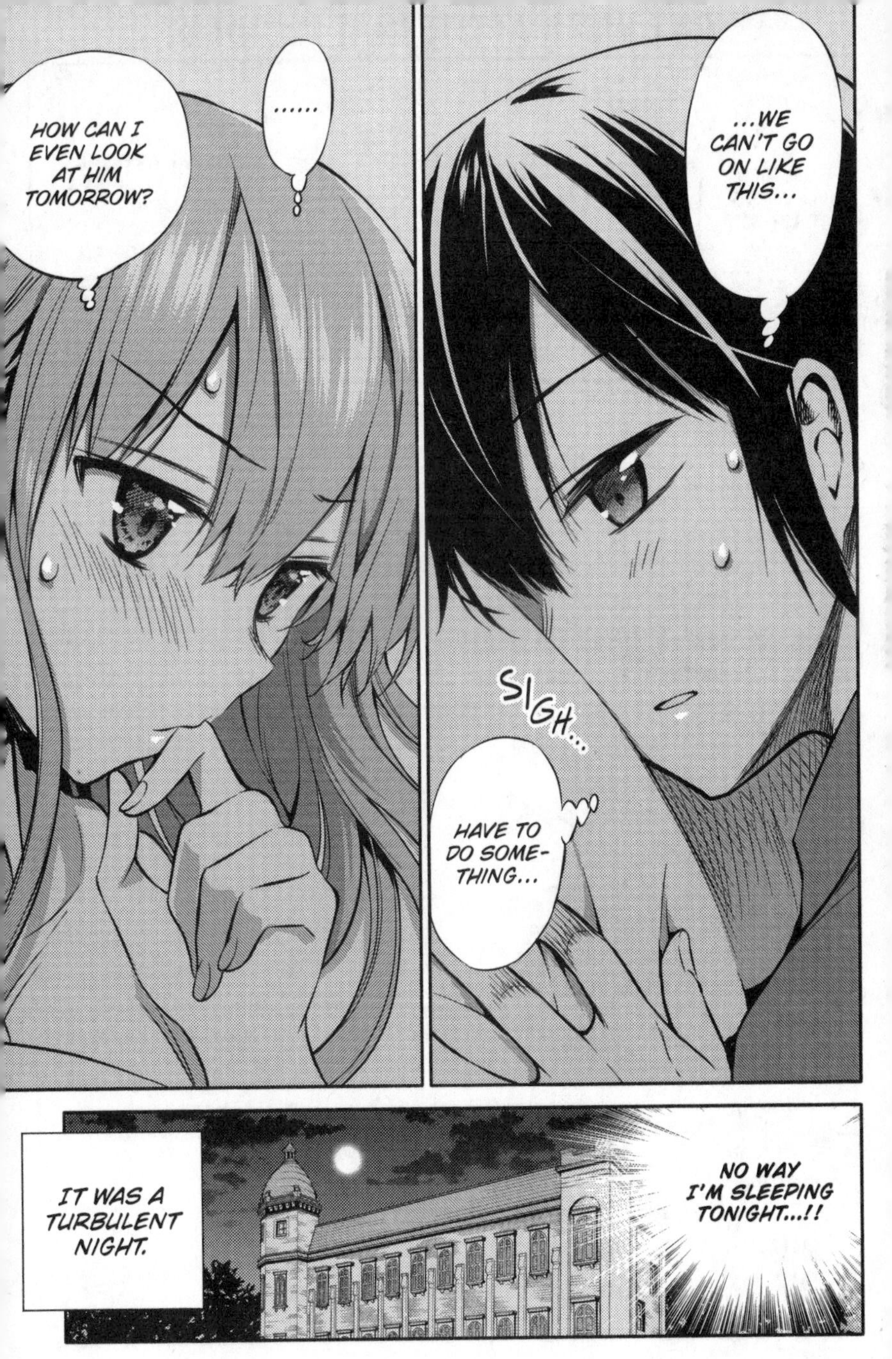
...WE CAN'T GO ON LIKE THIS...
SIGH...
HAVE TO DO SOME-THING...
......
HOW CAN I EVEN LOOK AT HIM TOMORROW?
NO WAY I'M SLEEPING TONIGHT...!!
IT WAS A TURBULENT NIGHT.

ONE WEEK AFTER THAT INCIDENT

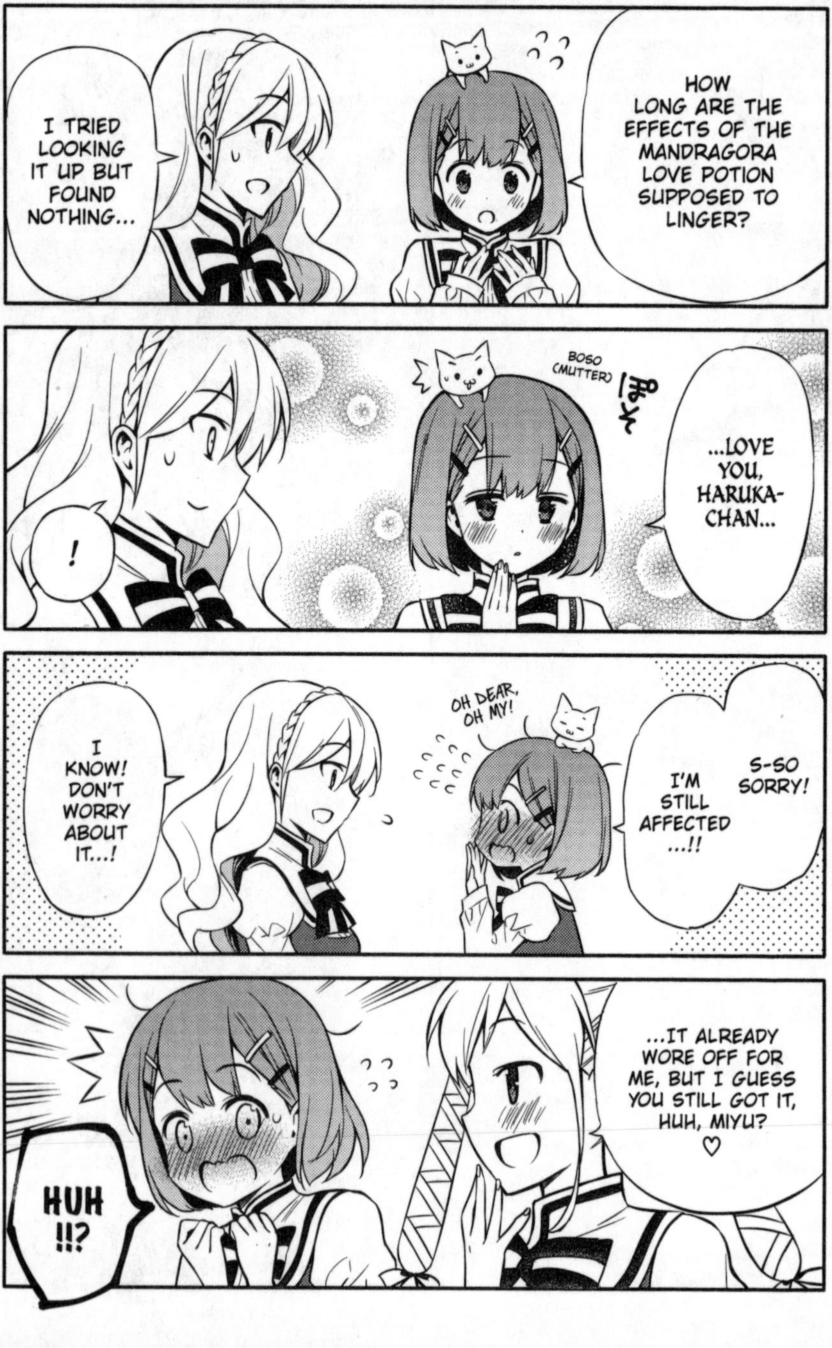
HOW LONG ARE THE EFFECTS OF THE MANDRAGORA LOVE POTION SUPPOSED TO LINGER?
I TRIED LOOKING IT UP BUT FOUND NOTHING...
...LOVE YOU, HARUKA-CHAN...
ぽそ
BOSO (MUTTER)
!
S-SO SORRY!
I'M STILL AFFECTED ...!!
OH DEAR, OH MY!
I KNOW! DON'T WORRY ABOUT IT...!
...IT ALREADY WORE OFF FOR ME, BUT I GUESS YOU STILL GOT IT, HUH, MIYU? ♡
HUH !!?

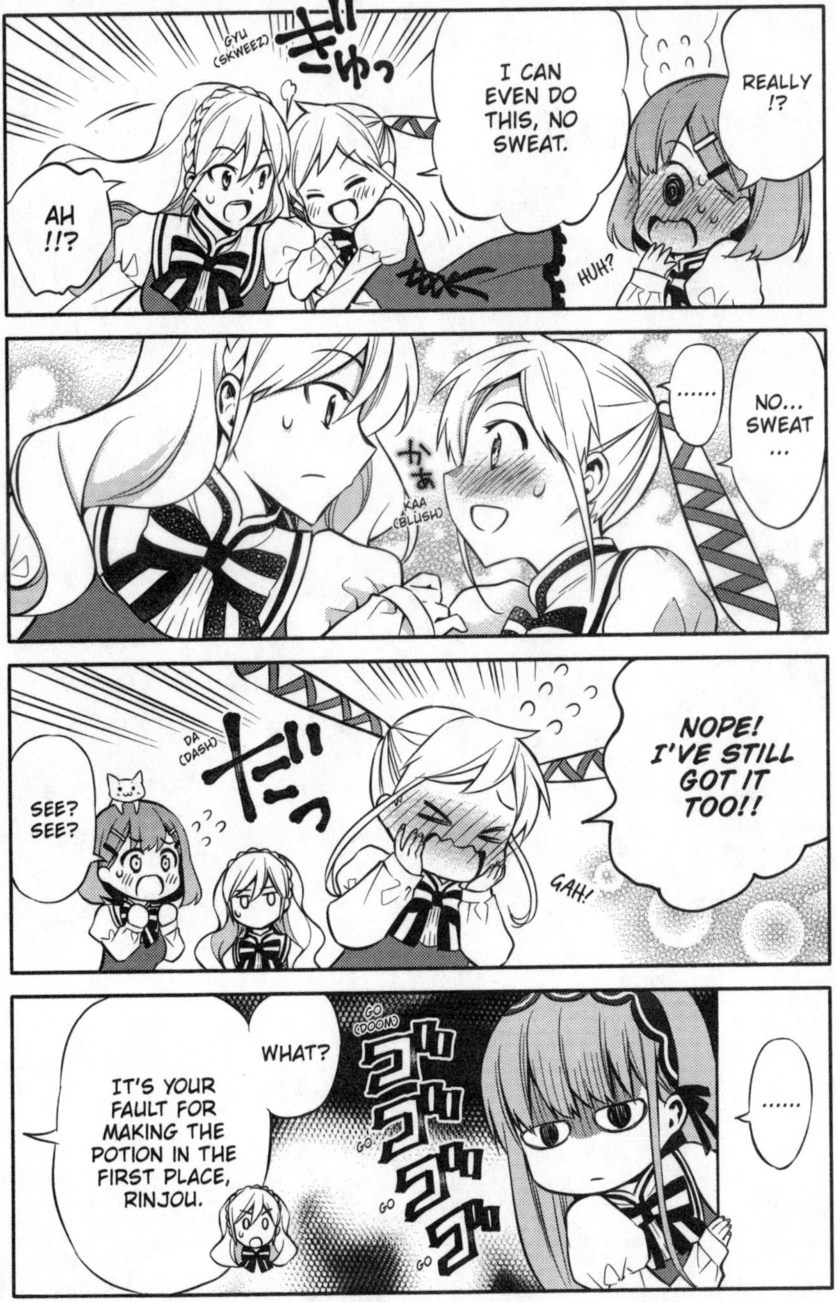
REALLY !?
I CAN EVEN DO THIS, NO SWEAT.
ぎゅっ
GYU (SKWEEZ)
HUH?
AH !!?
NO... SWEAT ...
......
かぁ
KAA (BLUSH)
NOPE! I'VE STILL GOT IT TOO!!
GAH!
だっ
DA (DASH)
SEE? SEE?
......
ゴゴゴゴ
GO (DOOM)
GO
GO
GO
WHAT?
IT'S YOUR FAULT FOR MAKING THE POTION IN THE FIRST PLACE, RINJOU.

I've Been Killing SLIMES for 300 Years and Maxed Out My Level

It's hard work taking it slow...

After living a painful life as an office worker, Azusa ended her short life by dying from overworking. So when she found herself reincarnated as an undying, unaging witch in a new world, she vows to spend her days stress free and as pleasantly as possible. She ekes out a living by hunting down the easiest targets—the slimes! But after centuries of doing this simple job, she's ended up with insane powers... how will she maintain her low key life now?!

IN STORES NOW!

Light Novel Volumes 1-9

SLIME TAOSHITE SANBYAKUNEN, SHIRANAIUCHINI LEVEL MAX NI NATTEMASHITA
© 2017 Kisetsu Morita
© 2017 Benio / SB Creative Corp.

Manga Volumes 1-6

SLIME TAOSHITE SANBYAKUNEN, SHIRANAIUCHINI LEVEL MAX NI NATTEMASHITA
©Kisetsu Morita/SB Creative Corp.
Original Character Designs:
©Benio/SB Creative Corp.
©2018 Yusuke Shiba
/SQUARE ENIX CO., LTD.

For more information, visit www.yenpress.com

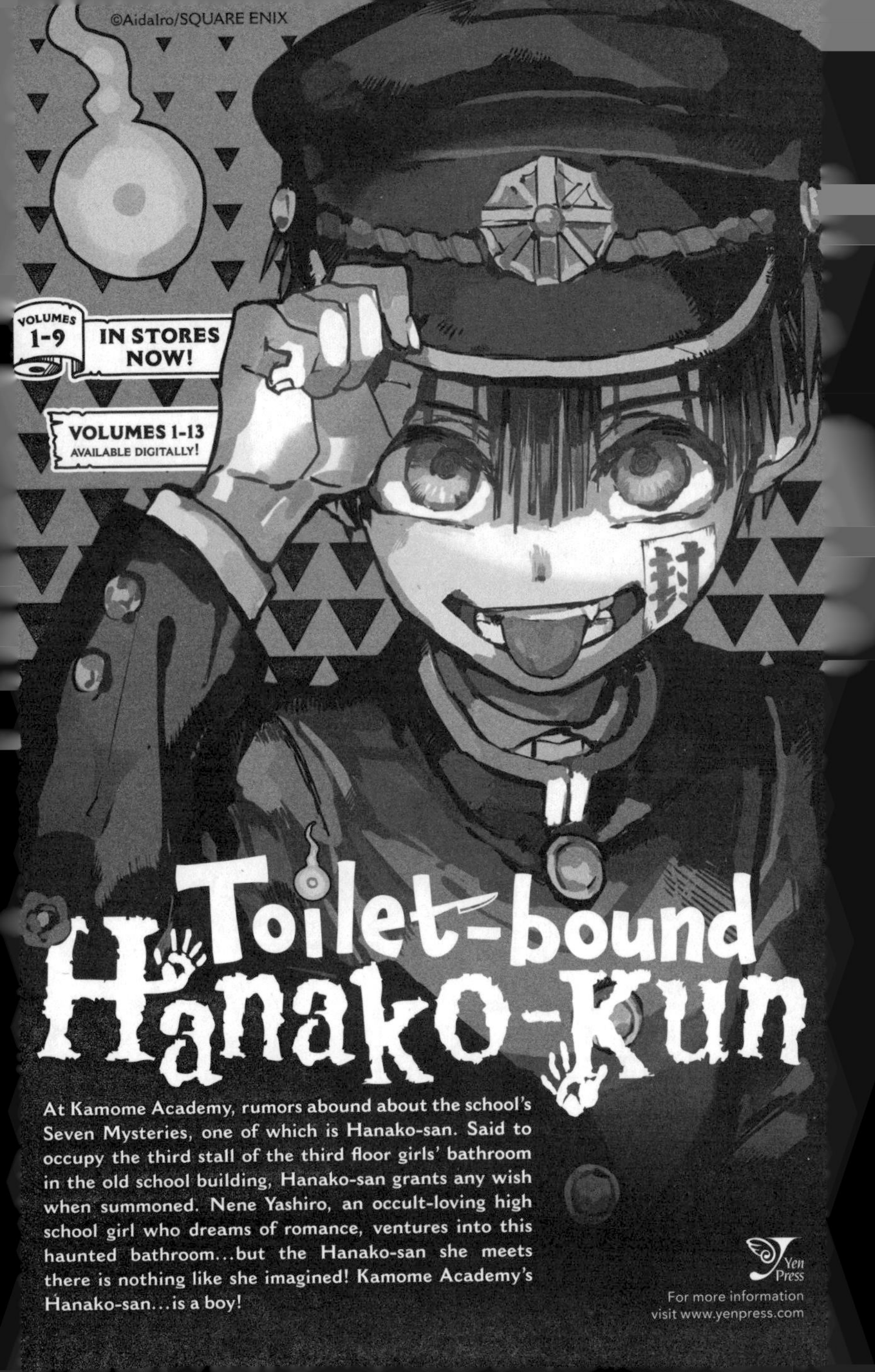
©AidaIro/SQUARE ENIX
VOLUMES 1-9
IN STORES NOW!
VOLUMES 1-13
AVAILABLE DIGITALLY!
Toilet-bound Hanako-Kun

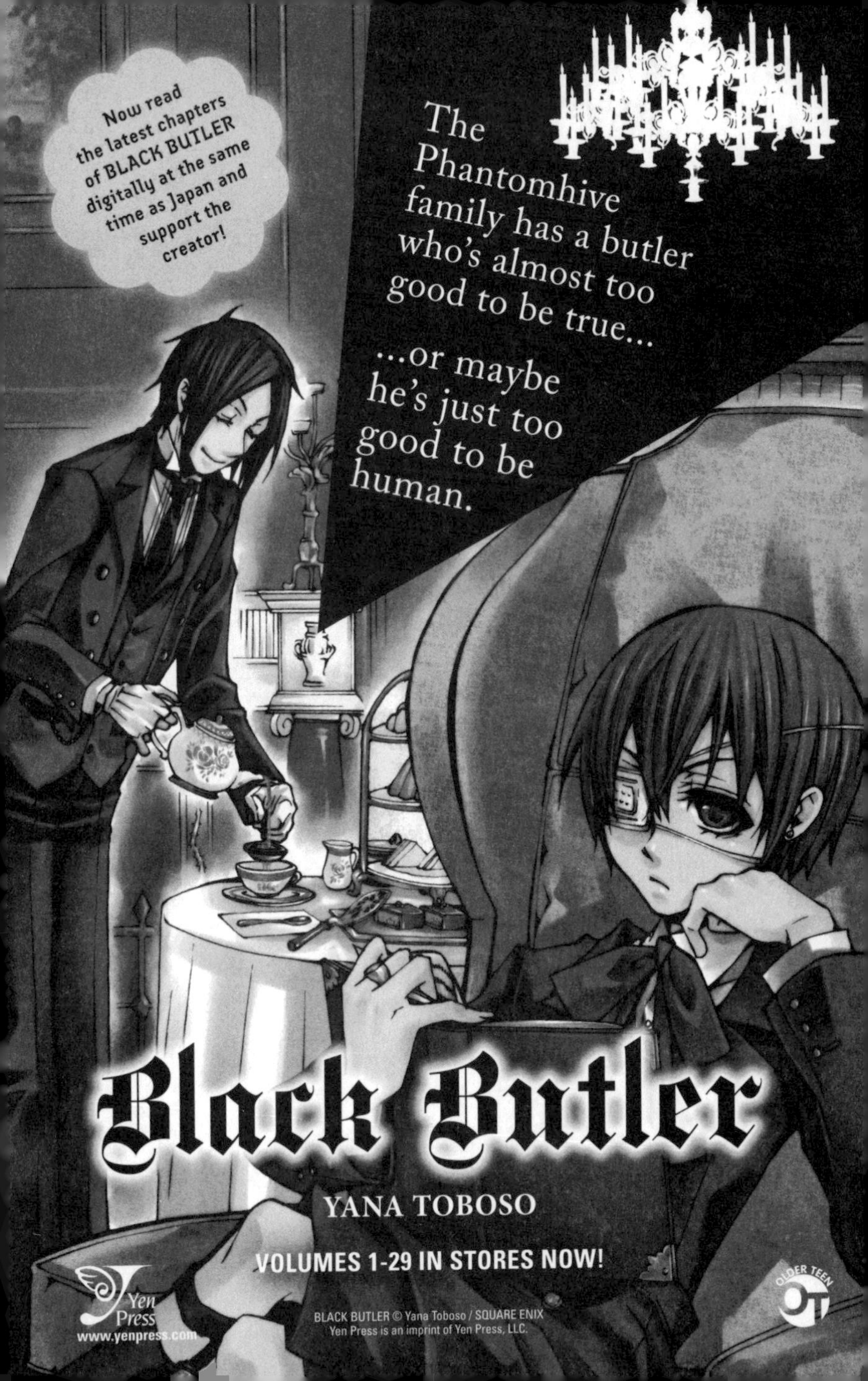
Now read the latest chapters of BLACK BUTLER digitally at the same time as Japan and support the creator!
The Phantomhive family has a butler who's almost too good to be true...
...or maybe he's just too good to be human.
Black Butler
YANA TOBOSO
VOLUMES 1-29 IN STORES NOW!
Yen Press
www.yenpress.com
BLACK BUTLER © Yana Toboso / SQUARE ENIX
Yen Press is an imprint of Yen Press, LLC.
OLDER TEEN
OT

If Witch, Then Which?

2 Ato Sakurai

Translation: CALEB D. COOK ★ Lettering: BIANCA PISTILLO

This book is a work of fiction. Names, characters, places, and incidents are the product of the author's imagination or are used fictitiously. Any resemblance to actual events, locales, or persons, living or dead, is coincidental.

MAJO RABA MAJO REBA Vol. 2
©2020 Ato Sakurai/SQUARE ENIX CO., LTD.
First published in Japan in 2020 by SQUARE ENIX CO., LTD.
English translation rights arranged with SQUARE ENIX CO., LTD. and Yen Press,
LLC through Tuttle-Mori Agency, Inc.

English translation ©2021 by SQUARE ENIX CO., LTD.

Yen Press
150 West 30th Street, 19th Floor
New York, NY 10001

Visit us at yenpress.com
facebook.com/yenpress
twitter.com/yenpress
yenpress.tumblr.com
instagram.com/yenpress

First Yen Press Edition: May 2021

Yen Press is an imprint of Yen Press, LLC.
The Yen Press name and logo are trademarks of Yen Press, LLC.

The publisher is not responsible for websites (or their content)
that are not owned by the publisher.

Library of Congress Control Number: 2020940350

ISBNs: 978-1-9753-1981-6 (paperback)
978-1-9753-1982-3 (ebook)

10 9 8 7 6 5 4 3 2 1

WOR

Printed in the United States of America